HOW TO DO YOUR SOCIAL RESEARCH
PROJECT OR DISSERTATION

Tom Clark · Liam Foster · Alan Bryman

HOW TO DO YOUR

SOCIAL

RESEARCH

PROJECT

OR

DISSERTATION

OXFORD

UNIVERSITY PRESS

OXFORD

UNIVERSITY PRESS

Great Clarendon Street, Oxford, OX2 6DP,
United Kingdom

Oxford University Press is a department of the University of Oxford.
It furthers the University's objective of excellence in research, scholarship,
and education by publishing worldwide. Oxford is a registered trade mark of
Oxford University Press in the UK and in certain other countries

Published in the United States of America by Oxford University Press
198 Madison Avenue, New York, NY 10016, United States of America

British Library Cataloguing in Publication Data
Data available

Library of Congress Control Number: 2019943975

ISBN 978–0–19–881106–0

Printed in Great Britain by
Bell & Bain Ltd., Glasgow

DEDICATION

In memory of Alan Bryman
(1947–2017)

Alan sadly passed away during the process of writing this book. But his insight, knowledge, and commitment to the learning and teaching of research methods was invaluable in developing both the idea and the content.

He has long been an inspiration to us, and his work has had a huge influence on what we have tried to do with our careers in higher education. We have always tried to follow his problem-focused approach, his interest in mixed methods, and the emphasis he placed on doing research of high quality. But perhaps most important to us were his attempts to make research methods more accessible to students by using clear and interesting explanations of what can be complex material. That is why we were delighted when Alan approached us to write a book that would complement his excellent and comprehensive methods text, *Social Research Methods*. Given our own interest in using enquiry-based approaches to help students develop their experience of research, we wanted to write a clear and concise guide that would help students to navigate through the whole process of undertaking a dissertation or project. Of course, the limitations of what we have written are entirely our own, but in following Alan's expertise we feel we have been able to deliver what we originally set out to do and hope he would be pleased with what we have achieved.

We actually first met Alan several years ago when we won him in a competition! We had been given an award from the Higher Education Academy for our methods teaching, and the prize was the opportunity for Alan to come and do a talk at our university. Although he was rather embarrassed to be a 'prize', given that he was based in Nottingham, he was also somewhat relieved that it was a trip to Sheffield rather than somewhere much further afield. We very much enjoyed Alan's talk, had a meal with him following the event, and met him several times during the process of writing. It was evident that Alan was a witty man, and humble in nature, despite his significant achievements. He had a love for sport and music—Spurs and the Human League in particular—as well as a deep passion for learning and teaching. We very much enjoyed his company and, even though we only knew him for a short time, we do miss him and it is very sad that Alan couldn't have played a fuller role in the project.

Tom once suggested to Alan that working with him was the research methods version of playing up front with Gary Lineker. Neither of us have ever met Gary Lineker, yet alone played football with him, but we can say with great pride that we did work with Alan Bryman. We hope that you find this book useful—and true to Alan's vision of problem-focused research design.

With much love
Tom and Liam

ABOUT THE AUTHORS

DR TOM CLARK is a Lecturer in Research Methods at the University of Sheffield, UK. He is interested in all aspects of method and methodology, particularly with respect to learning and teaching. His other interests have variously focused on the sociology of evil, student experiences of higher education, and football fandom. Tom's work has been published in a wide variety of journals, including *Sociology*, *Qualitative Research*, *Social Policy and Administration*, *Teaching in Higher Education*, the *Journal of Education and Work*, and *Qualitative Social Work*.

DR LIAM FOSTER is a Senior Lecturer in Social Policy and Social Work at the University of Sheffield, UK, who specializes in pensions and theories of ageing. Liam also has a long-standing interest in methods and has published widely in this area, including *Beginning Statistics: An Introduction for Social Scientists* (with Sir Ian Diamond and Dr Julie Jefferies). He has been an invited speaker at the Department for Education, Department for Work and Pensions, the European Parliament in Brussels, the House of Lords, and the UN in New York as a world-leading expert on ageing. Liam is a member of the UK Social Policy Association Executive Committee. He is also a Managing Editor of *Social Policy and Society*.

ALAN BRYMAN was Professor of Organizational and Social Research at the University of Leicester from 2005 to 2017. Prior to this he was Professor of Social Research at Loughborough University for 31 years. His main research interests were in leadership, especially in higher education, research methods (particularly mixed methods research), and the 'Disneyization' and 'McDonaldization' of modern society. Alan was also the author of the bestselling textbook *Social Research Methods* (Oxford University Press, 2015) as well as contributing to a range of leading journals: he was an extraordinarily well-cited and internationally renowned social scientist.

CONTENTS

DETAILED CONTENTS

GUIDE TO THE BOOK

WHAT DO I NEED TO KNOW?

A concise bullet-point checklist at the beginning of each chapter, with each point corresponding to a section in that chapter. It will help you navigate the content by highlighting the chapter coverage so you can quickly and efficiently find what is relevant to you and your research project. A short introduction accompanies each list to introduce you to the content and help you to place the material within the overall process of doing a research project.

WHAT DO I NEED TO KNOW?

- Planning your project
  - First steps of planning
  - Structure
  - Managing your time
  - Managing yourself
- Working with your supervisor
- Expecting the unexpected

I WISH I'D KNOWN . . . HOW LONG THE LITERATURE REVIEW WOULD TAKE TO COMPLETE 6.2

"*I wrongly presumed that the literature review was like another essay—but it isn't. I had to ask the question 'so what?' after each paragraph to ensure that all information I was using was relevant. This helped to ensure that I was being critical in relation to the knowledge gap.*"
— Megan Robinson, Student, Criminal and Forensic Psychology, University of Bolton

---

I WISH I'D KNOWN . . .

Snippets of advice from real students and supervisors across different disciplines. 'I wish I'd known . . .' tells you what students and supervisors wish they had known about their own research projects and what they learned from their experiences, so you can avoid the same pitfalls. We have also added a few extra tips from our own experience of supervising students.

WORKING WITH YOUR SUPERVISOR

Advice about how you might get the most out of the supervisior process. Drawing on our own experiences, as well as that offered by other supervisors, this advice will help you to understand how to make the most of your supervisor and how to best prepare for your meetings with them.

WORKING WITH YOUR SUPERVISOR 3.3

Preparing for each supervision meeting will ensure you get the most out of the sessions. It can also help you develop other transferable skills.

"*Make sure you plan for each meeting—have a rough agenda which you follow so that you get the most from your supervisor. This is a chance to practise your leadership and management skills.*"
— Dr Ruth Penfold-Mounce, Senior Lecturer in Criminology, University of York

FINDING YOUR WAY

Think of these as hints and tips for good research! We provide key pieces of advice designed to help you find your way through the journey of doing a dissertation. The advice provides insight that will help you succeed, and also enables you to react positively to those unexpected things that occur when doing research.

FINDING YOUR WAY 5.6

Many databases have an advanced search function. Once you have got used to the basics of searching, don't be afraid to use these tools as they can balance precision and sensitivity.

WHAT DO I NEED TO THINK ABOUT?

A series of questions that will help you to pause, anchor your thoughts, and reflect on the key issues in each chapter. Thinking through your answers – which will be personal to your project – will both consolidate your understanding of key issues, and how they relate to your project. You can find these at the end of each chapter.

> **WHAT DO I NEED TO THINK ABOUT?**
> - What key terms might be associated with your research idea?
> - What sorts of methods might be used to locate relevant literature?
> - What are the most relevant search engines available to you?
> - How might the challenges associated with searching the literature impact on your project?
> - What means of recording and storing identified items of interest are available at your institution?

> **WHAT DO I NEED TO DO?**
> - Make sure you understand the role of the literature review in the context of your dissertation or report.
> - Choose the most appropriate type of review for the purposes of your research.
> - Organize your literature thematically.
> - Plan your literature review.
> - Write the literature review.

WHAT DO I NEED TO DO?

A checklist of actions at the end of a chapter that we recommend you complete at each stage of your dissertation. It is an opportunity to take stock of your progress, and plan what you need to do. You can also find these at the end of each chapter.

DELVE DEEPER

A list of useful resources that can help you navigate the process of research. While we can't always cover everything in the way that we might like in a short book, we have provided an annotated list of further recommendations at the end of each chapter to direct you to other useful sources.

> **DELVE DEEPER**
> **Bryman, A. (2016). *Social Research Methods* (5th edition). Oxford: Oxford University Press.** Alan's book has a number of chapters devoted to qualitative analysis. There are extended discussions on grounded theory, analytic induction, narrative analysis, and discourse analysis, as well as a chapter devoted to getting to grips with NVivo, one of the most popular CAQDAS platforms. It will be of particular interest to those who are looking for a more extended discussion of the issues we introduce here.

> **Snowball sample** A *non-probability sample* in which the researcher makes initial contact with a small group of people who are relevant to the research topic and then uses these to establish contacts with others.
>
> **Spurious relationship** A *relationship* between two *variables* is said to be spurious if it is being produced by the impact of a third variable (often referred to as a confounding variable). When the third *variable* is controlled, the *relationship* disappears.
>
> **Standard deviation** A measure of dispersion around the *mean*.

GLOSSARY OF KEY TERMS

Short definitions of key terms are provided at the end of the book. Glossary terms are in bold and green when first used in the text.

GUIDE TO THE ONLINE RESOURCES

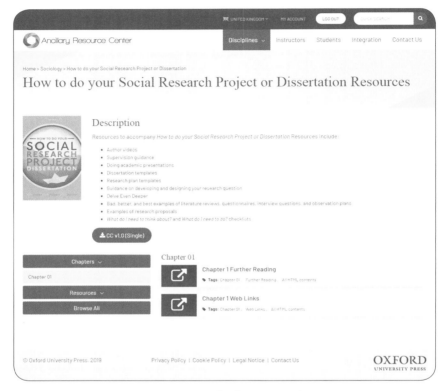

www.oup.com/uk/brymansrple

AUTHOR VIDEOS
Additional advice around key challenges for each chapter, including developing a research idea, managing your time, and writing up your dissertation.

SUPERVISION GUIDANCE
Advice and tips on how to approach your supervision meetings, including tasks to help you plan for meetings and to build a productive relationship with your supervisor.

DOING ACADEMIC PRESENTATIONS
Support with planning and delivering presentations, including tips on what a dissertation presentation might include, as well as author videos showing examples of a good and bad presentations.

DISSERTATION TEMPLATES

Templates for dissertations, showing how dissertations might look different depending on which theoretical and methodological approaches you use. This includes notes on chapter content and tips on dissertation structure.

RESEARCH PLAN TEMPLATES

Templates for you to use for planning your project, including helping you to get started and complete the dissertation, and to manage your time using key milestones and recommended timescales and targets.

GUIDANCE ON DEVELOPING AND DESIGNING YOUR RESEARCH QUESTION

A set of questions divided into categories and designed to help you formulate ideas, develop your thinking, set your research questions, and help you later on in the process to consolidate your argument and consider the contribution of your work.

DELVE EVEN DEEPER

Even more Delve Deeper recommendations and research suggestions, including a list of freely available data sets, links and resources to help you understand SPSS and NVivo processes and tools, analysis tools and help for specific research methods, and guidance on using vlogs, blogs, and other public resources, as well as using social media for your research.

BAD, BETTER, AND BEST EXAMPLES OF LITERATURE REVIEWS, QUESTION-NAIRES, INTERVIEW QUESTIONS, AND OBSERVATION PLANS

Examples of each of these key elements of your project deliberately designed to demonstrate how you can improve your work, and highlighted with annotations to help you gain a deeper understanding of how best to approach these stages of your project.

EXAMPLES OF RESEARCH PROPOSALS

Examples of research proposals for different social sciences to give you that extra support and an idea of what to expect. Here you will find tips on how to build a proposal and consider how this is useful for planning the dissertation.

WHAT DO I NEED TO THINK ABOUT? AND WHAT DO I NEED TO DO? CHECKLISTS

Digital versions of the end-of-chapter checklists for you to download and use.

ACKNOWLEDGEMENTS

Liam and Tom would like to thank members of the Department of Sociological Studies, University of Sheffield, for thoughts and ideas in relation to the content of this book. A special thanks to Calum Webb for his feedback on the quantitative analysis chapter, and Kitty Nichols for her work with us on the online resources. Liam and Tom would also like to thank all of the staff and students who have provided helpful feedback on the book and, in some cases, agreed to be quoted in the book. This feedback has been invaluable in improving the content.

A big thank you also goes to all the students we have taught over the years for their many comments, criticisms, and suggestions about how to improve the teaching of social research methods. We do listen, and we try to incorporate their ideas into our teaching.

Huge thanks, too, to Stephanie Southall and Sarah Iles at Oxford University Press for their patience, feedback, and guidance throughout the process of writing this book. They really have given so much time, effort, and enthusiasm and we very much appreciate their hard work.

Finally, thanks go to our families, Lydia, Betsy Lou (born while writing this book), Cassie and Chloe, and Kathy and Ian (who also proofread the book). Your support and encouragement have been invaluable.

Tom Clark and Liam Foster, 3 March 2019

The authors and Oxford University Press would like to sincerely thank all the students who formed part of our Student Advisory Panel for their comments and reviews. Your help in shaping the book, and sharing your experiences, was invaluable.

Anesu Mlauzi, BA Politics and International Relations, University of Hertfordshire

Antonia Panayotova, BA Communication and Media, University of Leeds

Ashley Neat, MA International Relations, University of Groningen

Ashley Taylor, BA Politics and International Relations, University of Limerick

Azhar Chaudhry, BA Politics, Philosophy and Economics, University of Exeter

Daniel Skeffington, BA Politics and International Relations, University of Bath

Danielle McMinn, BSc Criminology, University of Roehampton

David Coningsby, BA Geography, University of Chester

Eliska Herinkova, BA International Relations, University of Essex

Ellie Fitzpatrick, BSc Criminology and Sociology, University of Salford

Georgia Peterson, BA International Relations, Coventry University

Gerbrand Eefting, BA International Relations, Malmö University

James Rivett, BA Politics and International Relations, University of Kent

Jesse Hocking, BSc Criminology and Sociology, University of Surrey

Julie Keaveney, BSc Hons Counselling with Mentoring, Huddersfield University

Junayna Al-Sheibany, BA Politics, University of Kent

Justin van Lierop, Master International Security, Rijksuniversiteit Groningen

Katherine Bayford, BA Politics, University of Nottingham

Liisa Toomus, MSci International Relations & Global Issues, University of Nottingham

Mariana Matias, BA Politics with International Studies, University of Warwick

Megan Robinson, BSc Criminology with Forensic Psychology, University of Bolton

Parvez Minhas, BA Politics, Demontford University

Popescu Iulia Gabriela, BA International Relations, University of Essex

Roxana Dumitrescu, BA International Relations with Applied Quantitative Methods, University of Essex

Roxana-Claudia Tompea, BA International Relations, University of Essex

Sanzida Rahman, BSc Sociology, University of Surrey

Sophie Worrall, BA Politics with International Studies, University of Warwick

Stefania Irina Inoescu, BA Politics with International Studies, University of Warwick

Tan Wei Ern Sean, BA Politics and International Studies, University of Warwick

Vilde Bye Dale, BA Modern History and Politics, University of Essex

We are also immensely grateful to all the supervisors who gave their time and expertise to review draft material throughout the writing process.

Professor Alexander Dhoest, Communication Studies, University of Antwerp, Belgium

Dr Anna Tarrant, Reader in Sociology, University of Lincoln

Dr Ashley Dodsworth, Lecturer in Politics, University of Bristol

Dr David T. Smith, Senior Lecturer in Government and International Relations, University of Sydney

Dr Dominik Duell, Lecturer in Political Science, University of Essex

Dr Douglas Brown, Senior Lecturer in Geographic Information Systems and Human Geography, Kingston University

Dr Gethin Rees, Lecturer in Sociology, Newcastle University

Dr Ingrid A. Medby, Senior Lecturer in Political Geography, Oxford Brookes University

Professor Jackie Leach-Scully, Bioethics, University of New South Wales

Dr Jacqueline Dynes, Senior Teaching Fellow in Education Policy, University of Warwick

Dr Kate Burningham, Reader in Sociology of the Environment, University of Surrey

Dr Katharine A. M. Wright, Lecturer in International Politics, Newcastle University

Dr Magnus Feldmann, Senior Lecturer in Politics, University of Bristol

Dr Marie-Louise Glebbeek, Assistant Professor of Cultural Anthropology, Utrecht University

Dr Mark Holton, Lecturer in Human Geography, University of Plymouth

Dr Michael Pugh, Lecturer in Politics, University of the West of Scotland

Dr Neil Evans, Lecturer in Human Geography and Planning, Leeds Beckett University

Dr Patrick Diamond, Senior Lecturer in British Politics and Public Policy, Queen Mary, University of London

Ms Paula Surridge, Senior Lecturer in Sociology, University of Bristol

Dr Rebecca Westrup, Senior Lecturer in Education, University of East Anglia

Dr Ruth Penfold-Mounce, Senior Lecturer in Criminology, University of York

Dr Siobhan McAndrew, Lecturer in Sociology with Quantitative Methods, University of Bristol

Dr Victoria Foster, Senior Lecturer in Social Sciences, Edge Hill University

Thank you also to the numerous reviewers (both students and supervisors) who have chosen to remain anonymous, but contributed considerably to the final proposition. Thank you for taking the time to provide us with thoughtful feedback.

SUPERVISORS QUOTED IN THE BOOK

Dr Anna Tarrant, Reader in Sociology, University of Lincoln

Dr Ashley Dodsworth, Lecturer in Politics, University of Bristol

Dr Ingrid A. Medby, Senior Lecturer in Political Geography, Oxford Brookes University

Dr Jacqueline Dynes, Senior Teaching Fellow in Education Policy, University of Warwick

Dr Kate Burningham, Reader in Sociology of the Environment, University of Surrey

Dr Katharine A. M. Wright, Lecturer in International Politics, Newcastle University

Dr Michael Pugh, Lecturer in Politics, University of the West of Scotland

Dr Patrick Diamond, Senior Lecturer in British Politics and Public Policy, Queen Mary, University of London

Dr Ruth Penfold-Mounce, Senior Lecturer in Criminology, University of York

Dr Siobhan McAndrew, Lecturer in Sociology with Quantitative Methods, University of Bristol

STUDENTS QUOTED IN THE BOOK

Antonia Panayotova, Communication and Media, University of Leeds

Ashley Neat, International Relations and International Organisations, University of Warwick

Ashley Taylor, Politics and International Relations, University of Limerick

Azhar Chaudhry, Politics, Philosophy and Economics, University of Exeter

David Coningsby, Geography, University of Chester

Eliska Herinkova, Politics and International Relations, University of Essex

Georgia MarchbankPeterson, International Relations, Coventry University

Jesse Hocking, BSc Criminology and Sociology, University of Surrey

Junayna Al-Sheibany, Politics and International Studies, University of Kent

Liisa Toomus, International Relations and Global Issues, University of Nottingham

Mariana Matias, Politics and International Studies, University of Warwick

Megan Robinson, Criminal and Forensic Psychology, University of Bolton

Rachael O'Neill, Politics, and International Relations, University of Nottingham

Roxana Dumitrescu, International Relations with Applied Quantitative Methods, University of Essex

Sophie Worrall, Politics and International Studies, University of Warwick

Stefania Irina Ionescu, Politics and International Studies, University of Warwick

Vilde Bye Dale, Modern History and Politics, University of Essex

PERMISSIONS

The authors and publisher would also like to thank the following for permission to use copyright material:

Figure 13.4—data adapted from the UNESCO Institute for Statistics (UIS) (2019) http://www.uis.unesco.org/. Reproduced with permission from UNESCO.

Figure 13.5—data adapted from Office for National Statistics and Valuation Office Agency (2015) *Housing summary measures analysis.* https://www.ons.gov.uk/peoplepopulationandcommunity/housing/articles/housingsummarymeasure sanalysis/2015-08-05. Adapted from data from the Office for National Statistics licensed under the Open Government Licence v.3.0. Crown Copyright.

Figure 13.6—data adapted from Office for National Statistics (2016) *Conceptions in England and Wales: 2014: Annual statistics on conceptions covering conception counts and rates, by age group including women under 18.* Statistical bulletin. ONS. https://www.ons.gov.uk/peoplepopulationandcommunity/birthsdeathsandmarriages/conceptionandfer tilityrates/bulletins/conceptionstatistics/2015. Adapted from data from the Office for National Statistics licensed under the Open Government Licence v.3.0. Crown Copyright.

Tables 13.10 and 13.11—data adapted from the University of Manchester, Cathie Marsh Centre for Census and Survey Research, ESDS Government (2011). *British Crime Survey 2007–2008: Unrestricted Access Teaching Dataset* [data collection]. BMRB, Social Research, Home Office, Research, Development and Statistics Directorate, [original data producer(s)]. BMRB, Social Research. SN: 6891. Contains public sector information licensed under the Open Government Licence v.2.0. Crown copyright held jointly with the Economic and Social Data Service.

Chapters 11 and 13—include some content drawn from quantitative workbooks produced with the assistance of funding from a grant from the Higher Education Academy, now Advance HE (HEA Grant GEN1004).

PREFACE

One of the most satisfying elements of undertaking a qualification in the social sciences is, without a doubt, the opportunity to conduct a research project. Often positioned at the culmination of study, many colleges and universities will call such a project a dissertation. This is an extended piece of work on a particular topic, and it involves the written presentation of research that you have carried out. The thought of doing this might seem a little daunting at first, but with the right advice and some hard work, it is actually an enjoyable thing to do. It gives you the opportunity to investigate an aspect of the human world that you are interested in finding out about—and what could be better than that! However, a dissertation project also allows you to demonstrate a number of skills and capacities that are likely to be important as you graduate. Not only does it allow you to develop your expertise in a particular area, it also enables you to put the skills you have learned into practice and demonstrate that you can carry out an independent project through to completion.

The dissertation process is also one of the most rewarding elements of being an academic. It is really satisfying to see our students develop their ideas and produce interesting and insightful research. However, our experience of supervising dissertations suggests that there are many elements of doing a dissertation that can't feasibly be covered in a module handbook, or even the one-to-one supervision sessions we have with our students. We are also aware that not all supervision experiences are necessarily positive ones.

So, when Alan Bryman approached us about the prospect of writing a book that would take students through the whole process of doing a dissertation or research project, we thought it was an excellent idea. We wanted to produce a 'toolkit' that was as useful as it was accessible, and would allow students to write the best dissertation possible, no matter where they were or who they were working with. But we didn't want to just lecture. Instead, we specifically chose to work with Oxford University Press because of their innovative student panel. They really do care what their readers think about the textbooks they produce and directly engage with them to make sure that their books really meet the needs of students (see https://global.oup.com/ukhe/panel/). In writing this book, we deliberately drew on the experiences of the students on the panel who have been through the process of writing a dissertation. We also consulted with a number of academics who have supervised dissertations to make sure that we included their perspectives too. You'll meet some of these people as you make your way through the book.

We wanted to give you real insight into what it is like to do a research project, and how you can better navigate your own voyage of discovery. It was actually one of the students on the panel who came up with the metaphor of a 'voyage' that we have used as a theme throughout the book. Starting with the process of generating and developing your research ideas, we show you how to develop your project, how to collect data and analyse it, and how to think critically when writing it up. We believe that by reading this book, you will be in the best position to produce a dissertation that you can be proud of. We hope you agree.

Tom Clark and Liam Foster, 5 March 2019

CHAPTER I

INTRODUCTION

WHAT IS A DISSERTATION?

If you are reading this book, then you are likely to be doing a research project in the social sciences. Perhaps you are doing a dissertation, a 'final year project', or a piece of research in relation to a specific module. It is probably one of the most exciting, but challenging, tasks that you will undertake and it is likely to be the pinnacle of your programme. A dissertation or research project provides you with the opportunity to explore and understand a topic in great detail. It is likely to concern a subject that you are particularly interested in learning more about, and it will enable you to demonstrate that you have expertise in a particular area. But by undertaking a research project, you also have the opportunity to become a researcher, moving away from being a student or knowledge customer to being a knowledge creator. 'Doing research' is a key part of becoming a social scientist.

Focusing on a particular area of interest for the purposes of research can be extremely enjoyable and rewarding, but it is often approached with trepidation by students. This sense of fear is understandable given that it represents a larger piece of work than you are probably used to completing. Depending on the needs of your course, dissertations or 'final year projects' are likely to require anywhere between 8,000 and 15,000 words, and usually carry a larger number of credits than other modules. This means that it can have considerable impact on your final mark or classification.

Fortunately, this book has been written to help you to do your research. It takes you through each stage of the research process, providing advice and guidance along the way. As a form of independent learning, dissertation research is an opportunity for deep learning as you develop an in-depth knowledge of a topic. This will require quite a lot of effort and it is likely that your research will take place over a period of 9 to 12 months. Perhaps it is taking place over the whole of the final year of your degree. Of course, some courses may have a shorter time period, but it is still a big task. It might also have different requirements depending on your institution or department. For example, it will normally involve you carrying out your own analysis of data, although some courses may require you to undertake an extended literature review instead. Regardless, we will make sure you are clear about the requirements of your project and, in breaking up the research process into manageable chunks, help you develop a timetable for completing your dissertation which is attainable.

Dissertation research reflects and builds on many skills you will have directly developed throughout your course. It requires knowledge of research methods, a capacity to locate and use literature critically, and the ability to present a coherent and evidenced argument. But research also builds on your existing skills and we'll help you to develop the confidence necessary to explore your own research ideas, collect and analyse primary or secondary data, and present your findings in a critically informed manner. These are all things that can be developed with considered instruction. So if you have been doing well in your degree and you follow the dissertation guidance and work hard, then getting a good mark for your project is achievable. In fact, it might actually be an opportunity for you to improve your overall marks while working on something that you are particularly interested in—especially if you access the resources and support available to you. Again, we'll be highlighting these points of support throughout the book. In particular, we'll show you how you can get the best out of your relationship with your supervisor and/or module coordinator. Although dissertation research is independent in nature, you are not completely alone, and we'll make sure that you get the most out of whatever support you have in your particular institution. With a bit of dedication, hard work, and planning, we're sure that this book will help you rise to the challenge and develop the skills and capacities needed to become a great researcher!

WHY USE THIS BOOK?

As we have already established, the process of working on a dissertation can be daunting, even if you have the benefit of excellent supervision and guidance. It is for this reason that we decided to write a comprehensive guide that will help you to actually do a dissertation-style research project. We have developed *How to do Your Social Research Project or Dissertation* to help you to make all of the decisions that are needed to successfully produce your dissertation and complete your programme of study. We have designed it to map out the journey of doing a social research project, and we draw on a variety of examples from social science disciplines. So, whether you are studying sociology, anthropology, psychology, criminology, politics and political science, human geography, education, media studies, or even subjects like nursing, you should find the book useful.

The book will help you to move from a focus on the theory of research methods—which you are likely to have learned about in lectures—to the **process** of actually undertaking your own research. Learning about research methods is not always the same as actually doing research. So, we've written the book as a 'toolkit' to help navigate the dissertation process. We'll take you, step by step, through the processes of planning, designing, conducting, and writing up your research. By breaking the dissertation down into smaller linked stages, we'll show you how you can make research much more manageable. We will explain what you need to know, think about, and what you need to do (and how to do it!), as well as highlighting the potential challenges that might be encountered, and what you can do to avoid them.

However, this book should be used alongside discussions with supervisors, fellow students, and information provided by your university. It should act as an accompaniment, helping you to understand the dissertation process and get the most out of your supervision. Your university will normally provide you with a handbook outlining the requirements of the dissertation, including the word count, format, and expectations regarding your roles and responsibilities. Obviously, familiarizing yourself with your module handbook is a very good idea. However, completing a successful dissertation involves much more than adhering to those guidelines, and you will need to draw on a variety of skills and strategies to produce an excellent piece of research. We've designed this book to help you do just that.

HOW TO USE THIS BOOK

How to do Your Social Research Project or Dissertation is written in such a way as to help you conceptualize and manage the task of successfully completing a dissertation. It is structured to enable you to navigate the key stages in completing a dissertation. While the best way to use How to do Your Social Research Project or Dissertation is to read it from cover to cover, you can use particular chapters in isolation or miss out those that don't directly relate to your project. Individual chapters are designed to be 'detachable' so you can also use the book as a reference point in relation to particular aspects of the research process. You also need to be aware that although research is often presented as a linear process, starting with developing the question and finishing with the final product, the bits in between are not always as orderly as we might want them to be. So, while we have written the book in terms of the 'typical' stages of research, don't be surprised if your project deviates somewhat from this. This is not unusual!

Throughout the book you will also find a number of features that will help you to deal with the challenges of undertaking a dissertation, and that suggest how you might overcome them. These features are not only based on what we have learned from supervising students, but also draw directly on the experiences of students who have undertaken a dissertation, and the expertise of dissertation supervisors from different disciplines. These features include:

- **What do I need to know?**—At the beginning of each chapter, you will find a concise bullet point checklist. This will show you what you need to know, with each point corresponding to each section of the particular chapter. It will help you navigate through the content, and quickly and efficiently highlights what you will find in the chapter. A short section will accompany each list to introduce you to the content and help you to place the material within the overall process of doing a research project.
- **I wish I'd known …**—This feature has been written in collaboration with students and supervisors. It provides information about those little things that it would have been useful to know at the various stages of the dissertation process. It includes snippets of advice from a range of students and supervisors working in different disciplines, and tells you what they wish

they had known about their experiences, so you don't have to make the same mistakes. We have also added a few extra tips that we offer to our students.

- **Working with your supervisor**—Developing a working relationship with a supervisor can be hard, so we've put together some advice about how you might get the most out of the process. Drawing on our own experience, as well as that offered by other supervisors, this advice should help you to understand how to make the most of your supervisor and how to best prepare for your meetings with them.

- **Finding your way**—Think of this as hints and tips for good research! This feature provides key pieces of advice that are designed to help you find your way as you navigate the journey of doing a dissertation. The advice provides insight that will help you succeed, and also enable you to react positively to those unexpected things that occur when doing research.

- **What do I need to think about?**—This feature, located at the end of each chapter, provides a series of questions that will help you to reflect on the key issues in the chapter. Thinking through your answers—and they will be personal to your project—will consolidate both your understanding of key issues, and how they relate to your project.

- **What do I need to do?**—This provides a checklist of actions at the end of a chapter to take forward in your dissertation. It is an opportunity to reflect, take stock of your progress, and plan what you need to do.

- **Delve deeper**—There are a lot of resources available that can help you navigate the process of research. It is also true enough to say that the limitations on the size of this book mean that we can't always cover everything in the way that we might like. So, at the end of each chapter, we've provided an annotated list of further recommendations that will help direct you to other useful sources.

- **Glossary of key terms**—Short definitions of key terms are provided at the end of the book. The terms included in the glossary are in bold and green when first used in the text.

HOW IS THE BOOK ORGANIZED?

Following this introduction, **Chapter 2: The social research process** introduces you to the notion that research is a **process**. It has periods of plain sailing, but there are also unexpected developments that can throw you off course. Indeed, in some senses, the research process is a bit like undertaking a voyage across the sea, and this is an analogy that we develop in Chapter 2. The chapter also shows you how theory can be used in social research, so you can begin to explore, describe, and explain the human world with greater confidence. In **Chapter 3: Getting started**, we examine the more practical foundations on which all research projects are built and guide you through the realities of planning and managing your dissertation. This includes how to negotiate the workload of the research process, how to cope with unexpected problems, and how to best use your supervisor. **Chapter 4: Developing a research idea** takes you through a number of techniques that will help you to identify your research interests, develop project ideas, and build a rationale for research. We also consider how research is evaluated and explore the idea of quality in research. In following through this, you will begin to develop an understanding of what makes a good dissertation-style project.

The next two chapters focus on the role and uses of literature in research. **Chapter 5: Conducting a literature search** guides you through the process of literature searching, outlining how to develop a successful search strategy and how to search with greater efficiency. Once you have found this literature, you then need to use it, and **Chapter 6: Reviewing the literature** provides specific information about how to construct your literature review. We show you how the literature review plays an important role in framing your project; how it guides the emphasis of your data collection; how it informs your analysis; and how to situate your findings within a wider body of knowledge. Once you've developed an idea, outlined a rationale for research, and found the relevant literature, you need to know about different types of research strategy available to you, and the different research designs that flow from those strategies. **Chapter 7: Building your project** introduces you to these frameworks, and helps you to define the type of project that you are going to carry out.

Ethics are also extremely important in relation to social research. They provide a set of value-based principles that enable us to conduct research in an appropriate manner. **Chapter 8: Ethics** examines the basics of ethical practice—including informed consent, confidentiality, anonymity, avoidance of harm, and privacy—before introducing the nature and purpose of ethical review boards. At this point, you should now have enough knowledge to be able to construct a research pro-posal. **Chapter 9: Writing a research proposal** details the requirements of a typ-ical research proposal and offers useful advice about what information needs to go where and why. We then focus on who, or what, to focus on in your study in **Chapter 10: Sampling**. The chapter explores the process of identifying and designing your sampling frame, and we'll explain the key principles of both probability and non-probability sampling. This will show you why **who** you ask is just as important **what** you ask.

The next two chapters focus on data collection. **Chapter 11: Collecting quanti-tative data** discusses the basics of collecting information that is numerical in nature. Explaining the different levels of measurement that are associated with quantitative research, we will take you through the processes by which quantitative data can be designed and collected. **Chapter 12: Collecting qualitative data** then introduces you to the other side of the coin, qualitative data. Focusing on qualitative interviewing and participant observation, we discuss some of the common considerations that arise when thinking about qualitative data, and offer some useful advice about navigating the problems that can arise when collecting it.

The process of analysing the data you have collected then forms the basis of the next two chapters. **Chapter 13: Analysing quantitative data** focuses on how to organize and present numerical information using some of the basic techniques of quantitative analysis. We show you how to present your findings and, crucially, relate them back to your original research aims and objectives. In **Chapter 14: Analysing qualitative data**, we move on to discuss the analysis of qualitative material. We introduce you to the iterative processes of coding and categorization, as well as some of the major types of qualitative analysis. We'll show you how to identify key concepts in your data, and how those concepts can be connected to theory. **Chapter 15: Working with documents** provides a practical guide for those students who want to conduct research using documents. Exploring the many different types of document that can be used in social research, this chapter also outlines the processes by which they can be analysed.

The final set of chapters focus on reflecting on your research and the process of writing it up. **Chapter 16: Evaluating your project** shows you how to think through the value of your project, discussing the notion of reflexivity and demonstrating why critical thinking is necessary when evaluating your research project. The final chapter, **Chapter 17: Writing up**, takes you through the process of writing up your dissertation. It identifies the basic elements of writing a dissertation and introduces you to the structures, forms, and styles that are commonly used to create one. The chapter emphasizes the importance of creating an argument or narrative. This provides the core thread of the written dissertation.

Overall, *How to do Your Social Research Project or Dissertation* should provide you with the necessary guidance and skills to undertake a theoretically informed independent research project in the social sciences. By using this book, and taking into account the support of your supervisor and university guidelines, we're sure you can produce a dissertation that you are proud of and achieve a high mark!

CHAPTER 2

THE SOCIAL
RESEARCH PROCESS

WHAT DO I NEED TO KNOW?

- What is the process of social research?
  - Social research and the voyage of discovery
- The key characteristics of social research
- What are the main types of social research?
- What are the purposes of social research?
  - Describing the human world
  - Exploring the human world
  - Explaining the human world
- The role of theory in social research
  - Induction: from research to theory
  - Deduction: from theory to research

INTRODUCTION

This chapter will outline some of the basic features of social research. It will introduce you to the notion that social research is a process, help to clarify the reasons why you might carry it out, and explore the relationship between theory and research. Using the analogy of a voyage, it demonstrates that specific tasks associated with **doing** research tend to be ordered, but not always orderly. There are dynamic points of issue that need to be negotiated for you to move your dissertation project toward completion, or otherwise risk being blown off course. By understanding what is meant by the research process, and how theory can be used in social research, you can begin to explore, describe, and explain the human world with greater confidence.

WHAT IS THE PROCESS OF SOCIAL RESEARCH?

Social research is concerned with finding out about the world that we live in. It directs our attention to the things that people do as they go about their personal and professional lives and attempts to make some sense of them. The idea of 'social' specifically frames the focus of study on the individuals, interactions, and institutions that comprise human experience. This means that social research can encompass the disciplines of sociology, anthropology, psychology, criminology, politics and political science, human geography, education, media studies, or even subjects like social work and nursing. Given that people are a ubiquitous feature of the human world, there is actually very little that social scientists cannot be interested in.

Research, on the other hand, is a particular form of 'organized' discovery that conforms to a range of conventions associated with a wider community of knowledge-makers. As we will discover, while all social research is not the same, it does tend to follow an established and systematic process that is made transparent in the ways that it is carried out and communicated. This enables any single piece of research to be assessed within a wider framework of critique. That is to say that 'good' research should be subject to the evaluation, judgement, and discussion of significant others in the community. This helps to establish and sustain its integrity and veracity.

Social research is, therefore, a process that involves researchers and wider public communities. This will be a key theme throughout this book. What we mean by this is that social research is informed by a number of shared ideas **and** is characterized by a series of actions related to a specific goal. So, while there are general concepts and procedures associated with all social research, their realization in a specific project will often be quite different. There are any number of options and techniques available at each stage of a research project. This is exactly why the practice of social research is understood to be a process, rather than a standard or predictable routine.

To this end, it seems to us that the process of doing social research is actually a lot like a voyage of discovery.

Social research and the voyage of discovery

The research process is something of a journey into the unknown. Through doing a dissertation, not only are you discovering answers to the research aims and objectives that you set yourself, it might be the first time you have examined a topic in this much depth, and it may even be the first time you have conducted a piece of research. It also usually involves working with, and/or relying on, other people. This will include your supervisor, but during the process of research you are also likely to meet, and depend on, a myriad of people 'in the field'. These might be your participants or other people, such as librarians, key contacts, or associated professionals. Dissertation-style research also often takes up a significant proportion of the marks in a course or programme of study, and it is usually strictly limited by time. For all these reasons, the experience of actually **doing** research is often quite different from reading about it in a textbook—and, not too surprisingly, these pressures can create challenges. However, just like sailing on the ocean, if you are properly equipped with the right tools and knowledge, it is possible to navigate your way through your voyage of discovery with greater ease and precision.

Before you embark on your journey through the research process, you need a sense of where you are going, or at least to have a very good idea of the direction of travel. You will, for instance, need to develop a topic of interest and a series of research aims and objectives in relation to it. Sailing known routes will not lead

you to new places, and you are likely to need to demonstrate originality somewhere in your project. But while you could try to find new lands to explore new
problems, you could also try to find new routes to known destinations and
approach established problems from a different perspective.

Embarking on your research journey without sufficient preparation is likely to
leave you sailing into rough seas or simply getting lost. So you will need to chart
a course that will enable you to navigate your way through the reefs and shallows
that you will encounter. This is the purpose of understanding and **using** research
methods. Just like a compass, map, and sail, they give you the tools necessary to
respond to the demands of your intended destination.

But just like a voyage on the open ocean, you still might encounter some rough
seas and all might not be plain sailing. While the research process is ordered, it is
not always orderly. It is true enough to say that social research is characterized by
a sequence of tasks that need to be completed, and that these tasks tend to come
in a general sort of order. You start with an idea, conduct a literature search,
design a study, collect data, analyse your findings, and write up the project.
However, when you look beyond this typical 'research timeline', things can get a
little messier. There are certain things that can put wind in your sails and speed up
the process of discovery, but there are also those incidents that can blow us off
course or set us adrift. You might, for instance, find that a key participant pulls out
of an interview at the last minute, or discover that the direction that your results
have taken do not match your initial literature search and you need to conduct a
new one. On the other hand, you might discover you have access to a large number of participants, or use a form of computer-assisted analysis that allows you to
process your results with greater efficiency. If you find yourself sailing against the
wind, changing course might be necessary to navigate the conditions you
encounter.

On your voyage, you are also unable to sail off into the sunset—dissertation
research is constrained in a number of ways—so you need to know how long
your provisions will last so you can sufficiently meet your deadlines. Perhaps most
importantly, you need to know how your ship works so you can understand what
kind of research you're doing. Decisions made during the research process tend to
be related. One choice will often shape your options at a later stage of the process,
so being able to situate your project, and reflect on your progress, is likely to be
essential in arriving at your destination.

Of course, there are many ways in which the research process is different to
sailing on the high seas. However, it is a good way to begin to think about social
research, as it emphasizes the dynamic nature of the research process. It also highlights how you are intimately involved in the direction that the research project
takes, and how you will need to be responsive to the demands of your particular
project. We will return to this idea of the 'voyage of the research' as we move
through the book.

THE KEY CHARACTERISTICS OF SOCIAL RESEARCH

In order to fully understand what social research might entail, it is briefly worth considering how it is different from other ways of making claims about the human world. This will help us to articulate why research is considered to be a more secure form of knowledge production. Perhaps the key distinction to be made here is between social research and common sense. In its everyday form, common sense is well understood and often used with great impact. It can be considered to be something of a combination of intuition, intelligence, and experience. Common sense can be applied to problems to find solutions, or to explain or prevent mishaps. It is a heuristic device that helps us to navigate our everyday experiences of the human world.

However, while the idea of a 'sense' that is 'common' suggests that it is something that many of us possess, typically it is only noticed by its absence. Just think of all those times you've heard, 'Why does [so and so] have no common sense?' As a way to explain a failure of cognition, interaction, or communication, the meaning of common sense is almost always open to interpretation. Perhaps this is why it has been so successful as an idea. Without precise specification, it can be used to account for a multitude of situations, and to explain a multitude of sins.

Social research, on the other hand, is not subject to those important vagaries of circumstance. It is a much more refined practice that has well-articulated characteristics. Put rather bluntly, social research should always be subject to rigour, transparency, and community. It also often involves notions of **reliability**, **validity**, **replicability**, and **generalization**. But for now, we'll focus on those initial three characteristics. These are what really differentiate it from common sense.

Rigour encompasses notions of both thoroughness and precision. Research has to conform to conventions of both history and practice. This is, in essence, what 'social research methods' are all about. They are established, and specific, tools and techniques for finding out about the human world. Unlike the rather vague idea of common sense, the researcher's toolbox is packed with specific instructions and instruments that enable them to find things out in a systematic way. Central to this intellectual equipment is the notion of critical thinking. This does not mean we are going to point out the negatives in everything. Instead, it means that at each and every stage of the research process we are reflecting on our practice and not taking anything for granted. This is exactly what we'll be doing throughout this book: showing you how to ask appropriate critical questions about the research methods you have chosen to employ. In large part, critical thinking helps to ensure both thoroughness and precision because it clarifies what you are doing and why.

The second key difference between social research and common sense is transparency. Read any empirically driven research paper and you will see a section that details how the research project was conducted. Typically entitled 'research methods', 'methodology', or 'the present study', this will provide an overview of the process by which the results of the paper were produced. It's a sort of 'recipe for the research' and often includes important information on the approach taken, the sample, and the methods of data collection and analysis. It performs a valuable function in terms of knowledge-making because it provides openness about how the knowledge was generated. The methods of the research are made available for inspection to anyone with an interest so they can be examined and assessed with respect to other viewpoints and perspectives. The purpose here is not to 'catch someone out' and identify where they have gone wrong in their thinking or calculations (although this does happen from time to time). Instead, it is to encourage and promote critical discussion. This helps to ensure that there is confidence in the system.

I WISH I'D KNOWN . . . WHAT IS MEANT BY THE TERM EMPIRICAL RESEARCH? 2.1

Empiricism is an established school of thought in philosophy that argues for the virtue of knowledge that is based on sensory experience. Empirical research is simply research that is based on some sort of systematic observation of the world. This includes material produced by **surveys**, interviews, and '**participant observation**', as well as methods of analysis such as content analysis that make use of documentary sources. Dissertations tend to be empirical projects because they rely on **primary** or **secondary data**. However, more theoretically orientated dissertations are also possible.

The final distinction between social research and common sense is the notion of community. Social research is not produced, understood, or communicated in a vacuum. It draws on other work in the subject area; is created by established 'tools of the trade'; and follows well-drawn conventions concerning how it is disseminated. Social research is always conducted within a network of other researchers, both past and present, and is designed to be as open as possible so that it can be assessed and examined by that community in terms of its rigour, originality, and significance. Again, this helps to ensure that any knowledge claims are supported by both robust argument and evidence.

Given these three characteristics, it is possible to articulate key points of the social research process that differentiate it from 'common sense':

- The aims and objectives of research are specified beforehand, and directed toward specific aspects of the human world
- Use of established, but adaptable, methods of investigation

- Data are detailed, rich, and complex
- Theoretically informed by other research
- Reflective—the role and perspective of the researcher are acknowledged
- Ethically informed and positioned
- Outputs are disseminated in the form of peer-reviewed books, journal papers, and conferences

WHAT ARE THE MAIN TYPES OF SOCIAL RESEARCH?

While the principle of an open and inquiring community is a good one to uphold, this does not mean that researchers always agree. One key fault line that is often reproduced in the literature on social research methods is the difference between qualitative and quantitative work. The focus of this division is usually centred on the types of data that are typically used for research.

Briefly, data are the types of things that help social scientists to record social life in some way. From data, analyses are made, evidence produced, and conclusions made. It is an often overlooked point, but data are actually the very life-blood of social science. There are, however, any number of ways of thinking about data, not to mention collecting and analysing it. We will be dealing with many of these throughout the book, but for now it is worth highlighting that not all data are the same, and what you can do with one type is not the same as what you can do with another.

So, whereas quantitative research is often taken to be research that uses data that are numerable in form, qualitative research is much broader in its field of vision. Indeed, qualitative data can include textual information, visual images, material objects, and even more diffuse senses like smell or emotion. However, this distinction between qualitative and quantitative types of data leads to some further important differences between researchers in terms of how they under-stand the human world, what their research is actually trying to achieve, and how it should be carried out.

Depictions of quantitative research tend to characterize it as having an objectivist ontology, a positivistic epistemology, and a deductive approach. While such terms might sound a little daunting, what this means in practice is that there is a broad assumption that there is a world 'out there' that can be meas-ured (objectivism); that measurements can produce 'rule-like' generalizations concerning the human world (positivism); and that the function of research is to 'test' a particular rule and deduce an answer through observation (deduction). As a result of these assumptions, quantitative research tends to be associated with more stable forms of data collection like those found in relatively fixed surveys and questionnaires.

I WISH I'D KNOWN . . . WHAT IS MEANT BY ONTOLOGY, EPISTEMOLOGY, AND METHODOLOGY 2.2

Different approaches to research make different assumptions about social life and how to understand it. In some cases, these assumptions will concern the nature of the human world (ontology), the types of knowledge that are valued (**epistemology**), and the means by which research is actually carried out (**methodology**). That is to say that how we perceive the world influences the types of knowledge we are trying to create, which, in turn, has an impact on how we investigate it. This is an important recognition as it influences the extent to which we can evaluate research and how we might be able to make comparisons between research projects. Suffice to say, we might not always be comparing like with like.

On the other hand, qualitative research is often depicted as having a constructivist ontology, an interpretivist epistemology, and is inductive in its approach. Again, what this means in practice is more straightforward than it might first appear: the social world is made up of ideas that are, more or less, historically and socially contingent (constructivism); the purpose of research is to provide rich insight and understanding (interpretivism); and, that research proceeds first with the business of data collection, followed by the attempt to theorize (induction). This means that the research tools that are particularly suited to qualitative research are those that can adapt to the changing rhythms and flows of everyday life, like the rather more flexible techniques of interviewing and participant observation. Table 2.1 provides a useful summary of quantitative and qualitative forms of research and their typical characteristics.

Table 2.1 **Types of social research**

	Quantitative research	Qualitative research
Data	Counts and numerable scales	Textual, visual material, sensory material
Ontology	Objectivism	Constructionism
Epistemology	Positivism	Interpretivism
Typical methods of data collection	Surveys, questionnaires	Interviews, participant observation
Approach	Deductive (theory → research)	Inductive (research → theory)

While it is true enough to say that there are often differences between these two ways of finding out about the human world—not to mention the types of knowledge that are produced—there are also a lot of similarities and it is easy to overdetermine their separation. Thumbnail descriptions do not do justice to the huge variety of approaches that exist within both quantitative and qualitative research. It is perfectly possible, for example, to conduct inductive quantitative research using observational data. Many social scientists who employ quantitative techniques would also baulk at the suggestion that their work was 'positivist' in nature, or that they are aiming to produce 'law-like generalizations'. Social phenomena can, and do, change. It is also perfectly possible to do qualitative work with the data produced by an open-ended questionnaire, and many qualitative researchers would highlight that, in many ways and for a number of reasons, the human world is not infinitely malleable but is instead relatively stable. This is not to reject the idea that context is important, but it is to recognize that social patterns are not just possible, but actually help to define human experience.

All of this is to say that while there do tend to be some differences in the type of data used in quantitative and qualitative research, and in the underlying assumptions that are associated with those uses, these are not inevitable and should be treated with caution. Remember, critical thinking and those three important characteristics of rigour, transparency, and community, underpin all social research. With that in mind, it is worth taking some time to explore some of the differences in what social research is aiming to do. To this end, we now turn our attention to the ideas of description, exploration, and explanation.

WHAT ARE THE PURPOSES OF SOCIAL RESEARCH?

Not all research is the same with respect to what it is trying to achieve, and any single research project might have different purposes as it moves through the research process. Sometimes this will be a consequence of the particular research method employed; in other instances it will be as a result of something more serendipitous, like an insightful discovery. As such, the purposes of social research can be broadly characterized as being concerned with describing the human world, exploring it, or explaining it.

Describing the human world

Some research projects attempt to summarize aspects of the human world. There are, for example, an array of descriptive techniques within the quantitative canon that are entirely directed toward summarizing general trends and patterns. A histogram that demonstrates the ethnic population of a city, for example, is a direct attempt to describe a particular facet of that city. Elsewhere, research can be used to provide rich insight into the lived experiences of people in particular places. For example, the field notes that are produced in the practice of participant observation are, in essence, attempts to capture something of what happened at a particular gathering or event. Semi-structured interviews similarly provide a space for participants to articulate how they feel about aspects of their experiences and lives. What all of these techniques share is an attempt to describe aspects of interaction, understanding, and experience.

Descriptive approaches have three distinct uses in the research process:

1. Provide rich detail in arenas of interest
2. Useful in summarizing complex pictures
3. Allow us to 'defamiliarize the familiar'

Exploring the human world

Exploration, on the other hand, usually takes place in novel arenas where there has been little research conducted before. Exploratory modes of research are those that do not attempt to offer finite answers to research questions and instead try provide a better understanding of the issue under question. This kind of approach is particularly suitable when the researcher is attempting to get a feel of what is important in a particular area, and how it can be understood. This makes the more flexible techniques of data collection associated with qualitative research particularly useful for exploratory research. Semi-structured interviews, for example, provide a means for participants to articulate what they feel is important, rather than imposing an agenda on them. These are commonly used in dissertation projects. However, exploratory research is not limited to qualitative research. Not only do open-ended questions provide a similar purpose in survey research, analytical techniques like 'factor analysis' can similarly be used to help explore quantitative data and the various associations and relationships that may be present within it.

There are a number of advantages to this type of approach:

1. Flexibility, and the ability to adapt to emergent themes and issues
2. It is particularly useful in arenas where little is known about the topic
3. It can be used to provide a secure platform to build explanations

Explaining the human world

Explanatory research is directed toward providing an understanding of causal processes in more or less specific contexts. It often seeks to provide conclusive answers to very specific research problems. In quantitative arenas, the purpose is often to find causal explanations through the selection and rejection of research hypotheses. This search for cause and effect is common in 'experimental research'.

But again, explanatory modes of research are also more than possible using qualitative techniques. Analytical induction, for example, involves the systematic examination of a range of individual cases to generate more universal understandings, which can then be refined against further observations. Becker's (1953) analysis of marijuana users—and more specifically, how people become marijuana users—incorporated this type of approach. Reacting against a wealth of health-related research that had suggested a number of causes for smoking the drug, Becker conducted a series of 50 interviews with marijuana users to demonstrate the processes by which people learned to use the drug for pleasure. This involved explaining how users learned to smoke it so it produces real effects, recognizing those effects and relating them to the drug, and learning to value these effects as enjoyable. So, rather than looking for traits in people that would make them more likely to use the drug, Becker argued that use was instead related to a set of changes in the person's conception of the activity, and their understanding of the value of the associated experience.

To continue the theme, there are a number of advantages to these explanatory approaches:

1. It allows a causal relationship to be identified and investigated
2. Specificity of research questions
3. Clarity of findings

THE ROLE OF THEORY IN SOCIAL RESEARCH

Having introduced the overarching purposes of social research, we now need to think carefully about the role of theory in the practice of describing, exploring, and explaining. The relationship between theory and research is a complex one, not least because the meaning of both words can vary. Briefly, theory is a generalized form of understanding that is used to inform our worldview. It can be made to work retrospectively or prospectively in that it can account for something that has already occurred **or** be a way of seeing and interpreting events in the present and/or future. As an abstracted framework for thinking, theory provides a lens through which we view and interpret the human world.

Theory can also be made to work at different levels. So-called 'grand theory' attempts to explain and/or understand the whole of society. Combining the philosophical, political, religious, economic, and sociological, this type of theorizing is often perceived to be highly abstract because grand theory does not appear to use the language of everyday life. Instead, it articulates an arrangement of higher-order concepts which are then used to explain the overarching social structures that would otherwise remain hidden from view. Grand theory has often been considered to be so far removed from everyday life, that it actually has no bearing on reality.

Middle-range—or meso-level—theories seek to understand more limited aspects of social life. Typically, this type of theorizing occurs at a more substantive level. That is to say that it is the explanation of things that we can immediately recognize as organizing principles in everyday life. Labelling theory, for example, attempts to understand how the process of labelling operates in specific contexts and what its consequences might be. Middle-range theories are usually quite flexible and can often be applied to a number of topics or issues. Theorizing at this level is often intimately bound up with empirical research.

Micro-level theory, on the other hand, is very specific and concentrates its attention on everyday human interactions. Small-scale in focus, it largely uses interpretative techniques to examine how interpersonal encounters are achieved 'in practice'. As a result, it has a very close relationship with empirical research. Ethnomethodology, for instance, examines very specific interactions and/or conversations in order to try and understand how meaning is created and sustained in the practice of everyday life.

There are, however, two other considerations with respect to the role of theory and research that are worth articulating. Sometimes, research is considered to be atheoretical in that it largely ignores the issue of theory altogether. Instead, such research is directed toward answering very concrete problems. Much 'evaluation research', for example, is directed toward asking 'what works?' in the context of policy and practice, rather than concerning itself with high-order analysis of the data.

Another consideration occurs where literature is used as a proxy, or substitute, for theory. Here, a particular theoretical orientation is not directly articulated or advanced in a project. Instead, the research base is used to contextualize the project and inform both the research aims and the research findings. This is not to say that the research is necessarily or essentially atheoretical. It is, however, to approach theory from a pragmatic point of view and use empirically orientated work to connect the project with the wider literature. Much applied research—where the research focus is on tackling very practical problems—uses this type of approach.

So, theory can be directed to different levels of analysis, and be more or less present in a project. However, it can also be ordered differently within the research process. There are two directions; we'll deal with each in turn.

Induction: from research to theory

Induction is a process of knowledge construction that moves from research to theory. Data and analysis are used to build or inform theory. This is not, however, to suggest that research begins *tabula rasa*—on a blank slate. Indeed, such naive empiricism—observation that is entirely free from theory—has long been demonstrated to be impossible. Theory always guides what we see, and what we see as interesting. Instead, the emphasis here is on being open to the range of possibilities that are prompted by any given research aim. Explanation is guided by the data collection and analysis rather than being imposed on it. Inductive research is conducted in a spirit of openness and flexibility with respect to what to describe, explore, and/or explain. This is, perhaps, why it is often seen to be more suitable for qualitative research projects as they tend to have more open-ended research questions.

Perhaps the most obvious example of an inductive approach within the social science research canon is a form of research known as 'grounded theory'. First articulated by Glaser and Strauss (1967) in their book *The Discovery of Grounded Theory*, this approach begins with a general research aim or idea and then proceeds to collect exploratory data. As data are collected, repeating ideas are collated into codes, which are themselves analysed alongside emergent data and organized into higher-order categories. These higher-order categories can then be used as the building blocks to articulate a theory of the area under study. Theory is, therefore, a property of analysis and follows data collection.

Grounded theory tends toward qualitative techniques of data collection because of its requirement for rich and detailed data (we will discuss this more in Chapter 14). However, inductive approaches can be taken when using quantitative data too. The famous statistician John Tukey (1977), for instance, believed that there was too much emphasis on hypothesis testing in statistics and instead advocated a number of methods that, taken together, would form what he termed 'exploratory data analysis'. In turn, the results of such exploration could then be used to build hypotheses. A number of these principles can be seen in contemporary techniques of 'data mining'—which, broadly speaking, is the automated attempt to extract patterns and trends from huge data sets. It is predominantly used in digital research methods.

Deduction: from theory to research

On the other hand, theory can precede data. There are, perhaps, two versions of this deductive approach.

Firstly, research can be used to 'test' theory. This is typical of much psychological research, where experiments are designed to assess which hypothesis is more likely to be correct. Hypotheses are a key part of what is known as the 'hypothetico-deductive model'. This is an important element of the scientific method and is a form of theorizing that articulates a specific research question where two answers are possible. Explicitly identified before data collection takes place, these answers are typically labelled the 'null hypothesis' and 'alternative hypothesis'. Research is then designed to enable the question to be 'tested' against findings to determine which answer can be shown to be false. Logically speaking, this process of falsification does not 'prove' the remaining hypothesis, but instead serves to reject what is demonstrably 'wrong'.

Secondly, theory can be used to examine the topic under investigation. In this variant, data collection does not function as a means to choose between competing theories. Instead, there is some preselection involved in terms of preferred orientation, with research used to explore, develop, or critique the theory in question. Much research that is feminist in outlook, for example, seeks to explore gender inequality, and in doing so, makes the a priori assumption that women are necessarily disadvantaged in a patriarchal society. In some cases, the theory in question was always going to provide a focus of the research. In other cases, it is an emergent process that happens during the course of the project, where a particular theoretical direction is taken because it is thought it will help to illuminate the findings.

CONCLUSION

It is worth highlighting that the features of social research that we have outlined in this chapter are illustrative in nature. To return to our initial idea of 'the research process', dissertation projects are often 'messy' in that they will often develop and change over time. 'Mixed methods' are a regular occurrence in the literature, and it is perfectly possible, for example, for a project to begin somewhat inductively, before clarifying a theory and testing it more purposefully. This is, in fact, a central tenet of a technique called analytic induction. We'll talk about that in more detail later in the book, but the point here has been to introduce you to some of the overarching assumptions that help to structure the practice of doing social science research, and how we can begin to navigate that landscape.

It's also worth pointing out that much of this is only tacitly contained in research papers that you might read. This is largely because much of the 'messiness' of research is 'cleaned up' when research is written up. There are practical reasons for this—strict word counts being one—and a certain level of knowledge is often assumed to make room for higher-level discussion. From the bottom looking up, this can make research papers often seem very daunting things to read. But, to return to our idea of seeing the social research process as a voyage of discovery, having an awareness of some of those invisible building blocks will soon help you sail with the wind and on toward your destination!

WHAT DO I NEED TO THINK ABOUT?

- Why is it important to think about social research as a process?
- How is the knowledge produced by social research different to common sense?
- What type of data might you like to work with, and what sorts of research does that tend to produce?
- Why do we do social research?
- How can theory be used in the research process?

WHAT DO I NEED TO DO?

☑ Make sure you understand what we mean by the social research process, and what key characteristics make the knowledge produced by research more secure than common sense.

☑ Think about what types of data you might like to work with.

☑ Consider the type of research you find most interesting—descriptive, exploratory, or explanatory?

☑ Think about 'theories' you are familiar with. How might they help inform your social research project or dissertation?

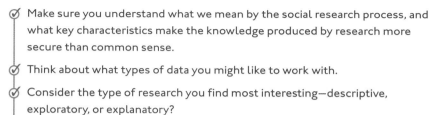

Access the online resources **www.oup.com/uk/brymansrp1e** to help you to successfully complete your social research project or dissertation.

DELVE DEEPER

Bryman, A. (2016). *Social Research Methods* **(5th edition). Oxford: Oxford University Press.** This is one of the most comprehensive textbooks on social research methods currently available—it's certainly one of the most popular among students doing dissertation-style research. Packed with empirical examples, it provides a thoroughgoing discussion of all aspects of research, including a detailed chapter on 'the nature and process of social research'. There is also a wealth of supporting material available online at www.oxfordtextbooks.co.uk/orc/brymansrm5e/ (Accessed 5 July 2016). We cannot recommend it highly enough—well, we would say that, wouldn't we!

Delanty, G. (2005). *Social Science: Philosophical and Methodological Foundations.* **Maidenhead: Open University Press.** For those of you who are interested in learning more about the philosophical assumptions that underpin different approaches to social research, Delanty's book is a great place to start. Written in a clear and unfussy manner, it is very readable and wide-ranging in coverage. It charts the development of social science from its beginnings in the sixteenth century right up to contemporary debates concerning constructivism and realism.

Dr Gerben Moerman's YouTube pages entitled 'Research methods and statistics' have a really useful playlist dedicated to issues of ontology and epistemology. Clear and engaging, the seven videos in the playlist are taken from a larger course on qualitative methods.
https://www.youtube.com/playlist?list=PLyLpEs0x9BnlSknrmaho Mrr7VI563CGX9 (Accessed 1 December 2018).

Graham Gibbs's YouTube pages have a lecture dedicated to 'the nature of social research' in which he discusses many of the issues we have explored in this chapter. It is quite detailed, but very informative. *https://youtu.be/pQ4RAHXtvS0 (Accessed 5 December 2018).*

Itsnotyouitsyourdata.com is a blog that explores different aspects of both undergraduate and postgraduate life. Written by a diverse array of academics—from PhD students to professors—it offers a wide variety of 'hints and tips'-style material directed toward many aspects of the research process. One of these blogs offers 'Top 10 hints for understanding your ontology, epistemology, and methodology'. Short, informative, and readable, it will help to consolidate your understanding of the relationship between ontology, epistemology, and methodology. You might also find some interesting material elsewhere on the site. *https://www.itsnotyouitsyourdata.com/undergraduates/top-10-hints-for-understanding-your-ontology-epistemology-and-methodology-2/ (Accessed 2 December 2018).*

Williams, M. (2000). *Science and Social Science: An Introduction.* **Oxford: Routledge.** This is another very accessible book about the philosophy of the social sciences, and how these debates have shaped the practice of social research. It outlines the development of natural science, and demonstrates how the social sciences have attempted to both retain and reject aspects of its distinctive methodology. Detailed, but always readable, Williams provides a number of short examples to illustrate the discussion and demonstrate how theoretical debates are realized in empirical research.

CHAPTER 3

GETTING STARTED

WHAT DO I NEED TO KNOW?

- Planning your project
  - First steps of planning
  - Structure
  - Managing your time
  - Managing yourself
- Working with your supervisor
- Expecting the unexpected

INTRODUCTION

We understand that you want to get on with doing your research, but carefully planning your dissertation or project is crucial to its success. As such, this is potentially the most important chapter in the whole book! It will examine how to negotiate the workload of the research process, how to cope with unexpected problems, and how you can best use your supervisor to support you through this process. If you can start your dissertation with a clear plan, and an agreement about your working relationship with your supervisor, it will limit the problems you might encounter further down the line and give you the best chance to fulfil your potential.

PLANNING YOUR PROJECT

A dissertation is a significant piece of investigative work. It requires the use of many basic skills. These include analytical and critical thinking, but also the ability to organize and plan your time. In many ways, you will prepare for your dissertation using skills you have developed when planning to write other assignments. However, there are key differences between dissertation research and other assignments, not least the amount of time you will spend on it. Dissertations require tenacity, hard work, and careful planning. While you may be good at writing short essays the night before they are due, this is not going to happen with the dissertation. Writing a dissertation is a complex process, which begins with the initial idea and continues with the research design, ethics approval process, data collection, analysis and write-up. All of these components require careful planning and execution. You will also need to make sure you are suitably prepared to deal with any obstacles that might come your way during the process. While we wouldn't go as far as to say 'fail to prepare, prepare to fail', failure to plan properly is likely to result in problems further on in the research.

FINDING YOUR WAY 3.1

Having a well-thought-out plan is integral to undertaking a successful research project. Without one, it is easy to lose focus, come up against unexpected changes, and struggle with time management.

First steps of planning

When you do a dissertation, the process begins long before you actually start collecting data—and the preliminary stages of planning are certainly just as important in enabling your project to run smoothly. There are a number of things you should do when planning your dissertation:

1. Identify your topic area and a potential title
2. Make sure your aims are achievable
3. Think about what kind of theoretical approach and methods to employ
4. Make sure your aims are ethically suitable
5. Familiarize yourself with dissertation guidelines and requirements, including the format that your dissertation should take

Firstly, you will need to identify your research interests. We're going to discuss how to develop a research idea more fully in Chapter 4, but it's worth highlighting here that it is often a good idea to make sure the topic you choose is something you find interesting, as you are going to spend a considerable amount of time researching it. You'll also need to narrow down this interest so that it is manageable. This can be a challenging process. We have seen many students come to us with initial ideas that are so broad they were more like three or four dissertations! Let us suppose, for example, that you were initially interested in the expansion of the use of social media across the western world, which groups were not using social media as frequently (for example, older people) and why, as well as types of training to encourage social media use. This kind of focus would need narrowing substantially because it is far too broad in scope. You would be much better off looking at a local initiative that was designed to teach older people how to use social media. You could then use semi-structured interviews to explore some of the barriers older people face in using social media and how they might be overcome. Familiarizing yourself with the literature in relation to the topic area (see Chapter 6) is crucial in both helping you to see what has already been written about an area, and in defining your scope. It will help you to develop your research ideas and position your research. This knowledge provides you with a platform to identify a research gap, and to introduce the aims and objectives of your project.

I WISH I'D KNOWN . . . THE IMPORTANCE OF CHOOSING A TOPIC OF INTEREST 3.1

The dissertation can be a much more enjoyable and rewarding process if it is based on a topic of interest that you can explore in detail.

"*Choose a topic that you are passionate about and that you want to understand more about. I still follow this advice in my own research. If I wasn't interested in my topic I wouldn't be able to sustain a critical interest in it.*"

— Dr Anna Tarrant, Reader in Sociology, University of Lincoln

WORKING WITH YOUR SUPERVISOR 3.1

Your supervisor should be a valuable resource when developing and focusing your dissertation idea. They will be able to advise you whether your dissertation topic is likely to be too broad or too narrow in focus. They can assist in relation to whether it is likely to be achievable.

"*Mistakes most commonly arise at the topic selection stage. Students choose a theme that turns out to be too broad, or a research question that proves impossible to answer. They are reluctant to narrow down their ideas, and become increasingly frustrated. The nature of the research process means that it can be difficult to pull students back from early mistakes. That makes the topic development stage at the outset absolutely critical to effective student performance.*"

— Dr Patrick Diamond, Senior Lecturer in British Politics and Public Policy, Queen Mary, University of London

To formulate the specific research aims and objectives, firstly you need to have a good idea of what you want to find out and how you are going to do it. Outlining a clear idea of what you want to achieve will play a valuable role in keeping you on course. The process of formulating a rationale for research is discussed in detail in Chapter 4, and the process of writing a research proposal is the focus of Chapter 9.

Secondly, when starting to outline your research, you need to think about whether your project is achievable. You need to find out what sorts of things are typical for a dissertation in your department, and how your research idea compares. This includes the number of people you might need to interview or survey, the methods of data collection and analysis, as well as more practical concerns around cost.

I WISH I'D KNOWN . . . TO LOOK AT AN EXAMPLE DISSERTATION 3.2

Many universities will provide examples of dissertations, which can provide a good indication regarding these types of expectations.

"*Read examples of past good dissertations and journal papers reporting empirical research—both will give you a good guide for what you are trying to achieve in your dissertation. Looking at how other people have presented and reported their research is definitely something I still find useful!*"

— Dr Kate Burningham, Reader in Sociology of the Environment, University of Surrey

Making sure your dissertation is achievable also means finding a balance between originality, ambition, and the expectations around an undergraduate dissertation or research project. This is the pinnacle of your degree so it is important that you are proud of your work at the end of it! However, speaking to your supervisor and looking at past dissertations will help you manage your expectations, and avoid taking on a project that reaches beyond what is expected of you. It will also help you identify any issues that might impede you in carrying out your intended research, and the likelihood of you being able to navigate them.

Thirdly, you need to think about the theoretical approach and method(s) to employ. Try to consider how the methods you want to use will help to address the aim(s) and objectives of the research. Draw on your existing knowledge of research methods to do this. Think about what kinds of methods you enjoy using and what types of methods will be most effective in addressing your aims. Be aware that you may need to undertake additional training to improve your knowledge of a particular method, or read about it in more depth. Also think about issues around sampling and access when planning your research. What might be an appropriate sample and how can they be accessed? Without careful consideration of these issues, you are likely to encounter problems later on (see Chapter 10). Theoretical considerations should also not simply be an 'add on' to your dissertation. Think about what kind of theoretical approach is suitable for your research, if this is required in your discipline, and how it may influence the methods you use.

Fourthly, you will also need to ensure that the project is suitable in terms of ethics. Ask yourself whether your project is likely to cause any harm to the participants. Is informed consent required, and will your participants be in a position to give it? Can you make sure that anonymity and confidentiality are maintained? You will find a detailed discussion of ethical issues in Chapter 8, but we'd also again advise you to look through previous dissertations and see the types of projects that were completed. This will give you an idea of the types of things that are ethically plausible for a dissertation.

Fifthly, another good place to start when planning a research project or dissertation is with the guidance you are provided by your university or college. There may be, for instance, particular requirements regarding the structure of the project, the word count, and rules regarding contact with your supervisor. You don't want to end up wasting time doing research that fails to satisfy the requirements set out by your institution. If you are only allowed to see your supervisor on four occasions for half an hour during the process of writing your dissertation, then you don't want to ask questions about things that are covered in the guidance, or use up all these contact points at the beginning of your project. Our advice in relation to the guidance is simple: follow the requirements you are given in your handbook.

Some of the key requirements that are likely to be in the guidance include:

- **The deadline**—Like other assignments, your dissertation will have a deadline. This is likely to seem a long way off when you start, but it will soon begin to appear on the horizon. If you need an extension, you will also need to familiarize yourself with the procedures and ensure that you submit any request on time.
- **Word limit**—While the word limit will differ depending on where you are doing your dissertation, it needs to be adhered to. Though it is often difficult to remove words that you have lovingly crafted, cutting them is better than being penalized for failing to follow the rules. It is also worth noting that if you are a long way under the limit, you may be more likely to be criticized for leaving something crucial out of the dissertation.
- **Structure**—Look for information regarding the structure of the dissertation that you need to follow. This often differs between institutions, but is generally provided in the handbook. This will help you to get a sense of what the final dissertation will look like and can assist you in thinking about the amount of words (roughly) you expect to see making up each section. Your supervisor can help you think about this process.
- **Ethics approval**—Without ethics approval you are unlikely to be allowed to undertake empirical research. Each university has its own ethical review process, and you need to make sure you follow these processes.
- **The role of the supervisor**—The handbook often provides guidance about what you can expect from your supervisor, and what your roles and responsibilities are in this relationship. This may include information about what work your supervisor can look at. For instance, there may be a limit to how much of your dissertation your supervisor can look at prior to marking it. If there is a limit, then you need to be aware of it. This will enable you to consult with them about what work is most useful to obtain feedback on.
- **Marking criteria**—The handbook may also include some information about what your dissertation will be assessed on. The marking criteria act as a guide for examiners to help them make judgements about the quality of the work. It will often refer to things like appropriate use and understanding of methods, strength of the argument, use of evidence, and originality. When writing your dissertation, it is a good idea to refer back to this to make sure you are fulfilling these requirements.

- **Format**—All universities have different requirements about how the dissertation should be presented. This will include the type and size of font, the style of referencing, and instructions regarding binding. Again, it is important that you familiarize yourself with these requirements as it can help you avoid having to make unnecessary changes.

FINDING YOUR WAY 3.2

In addition to providing a maximum word count, guidance is likely to include information as to what is included in the word count. Familiarizing yourself with this is really useful in your planning. For instance, an appendix doesn't always count in the word count and can be a useful place for additional sources, such as information and informed consent sheets and the interview questions used. Also check to see whether your footnotes and bibliography are included in your word count.

Structure

In order to plan your project, you will need a good understanding of what a dissertation looks like, and institutions will usually have specific requirements regarding structure. Therefore, it is useful to have an idea of a typical structure when planning your dissertation and to think about the time allocated to each task.

Although the structure can differ, it is common for a dissertation to be structured in the following manner:

- **A title page**—This includes (at a minimum) the title of your project and your name (or registration number).
- **A contents page**—This contains (at a minimum) a list of chapters and page numbers.
- **Introduction**—A section providing an overview of your project. It explains your interest in the topic and sets out the structure of the dissertation.
- **Literature review chapter(s)**—Your literature review sets out the existing work in this area and what has previously been identified, as well as highlighting any gaps in the literature.
- **Methodology**—This includes a discussion of the methods chosen and the theory behind them, as well as justification for your decisions. Drawing on methods literature throughout, this section also discusses the sample and ethics. There is more to a dissertation than the communication of the results of your research. It is just as important to show the examiners that the methods underpinning your research are appropriate.

- **Findings chapter(s)**—Both a description of the data and the presentation of it. Often this chapter is combined with the following one, as it can be difficult to separate your findings from the analysis.
- **Analysis/discussion**—This contextualizes the findings. It brings the different elements of the dissertation together, linking the research questions to the findings, building on the existing literature in the process.
- **Conclusions**—This draws your conclusions together, stating clearly what the work has identified and how the research questions were addressed. It is also likely to reflect on possible areas for future research.

Having an idea of this structure will help you to get a sense of what the final dissertation may look like, and thinking about your dissertation in this manner—with separate but interrelated chapters—can make doing your dissertation a less daunting and more manageable prospect.

I WISH I'D KNOWN . . . TO BREAK THE DISSERTATION INTO MANAGEABLE CHUNKS 3.3

Thinking about your dissertation structure as a series of discrete, but interconnected tasks can make the business of actually doing it much less imposing. By breaking up the writing, for example, it can feel more like a collection of shorter essays, similar to those you have previously written, which link together to make a coherent whole. This can be helpful when planning your dissertation too, where you can break the process up into smaller, more manageable chunks.

"*I wish I'd been told to think of a dissertation as the equivalent in content to three or four related essays linking to a similar number of research questions, rather than as a magnum opus. This is something I still emphasize to my students.*"
— Dr Michael Pugh, Lecturer in Politics, University of the West of Scotland

Managing your time

One of the challenges of completing a good dissertation is that while the long-ranging nature of the deadline creates a sense of dread, it often fails to create an immediate feeling of urgency—until it is almost upon you, that is! Often, the main reason why some students do not fulfil their potential in their dissertation project is a lack of planning, rather than a lack of intellect or ability. So, when you are beginning to think about your research project, it is important to firstly think realistically about when you work best; whether you feel at your most productive in the morning, afternoon, or sometimes even later at night. Ask yourself what sort of tasks should be planned for those more productive time slots. Then, think about what you can do with the time that is available to you before your submission date. It is common for research projects to take longer than expected, and it is possible to get carried away with your research and find out later that you are running out of time. It is all too easy to do lots of reading for the literature review at the beginning, and then delay data collection. At some stage, a decision has to be made to stop reading and start writing. Forcing yourself to move on is important and a well-developed plan can be helpful in this.

A timetable is a very useful tool for keeping you focused on your dissertation and the different elements of it that you will be required to complete. If you can create a schedule that articulates the time needed for each part of your dissertation, it makes it easier to ensure you have space to complete each task.

I WISH I'D KNOWN . . . TO FACTOR IN OTHER ASSIGNMENTS WHEN DEVELOPING A TIMETABLE 3.4

If you have other university assignments to complete while doing your dissertation it is useful to think about their hand-in dates and factor them into your dissertation planning.

"*I wish I had known the real practicalities of balancing my dissertation with my coursework demands.*"

— Georgia Marchbank Peterson, Student, International Relations, Coventry University

To create a timeline, identify the start and finish dates of the dissertation process, and then begin to consider the units of time that you will use to allocate sections of work. For instance, you could use standard months or weeks, but you might also want to base it around weeks in the university calendar. Once you are happy with this, you then need to identify the major aspects of your research and the time they will take. This should include leaving plenty of time to check through your dissertation, as well as more practical tasks like checking references. Factor in things like waiting for questionnaires to be returned—and probably sending out reminders—or negotiating access with participants. Don't forget to allow plenty of time for writing and getting your drafts of work checked by your supervisor. Also always build in some room for contingency.

FINDING YOUR WAY 3.3

Remember to include any holiday periods in your timeline. These are important to you too as they will refresh and revitalize you, helping you to complete your dissertation!

Many institutions require you to get your dissertation professionally bound. You need to make sure that you factor in time to do this; otherwise you could end up missing the deadline. Remember, many other students will be looking to have their dissertations bound at around the same time, so the binders are likely to be fairly busy at that time of year.

I WISH I'D KNOWN . . . TO MAKE AN ACHIEVABLE TIMETABLE 3.5

Once you have sketched out your timetable, look to see if it is realistic. Be honest with yourself about your milestones and whether they appear feasible. Your supervisor should also be able to give you guidance on whether your plans are realistic.

"*I wish I'd known how important it was to make an achievable timetable and stick to it.*"
— David Coningsby, Student, Geography, University of Chester

While it is better to try and stick to your plan, it does not have to be definitive. You may need to revise the timetable as you go along, and every researcher comes up against unexpected problems and pitfalls at some point. Expect some uneven progress and uneven patterns of success. It may be that feedback from your dissertation supervisor means that you need to spend more time focusing on a particular chapter of your dissertation. The important thing is that you are still aware of what needs to be completed and how much time you have left. You don't want to let things drift and then have a last-minute rush.

There are innovative options for creating timelines and tracking progress using software that you may wish to consider using when creating a plan. There are, for example, a number of online calendar apps that can be used to map out your dissertation timeline. Many can be connected to your email so that reminders are automatically sent to you.

FINDING YOUR WAY 3.4

You may find it helpful to look at the example of a sensible and realistic time plan detailed in Figure 3.1. This is called a **Gantt chart**. This example involves the use of interviews, and you can see that some tasks overlap on the timeline. This means that you could begin transcribing while you're still collecting data. You may find it helpful to study this timetable and adapt it to your own research plans, in discussion with your supervisor.

Figure 3.1 **Example dissertation timetable**

	Aug	Sep	Oct	Nov	Dec	Jan	Feb	Mar	Apr	May	Jun
Completing the literature review	X	X	X	X							
Obtaining ethical approval	X	X									
Recruiting participants		X	X	X	X						
Conducting interviews					X	X	X				
Transcribing interview data					X	X	X	X			
Data analysis						X	X	X	X		
Follow-up interviews								X	X		
Writing up the research							X	X	X	X	X
Thoroughly checking the work											X

Managing yourself

Of course, you may be good at drawing up a comprehensive plan for your research, but it is important to remember that **you** then have to make it work. So it is worth taking some time to think about **how** you like to work, and the types of working environment that are most productive for you. Remember that there is often a difference between where we like to work and where we are most productive. Are you able to work in the university library, or do you find that you are easily distracted by other people around you? Are you able to work more effectively at home when nobody is around?

One of the most difficult things about your dissertation is getting started, and there are a million and one reasons why you might put it off. So, you need to develop strategies to self-motivate. Developing and sticking to a timetable is one way of ensuring that you get started. You can also show this to your dissertation supervisor and use it to agree some dates, which fit with your plan, for producing pieces of work. It is also no use trying to read everything about your topic area and then not writing anything down. You need to be systematic in how you search for literature (see Chapter 5) and what literature to include in your dissertation (Chapter 6). Reading endless amounts of literature can be one way of putting off getting started.

Struggling to get started—or 'writer's block'—is often the result of wanting your writing to be perfect, especially when you are handing your research to expert academics. You may be afraid your work won't measure up to your supervisor's expectations. These feelings are natural and normal. Remember that your supervisor is there to help, and in the first instance you need to 'get it written', not necessarily 'get it right'. Drafting your writing, as we show in Chapter 17, is an important part of the research process.

It is very easy to procrastinate about different elements of your dissertation. While some procrastination is normal, you are likely to risk getting behind in your study timetable. Being proactive about making decisions will help your progress, and seeking advice from your dissertation supervisor is also likely to be important because they might be able to help you develop more effective writing strategies. Indeed, many writers compound their problems by employing weak writing strategies. Fortunately, there are a number of other things you can do to help you get going:

- Try free-writing, which involves writing down anything that comes into your mind regarding the topic for 10–15 minutes. Don't worry about spelling mistakes and full sentences—just get it written. You can then begin to work with what you have produced. While personal preferences are a factor, we find it useful to do this on a word processor as it is much easier to keep and edit at a later date.
- Break up study time into blocks of different lengths, and set yourself challenges or targets within each block. You could also set yourself targets in terms of the number of tasks you achieve in a day or a week.
- Be clear about your boundaries, so when you are working, ensure that you are indeed working. Make sure people understand this and don't interrupt you unless absolutely necessary.
- Consider using rewards or treats—perhaps watching your favourite TV series with a takeaway—but make sure you have earned it! Try to be disciplined with this. If you have allowed yourself ten minutes to go for a walk, don't then get distracted by going shopping for an hour. This certainly won't help your progress.
- It is important to monitor distractions. So take some time to think about how long you spend on things that distract you from your work, and then consider how long it then takes you to settle down to work following them. It can often be quite a lot of time that you didn't realize you were wasting! But, now you've identified what distracts you, and how much time it takes to negotiate these things, you should be able to recognize when you are going into 'distraction mode' and reverse the process.
- Think about how you are organizing the notes you make. For instance, are you using headings so you can find things? Are you repeating information? You need to work efficiently—and that includes being able to locate material easily.

- While we all like to have extended periods of time to get stuck into our work, sometimes that is simply not possible. Try to identify where these shorter periods of opportunity occur during your working week, and plan to do less arduous tasks then. For instance, some people like to timetable 'email activity' toward the end of the day when they have less creative energy. This means they can ignore the irregular distraction of checking their email throughout the day and deal with it all in one 'timetabled' event. We also have other colleagues who never schedule meetings in the morning, and others who use their commute to work as an opportunity to read.
- You may find it helpful to keep a research diary to record the practical steps that you went through during your dissertation. It will be much easier to write up a methodology chapter if you have something like this to remind you of what you did, when, and how.
- Think about your reference management strategy and what works for you. You could save valuable time at the end of your dissertation by writing down references properly when making notes. You might also choose to use reference management software to help keep track of important work in the field.
- It is important to recognize that your mood or energy levels can affect your progress at various times throughout the dissertation. There may be times when you need to give yourself a break or focus on dissertation tasks that you may find easier. For instance, if you are struggling to be in the right frame of mind for writing a difficult aspect of your dissertation, you may find it easier to work on an element of the dissertation you find more straightforward and leave the more challenging component to another day. This is better than not achieving anything, and is perfectly acceptable. However, at the same time, don't put off the difficult part indefinitely!

I WISH I'D KNOWN . . . HOW TO DEVELOP WRITING STRATEGIES 3.6

Developing realistic writing strategies from the start will ultimately help you to complete your dissertation. This involves developing personal writing goals.

"*I wish I'd known to set myself smaller, achievable goals as I progressed with my dissertation so it wasn't all down to the last days of writing. A goal could be to read three journal articles today and write down three main points for each, something which is achievable.*"

— Sophie Worrall, Student, Politics and International Studies, University of Warwick

"*I wish I'd known to make sure I have set times to work on the dissertation every day.*"

— Junayna Al-Sheibany, Student, Politics and International Studies, University of Kent

WORKING WITH YOUR SUPERVISOR

At the start of the dissertation process, many departments will allocate you to an academic member of staff who will act as a guide through the dissertation process. This is your supervisor and they will be one of many 'resources' you can use to make your project more successful. They are there to provide practical advice and suggestions, give feedback on your work, and offer general support and encouragement. Supervisors can also act as a calming influence if needed.

WORKING WITH YOUR SUPERVISOR 3.2

Effective use of dissertation supervision will enhance your prospects of successfully completing your dissertation.

"*Every student can and will succeed as long as they are willing to invest the required time and effort—and that also means using the support and resources available to them, including the help of supervisors and lecturers.*"

— Dr Ingrid A. Medby, Senior Lecturer in Political Geography, Oxford Brookes University

Working with your supervisor is likely to be very different to your experience of working on other modules, and it is important that the process of being supervised is a positive one. Indeed, it is important for both staff and students to develop strategies to ensure the relationship is as productive as it can be. In order to do this, you need to understand what your supervisor is, and isn't, there to do.

In the first instance, you will be able to get a feel for the nature of the relationship by reading the guidance your institution provides about expectations placed

FINDING YOUR WAY 3.5

Supervisors are normally assigned students who have chosen a topic area they are familiar with. However, if too many students want to do the same topic area for one supervisor to supervise them all, or if someone changes their topic, a non-specialist supervisor may be assigned to some students. Fortunately, this is unlikely to impact on the quality of support you receive. Not only do social scientists have to specialize in many areas—and therefore have wide-ranging knowledge—their primary role is to oversee the process of the dissertation, and all should have relevant experience in managing research projects. It can also be worth consulting other academic staff on ideas for your topic, such as key reading. But remember that they are likely to be busy and can sometimes take a while to respond. They are more likely to be receptive if they think you are well prepared and genuinely interested in the topic rather than trying to take shortcuts.

on both students and supervisors. Then, once you meet your supervisor for the first time, you will be able to establish the 'ground rules' of the supervision process. This should include a discussion about how you work best, and how this may impact on the timing and structure of supervision meetings. It is worth noting that students often have very different expectations and needs in relation to the role of their supervisors, meaning that communication is vital in clarifying the nature of the relationship from the outset.

You also need to discuss typical expectations regarding contact arrangements, such as when you will be expected to complete work, as well as the nature of the feedback you will receive. This will ensure that you are working to an agreed plan with specific targets. When students attend meetings, many supervisors will expect them to bring something to discuss. So make sure you have a list of items that you can take into the meeting. This could take the form of general ideas or specific written work. The sessions should conform to the departmental guidelines in terms of frequency and you may find it useful to take notes about the event to provide a clear record of what was agreed.

WORKING WITH YOUR SUPERVISOR 3.3

Preparing for each supervision meeting will ensure you get the most out of the sessions. It can also help you develop other transferable skills.

"Make sure you plan for each meeting—have a rough agenda which you follow so that you get the most from your supervisor. This is a chance to practise your leadership and management skills."
— Dr Ruth Penfold-Mounce, Senior Lecturer in Criminology, University of York

"When you meet with your supervisor, make sure you come prepared, for example bring a list of questions and use that to help guide the discussion. This book could provide a useful starting point for thinking about what you need to know or find out from them."
— Dr Katharine A. M. Wright, Lecturer in International Politics, Newcastle University

There are a number of good practices that supervisors and students should adhere to in order for the supervision process to operate effectively—these are set out in Working with your supervisor 3.4.

WORKING WITH YOUR SUPERVISOR 3.4

Supervisors should . . .
- inform students of their rights and responsibilities
- clarify what they expect from their students
- undertake necessary training
- foster a relationship of trust with their supervisees
- make sure (wherever possible) interruptions don't occur during meetings

- give students sufficient time in meetings (in accordance with any guidelines)
- schedule regular meetings, with clear expectations
- review students' progress regularly
- offer constructive criticism

Students should . . .
- always prepare sufficiently for meetings
- read the student handbook
- recognize their responsibilities in the supervision relationship
- foster a relationship of trust with their supervisor
- schedule regular meetings, with clear expectations
- attend regular sessions and come prepared for these sessions
- attempt to complete set work and work to agreed deadlines
- make notes on the meetings (where appropriate)
- be honest about progress

If you have any uncertainty regarding these processes, you should ask your supervisor.

Some supervision sessions may also take the form of group meetings. This sort of supervision is particularly useful for providing more general advice on a range of issues, such as literature searching techniques, writing up, etc. There is also some benefit in hearing about issues raised by other people, that you may not have thought about, as well as the responses to these issues. However, remember that all dissertations are different and not all the concerns that other students identify will apply to your research. Dissertations also often progress at different speeds, so comparing and contrasting 'where you're at' is not always helpful.

I WISH I'D KNOWN . . . NOT TO WORRY ABOUT WHAT OTHER PEOPLE ARE DOING 3.7

"*Don't focus too much on what other people are doing. I often got disheartened by hearing that other people were way ahead of me, which was silly as it was not productive and only hindered me in getting on with my work.*"
— Vilde Bye Dale, Student, Modern History and Politics, University of Essex

You can also email your supervisor to make quick queries, but make sure you have thought carefully about your question first. For instance, don't email them about the hand-in deadline if this information is already available to you in the handbook. This is unlikely to endear you to them, given their already busy schedule. Also, be realistic in your expectations regarding their response time. Emails can avoid the problem of having to wait for a meeting, but there are also limitations, such as the time needed to write a response. For more substantive issues it is often better to arrange a meeting.

WORKING WITH YOUR SUPERVISOR   3.5

Don't forget it is not your supervisor's job to choose your topic (something some students seem to expect!). It is your decision what topic to choose, while taking on board guidance from your supervisor.

"Some students struggle with taking responsibility for their project. They can be inclined to blame their supervisor and the institution for their lack of progress. It's helpful to remember that the academic credit is awarded on the basis that it is an independent project."

— Dr Siobhan McAndrew, Lecturer in Sociology with Quantitative Methods, University of Bristol

When you are in a position to do so, and you have the opportunity, try to get some feedback on your written work. But make sure that you leave your supervisor sufficient time to read your work in advance of meetings. Don't send them something on the morning of the meeting and expect to have immediate feedback. The more time you can give your supervisor the more likely they are to be able to make thorough comments. From a supervisor's perspective, there is nothing more frustrating than being sent work to read over the weekend for a Monday morning meeting. Be fair with your expectations.

WORKING WITH YOUR SUPERVISOR   3.6

It is very important to keep appointments. You would be amazed how many students arrange meetings and then don't turn up, without letting their supervisor know. You wouldn't do it elsewhere, such as at work, so why do it at university? It is also an easy way to frustrate your supervisor.

"Students will often communicate less with their supervisor in the middle of the project—consistent attendance at meetings and responses to communication is vital throughout the research process."

— Dr Ashley Dodsworth, Lecturer in Politics, University of Bristol

It can sometimes feel quite scary handing work to your supervisor, but you are not going to get the value of their feedback if you don't show them anything—and your work might be much better than you think. And don't worry too much if they make critical comments: these are intended to be constructive and to provide you with helpful suggestions that will help you improve your work. Feedback should also be directed toward positive aspects of your work, as well as where you might improve. It is certainly not a personal attack against you. It is also a lot better to have feedback early in the process, rather than waiting until it is too late to do anything about it.

WORKING WITH YOUR SUPERVISOR 3.7

"I think it is better to ask your supervisor for guidance you think you may need, rather than spend time struggling to try and do it on your own. Supervisors are there to help, and they are used to working with students just like you—let them! It's easy to get Imposter Syndrome, but everyone feels like that at some point. Don't suffer because you are afraid to ask for help!"

— Ashley Taylor, Student, Politics and International Relations, University of Limerick

It is also your decision as to what you take on board in relation to your supervisor's comments. It can be OK if you feel that the advice is unwarranted, but you will need to take responsibility for this decision, and it may be worthwhile to revisit the issue with them before making a choice about the direction to take. Remember that your supervisor could be involved in marking the dissertation, so you may want to take this into account in your decision-making.

Dissertation study requires a high level of independence and often feels like a solitary pursuit. Your supervisor is not there to spoon-feed or micromanage you. They should, however, be providing you with support and guidance while seeing you regularly. You should also not keep putting off meeting with your supervisor if you have not done the required work. Instead, discuss reasons for this with them. It is not their job to chase you regarding your dissertation, and it is your responsibility to organize meetings. While they are not your counsellor, they do need to know about any issues affecting your well-being and ability to complete your dissertation. For instance, can deadlines be restructured to more accurately reflect your ability to meet them? Can they advise you in relation to an extension? Don't expect them to guess that you have issues about something or need additional advice or support.

I WISH I'D KNOWN . . . ABOUT THE EXPECTATIONS OF SUPERVISION 3.8

"I think it took me a couple of sessions to understand that I cannot expect my supervisor to give me the right answers to my questions and my confusions, but rather to just provide me with the guidance to identify issues and find the answers myself."

— Stefania Irina Ionescu, Student, Politics and International Studies, University of Warwick

Unfortunately, sometimes the student–supervisor relationship does break down. In the case that you do not receive the kind of supervision that you expected and agreed on, then there should be processes in place for you to raise this as a point of issue. In the first instance you could discuss these matters with your supervisor. However, if you do not feel comfortable doing this, look for the named contact in your handbook. This will probably be the module convenor. They should be able to offer you further advice. You could also speak to your personal tutor or programme manager. There may also be a dedicated student support office that you could visit.

WORKING WITH YOUR SUPERVISOR 3.8

The importance of effective communication in maintaining a good supervision relationship can be seen in this hypothetical example of notes made at a meeting by a student and a supervisor. You should be able to see their different perspectives on the supervision process. Asking your supervisor about the expectations regarding supervision can help avoid these complications.

STUDENT MEETING NOTES (JOHN SHERIDAN)

I finally got to see Professor Waddle today; she is a busy woman! The phone didn't stop ringing during the meeting and she seemed to be having really important conversations about her research. Unfortunately, this meant I didn't have much time to talk about what I was doing. I wish she had a bit more time for me. I suppose I am only a student and I know she has lots of important people to see before she goes away. I really did hope she was going to explain what she wanted from my literature review. She seems to think it's 'best to get on with it', but I'm not really sure what that means in practice, or how to do it. Now I feel like I've missed the opportunity to ask her about it. I don't want her to think I'm stupid!

She also wants me to start looking at the data sets after Christmas, but I don't really understand what she's talking about most of the time. When I do start looking at them I feel like I'll need a lot of help as I know that I'm not that great at stats. Unfortunately, she said she's going away for a month after Christmas, so I am not sure what I will do. I'm dreading it, to be honest.

I've also overheard other students talking. They've already started their data collection and I feel like I'm falling behind already. It's going to get a lot worse after Christmas. I just seem to have a pile of notes. It's not like I haven't been working. In fact, I've read lots and lots. But the more I read the less I know what to write. There is so much research out there! What should I focus on?

Professor Waddle is nice, but it's rather intimidating speaking to her about my own research. I'm even more scared of sending her something! I just seem to lose my tongue in supervision and think of lots of questions afterwards. At least she gave me a very good reference for that job I got in the library. However, I'm finding that doing all these night shifts makes me rather tired and I keep getting horrible headaches. Maybe I am not cut out to be able to do a dissertation. I knew I would find it tough, but not this tough.

SUPERVISOR MEETING NOTES (PROFESSOR WADDLE)

John seems to be getting on fine with his dissertation, although he seems a little reluctant to hand me his work. I have been very busy recently so when he does make an appointment to see me, I wish he would make the best use of my time. I think that it's been two and a half months since our last meeting. I was under the impression that the literature review was nearly done and he would have sent it for this supervision meeting. Never mind, it must be pretty much done. He also needs to start his empirical research soon as I don't want him to get behind. John has a tendency to wander off topic quite a bit, and he seemed more comfortable talking about my research. Of course, I think my results are fascinating, but I can't see why he's so interested. I'm glad he's interested, but I would have liked to know more about his progress. I think he knows what he is doing though.

Unfortunately, there were a couple of phone call interruptions during the supervision session which reduced our time a little, but John didn't seem to mind. On another note, I did a reference for John and I was pleased to hear he got the job in the library. I think he was probably struggling a bit financially and I am sure the money will come in handy with Christmas coming up. I am away for a month after Christmas and I hope John sends me his literature review before I go away. I could do with it soon as I have lots to do before then. And by the time I get back he should have started to work with the data set too. I think his topic is really interesting and I am looking forward to hearing what he finds out.

It is quite evident that much is not going well with this relationship and how the supervision is taking place. John lacks openness and honesty with his supervisor, while Professor Waddle is not doing enough to ensure the student is focused in his approach. If you refer back to the good practice on supervision (Working with your supervisor 3.4), it is apparent that if they followed the principles set out they would be much less likely to encounter problems in the supervision process. This emphasizes the importance of establishing these ground rules.

It should also be noted that it is becoming more common for supervisors and students to come from diverse cultural and linguistic backgrounds. This can have implications for the interactions that occur during supervision. Various supervision strategies may be adopted where such differences exist—although these strategies may also be useful where there are no cultural or linguistic variations.

There may be different expectations regarding turn-taking, for example, with some students expecting supervisors to frame meetings and take the lead. This may be a cultural deference to those in senior positions. Equally, there might be a reluctance to admit when there is a lack of understanding. These misunderstandings can be minimized by emphasizing the value of interaction in supervision, and in confirming expectations regarding the role of supervisor and student through 'establishing ground rules'. Supervisors expect to have to clarify thoughts and ideas to students, so there is no issue with requesting additional explanation.

There might also be cultural differences in relation to the physical proximity between students and supervisors. These need to be clarified and dealt with sensitively. Body language is a significant aspect of all cultures, with various meanings associated with different gestures—and it is possible for misunderstandings to occur. Both students and supervisors need to be aware of their body language and how this may be interpreted.

EXPECTING THE UNEXPECTED!

It would be unrealistic to complete the whole dissertation process without encountering any sort of challenges. But that does not mean that it is easy to anticipate what those difficulties might be! At some point it is likely that you will lack the motivation you feel is necessary, or you might become fed up with the whole thing and just want it done and out of the way. This can even happen when you have chosen a topic that you are really interested in.

I WISH I'D KNOWN . . . ABOUT SUBJECT FATIGUE 3.9

"*I chose a topic that I am highly passionate about—Mexican drug cartels and narco-trafficking—based on having grown up with Mexican friends and heard stories about the Drug War. I have also learnt the language and spent time in México. I thought it would only be beneficial to have had such a big interest in a topic, but upon studying it more in-depth I often felt really bored and tired of it, and as if pursuing my dissertation project had taken away the fun from one of my specialist topics.*"
— Liisa Toomus, Student, International Relations and Global Issues, University of Nottingham

Speaking to your supervisor or taking a little time out can help, as can speaking to your peers, who may well have similar feelings. This is partly why it is important to allow for some slippage in your timetable. This can help at times when, for whatever reason, you are progressing more slowly than expected. Sometimes it is just a process of stepping back, giving yourself a break, and then immersing yourself back in the work. 'Passive thinking'—where you go away and do something completely different—might seem like a waste of time, but it can actually be a very productive part of the creative process.

I WISH I'D KNOWN . . . TO MAKE A START EARLY ON 3.10

Aim to do more than you think is necessary in your project early on. In fact, getting ahead of your schedule is positive. This will provide you with some leeway later on in the process.

"*Get started early so unexpected setbacks do not impede your progress.*"
— Rachael O'Neill, Student, Politics, and International Relations, University of Nottingham

Dealing with unforeseen challenges can obviously eat into valuable time and resources, and you may have to develop solutions or change direction. This flexibility is important. A good management strategy is to consider what (realistically) might go wrong, and what contingencies you might put in place to deal with any delays. Recruiting participants, for example, can often take much longer than anticipated. Thus it is often worth thinking about what 'plan B' would look like. If you have planned to conduct research on what 'Housing Officers' thought of a new social housing initiative in your area, for example, but couldn't find enough people to interview, it might be worth scaling back your research. Could you examine how the policy had been represented in the press? Or perhaps you could interview local residents who might be affected by the scheme? It may be that you never need to put these plans into place, but it is always good to have them there just in case. Sometimes changes are needed as a result of things that are well out of your control and that couldn't have been predicted. This is not uncommon and should be seen as part of the research process.

CONCLUSION

Planning will help you to feel more confident about getting your dissertation in on time; it can also help you to negotiate challenges as and when they arise. Techniques like timetabling your planned progress, setting out your expectations of the student–supervisor relationship, and thinking about 'plan B' will provide you with a solid foundation for your research. Together they will help you negotiate the practical realities of planning and managing the research project.

WHAT DO I NEED TO THINK ABOUT?

- What areas of research are you interested in and what might the aims and objectives look like? Taking into account the dissertation requirements, including the handbook, do these areas of research seem feasible for this type of research project?
- Are you clear about how you work most effectively, and how this may differ in relation to an extended piece of work?
- What writing strategies might be useful to you?
- Do you understand how to create a dissertation timetable which also takes into account your other commitments?
- Are you clear about supervisory expectations and how to get the most out of the supervisory relationship?
- Do you know what your 'plan B' might look like?

WHAT DO I NEED TO DO?

- Read the dissertation handbook to make sure you are familiar with your department's requirements.
- Decide on the subject area of your research, and establish your research aims and objectives.
- Identify how you work best in terms of timing and location.
- Construct a dissertation timetable to plan your project.
- Develop writing strategies to assist you with getting started.
- Establish the 'ground rules' of supervision with your supervisor once they are allocated.
- Develop a 'plan B' in case there are unexpected developments in your dissertation.

Access the online resources **www.oup.com/uk/brymansrple** to help you to successfully complete your social research project or dissertation.

DELVE DEEPER

Becker, H. (2007). *How to Write for Social Scientists: How to Start and Finish Your Thesis, Book or Article.* **Chicago: University of Chicago Press.** While this is aimed at more advanced students than undergraduates, it is excellent in terms of getting you to think about what research means and what it will look like in the context of an independent project.

Michael, P. (1992). **'Tales of the Unexpected: Supervisors' and Students' Perspectives on Short-term Projects and Dissertations'**, *Educational Studies,* **18(3): 299–310.** This interesting journal article, based on inter-views with 22 staff–student undergraduate and postgraduate supervisory dyads, focuses on the students' and supervisors' expectations in super-visory relationships. It highlights variations in expectations. Ultimately, it shows the need for both students' and supervisors' needs and expect-ations to be continually reviewed in a supervisory relationship.

Mind. It needs to be acknowledged that student life in general, and the dis-sertation in particular, can be a challenging and stressful time. This can result in feeling rather pressured. While some of the tips throughout this chapter will help manage this process, it is important to develop strategies to keep yourself healthy and well while doing your dissertation (and in general!). This guide from Mind aims to support you during your time as a student and provides useful tips and guidance on how to keep yourself healthy and well.

https://www.mind.org.uk/information-support/tips-for-everyday-living/ student-life/#.XAENvPZ2s2w (Accessed 26 November 2018).

The Pomodoro Technique. There are a number of techniques for managing your time during the dissertation process. One of these is the Pomodoro Technique. It is something you may find really useful. However, you must find a technique that works best for you.

https://francescocirillo.com/pages/pomodoro-technique (Accessed 21 November 2018).

The Royal Literary Fund. This resource provides support and advice on writing skills for those writing a dissertation. It is not presented as a conventional how-to guide, but rather provides a variety of voices on the processes of writing. These come from interviews with professional writers, successful doctorate students, and writing experts. These are particularly useful in thinking about the process of writing, drafting, and rewriting, crucial elements of a dissertation.

https://www.rlf.org.uk/resources/introduction-dissertation/ (Accessed 10 November 2018).

Todd, M., Bannister, P., and Clegg. S. (2004). 'Independent Inquiry and the Undergraduate Dissertation: Perceptions and Experiences of Final Year Social Science Students', *Assessment and Education in Higher Education,* **29(3): 161–173.** If you want to look at supervision experiences and perceptions from a supervisor's perspective you may find this of interest. This article uses interviews to draw on the experiences and perceptions of staff supervising final year social science undergraduates.

The University of Leicester. A number of universities provide dissertation guides which are available online. This is one of the better ones. It addresses the process of planning and conducting a small research project, providing support for you in organizing, planning, and monitoring your project. It also includes examples of Gantt charts.

https://www2.le.ac.uk/offices/ld/resources/writing/writing-resources/ planning-dissertation (Accessed 1 December 2017).

CHAPTER 4

DEVELOPING
A RESEARCH IDEA

WHAT DO I NEED TO KNOW?

- What is meant by the term research 'quality'?
  - Reliability
  - Validity
  - Generalization
  - Reflexivity
- Identifying your research interests
- How to develop a research idea
- Developing a research rationale

INTRODUCTION

Social research is concerned with developing defensible knowledge about people and all of the things that they do. This means that the landscape for social research is both wide and varied. In some cases, your research gaze will be directed by disciplinary interests; in others it will be much more open. Criminologists, for example, are interested in crime, criminals, and criminal justice. Other disciplines, however, are more conceptually driven. Politics, for example, is broadly concerned with power—its organization, its distribution, and the impact this has on people. Some disciplinary fields emerge from more professional interests. Social work research, for instance, is concerned with the activity of social workers specifically, as well as the field of social care more generally. Then there are those disciplines, such as sociology, that are so incredibly broad they have the potential to be interested in anything and everything that involves human activity! As exciting as all of these possibilities may be, it can make deciding what to study in your dissertation a little bit daunting. There is often so much that you could do, knowing what to do and how to justify that decision can be a difficult process—and one that requires you to develop the confidence necessary to explain the reasons why your research is interesting and important. In this chapter we'll go through a number of techniques that will help you to identify your research interests, develop project ideas, and build a rationale for research. But first, we need to deal with a question that many students ask us at this stage of the process—what makes a good dissertation project? And to answer this question we need to introduce the idea of research quality.

WHAT IS MEANT BY THE TERM RESEARCH 'QUALITY'?

The notion of quality in research is a contested concept. While we can probably all agree that social research should have quality, what that means in practice is often harder to articulate. Much early debate focused on the ideas of reliability, validity, replicability, and generalization. However, more recent discussion has introduced a number of other ways of thinking about what makes for good research. The central point of contention associated with all of this discussion is that different types of researchers have conflicting ideas about the nature of the human world, the value placed on different forms of knowledge, and how we should carry out social research. As we saw in Chapter 2, these are the interrelated concerns of ontology, epistemology, and methodology.

This means that different research communities have different ideas about what, exactly, makes for 'quality' research. As such, there are no absolute constants that are applicable to all research. What makes a good dissertation-style project is actually relative to the field you are working in, what conventions there are within the particular approach you are taking, and, as suggested in Chapter 3, the expectations of your particular department/faculty or school.

That said, there is now a long list of terms that have been associated with quality that we might want to concern ourselves with. These include: credibility; authenticity; verisimilitude; confirmability; and dependability. While some of these terms are associated with particular types of research, others have been specifically designed to be more cross-cutting in nature. What is clear, however, is that there is not much agreement about where, when, and how they should or can be applied. It is for this reason that Seale (2002) uses the term **'criteria-ology'** to describe the diverse ways of thinking about quality. Rather than providing a critique of the notion of quality, his point is to highlight the importance of methodological awareness when thinking about criteria of quality, together with being able to situate projects within particular **paradigms at the same time** as being able to learn from other approaches. So, whether you are working within a positivist, interpretivist, or **postmodern** framework, you can ask broader questions about quality in order to improve the critical dynamics of your research.

For Seale the important thing is to ask the following questions:

1. How might approaches to quality be relevant to your research?
2. How might they help to inform your research design?
3. How can they be used in your dissertation more generally?

It is this methodological awareness that helps to make our research rigorous, transparent, and critical.

FINDING YOUR WAY 4.1

There's more to the question of 'what makes a good dissertation?' than the concepts associated with research quality. We'll be dealing with these elsewhere in the book, but the sorts of things you might need to look out for include the following:

- ✓ Can you appropriately situate your project in the literature? (Chapters 5 and 6)
- ✓ Do your chosen research strategy and design allow you to respond to your stated aims and objectives? (Chapter 7)
- ✓ Is your sample size appropriate and realistic? (Chapter 10)
- ✓ Are your chosen methods of data collection appropriate and robust? (Chapters 11, 12, and 15)
- ✓ Is your analysis of the data appropriate and insightful? (Chapters 13, 14, and 15)
- ✓ Are you likely to be able to make good use of theory and concepts in your analysis? (Chapters 13, 15, and 16)
- ✓ Have you complied with relevant ethical requirements of research? (Chapter 8)
- ✓ Have you made some effort to think critically in relation to the limitations of your study, as well as its originality and significance? (Chapter 16)
- ✓ Is your dissertation written up appropriately? (Chapter 17)

With this idea of criteria-ology in mind, we'll review four of the most common considerations of research quality that we think will help you to think critically about your research ideas, and understand what makes for a good dissertation project.

Reliability

The issue of reliability is associated with the extent to which your research is stable, consistent, and, broadly speaking, repeatable. It is to consider whether, if you asked the question in a different context, you would find similar results. It is often associated with quantitative methods, where there are a range of techniques that can be used to make a direct assessment of reliability, usually in numerical form. There are also different types of reliability that can be variously directed toward research instruments, participants, or the researchers themselves. In addition, issues of reliability also inform more qualitatively oriented projects. Much research would actually be relatively pointless if we couldn't rely on our data to be somewhat stable beyond the point of its realization. Therefore, the point of thinking about reliability is to consider where you might be able to judge or enhance the stability of your research instruments, data, and findings.

Validity

Validity is broadly concerned with the meaningfulness of your research. Again, it can be applied to research instruments, data, analysis, and even your attempts to write up your research. This isn't necessarily a concern with truth—logically speaking, an argument can be false and valid at the same time. Instead, validity refers to the ability of something to do what it actually suggests it does. To use an everyday English phrase: does it do 'what it says on the tin'? That is, do the inferences, interpretations, and arguments that you make in your research reflect reality, or are you shaping your research in particular ways so that your view is somehow skewed?

I WISH I'D KNOWN . . . THE DIFFERENCE BETWEEN RELIABILITY AND VALIDITY 4.1

A useful way of thinking about the relationship between reliability and validity is to think about some broken weighing scales that always under-report weight by 3 kilograms. These particular scales might be reliable because they are consistent, but they are not valid because they do not correspond to the accepted conventions of measuring weight.

For example, we might want to use the principle of validity to think critically about the nature of interviewing friends and family for the purposes of research. This is something that is common in undergraduate dissertations, but rarely written about in textbooks. Are they likely to answer questions in ways that are implicitly sympathetic to you and the requirements of your research, or are they likely to be less guarded in their answers because of your association with them? It is also possible that they may say very little because they presume you already know how they feel. In each case, the validity of the information they provide is in question because their answers are shaped around your pre-existing relationship with them.

This is not to suggest that you can't interview family and friends for the purposes of your project. But you would need to be very careful in making an assessment of your ability to interpret that information as somehow instructive of the wider world because of the very nature of the research relationships you have developed. In other words, you will need to acknowledge the limitations of your research and be cautious about the kinds of conclusions you make from your data. This kind of awareness will be well received in your dissertation.

Generalization

This brings us to the issue of generalization—the extent to which your research is able to 'travel' across different situations. This is about the capacity of the research to be instructive of people, interactions, and situations beyond the initial context of the research. We are not necessarily talking about statistical generalization here, which is broadly interested in the likely representativeness of sample to population. Instead, we are concerned with making some assessment of the capacity of your research to resonate with interests, people, and situations elsewhere. This will allow you to make what Williams (2000) refers to as 'moderatum generalizations'—the ability of your findings to be instructive, but not exhaustive of situations elsewhere. Again, if our research is only relative to the context in which it is produced, then the enterprise of social research would be pretty limited in scope. But this is not to say that our research **necessarily** corresponds to the outside world. Thinking critically about the nature of our research, and its ability to inform beyond its immediate point of reference, is crucial in demonstrating methodological awareness.

Reflexivity

The practice of doing research is social, just like the world it seeks to investigate. Reflexivity is the attempt by researchers to reflect on the process of research to consider how our research findings might be shaped by the decisions we take. It is not a measure of research quality per se, but it is a 'tool' that can be utilized to recognize and assess the political, social, and personal context within which research is produced. Law (2000) puts it more simply: research is a messy business and often quite unlike the process described in research methods textbooks. Reflexivity is about thinking through some of that messiness. This is why we emphasize the social process of doing your dissertation research throughout this book.

You can see how this 'research self-awareness' works in practice by reading some of the reflexive literature that describes the process of social research. A combination of 'thick description' and case study, reflexive accounts are personalized histories of the research process in which the researcher is fully implicated in the data gathering, the analysis, and any subsequent writing up. Going beyond the technical description of method, they are 'warts and all' accounts of the process of doing social research. According to Bell and Newby (1977: 10), two British sociologists who collected a seminal series of reflexive accounts in their book *Doing Sociological Research*, these recognitions can be everything from the micropolitics of interpersonal relationships, to the politics of research units, institutions, universities, and government departments: all of which 'vitally determine the design, implementation and outcome of [research]'.

While you might not include a formal presentation of such reflexivity in the write-up of your dissertation, the purpose of being reflexive during your project is twofold. Firstly, and as Letherby et al (2012) highlight, 'theorised subjectivity' is better than assumed objectivity. This means being explicit in terms of our values and, where necessary, holding them in check or challenging them. In part, 'theorised subjectivity' is why it is so important to make sure that your research is theoretically informed. 'Theory' situates your project within particular traditions of research that have their own means of thinking about quality.

Secondly, and to return to Seale (2002), being reflexive is a key step in being methodologically aware. It can enhance the critical nature of the research process, and helps to ensure both rigour and transparency. A good dissertation project is one that allows you to be thorough, clear, and critical.

IDENTIFYING YOUR RESEARCH INTERESTS

Having reviewed some of the issues involved in thinking about research quality, we can now turn toward answering two more practical questions: how do I identify my research interests and how do I develop a research idea?

Some of you may already be quite clear about what you are interested in, and what type of study you may want to do for your dissertation, but many people will have lots of interests and ideas, to the point that navigating them becomes unmanageable. Other people become a little daunted by the prospect of having to pick a single point of development. So how might you go about choosing?

One means of developing a dissertation project is to first identify your research interests—and social researchers tend to generate their projects using different points of reference. These include: personal interest; professional experience; recommendations; and using the research literature. We'll take each one in turn.

We all have things that we enjoy doing when we are away from work, and in many cases these things can serve as a useful starting point for research. You might, for instance, have noticed something that has puzzled you in your everyday life and wish to find out more. Alan's interest in the process of 'Disneyization' that he developed in his book *The Disneyization of Society* (Bryman 2004) was, at least in part, due to his love for roller coasters!

In other cases, researchers may also have a particular identity that leads to them working in a research area. As a devoted supporter of Scunthorpe United, Tom's research interests have occasionally been directed toward exploring football fandom cultures, and why people support relatively unsuccessful sports teams. Some of Tom's other work on the relationship between class and higher education, for example, is based on his own experiences as a working-class student and his belief in the transformative power of higher education. So it is also possible to take your cue from important issues in wider society and use them in your own research ideas.

TASK 4.1

Write a list of some of things that you are interested in in your daily life—try to be as imaginative as possible.

Other projects, however, are developed through more professional associations and experiences. A researcher might develop a project because they have previous experience of working in a particular area or because of their professional background. Many researchers with an interest in social work, for example, are actually qualified social workers with professional experience in the field. Similarly, Liam's research interests in teaching statistics emerged from his own experiences teaching quantitative methods to sociology students. Things like retail, and sport and leisure can also be used as a base to develop research projects. You might choose to build a research project around an area that you specifically want a career in. Perhaps you have a part-time job and something stands out as particularly puzzling and is worth further investigation. Maybe you volunteer and have experience of particular pressures that exist in the sector you are familiar with.

TASK 4.2

List your professional interests. Think about both your previous occupational experiences and what you might like to do as a career. If you are considering a career in teaching, for example, try to think about what particular areas of education interest you.

Research can also be commissioned by certain people and institutions. Of course, at this stage of your career you are unlikely to be asked to carry out research on behalf of someone. However, you can do something similar by asking researchers if they have any projects that you could carry out for them. Many will have ideas for things that they do not have time to develop and it might be worth contacting them to see if they have some ideas that you might be able to take forward. But before you do this, make sure that you have read their work and made some attempt to identify the things that interest you. This will help to ensure that your relationship starts off on the right footing.

The final way to identify research topics that interest you is to simply adapt an existing study that has inspired you. Little social research is truly unique, and many studies are actually variations on a theme. In these terms it is possible to do something of a 'restudy' (or 'replication study'), albeit with a few tweaks. For example, you might want to employ a different methodological technique, introduce a different variable, use a more up-to-date data set, conduct research in a different location, or even with a different age group. All of these are viable methods to generate original research. One example of this in the literature relates to a project that was undertaken by Johnson et al (2010). Their study involved replicating Peter Townsend's (1962) classic study 'The Last Refuge'—albeit 50 years later. In the original study, Townsend depicted residential homes as being large, impersonal institutions which isolated older people from the outside world, routinized activities, and bred poor staff attitudes. By employing the same techniques as Townsend in a different time and place, Johnson et al were able to replicate his research to investigate whether, and how, practices had changed. Unfortunately, they found that much remained the same almost half a century later.

I WISH I'D KNOWN . . . HOW TO IDENTIFY A RESEARCH GAP 4.2

"*A research gap does not only mean finding a literal gap in the literature. Sometimes previous research on a topic can be so exhaustive that there is not much left to 'find out'. Instead, I realised that you can also approach previous research from a different angle, perhaps using a different theory, and if it's old research, applying it to a contemporary case to see if anything has changed. Once I learnt that identifying a research gap is not so restrictive, it came a lot easier to me.*"

— Ashley Neat, Student, International Relations and International Organisations, University of Warwick

See Chapter 6 for further discussion about identifying a research or knowledge gap.

HOW TO DEVELOP A RESEARCH IDEA

You should now have an emerging list of things that could count as your research interests. Some of these may be pointing toward a very specific research project already, but others will still be in need of some development. Here's one way of developing your interests into a project.

I WISH I'D KNOWN . . . HOW TO DEVELOP A RESEARCH IDEA 4.3

"*It would have been really helpful to have been aware of the different ways that can be used to develop research topics—as is outlined here. I found it very challenging trying to come up with an interesting topic, this would have been much easier if I'd started by writing down my interests.*"

— David Coningsby, Student, Geography, University of Chester

Suppose that your favourite subjects in your degree have been 'race and ethnicity', 'social inequality', and 'ageing in society'. Let's pretend that these interests emerge from the volunteering you do in an old people's home, the fact that you grew up in a multicultural inner-city environment, and your desire to work in some aspect of public administration in the future. So, having identified your research interests, how might you combine them to build a research project with achievable aims? One way is to look for common threads that might allow us to connect these areas.

TASK 4.3

Using the knowledge you have of these subject areas, quickly list some keywords
that you can associate with these subjects.

The literature on 'race and ethnicity' is often concerned with the disadvantages
ethnic groups can face in areas such as health, work, and education. There is also
much interest in determining what is meant by the term 'race' and 'ethnic group'.
'Inequality', on the other hand, is often associated with things like welfare, tax,
benefits, capitalism, and money, while the literature on ageing is interested in
differences between and within groups like children and pensioners, or concepts
such as the life course more generally.

It is now possible to see some emerging themes. Generally speaking, you may
appear to be interested in the economic and welfare inequality of ethnic groups across
the life course. Therefore, your headline research interest might be: to explore the
experience of inequality in ethnic groups across the life course. This is still quite broad,
but it provides an overarching research interest that has a number of possibilities.

In truth, there are many ways through which you might use your research
interests to develop a research idea, and it is often a process of perspiration as
much as inspiration. Sometimes an idea will follow an interest very easily; sometimes it will take more work. Although research textbooks and research papers
will take this process for granted, it often takes time and a lot of thought. Indeed,
developing a research idea is a process rather than a 'eureka'-type event. Did you
also notice how the process of moving from an interest to a research idea necessarily involved some working knowledge of the subjects we were interested in?
Developing some familiarity with the area you are thinking about is a crucial part
of the process of 'getting to know the field'. It is one thing to have an interest, but
it is another to develop a good idea for research. Having some 'theoretical sensitivity' to the theories, issues, and debates in the literature is crucial to the process
of developing a research project. It requires gradual and repeated development
over a period of time, and some dedicated thinking, reading, and planning. Many
ideas begin broadly, but through further reading they are refined and reduced in
scope to something more manageable and focused.

I WISH I'D KNOWN . . . THAT TALKING ABOUT YOUR
IDEAS HELPS TO DEVELOP THEM 4.4

*"Talking to my course mates about my different ideas was very motivating. It helped me
to clarify my topic because speaking about it out aloud meant I had to be clear about
what I was trying to do."*

— Antonia Panayotova, Student, Communication and Media, University of Leeds

DEVELOPING A RESEARCH RATIONALE

For now, let's presume that you have identified your research interests, and that you have some idea of the overarching theme of a potential dissertation project. You now need to develop a research rationale that contains some achievable research aims.

I WISH I'D KNOWN . . . TO DO LESS, MORE THOROUGHLY 4.5

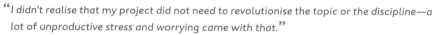

"I didn't realise that my project did not need to revolutionise the topic or the discipline—a lot of unproductive stress and worrying came with that."
— Stefania Irina Ionescu, Student, Politics and International Studies, University of Warwick

A research rationale is a very short written overview of our research idea that introduces the project, justifies the reason for it, and provides an outline of what it will achieve. Together, this builds a frame for the research, specifying what it is trying to achieve and why. Once you have this in place, you can begin to elaborate on it to produce a more fully formed **research proposal** (see Chapter 9). Think of it as the detailed sketch that you make before painting the big picture.

The following is a research rationale from one of Tom's projects:

Within the field of Higher Education, there is currently much policy and practice interest in the attainment gap between BAME (Black Asian and Minority Ethnic) and White students. This gap is generally taken to be the difference between the proportion of White students who gain higher degrees and the proportion of BAME students who gain the same degrees. Using a mixed methods approach, this project will explore how differential levels of attainment might be experienced within Higher Education. Drawing on quantitative data within an English University to examine the nature of the gap, and a range of qualitative interviews with BAME students to understand the experience of it, the study will attempt to explore how BAME students negotiate their way through university landscapes.

With this in mind, you can break down a research rationale into three distinct parts:

- Context
- Method
- Aims

In the first instance, sentence one and sentence two provide the context of the project.

> *Within the field of Higher Education, there is currently much policy and practice interest in the attainment gap between BAME (Black Asian and Minority Ethnic) and White students.*

And:

> *This gap is generally taken to be the difference between the proportion of White students who gain higher degrees and the proportion of BAME students who gain the same degrees.*

Taken together, the context part of the rationale is essentially a statement that demonstrates why this might be an interesting thing to do. There are two dimensions to think about when trying to answer these questions. The first is to think why a layperson or a professional practising in the area might be interested in the project. The second is to directly outline why this is of specific academic interest, perhaps even lightly citing academic literature. Given the cursory nature of a research rationale, either approach is fine. In this particular instance, it is a mix of the two as it draws attention to both policy and practice interest, with the second sentence clarifying what is meant by the attainment gap. If we wanted to reinforce the points further, we could add a reference to relevant academic literature at the end of both the first and second sentences.

In the second instance, we need to provide a very brief outline of our research design, with particular focus on the methods of data collection it will use. The first clause in the third sentence in the example—'*using a mixed methods design*'—is an attempt to introduce the overarching approach. This is then reinforced further by the first and second clauses of the fourth sentence which outline the data-collection techniques more clearly.

> *Drawing on quantitative data within an English University to examine the nature of the gap, and a range of qualitative interviews with BAME students to understand the experience of it …*

You may have noticed, however, that the third and fourth sentences also contain key information about the aims of the research. This material is directed toward defining the parameters of research, for instance what the purposes of the study will be. In this instance, the overarching aim is given in the second clause of the third sentence:

> *this project will explore how differential levels of attainment might be realised within Higher Education*

This is then elaborated on in the final sentence—and given the mixed methods design, the purpose of this study is twofold. First, it is to '*examine the nature of the gap*' and second, '*to understand the experience of it*'. The quantitative element of the study will assess the general existence and level of the gap, with the qualitative element directed toward understanding the experiences of those who might be subject to it.

I WISH I'D KNOWN . . . THAT THE AIMS OF RESEARCH CAN CHANGE 4.6

Sometimes, as a result of further reading, conversations or collection of data, you may refine your research as you go through the process.

"*Be prepared to change your research aims and objectives as you move through the research process.*"

— Azhar Chaudhry, Student, Politics, Philosophy and Economics, University of Exeter

"*Don't be afraid to revisit these and refine them as needed as your work progresses. Talk to your supervisor if you are worried about your focus shifting.*"

— Dr Michael Pugh, Lecturer in Politics, University of the West of Scotland

Of course, it is possible to develop the rationale further by specifying where the secondary quantitative data will be obtained, what techniques of data collection will be used, how many people will be in the sample and the type of sampling that will be employed, how ethics will be addressed, and so on. However, the purposes of a research rationale are to provide you with a foundation with which you can 'think through' the finer detail in a larger research proposal (see Chapter 9).

TASK 4.4

Here's another rationale. See if you can identify the context, method, and aims of the research.

According to Peach (1999: 391), 'ethnic segregation is a marked feature of western cities'. Dismissed as a negative and divisive social phenomenon that prevents social integration and understanding, the likes of Paris, Chicago, and the Bronx are often used as examples of problematic 'urban ghettos' (Wacquant, 2008). Sheffield is no different in this respect with many areas often being referred to in such stereotypical terms (Lee and Dorling, 2011). This study will make use of decennial census data between 2001 and 2011 to explore segregation and dispersal patterns of ethnic groups in Sheffield. It will aim to assess the changing geographical pattern of ethnic groups in the local wards of the city, and, in doing so, assess whether the city can be considered to have 'ghettos'.

Can you see how the first sentence establishes the field of vision (ethnic segregation), using an example from the literature? The second sentence reviews the key aspects of the phenomenon, and again reinforces the point with a key reference from the field. The third provides further context about the nature of the study, drawing on some literature to help to evidence the point. The first part of the fourth sentence outlines key detail about the research design in terms of the data that will be used, with the second part providing the overarching aim of the study.

The final sentence is dedicated to the further articulation of those aims. It first specifically outlines the remit of the study—'*to assess the changing geographical pattern of ethnic groups in the local wards of the city*'—before linking the purpose of the study to the context previously introduced: '*assess whether the city can be considered to have "ghettos"*'. Together, these sentences provide a sound rationale for the research.

There are, of course, other ways to build rationales for research. Many will keep the aims and methods quite separate in terms of sentence structure. Some rationales will place the research aims first, followed by a justification for those aims, and then some detail about the methods. In these respects, there are no hard-and-fast rules about building research rationales. However, what they always do is help you to 'think through' the basic elements of what your study might involve, and help you to sketch that out. In turn, this provides you with an initial framework for further thought, further articulation, and further discussion.

CONCLUSION

This chapter has explored how you might want to go about developing an idea for your dissertation. Introducing you to some notions of research quality that you might want to consider when beginning to think about a project, it then detailed a few techniques to help you identify your interests and how you might turn them into an idea for dissertation research. Developing and writing a research rationale is a key phase of development for your research as it provides a point of lift-off for other aspects of the research process. Once you have this 'sketch' of your dissertation project, not only do you have something that you can use to discuss what you are thinking of doing with a supervisor, it also allows you to think about: a literature search strategy (Chapter 5); how you might review the literature associated with your project (Chapter 6); how you might actually design the specifics of your project (Chapter 7); and how you will ensure you carry it out ethically (Chapter 8). This will then help you write a fuller 'research proposal' (Chapter 9). Completing a dissertation can feel like a long process, and actually writing a research rationale might seem like unnecessary work. However, taking the time to work through your interests and develop ideas that you have some investment in will help you start the dissertation process with a strong foundation.

WHAT DO I NEED TO THINK ABOUT?

- How might you develop your methodological awareness?
- What types of things make for a good social science research project or dissertation?
- What sorts of areas of research are you interested in?
- How might you develop these interests into ideas that might be suitable for dissertation-style research?

☑ What might a rationale for your research idea look like?

☑ How might different approaches to research quality be relevant to your research ideas?

WHAT DO I NEED TO DO?

☑ Make sure you understand the key issues related to research quality.

☑ Identify your research interests.

☑ Develop your ideas for research.

☑ Sketch a research rationale.

⬤ Access the online resources **www.oup.com/uk/brymansrp1e** to help you to successfully complete your social research project or dissertation.

DELVE DEEPER

Punch, K. (2016). *Developing Effective Research Proposals* **(3rd edition). London: Sage.** This book provides a step-by-step guide to developing and writing proposals. Chapters on 'understanding readers, expectations and functions' and 'developing a general framework for proposals' will be particularly useful for those looking to develop their ideas into projects.

Rojon, C. and Saunders, M. N. K. (2012). 'Formulating a Convincing Rationale for a Research Study', *Coaching: An International Journal of Theory, Research and Practice,* **5(1): 55–61.** This research note provides practical and detailed guidance on how to build a rationale. Relatively short and very readable, it explains the role of a rationale in research, and offers specific advice on contextualizing research and building aims and objectives. It is nominally directed toward issues of 'coaching', but this does not obscure the discussion and it will be relevant to students regardless of discipline.

Saunders, M. and Lewis, P. (1997). 'Great Ideas and Blind Alleys? A Review of the Literature on Starting Research', *Management Learning,* **28(3): 283–299.** There isn't that much literature on developing an idea for research, so finding tips and tricks is not always easy. Fortunately, Saunders and Lewis have reviewed the literature on the topic and provide a handy overview in this paper. It is focused on management research and the paper is a little old now, but the ideas they present don't really go out of date and do travel, so age and discipline are not a concern. And you can always do a citation search on it and see other work that has referenced it (see Chapter 5)—you might just find things of interest!

The Centre for Innovation in Research and Teaching. Based at Grand Canyon University, they have some really useful web pages on 'generating ideas'. There is some useful context about the research process, as well as an online lecture, accompanying slides, and links to other resources. The examples are orientated toward business management, but the principles they discuss are relevant across the social sciences.
https://cirt.gcu.edu/research/developmentresources/tutorials/ideas (Accessed 15 December 2018)

The Web Centre for Social Research Methods. This has some short useful summaries concerning various aspects of the research process. They are a little bit 'on the quantitative side', but are always very readable. There is a good overview of some of the issues associated with validity, and some specific information about the different types of reliability.
http://www.socialresearchmethods.net (Accessed 16 December 2018)

White, P. (2009). *Developing Research Questions: A Guide for Social Scientists.* **Basingstoke: Palgrave Macmillan.** This is a fantastic book. It provides a range of handy hints and tips to help you start your research project. With chapters on 'where do research ideas come from?', 'what makes a research question?', and 'what makes a question "researchable"?', it will certainly help you get your project up and running. However, it also has material on other parts of the research process. Of particular note is a chapter on 'answering research questions'. This details how to use evidence and make claims about your research, something that is likely to be of interest when you are analysing your data and writing up your project. You can watch a short video of Patrick White giving some tips for research questions in the following link:
https://www.youtube.com/watch?v=21qiGXIO70I (Accessed 13 December 2018)

CHAPTER 5

CONDUCTING
A LITERATURE SEARCH

WHAT DO I NEED TO KNOW?

- What is literature in the social sciences?
- What counts as literature?
- Different 'types' of literature searching
- How to develop a literature search strategy
  - Establish the search terms
  - Using Boolean logic
  - Identify relevant databases, engines, and locations
  - Find the material and assess its relevance
  - Record and store your results
- Common problems associated with literature searching

INTRODUCTION

The digital realm has revolutionized the practice of searching for academic literature. Gone are the days of going to the library to look through index cards for books that might be relevant to your research. Today, the world of research is quite literally at your fingertips through the touch of a few buttons. But this increase in access and availability is not without its challenges. With 'hits' that can run into millions, unless you know how to search effectively and efficiently, the information that you find can quickly become overwhelming. This chapter will guide you through the process of literature searching for your dissertation. It will outline how to develop a successful search strategy and what to do with the literature once you have discovered it.

WHAT IS LITERATURE IN THE SOCIAL SCIENCES?

A literature search is an organized exploration of the academic work relating to a particular topic or issue. When conducting a literature search you are attempting to identify the key research in your arena of interest. This material could be theoretical, empirical, or reflective in nature, and can include journal articles, books, and reports.

FINDING YOUR WAY 5.1

Good literature searches are:

- well-planned
- dynamic
- sensitive
- precise
- comprehensive

Not only will this literature help you to inform your thinking and frame your dissertation, it will also allow you to identify the 'knowledge gap' that will enable you to justify your study. To this end, literature plays an important role in the research process. It will:

- help you generate ideas and help to inform your thinking about your topic
- help you establish a context for your dissertation and enable you to situate it appropriately in the wider field
- help you understand what has previously been written (and what has not) in your research area
- support the development of the rationale for your research
- inform the design of your data collection and analysis
- help you substantiate and/or legitimate your arguments

You can see from this list that undertaking a successful literature search is crucial to the development of your dissertation.

I WISH I'D KNOWN . . . TO SPEND MORE TIME RESEARCHING MY TOPIC 5.1

"*I should have spent more time researching my initial research idea before deciding on doing research into it. It would have saved me a lot of time and trouble if I had done this before committing to the project.*"

— Eliska Herinkova, Student, Politics and International Relations, University of Essex

WHAT COUNTS AS LITERATURE?

Academic literature in the social sciences is broadly directed toward presenting, discussing, and/or critiquing knowledge about the human world. It is concerned with creating, establishing, and evaluating both theory and research. Given these purposes, it is important to recognize that literature can take a number of forms, and that it can also be of variable quality. Just because the literature is available to you does not mean that it is necessarily of good standing, and there is a danger in thinking that just because it has been published it will be worth using. This is partly why social scientists make an overarching distinction between 'peer-reviewed literature' and 'grey literature'. We'll take each in turn.

'Peer review' is concerned with ensuring research integrity and refers to the process of evaluation that occurs before publication. It is often considered to be the best form of academic publishing because it involves other experts in the field being invited to comment critically on the value and veracity of the work. These reviews result in either the work being rejected for publication, or the authors being invited to make amendments suggested by the reviews. These changes are then approved by the editor and/or other reviewers. This process helps to secure the integrity of the subsequent publication.

There is no 'kite mark' that will immediately tell you that the research you are looking at has gone through peer review. Instead, the information is usually contained in the small print of the journal or book you are looking at. There are, however, some basic rules of thumb that can be used to guide you as to what sorts of things are likely to have gone through this process. Peer-reviewed work often includes:

- books from recognized academic publishers, such as Oxford University Press
- articles published in refereed academic journals
- conference papers from recognized academic or research institutions
- doctoral theses from reputable universities

While it would be unwise to assume that all literature that has been through the peer review process is of an equal standard, peer-reviewed literature is generally viewed as being the most trustworthy form of publication given the emphasis on quality control.

On the other hand, 'grey literature' is something of a catch-all term for everything that hasn't been through the process of peer review. In many ways, using this material is more difficult because it requires considerable levels of critical literacy to be able to understand and evaluate the constraints on quality. You will need to think about any potential biases or flaws in the work that might compromise its usefulness. For instance, if you used material taken from a political 'think tank' about a particular policy, the information is likely to be presented in a way that resonates with their political position. This may compromise the quality of the work.

Grey literature is also not an excuse to use anything that is returned on an internet search. Instead, you are looking for reputable material rather than polemic or dogma. This might include:

- technical reports
- working papers
- newspaper articles

- magazine articles
- websites of research agencies and organizations
- university, government and company websites

But it is important to note that over-reliance on this type of literature is likely to mean your work lacks the required critical depth and academic insight. This will inevitably affect your dissertation mark.

WORKING WITH YOUR SUPERVISOR 5.1

Information literacy is concerned with your capacity to recognize when information is needed, and how you can locate, access, and retrieve it. On the other hand, critical literacy refers to the capacity to understand and evaluate information. It often involves adopting a 'critical' approach toward what might otherwise be taken for granted. Fortunately, many university libraries offer resources that can be used to enhance both your information literacy and your critical literacy. Ask your supervisor to direct you towards such material.

Generally speaking, the nature of the peer review process means that you should be aiming to place the emphasis of your search on this type of material. While you should engage with all literature in a critical manner, grey material should really only be used to augment peer-reviewed literature, and only when you clearly understand the specific limitations of the work.

DIFFERENT 'TYPES' OF LITERATURE SEARCHING

Now that you know what you are looking for, we can turn to the question of where you might go to find it. There are three overarching approaches you can take: internet searches, database searches, and manual searches.

Internet searches use digital platforms to enable you to discover online material that relates to particular keywords. Basically, these search engines allow you to access a massive index of websites created by web crawling programs that automatically seek out and store information about particular internet addresses. An index is basically a list of things—names, subjects, and topics for instance— that is cross-referenced with the places that they are mentioned. So, when you type a word into a search engine you are actually reaching into a vast digital index of keywords that are associated with particular websites. Keywords are compared and matched to the index which, in turn, is linked to the websites.

Unfortunately, there are any number of websites associated with keywords and search returns into the millions are not uncommon. To solve this issue, the search engine will often use complex algorithms to try and work out which of those

I WISH I'D KNOWN . . . TO START THE LITERATURE SEARCH EARLY 5.2

"*I did not initially work on my dissertation at the beginning of term. However, one of my lecturers forced us to think about our research topic and explore how to approach it from different directions using the literature. Once I started to actually work on my research and reading the literature, I have found the process much easier.*"
— Eliska Herinkova, Student, Politics and International Relations, University of Essex

'hits' will be most relevant to you. This often involves drawing on your own search history, the history of other people who have conducted the search and/or looked at websites that were returned, how often the page is updated, how often it is viewed, and whether it comes from a trusted domain.

For the purposes of social science dissertations, there are two major problems associated with this type of internet searching. In the first instance, there is no quality control. Even on those more specific platforms that brand themselves as scholarly, it is not clear what material is, and is not, being included in the search— not to mention whether it has been through a robust process of peer review. Second, while general search engines are often perfect for everyday purposes, the lack of clarity on what is being returned, and how those returns are being ranked, makes the returns very difficult to evaluate, particularly where the number of 'hits' is very large. Very few people go beyond the first few pages of the search results. Terms may also have multiple meanings and result in many unrelated hits. For instance, if you were interested in training for professional courses such as nursing, teaching, or social work and you simply typed in 'training', you will be provided with links about dog training and first aid training. While these may be interesting, it is unlikely they will be useful for your dissertation.

To put all of this more succinctly, there are too many 'known unknowns' when using general internet searches for the purposes of dissertation research. So, they should not be relied on if at all possible. We often find that when we mark

I WISH I'D KNOWN . . . ABOUT GOOGLE SCHOLAR 5.3

Google Scholar is a freely accessible web search engine that indexes academic literature. It includes academic journals and books, conference papers and theses. It is estimated to index 389 million documents. However, access to those papers will still depend on institutional subscriptions. Fortunately, there is an 'all versions' function that allows you to see where alternatives might be located. The 'cited by' function is also an extremely helpful tool in seeing where literature of interest has been cited.

https://scholar.google.co.uk (Accessed 10 December 2018)

dissertations it is easy to identify where these more general literature searching strategies have been employed. This is because there is a tendency for them to result in an over-reliance on grey literature and an inadequate engagement with academic sources.

Thankfully, there are a number of academically oriented databases that are more transparent in terms of the items they curate, and they host a huge number of peer-reviewed publications you can access. These databases record keywords, the title, the abstract, author(s), the date of publication, and the publisher, and all this information feeds through as a searchable index for you to explore according to your research needs.

WORKING WITH YOUR SUPERVISOR 5.2

There are now so many different databases it is difficult to recommend a single one. It is also worth highlighting that universities will often subscribe to different databases and providers. We recommend that you consult with your supervisor about which databases to use.

Given the volume of publishing, working out what sorts of things to search for in academic databases needs careful attention, and we'll deal with the specifics of doing this in the next section. But before we get there, we also want to highlight a few other methods of searching that can be very useful: what we are going to call 'manual searching methods'. These types of searching tend to be a little more haphazard than the systematized searching of digital databases, but they can prove invaluable, particularly in cases where you are overwhelmed with research and need to find key points of reference, or where finding anything is proving particularly tricky. We'll introduce you to three key methods of manual searching: library searching, hand searching, and using informants.

All contemporary universities should have a library containing books about all sorts of different things. But such a range of different topics creates something of a problem for librarians tasked with helping people to find what they are looking for—how do you organize a library? Fortunately, a very forward-thinking individual by the name of Melvil Dewey was determined to try and solve this issue. In 1876 he produced a standardized system of classification that could be used by all libraries, called the **Dewey Decimal System**, or DDS for short. This is basically a numbering system that catalogues and arranges collections of books into themes. Essentially, each number in the system corresponds to a particular subject. So, for example, the number for social science is 300—and 300.72 is the number for social research in particular. This means that in every library that uses the DDS you can go directly to the shelf that corresponds to these numbers to find books about social science generally, and social science research methods more specifically. The DDS can be applied to both books and journals, making the job of navigating any library very easy.

There is an added benefit to this system for those of us who are doing literature searches. Once you have found an item of interest, you can return to the place on the DDS where it is usually shelved and look through all the books or journals that are close by to see whether they are also relevant to your interests. This can be done quite quickly by looking through the contents or browsing the index of the book for relevant terms and material. Many libraries will also have an online cataloguing system that can also be used to search keywords, effectively allowing you to browse the shelves electronically.

FINDING YOUR WAY 5.2

Library Hub Discover is a 'union catalogue' of over one hundred different research-related libraries. Based in the UK, it allows you to search the content of many different university libraries at once. This service can be invaluable if you discover a book that isn't in your local library, because you can find out exactly which UK libraries do hold the material you require. Other countries have similar services—ask your local librarian for further information. For more details, visit: https://libraryhub.jisc.ac.uk/discover/

You can do a version of this manual searching with journal articles too. This basically works on the assumption that all journals have specific, and stated, subjects that they are interested in. For instance, you will find journals specifically focused on areas such as children and families, care provision, ageing, race and ethnicity, gender, accounting, ethics, criminology, economic geography, comparative politics, media studies, and cultural anthropology. Therefore, if you discover an article relevant to your needs, there is a good chance that that journal will have published articles on similar topics. In many institutions, physical copies of journals are still sent for binding on an annual basis, so you can also actually browse journals for relevant articles. However, given that the major journals are now online, it is much easier to click through electronic issues and assess the titles and abstracts for relevance. You can then read the abstract to decide whether an article is likely to be useful.

The final form of manual searching simply involves asking people for advice, either in terms of specific books and articles on a topic, or where to begin looking. Your first port of call here is your supervisor. They will be able to advise you not only on what literature might help to inform your project, but also on where and how to search. Beyond that, there may be other experts in your department, school, or faculty that might be able to help. However, remember that you are asking them to take their own time to help you. Always be polite when making a request, and it's often worth reading some of their research before you approach them. This will help you to articulate why you are seeking their advice.

I WISH I'D KNOWN . . . TO REFERENCE RAID 5.4

Once you have discovered relevant material, you can employ citation searches to expand your search. Citation searches are available in many academic databases. They basically search for literature that has cited the work you are interested in. This allows you to specifically target publications that are much more likely to be of relevance to you. You can also 'raid the references' in any given publication of interest to discover more material that might be useful—and, of course, if you find something useful, you can do a citation search and 'reference raid' on that too!

"When doing a literature review, use the citations of the works you're reading to further guide your reading. If you are interested in a point the author made, look at citations connected to that point and see if they could inform your research further."

— Ashley Taylor, Student, Politics and International Relations,
University of Limerick

HOW TO DEVELOP A LITERATURE SEARCH STRATEGY

A literature search is a planned and organized examination of a particular research topic. It is planned in the sense that you make predetermined decisions about what, where, and how you will search for information, and it is organized in that you systematically work through a series of processes to achieve the aims of the search. To make sure your search covers as much of the literature as possible, it is a very good idea to develop what is known as a literature search strategy. This allows you to identify and articulate the specific parameters of your search, and enables you to critically reflect on the process. Good literature searches have four separate component parts:

1. Establish the search terms
2. Identify relevant databases, engines, and locations
3. Find the material and assess its relevance
4. Record and store the literature

It is also worth highlighting that many searches will be dynamic in terms of process. This means that you will need to be responsive to the results of your search and may have to change, expand, or constrain your strategy as required. In this respect, literature searches often comprise sequential phases of development rather than stand-alone 'one-off' events. We'll deal with some of the problems of literature searching later in this chapter, but the nature of social science knowledge often requires searching to have both sensitivity and flexibility.

Establish the search terms

In order to establish your search terms, you will need to decide on your research topic, and formulate a broad question or statement to define your key foci. This will often mean pulling out the key concepts and topics that you are interested in. You can then use these terms to begin to identify a list of keywords that relate to your research idea. This involves listing key concepts and terms and thinking about how they might be expressed differently elsewhere.

Using synonyms that you might find in a thesaurus is one way of doing this. Inspecting a journal article for keywords that are similar in nature is another approach. At this stage, you might also want to think about any alternative ways of spelling for your terms, or how terms can be used differently according to place. Perhaps the easiest example of this is football. What is known in the UK as 'football' is known in the USA as 'soccer', and what is known in the USA as 'football' is known as 'American football' in the UK. Another example is the term 'kindergarten', which is not used in the UK to describe modern preschool education or the first year(s) of compulsory primary school education, but it is used in many other countries. In the UK, preschool is usually referred to as crèches, nursery schools, or playgroups.

To see how this might work in practice, let us return to the example of ethnicity and attainment in higher education that we looked at in Chapter 4. This was the research rationale:

> Within the field of Higher Education, there is currently much policy and practice interest in the attainment gap between BAME (Black Asian Minority Ethnic) and White students. This gap is generally taken to be the difference between the proportion of White students who gain higher degrees and the proportion of BAME students who gain the same degrees. Using a mixed methods approach, this project will explore how differential levels of attainment might be experienced within Higher Education. Drawing on quantitative data within an English University to examine the nature of the gap, and a range of qualitative interviews with BAME students to understand the experience of it, the study will attempt to explore how BAME students negotiate their way through university landscapes.

FINDING YOUR WAY 5.3

It is important to recognize when developing your literature searching strategy that many databases will allow you to search by date range or author. Searching by date is particularly useful if you are updating a search you have previously carried out to see if there is anything new in the field. Author searches can also be very helpful when you discover a key piece of literature. There is a very good chance that the author will have written something else in the area that may be suitable for your needs.

It is possible to quickly identify a number of keywords from this rationale. They broadly circulate around 'ethnicity', 'attainment', and 'higher education'. From here, we can begin to build a list of key search terms (see Table 5.1).

Table 5.1 **List of search terms relating to the BAME attainment gap in higher education**

Ethnicity	Attainment	Higher education
Ethnic group	Outcome	University
Minority group	Results	Degree
BAME (Black Asian Minority Ethnic)	Classification	Post-compulsory education
BME (Black Minority Ethnic)	Marks	Further education

Using Boolean logic

We could conduct single item searches using these terms. However, there are some advanced methods that can help you to build more sophisticated searches. These techniques are often associated with what is often referred to as 'Boolean logic'. George Boole was a nineteenth-century mathematician who developed a system of logic that was designed to explicate the relationship between probability and reasoning. In fact, he created what is now known as 'Boolean algebra' to help him solve logical problems. His system was based around three basic operations—AND, OR, and NOT—that would provide one of two answers, TRUE or FALSE.

You don't really need to understand much more about this, but Boole's ideas have been extraordinarily helpful in the field of electronics and in the processing of digital information. Search engines also make use of this logic so we can search for more than one term at a time.

Remember our rationale? We had three key elements of focus: ethnicity, attainment, and higher education. Using Boolean logic, we can begin to put together those terms to create more complex searches. For example, we could specifically search for the following:

ethnicity AND attainment AND higher education

This is an example of a single search string. If we were to search for this it would return all the 'hits' where ethnicity, attainment, and higher education were found in a given database—but only where all three appeared. These are essentially all the TRUE matches. Everything else would be FALSE so would not be returned.

However, we could actually go a lot further and use Boolean logic to put together an even more complex search by using parentheses to combine search strings. In fact, we can use Boole's system to express all of the words in Table 5.1. It would look something like this:

(ethnicity OR ethnic group OR minority group OR BAME OR BME) AND (attainment OR outcome OR results OR classification OR marks) AND (higher education OR university OR degree OR post-compulsory education OR further education)

This search would return all the hits where any combination of these three elements were returned as TRUE. If we were to conduct this search using single strings, we would need to conduct 125 different searches. By taking advantage of Boolean logic, we can conduct the search in one single go, and our search is quickly becoming much more efficient and much more comprehensive.

But it gets even better. Many search engines have expanded Boole's system to include ways of searching for exact phrases (" "), using wildcards to search for truncated words (*), and automatically searching for synonyms (~). This means you can use Boolean logic to express your search a little more concisely:

~ethni* AND ~attainment AND ~"higher education"

You can often specify whether you want to search for your terms in the title, the abstract, and in some cases, the entire document. Table 5.2 provides a summary of Boolean commands, their function, and the commonly associated special characters.

Unfortunately, while Boole gave us a very handy system for expressing the logic of literature searches, there is a problem. Remember how we said there were a great

Table 5.2 **Search terms using Boolean logic**

Command	Function	Special Character
AND	Returns all hits with term1 AND term2	+
OR	Returns all hits with either term1 OR term2, or both	|
NOT	Excludes returns with term2 where it occurs in close proximity to term1	-
NEAR	Proximity search that returns term1 where it occurs NEAR to term2	*See specific instructions for the platform*
Synonyms	Returns terms similar to term1	~
Wildcards	Can be used in place of a missing word or part of a word	*
Parentheses	Combines search strings	( )
Quotation	Searches exact phrase	" "

many different databases and search engines? Although they all make use of Boolean logic, they represent it in different ways—and few will actually respond to the search strings as we have expressed them above. Some will use drop-down menus to make Boole's system a bit more user-friendly, others will not include all of the functions, whereas some might use different symbols to replicate functions.

That said, many platforms will provide help or 'frequently asked questions' where they will detail, exactly, what functionality they offer and how to use it. When using a database or an engine for the first time, we recommend familiarizing yourself with these pages before you begin your search.

FINDING YOUR WAY 5.4

Many university libraries will have information sheets and/or tutorials that can help you learn about the different functionality available within particular databases. Check with your local librarian to see what they offer.

Identify relevant databases, engines, and locations

We've already hinted at the fact that there are many different databases that you could use in your search, and that they operate in different ways, so it is worth explaining how these academic databases 'work' in practice.

Databases have different interfaces and operate differently. This is partly because different companies own and operate them. So, while they all run along similar lines, they all have different decoration in terms of how they look and feel. They also specialize in different literatures. Some focus on a specific discipline, others are focused on the social sciences more generally, while some are multidisciplinary and actually contain material on all major subjects. Table 5.3 provides a list of the major databases you might make use of in your search for your dissertation.

Table 5.3 **Major academic databases of research**

Database	Subject(s)	Platform
Social Science Citation Index	Multidisciplinary	Web of Science
International Bibliography of Social Sciences	Social science	ProQuest
JSTOR	Multidisciplinary	JSTOR
PsychINFO	Psychology, behavioural science, and mental health	OvidSP
Sociological Abstracts	Sociology	ProQuest
Criminal Justice Abstracts	Criminology/law	EBSCO
Scopus	Multidisciplinary	Scopus
MEDLINE	Health-related research	PubMed

This is worth thinking about in a little more detail as it can impact on the relevance of your results. Different disciplines look at issues and problems in different ways. That is to say that they have particular histories, different foci, **and** different epistemologies associated with them. This means that, for example, sociological research and psychological research think and act differently, as do politics and criminology. Where disciplines are close—like (British) sociology and (British) criminology— these differences **and** similarities can be very difficult to spot. Elsewhere, the differences between, for example, economics and psychology are more obvious.

Find the material and assess its relevance

The point of highlighting this is to make you aware of some of the complexities of assessing the relevance of your results. Not all research on a given topic has the same nature, and not all will be relevant to the approach that you are taking, or the discipline that you are working in. This means that you will need to be aware of the types of disciplines and approaches associated with the topic that you are interested in.

I WISH I'D KNOWN . . . HOW TO REFINE A SEARCH 5.5

Sometimes the number of results obtained from a search can be very daunting. However, there are ways to limit the number of hits and to make sure you target the most relevant literature. For instance, many databases allow you to identify the year of the publication. This can be particularly useful in enabling you to focus on recent literature, especially if you are looking at a particular policy or development and you want to focus on literature following this.

You also need to think about the types of literature you want to engage with. In general terms, monographs tend to provide an in-depth discussion of an area, often illuminated with empirical research. Usually written by a range of different authors, so-called 'edited collections' tend to provide a range of different perspectives or issues associated with a particular topic. Papers in academic journals tend to be much more specific in terms of the issues or problems being addressed. Table 5.4 details some of the different types of literature you may encounter.

Table 5.4 **Types of literature**

Type of literature	Description
Theoretical	An explication of a particular framework for thinking about a specific topic. In some cases, this will be entirely novel; in others, it will be an extension of an approach used elsewhere and applied in a different context.
Literature reviews	Provide a general overview of the field and the different approaches associated with it.

Type of literature	Description
Scoping studies, meta-analyses, systematic reviews	Often associated with medicine, health and social care, and education, these are a comprehensive attempt to review all known research in a specific area. They are broadly concerned with 'what works' in a given area.
Discussion papers	Examine a particular aspect of the field in depth, often introducing or justifying a particular perspective.
Empirical research	The presentation of the results of a research study that makes an original, significant, and robust addition to the body of knowledge.
Evaluations	Descriptive rather than critical; they provide a presentation of outcomes from a very specific programme of work or intervention.

Again, not all of these outputs will be relevant to your interests and it is likely that you will need to be somewhat selective in the types of output you engage with.

Record and store your results

Before you begin your search, you will also need to decide on a means of both recording the results of your search and storing any associated items of interest. There are a number of ways of doing this. In the first instance, academic databases will often allow you to 'mark' items of interest. This provides a means of narrowing down your search to include items that you have specifically chosen as being of interest as you process the relevance of your hits. Once you have compiled your list of 'marked' items, it is then relatively easy to click through associated links to access the relevant articles and save any documents directly to your hard drive. These lists can then be emailed or printed to give you a written record of things you have downloaded, or you can also save these lists for future reference.

I WISH I'D KNOWN . . . TO RECORD MY READING EARLY ON 5.6

Recording your literature searches from the onset is important in organizing your work.

"*I should have established a system for all of my reading, including page references, searchable key words etc. It is definitely best to do this very early on as it helps to organise your work.*"

— Vilde Bye Dale, Student, Modern History and Politics, University of Essex

However, there are now a number of platforms that will allow you to record and store citations electronically. Effectively, this 'reference management software' allows you to create and curate your own database of material associated with your research. This software can be used to import material from databases for viewing, as well as allowing you to export any selected references to create specific bibliographies. Many will also interface with word-processing software to automatically produce reference lists in the particular format you require. Writing references is quite a laborious job, and making use of these platforms can save you much time when it comes to 'writing up'. However, there are some substantial entry costs. Firstly, you have to be able to access the software. Not all higher education institutions make these platforms freely available, so you will need to check with your library to see what might be available. Secondly, you will have to learn how to use it. Generally speaking, the usefulness of any information extracted from a database is only as good as the information that is put into it. While some databases will allow you to download citations directly into the software, other more manual techniques will rely on you to input the relevant data. You will need to input all of this information correctly.

FINDING YOUR WAY 5.5

When creating a bibliography, avoid the temptation to simply 'cut and paste' references from other sources. This creates numerous problems with style and form as there are many small inconsistencies within and between specific referencing formats. Even in the Harvard system of referencing there are many 'house formats' that are used by publishers—and they are not all the same. If you do decide to 'cut and paste' make sure you go through your references to ensure they are consistent with the required format.

COMMON PROBLEMS ASSOCIATED WITH LITERATURE SEARCHING

As you will no doubt find out for yourself, there are any number of difficulties associated with literature searching. These include problems of coverage, terminology, sensitivity, and selection.

In the first instance, research outputs in the social sciences can be quite diverse, and although academic databases do contain a lot of information, they are rarely exhaustive of everything that is available. This is the problem of coverage, and it means that good searching will necessarily involve using more than one resource because this will help to ensure that you are surveying as much of the field as possible. In turn, this means getting to grips with how particular databases and engines work. Taking time to learn how to use databases is important; don't expect to be an expert immediately.

Second is the problem of terminology. Unlike the sciences, which usually have discipline-specific words for the things they study, the social sciences often draw on everyday language for the purposes of research. As a result, the language of social sciences is often imprecise. Methodological terms like bias, representation, and subjectivity have similar meanings and are, more or less, understandable from a lay perspective. Concepts like poverty, exclusion, and inequality are similarly multifaceted. You can do a fairly comprehensive search of the literature on, for example, the side effects of the drug ibuprofen because that term is always how the drug is referred to in an academic context. Try to do a search on the impact of bias on research results, and not only will you be inundated with hits because of the generic word 'research', but also you are unlikely to discover any of the literature on representation and subjectivity. Overlay this problem with the fact that social science authors can be creative with the way they word titles and abstracts, and the idea of an absolutely systematic search quickly sails away over the horizon.

In part, this is why taking the time to develop your keywords is so important. You need to think carefully about how a term might be used and what it might encompass. On the surface of it, poverty might appear to have a straightforward meaning, but it actually covers a range of economic, cultural, and political issues that are associated with wealth, living standards, and human need—and this is before we consider how it is actually measured. Problems of terminology also emphasize why literature searches in the social sciences are rarely static. This is because some familiarity with the literature, and how terms are being used in a given area, is crucial to the process of discovery.

Third is the related problem of sensitivity. Broadly speaking, this refers to the capacity of a search to identify as much relevant material as possible, as precisely as possible. That said, the initial results of a search will often dictate the exact nature of what precision means in the context of your research project. Perhaps the easiest way to explain this is to take two extremes. Let's suggest that your first search returns over a million hits. This is clearly unmanageable. It also suggests that your search is too sensitive. To try and rectify this you would need to change your search terms to make them more precise. Unfortunately, you have been a little too exacting and your search now returns no hits. It is now not sensitive enough. There is a fine line between too vague and too specific.

Generally, if you increase the sensitivity, you decrease the precision. This process of trying to get more hits is often termed 'searching up'. It often means adding more terms or broadening search terms. On the other hand, if you decrease

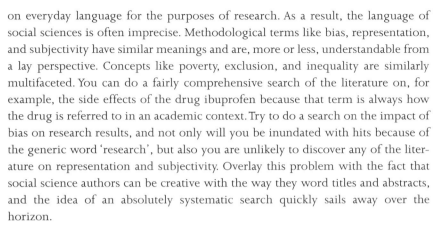

FINDING YOUR WAY 5.6

Many databases have an advanced search function. Once you have got used to the basics of searching, don't be afraid to use these tools as they can balance precision and sensitivity.

the sensitivity you will increase the precision. Effectively, this will lower the number of hits, and is known as 'searching down'. This might mean developing exclusion criteria or using more precise terms and strings. Good searching is a process of getting a good balance between these two outcomes, and some fine tuning is often necessary to achieving it.

There is a further complication here: not all literatures are the same. In some cases there will be a plethora of studies to look at. This is particularly likely in arenas that have a long history. In practice, this allows you to be very specific in terms of the literature that relates to your study. In other cases, there may be very little work in the area and you will not only need to broaden your search terms, but also broaden the general scope of your search.

In some cases, the results of your literature search might actually indicate that you should refocus your topic, either because it is too broad or too specific. The literature searching process could also lead to you identifying another related area that you are actually more interested in, where there may be a clearer justification for a potential project.

The final problem relates to the issue of what to include or exclude in your search. Somewhat inevitably, the answer to this question will depend on your particular search. There are, perhaps, three considerations: discipline/approach, quality, and manageability.

Firstly, you will need to consider whether you need to include material from different disciplines to substantiate your research aims, or whether you can rely on the material written from your particular discipline. If so, you may need to ask a further question concerning whether you need to acknowledge different approaches within your discipline. Where there is a lot of literature on a topic, it may be the case that you can actually stay inside a particular perspective.

Secondly, you might wish to consider the quality of the literature. This might involve making an assessment of your results with respect to source, relevance, rigour, and/or significance. You could, for example, choose to exclude conference papers because you cannot guarantee they have been subject to peer review. Similarly, you might choose to exclude research where the sampling strategy has not been explained in enough detail because it does not allow you to consider how the conclusions might be instructive in similar situations.

Finally, and most practically, there is the issue of manageability. How much time do you have? What are the general expectations in your department? You can't do everything, and you will not be expected to. But you will need to exercise your academic judgement and be responsive to the needs of your project, the discoveries you have made, and the wider demands of the learning objectives that you are working under. And do you have the confidence to know when to stop? If you feel like you are reading the same article again and again, or that you are going around in circles, then you probably don't need to carry on. Trust your own judgement.

FINDING YOUR WAY 5.7

Remember that good literature searching involves:

- practice
- diversity
- dedication and detective work
- flexibility and patience
- ingenuity and imagination

CONCLUSION

Good literature searching in the social sciences is very much a developmental process. It involves thinking, searching, rethinking, searching again, and learning from discovering. You will need to be flexible and be prepared to use your academic judgement to make choices in response to your discoveries. You will need to build search strategies that suit you, your topic area, **and** what you discover. Literature searching is a time-consuming process, but it is worth the effort. Remember, you have a whole world of interesting research at your fingertips!

WHAT DO I NEED TO THINK ABOUT?

- ☑ What key terms might be associated with your research idea?
- ☑ What sorts of methods might be used to locate relevant literature?
- ☑ What are the most relevant search engines available to you?
- ☑ How might the challenges associated with searching the literature impact on your project?
- ☑ What means of recording and storing identified items of interest are available at your institution?

WHAT DO I NEED TO DO?

- ☑ Develop a literature searching strategy.
- ☑ Carry out your literature search.
- ☑ Change your approach depending on your results.
- ☑ Identify key literature relating to your topic by recording your results appropriately.

Access the online resources **www.oup.com/uk/brymansrple** to help you to successfully complete your social research project or dissertation.

DELVE DEEPER

There's a wealth of online material dedicated to literature searching. This is partly because many university libraries produce information for their students. So it is worth visiting your **institutional library** to see what resources they offer and how they might be able to help conduct your literature search.

Nexis provides a range of sources from the print media. This includes UK national and regional newspapers, international newspapers and newswires, and foreign language news sources in Dutch, French, German, Arabic, Spanish, and Portuguese. It is possible to search groups of sources (for example, UK Broadsheets, Major World Newspapers) or individual publications. Coverage is from the 1980s onwards and it is updated daily. Helpfully, there are a range of tutorials that help you to get to grips with the database, available from the Help link on the Nexis website. Unfortunately, an institutional subscription is required. Check with your local librarian to see if you have access.
https://nexis.com (Accessed 10 December 2018)

Open Grey is a multidisciplinary open access database of grey literature that contains over 700,000 bibliographical references produced in Europe. Academic in nature, it covers issues relating to science, technology, bio-medical science, economics, social science, and the humanities. While the database does not always actually contain the material of interest, it does allow you to export records and locate the documents. Examples of grey literature in the database include technical or research reports, doctoral dissertations, some conference papers, and some official publications.
http://www.opengrey.eu (Accessed 10 December 2018)

The Open University has some particularly helpful pages on literature searching. This includes help on selecting sources and using advanced search terms, as well as evaluating material.
http://www.open.ac.uk/library/help-and-support/how-do-i-do-a-literature-search (Accessed 10 December 2018)

Sage Research Methods website has much material on social research methods. However, as a part of their project planner, they provide some helpful advice about the practicalities of literature searching. Written by David Byrne in an accessible and engaging way, there is much advice on building a search strategy, as well as what makes a good literature search. Unfortunately, you might require an institutional subscription to access the material. If you are uncertain about this, ask your local librarian for help.
http://methods.sagepub.com/project-planner/reviewing-the-literature/i340#i348 (Accessed 10 December 2018)

Zotero is freely available reference management software that can be used to help you manage bibliographic data and references. It allows you to store papers and websites so you can curate your own custom database of material. You can then use this to generate in-text citations, footnotes, and bibliographies. Fully compatible with Microsoft Word and Google Docs, you can choose the format of your references. Zotero can even be incorporated into your web browser!
https://www.zotero.org/ (Accessed 10 December 2018)

CHAPTER 6
REVIEWING
THE LITERATURE

WHAT DO I NEED TO KNOW?

- What is a literature review?
- The relationship between literature and theory
- Types of literature review
  - Systematic reviews
  - Scoping studies
  - Narrative reviews
- Key components of a literature review
  - Why is this topic interesting?
  - What are the key themes from the research base?
  - What knowledge gap will you address?
  - Research aims and questions

INTRODUCTION

The literature review is a key component of a dissertation. It serves to contextualize the aims and objectives of the project, and in terms of the research process it helps to sensitize to issues of interest that you might want to direct your attention towards when you begin collecting and analysing data. A literature review is also dynamic in that it can change during the process of research and in response to the demands of the field. This chapter will introduce you to the literature review and examine its purpose in relation to the research process. Beginning with a short exploration of the nature of a literature review and its relationship with theory, the chapter will go on to examine the different types of review before detailing the key content. By the end of the chapter you should have a good understanding of the role of the literature review in research and how it informs every aspect of the research process.

WHAT IS A LITERATURE REVIEW?

A literature review is a key component of all research projects, including a dissertation. It is more than just a written summary of research in a particular area. Not only does it reflect the results of a literature search, it also functions as a framing device that creates 'the knowledge gap' together with the research questions that follow. Literature reviews are a key part of the research process because they situate a project within a wider body of knowledge and demonstrate how the aims of the project will contribute to the field. They show the reader why the research is important.

I WISH I'D KNOWN . . . ABOUT THE IMPORTANCE OF THE LITERATURE REVIEW 6.1

"*Start reading for your literature review as soon as you've decided your title or topic area. It's important to do this first as other parts of the research process relate heavily to this material.*"

— Rachael O'Neill, Student, Politics, and International Relations, University of Nottingham

In this respect, literature reviews tend to have both passive and active elements. They attempt to describe key research in the field, but also provide some critical commentary in relation to that literature. This enables the review to both provide the background to the research **and** outline a justification for the proposed research.

Given these purposes, it might seem obvious to point out that literature reviews are always positioned toward the beginning of a dissertation, usually between the introduction and methods sections, and it is common for literature reviews to be written at the start of a project. However, in practice, the actual writing of the review can also happen at other points in the research process. While familiarizing yourself with the literature before you enter the field is usually desirable, it is not always necessary to complete the formal presentation of that review at the beginning. Indeed, one of the dangers of writing a literature review early on is that your focus may shift during the research process, particularly when you start collecting and analysing data. If your review is completely fixed beforehand, it could mean that the literature doesn't correspond with your findings. In fact, there is nothing wrong with returning to and adapting your literature review later in the process of writing your dissertation.

WORKING WITH YOUR SUPERVISOR 6.1

Discuss your literature review strategy with your supervisor. Ask them when you should be completing drafts and making revisions in the context of the whole research process. Make sure you include some contingency in your planning. This can provide you with the time necessary to make changes to your review if necessary.

THE RELATIONSHIP BETWEEN LITERATURE AND THEORY

As we've highlighted, the literature review provides a framework within which your research project can be situated and understood. In writing a review, you make choices about what sort of literature will help orientate the reader to your field of study, your argument in relation to it, and how you position that all-important knowledge gap and the aims and objectives that follow from it.

In doing so, you will make decisions about your position in relation to the field and how you are approaching it. This is, once again, concerned with ontology, epistemology, and methodology—but there's no need to get unduly worried by the terminology. Basically, we all work within disciplines. These disciplines have their own particular ways of seeing and doing. That is, they are interested in different things **and** act differently in relation to those interests. But **within** those disciplines there are often different kinds of approach that can be taken. These approaches are sometimes called schools, traditions, paradigms, perspectives, or theories. For example, the vision of criminology is directed toward various aspects of crime—but radical criminologists are interested in the critical appreciation of how power creates and sustains particular forms of crime, and who benefits from the reproduction of those relations. This approach is different from so-called subcultural theories that choose to emphasize how particular groups in society develop their own norms and routines in relation to crime and deviance, and how those norms might be, at least in part, structured by society.

With this in mind, before you begin writing your review, you need to think carefully about what sort of researcher you are, and what sort of approach you are taking in your research. You need to ask yourself, 'what is my theoretical focus?', because this will influence the way you present **your** field of interest. There are two ways of answering this question. The first is relatively straightforward; the second is a little more nuanced.

In the first instance, you simply need to recognize the particular theoretical tradition you are working in. That is to say, what sorts of theories are informing the direction of your project?

In some cases, identifying your theoretical position will be relatively easy. For example, if you were trying to use labelling theory to explore how students 'fail' at university, you would be working in the broad tradition of symbolic interactionism. This body of work emphasizes the role of symbols in everyday life, and how people interact with them to produce meaning and experience. Labelling theory emerged from this particular body of literature and continues to be a core theme within it. Identifying your theoretical position is very important as it will influence the way you represent your field. In this case, you would probably wish to orientate your review around the literature on 'failing' generally, followed by labelling theory more specifically, including some justification of why it is likely to be a fruitful approach to take. Broadly speaking, you would then be writing your review along these lines: 'Working within the broad tradition of symbolic interactionism, this dissertation aims to examine the capacity of "labelling theory" to account for how students "fail" while studying in higher education.'

In other cases, identifying your theoretical position might be more nuanced. Rather than using theory per se, some studies use literature as a proxy for theory (see Chapter 4). Relevant background literature associated with the topic is used to provide the context for the research, not an explicit theory. For instance, you may use your literature review to outline different areas of research in relation to the use of art and music therapy with people diagnosed with dementia. It may be that research questions arise from an examination of the literature, with data collection and analysis specifically designed according to the demands of the research base.

It would be easy to dismiss this use of literature as a form of naive empiricism—blind fact gathering—or as an exercise in unreflexive post-positivism. But we feel that this would be an unfair criticism, largely because social research can have a strong rationale without recourse to an explicit theory. It also does not mean that your work is lacking theoretical direction. Instead, using literature as a proxy for theory is a more iterative form of working whereby the literature review is designed to be responsive to the emergent requirements of the literature. In the first instance, this means contextualizing the research problem with related literature; and, in the second, using literature as and where appropriate during the course of the study to further explicate data or the findings.

You're unlikely to explicitly state that you are using literature as a proxy in the review itself. This is largely because it would be a little awkward in terms of the flow of your writing. Instead, it can be inferred from the way you frame your study around a range of literature. For example, we can amend the previous example to produce a very general rationale: 'Within both policy and practice, there is currently much interest in retention rates at university (see, for example, British Council, 2014). Using data generated from semi-structured interviews, this dissertation will explore the experiences of "failing" students to determine the processes through which "failure" is achieved.' Of course, your review will be much longer in practice, but you should now have a better idea of what is meant by using literature as a proxy for research.

FINDING YOUR WAY 6.1

To get the most from your reading:
- Take good notes—try to summarize ideas in your own words (close the book!), and remember to record page numbers and references. Colour coding and mind-maps can also be used to help organize information.
- Develop your critical reading skills.
- Select the most appropriate literature for your purposes—you don't have to include everything.
- Don't stop reading after the initial stages of the literature search!

TYPES OF LITERATURE REVIEW

Having discussed the overarching purpose of literature reviews and the relationship between literature and theory, we can now move on to introduce the different types of reviews that exist. Not all literature reviews have the same characteristics or share the same relationship with the literature search strategy. Some are quite tightly bounded by rules and conventions, others follow certain general processes, while some operate with less constraint. There are actually a quite a few different approaches to reviewing, but we'll discuss the three main types you are likely to encounter: systematic reviews, scoping studies, and narrative reviews. Different approaches are more likely to be employed in particular disciplines, so you will need to identify whether your course has specific requirements as to the type of literature review you undertake.

I WISH I'D KNOWN . . . HOW LONG THE LITERATURE REVIEW WOULD TAKE TO COMPLETE 6.2

"*I wrongly presumed that the literature review was like another essay—but it isn't. I had to ask the question 'so what?' after each paragraph to ensure that all information I was using was relevant. This helped to ensure that I was being critical in relation to the knowledge gap.*"

— Megan Robinson, Student, Criminal and Forensic Psychology, University of Bolton

Systematic reviews

The Campbell Collaboration is an organization that promotes evidence-based policy and practice in the social sciences. It aims to provide policy-makers and practitioners with the research evidence that will help them make better decisions about the effectiveness of particular programmes of intervention. They use systematic reviews and other forms of evidence synthesis to help them do this.

Systematic reviews adopt explicit procedures to search for, organize, and review literature. They were originally developed for the purposes of medical and scientific research and are implicitly bound up in policy and practice discourse around questions of 'what works?' In this respect, the use of systematic reviews is something of a reaction to accusations that reviews in the social sciences are poorly conducted and/or misrepresent the literature they purport to cover. Often this is because there is no transparent search strategy or there are no clear procedures for the selection of sources used. In part, this is why organizations like the Campbell Collaboration have quite strict rules on the types of review that they will support, conduct, and/or disseminate.

Partly due to their successful use in the natural sciences, systematic reviews are often associated with 'the gold standard of reviewing'. In many cases, they can be considered to actually be a form of research in themselves as they attempt to comprehensively synthesize literature on a particular topic in order to answer a very specific research question.

Broadly speaking, systematic reviews have at least five key components:

1. Definition of the purpose and scope of the review
2. Development of an explicit literature search strategy that is appropriate to the purpose and scope of the review—including explicit inclusion and exclusion criteria
3. Appraisal of the quality of each study found by the search with respect to any criteria outlined
4. Extraction of results
5. Research synthesis

Literature search strategies for the purposes of systematic review are usually very detailed and also very explicit in terms of the criteria for inclusion and exclusion. This is to aid the transparency of the review. There are also highly specialized techniques used to aggregate research results, particularly where studies have incorporated quantitative data. Meta-analyses, for example, attempt to combine the results from a number of studies. Qualitative research synthesis is, perhaps, less well developed than its quantitative counterpart. However, there are a range of techniques associated with the attempt to combine qualitative results, which include: narrative synthesis, thematic synthesis, meta-ethnography, and qualitative meta-synthesis.

In all likelihood, the complex techniques associated with systematic reviewing make it an approach that is seldom seen in undergraduate or even postgraduate work. However, the terminology associated with systematic reviewing is commonly seen in research methods textbooks. It is important that you understand the complexities of systematic reviewing so you don't inadvertently claim you are doing something that you are actually not equipped to do. This is a common mistake made by students, and is the reason that we've introduced it here.

Scoping studies

While systematic studies are, perhaps, beyond the remit of a dissertation project, there are other relatively robust methods of reviewing that might be more appropriate. Scoping studies are one such possibility. According to one influential review conducted by Arksey and O'Malley (2005), scoping studies can be used to:

*   map the extent, range, and nature of research activity in a given area
*   assess whether a full systematic review is possible or desirable
*   summarize and/or disseminate research findings
*   identify gaps in the literature

FINDING YOUR WAY 6.2

In their review of scoping studies, Arksey and O'Malley (2005) recommend that you use a spreadsheet to record the results of your literature search. This is because it allows you to clearly evidence the themes you discover, but also because it helps to organize the results in a transparent manner. They recommend recording the following:

- Author(s), year of publication, study location
- Intervention type, and comparator (if any); duration of the intervention
- Study populations (eg carer group; care recipient group)
- Aims of the study
- Methodology
- Outcome measures
- Important results

Generally speaking, a scoping study tends to focus on broader topics of investigation than the specific research questions of systematic reviews. There also tends to be less emphasis on research quality. That is not to suggest that issues of inclusion and exclusion are not important. However, the more exploratory nature of a scoping study necessarily requires more flexibility than the fixed requirements of systematic review. Arksey and O'Malley (2005) outline five key stages of a scoping study:

1. Identifying the research question
2. Identifying relevant studies
3. Study selection
4. Charting the data
5. Collating, summarizing, and reporting the results

It's easy to see how the process of scoping studies resonates with systematic reviews. The differences, however, lie in the specificity of the focus, the broader range of techniques associated with discovering the literature, the less stringent nature of quality, and the more flexible means through which results are synthesized. Collectively, this makes them much more suitable to undergraduate and postgraduate projects. Indeed, they provide a very handy road map of how to do a literature review that is both comprehensive and transparent in nature.

Narrative reviews

Narrative reviews are the most common type of literature review used in student projects. As the name suggests, they provide a narratively driven overview of research in the area of interest. They 'set the scene' for you to tell the story of your research, but don't just list studies, or simply review key studies in bullet point format. Instead, narrative reviews use literature to develop an argument in relation to the body of knowledge. This argument clearly specifies why the research is necessary by outlining the significance of the project and detailing how, and where, it contributes to the field.

Narrative reviews need to be comprehensive in nature, but not necessarily exhaustive. This is because they have to review the key approaches and issues that exist in a field **and** demonstrate where and how the proposed project 'fits in' within that overarching narrative. Not every piece of literature on a topic will be necessary to do this, as many of the key themes will be repeated across studies. So, if you are going to adopt a narrative strategy in your research, you will need to be selective **and** transparent about the literature that you do and do not include. This might mean providing a copy of the literature search strategy in your dissertation.

I WISH I'D KNOWN . . . EVERYTHING I READ WAS HELPFUL 6.3

"All research is useful research. I did so much research months before I started writing, and felt disheartened that a lot of it was not relevant as my dissertation gradually changed. But when I started writing, I realised that the research that isn't included in my project was still useful as it contributed to my overall knowledge on the topic."

— Vilde Bye Dale, Student, Modern History and Politics, University of Essex

A narrative review should also not be interpreted as 'anything goes'. While they are more subjective than either scoping studies or systematic reviews, that does not mean that you can leave ideas out that you find difficult, or ignore studies that might otherwise compromise your knowledge gap. Instead, narrative reviews utilize some of the techniques associated with systematic reviewing in order to enhance the coverage and sensitivity of the search. This is exactly the approach we have taken in Chapter 5. By introducing you to some of the techniques associated

FINDING YOUR WAY 6.3

When undertaking a narrative review bear the following key points of interest in mind (adapted from Bryman, 2016: 94):
- What is known about the area?
- What theories and concepts are relevant?
- What research designs and methods are usually associated with the topic?
- Are there any significant controversies?
- Are there any inconsistencies in the research findings?
- What unanswered research questions exist in the area?
- How does the literature relate to your research project?

with more sophisticated literature searching, as well as some of the issues around inclusion and exclusion criteria, you should be able to expand your field of vision beyond what is in easy reaching distance. This will enable your review to be as comprehensive as possible and allow you to clearly demonstrate the originality and significance of your project (see Chapter 16).

KEY COMPONENTS OF A LITERATURE REVIEW

Now that you're familiar with some of the key terminology associated with the different types of literature review, we can begin to think about what they actually look like. Of course, all literature reviews are different. In the first place, they are about different topics and issues—and each of those topics will have different histories, debates, concepts, and approaches. This means that the structural requirements of the review will also vary by subject. Reviews will 'look and feel' different just as much as they are about different things.

That said, it is possible to provide an overview of the sorts of things they contain, even if the exact content will vary in shape and form. Generally speaking, there are four component parts of a literature review—and when put together they tell the background story to the research. The narrative arc runs thus:

- This area is interesting because . . .
- So and so have said this about it; so and so have said that . . .
- However, no one has said . . .
- Therefore, this project will . . .

This story broadly equates to context, content, knowledge gap, research aims, and questions. We'll take each in turn.

Why is this topic interesting?

In the first instance, literature reviews tend to begin with some description of the nature of the issue under investigation. To put this more simply, why is the topic interesting? There are a number of reasons why something might be interesting to research, including:

- Are lots of people involved?
- Does it cost, or generate, money?
- Does the issue impact on people's lives?
- Is there lots of policy, practice, or public interest in the issue?

The aim here is to provide some context about why the topic is important. This discussion does not have to be laboured or particularly lengthy, but it does need to provide a lead into the more academic discussion because it helps to justify that research interest. From the perspective of the reader, it also provides a rolling

FINDING YOUR WAY 6.4

Academic work can sometimes be difficult to understand. However, it is always worth remembering that complex ideas do not need to be communicated through complex sentence structures. If you write a sentence that has more than three clauses, it is probably worth thinking about whether you could make the sentence structure less complex. This will enhance the clarity of your writing.

introduction into the material. It helps to familiarize them with the issue before starting on what is likely to be more complex debate.

Given the contextual purposes of 'setting the scene', it is often the case that you will need to draw on more grey literature here than you might do elsewhere in your dissertation. This is because you are trying to connect a research issue to everyday or professional life, and to do that you will need to use those vehicles of publication that are more connected with those arenas. Figures taken from official documents, for example, can help you to justify the scale of an issue. Similarly, newspaper headlines can provide evidence of public interest, while governmental debate is indicative of policy and/or practice interest. You will still need to maintain critical vigilance when using these sources, and you should not take them for granted, but there is a very good case for using them to provide the wider context for your research.

What are the key themes from the research base?

The biggest part of your literature review will be your review of the academic literature. This is also the most difficult component of a literature review to explain as there will be much variance in exactly how you go about doing this.

Essentially, what you are trying to do is identify the key themes in your area and how those issues lead to your knowledge gap. What constitutes a key theme can be quite varied. Studies, concepts, theories, people, events, intellectual traditions, and even disciplinary approaches can all function as a theme in a particular research area.

One way to try and develop your themes is to use the notes you have made from your reading to develop keywords that summarize particular ideas, approaches, and studies. Stand back from what you have read and try to think of words that succinctly describe your thoughts. Once you have thought of a term, try to write one or two sentences that explain what it refers to. At this point you shouldn't really try to constrain your list because you are trying to summarize the totality of your reading.

It can be a good idea to do this alongside your literature search. Of course, if you are adopting more of a scoping study style this would actually be a requirement of the process. One of the advantages of taking such an approach is that it makes the job of synthesizing the research field more organized. In turn, this process can help you to review the literature you've found.

Regardless, once you have a list of keywords, try to think about what sorts of things in that list might go together to create higher-order items that summarize a range of keywords. How are your keywords similar or different? Are there different ways of putting them together? What issues appear to be key, and which ones are tangential? Once you have these higher-order sets of key ideas, can you think of a label that adequately summarizes that category?

Another method of generating your themes involves looking at studies that are similar to yours. These studies will also have to position their research with reference to other literature. If you look at both the content, and the way the review is put together, you should be able to pick up a few clues about what you might need to include and what you can leave out. However, there are two things to be aware of here. The first is **plagiarism** (discussed further in Chapter 8). While it is fine to take inspiration from the structure of another review, it is not OK to copy words from elsewhere and pass them off as your own, even if you do so indirectly or unknowingly.

The simplest way to avoid plagiarism is to 'shut the book' before you start writing. This means that you cannot inadvertently copy passages from the reference into your notes, and then from your notes into your review.

The second issue is concerned with relevance. Even similar studies will be working in different contexts, and what is relevant to one need not be relevant to another.

FINDING YOUR WAY 6.5

Common considerations related to the writing of a review, that you may see in your feedback, include: structure, style, and form. Paying attention to all three during the process of writing your review can help you to develop your writing style.

- Structure refers to the way that an argument is built in the dissertation. It's a good idea to identify the argument you are making when planning your review, and then think about the role of each paragraph in relation to that greater purpose.
- Style refers to the way the review is written. It includes issues of syntax, word choice, and tone. Reading your review out loud can help you think critically about your style of writing and how it will sound to the reader.
- Form refers to the way that the writing is organized.

Dissertations will often utilize objective presentation, formal structure, and use clear language.

You've also got to remember that your supervisor may be an expert in the field and may mark you down if you are simply reproducing arguments taken from elsewhere: a dissertation is meant to have aspects of originality. So, try to read across your subject, including different studies. Your review is more likely to be comprehensive if you look at the different things you find in different places and then amalgamate the most relevant material in your review.

WORKING WITH YOUR SUPERVISOR 6.2

"*Most students overdo their literature review. You should definitely read widely, but keep the written review section highly focused—then refer to the literature again in your discussion and interpretation of results. The bulk of your dissertation should be your own research rather than summarizing what others have said.*"

— Dr Siobhan McAndrew, Lecturer in Sociology with Quantitative Methods,
University of Bristol

What knowledge gap will you address?

This part of your review will often be quite short. It will usually offer a succinct overview of the literature you have discussed and underline the key argument in relation to it. Your literature review asks the reader to consume a lot of information in a short period of time, and it is easy for some of the key detail to be lost in all this discussion. Therefore, taking the opportunity to remind the reader what key points to take away from the review is often a good idea, not least because it enables you to shape their understanding of the problem towards the knowledge gap.

Your summary will then provide the platform for you to state, often quite explicitly, what is missing from the body of knowledge and what you intend to do about it. You may be seeking to:

- resolve an inconsistency between different interpretations of findings
- identify a neglected aspect of the topic that hasn't been researched before
- examine certain ideas that may not have been tested with much veracity across time and place
- resolve a deficiency in existing approaches

I WISH I'D KNOWN . . . TO START READING EARLY 6.4

"*You should start by reading as much literature as possible in order to identify a research gap/question. Many of my classmates jumped straight into their project and tried to form a research gap/question around their idea, which was a much more difficult way of approaching the problem because they struggled to situate their ideas.*"

— Ashley Neat, Student, International Relations and International Organisations,
University of Warwick

I WISH I'D KNOWN . . . THE MARKING CRITERIA 6.5

Understanding what markers look for in a literature review will help you construct your literature review. Markers are likely to consider whether you:

- demonstrate comprehensive familiarity with the field
- have any major omissions in the review
- show any errors of understanding
- use the literature to outline a case for the project
- have positioned the review appropriately with respect to theory and/or the literature
- have produced a well-written review

Research aims and questions

In turn, this leads to the final part of your review. Again, this is likely to be the shortest component in length, but is most important in terms of outlining what your project will focus on. You should already have developed some research aims and questions when writing your research rationale or your research proposal (see Chapter 4 and Chapter 9). Be careful to make sure they still reflect your research intentions and, if so, add them to your review. It is not unusual to see research questions included at the start of the methods section. However, we tend to prefer them at the end of the review because it aids the narrative arc we introduced earlier. Indeed, if the purpose of a literature review is to state the research problem, putting the research aims and questions at the end of the review allows the methods section to function as a place that details how you answer those questions, with the findings working as the answer.

CONCLUSION

A literature review provides an important foundation for the rest of your dissertation or project. Not only does it provide a foundation for your aims and objectives, your subsequent findings and analysis will build on, and link to, the literature review. But beyond the issue of writing up (see Chapter 17), the literature review allows you to develop familiarity with a topic, not to mention the ways in which it can be approached. This means you are better able to situate your project within the intellectual traditions that help shape your dissertation research, and you will be better prepared to enter the field. However, it is also important to remember that while your literature review does come at the beginning of your written dissertation, it can change during the process of research. So be prepared to revisit your review at different points in the process to make sure that it continues to reflect what you are actually doing in your research.

WHAT DO I NEED TO THINK ABOUT?

- What types of literature review could be suitable for your project?
- Why is your project an interesting thing to do?
- Can you identify the key themes in the literature?
- Can you use the literature to identify a knowledge gap?
- How might you use the literature to position your research aims and objectives?

WHAT DO I NEED TO DO?

- Make sure you understand the role of the literature review in the context of your dissertation or report.
- Choose the most appropriate type of review for the purposes of your research.
- Organize your literature thematically.
- Plan your literature review.
- Write the literature review.

 Access the online resources **www.oup.com/uk/brymansrp1e** to help you to successfully complete your social research project or dissertation.

DELVE DEEPER

Hart, C. (2018). *Doing a Literature Review: Release the Research Imagination* (2nd edition). **London: Sage.** This is a 'classic' text that has no doubt seen many students through the process of conducting a review. Now in its second edition, it has been thoroughly revised and updated, and now has online resources dedicated to it. There are similar books on the topic that are now available, but this text remains as popular as it was when it was first written. There is a companion book on literature searching that many students also find very useful.

Lynch, T. and Anderson, K. (revised and updated Elloway, A). (2013). *Grammar for Academic Writing.* **Edinburgh: English Language Teaching Centre, University of Edinburgh.** This thoroughgoing guide to the grammar of academic writing is a brilliant step-by-step introduction. Written around a series of units, it details each component necessary to understand how writing works in practice. To go through each task would

take up a lot of time, but you would certainly improve your writing skills—and it is freely available. Highly recommended.
https://www.ed.ac.uk/files/atoms/files/grammar_for_academic_writing_ism.pdf (Accessed 1 November 2018)

Patter is a blog written by Pat Thompson, Professor of Education at the University of Nottingham. Always very insightful and clearly written, the blog is dedicated to aspects of academic writing. In the past, this has included entertaining posts on 'becoming friends with theory', 'aims and objectives—what's the difference?', and 'I can't find anything written on my topic . . . really?' Collectively, it provides an interesting insight into the challenges of writing and is well worth your time.
https://patthomson.net/ (Accessed 13 December 2018)

RMIT University. The Learning Lab at RMIT University has produced a very engaging overview of the process of writing a literature review. This includes multimedia material on 'choosing, defining, and refining your topic', 'the research timeline', and 'writing a literature review'. Engaging, interesting, and very well presented, it provides a wealth of useful material at the click of a button.
https://emedia.rmit.edu.au/learninglab/content/literature-review-overview (Accessed 1 October 2018)

The Royal Literary Fund has a number of pages dedicated to literature reviews for the purposes of undergraduate research. These include detailed material on the structure of a literature review, but also tips on reading and researching, and drafting and editing. There is also material relating to writing more broadly, and a link to a very useful essay writing tool called ALEX that takes you through each stage of the writing process.
https://www.rlf.org.uk/resources/the-structure-of-a-literature-review/ (Accessed 12 December 2018)

The University of Leicester. There are many guides to literature reviews on the internet—mainly produced by those working in higher education institutions who have some responsibility for study skills. We particularly like the material provided by the University of Leicester. Readable, concise, and informative, it covers searching for literature and reviewing it, as well as answering some common concerns that students have when putting a review together. There are also links to other material related to writing. It is an excellent resource.
https://www2.le.ac.uk/offices/ld/resources/writing/writing-resources/literature-review (Accessed 1 December 2017)

CHAPTER 7

BUILDING
YOUR PROJECT

WHAT DO I NEED TO KNOW?

- What is a research strategy?
  - Quantitative research strategies
  - Qualitative research strategies
  - Mixed methods
- What is a research design?
  - Experimental design
  - Cross-sectional design
  - Longitudinal design
  - Case studies
  - Comparative design

INTRODUCTION

Once you've developed an idea, outlined a rationale for your research, and found the relevant literature, you then need to start mapping out what your project will look like. To do this, you will need to make a few important decisions about how you will answer your research questions. This is, perhaps, one of the most important stages of the research process as it defines the type of project that you are going to build and carry out.

Research can be approached and conducted in many different ways. Broadly speaking, there are four interrelated stages of building a social science dissertation:

- Research strategy: the type of data under investigation (qualitative, quantitative, or mixed methods)
- Research design: the framework through which that data will be collected
- Research methods: the methods associated with collecting the type of data selected
- Type of analysis: the techniques through which the data will be analysed

There are many different options at each stage, and your decisions at the first stage will influence your choices in respect to the other three. We will be detailing some of those choices later on in the book, but this chapter is concerned with the decisions you can make in relation to the first two of those stages: the research strategy and the research design.

WHAT IS A RESEARCH STRATEGY?

A research strategy is simply the means by which you orientate your research to the data you are going to collect and analyse. This is primarily a decision about whether you will take a qualitative, quantitative, or a mixed approach to your research.

There are some researchers who would regard the distinction between qualitative and quantitative research as problematic, either because they believe that it is no longer a useful way of framing research, or that it is simply misleading. However, the distinction between qualitative and quantitative research remains useful because it provides a straightforward way of introducing a range of issues associated with actually **doing** social research that broadly correspond with these categories. It is also worth highlighting that for many social science researchers, the association with qualitative or quantitative research provides them with a sense of their professional identity.

Regardless, in using the term 'research strategy', we are simply referring to the general orientation that you take toward your research project and the type of data you will collect. We'll take quantitative, qualitative, and mixed methods in turn.

FINDING YOUR WAY 7.1

When building your project, it is crucial to distinguish between your research strategy, research design, research method, and type of analysis.

- A research strategy is the broad orientation to the study in terms of whether it is qualitative or quantitative in nature, or both.
- A research design provides a structure through which data collection can be organized and arranged. Typical research designs include: **experiments**; **cross-sectional**; **longitudinal**; case studies; and **comparative research**.
- Research methods provide the means through which you actually collect the data. Among many others, research methods include: surveys, semi-structured interviews, **ethnographies**, and **focus groups**.
- Type of analysis refers to the techniques associated with describing, interpreting, and processing your data. They are often closely allied with methods of data collection.

Quantitative research strategies

Quantitative research strategies make use of information that is, in one way or another, numerable in form. While there are variations on the theme, this type of approach transposes the things people feel, say, or do into values that can be measured with numbers. For example:

- Beliefs about climate change can be placed on a numeric scale and comparisons made against the way people vote in elections
- Assessments of the number of people in part-time employment can be taken over time and cross-referenced with characteristics like gender, ethnicity, and age
- The types of people who live in one area of a city can be counted to see how they differ to other areas in terms of wealth and occupation
- The total number of times certain words appear in tabloid newspaper stories about crime can be set against the types of criminal activity that people are most fearful of experiencing

Given the reliance on numeric data, the techniques of data collection associated with quantitative research have traditionally been those that are suitable to counting or scaling. This typically includes:

- 'closed' interviews with people in the form of surveys or questionnaires
- the 'structured observation' of what people do
- the analysis of secondary material that is already quantitative in nature (crime statistics for example)
- any other material that can, in some way, shape, or form, be counted

The measurement of attitudes, beliefs, and practices, not to mention the interactions between them, are common goals of quantitative research strategies.

As we suggested in Chapter 2, quantitative research strategies tend to have an objectivist ontology and a positivist epistemology. There is, so to speak, a human world 'out there' that is relatively independent of our knowledge of it—and we can use numbers to measure that world because it is, more or less, stable enough to produce meaningful data. In these objectivist terms, the goal of social science is to broadly follow the scientific method and conduct empirical research. This also means that quantitative research tends to be deductive in nature. Specific predictions are made about some aspect of the human world, and observations are then made to see whether these predictions resonate with how things actually are. This helps us to produce explanations of society that correspond to the people, things, and relationships that exist in that world—the so-called 'correspondence theory of truth'.

The relative ease by which numeric information can be collected means that quantitative research often draws on large-scale data sets that are provided by external organizations. Some of these are international in nature, like the 'World Values Survey' and the 'International Social Survey Programme'. Others, like the Census in the UK, the Baylor Religion Survey in the USA, and the German General Social Survey, are more national and/or specific in scope. However, well-distributed local surveys that might be designed specifically for the purposes of an undergraduate dissertation can have samples in the hundreds, and sometimes in the thousands. The size and scope of quantitative strategies can result in very powerful forms of research.

To be clear, this is a thumbnail description of the general tendency of quantitative research. There are techniques of quantitative analysis that emphasize exploration rather than explanation, and many quantitative researchers would baulk at the portrayal of their research as positivist. However, the purpose here is to highlight the rather broad trends of quantitative research rather than describe every particular realization of it. We will spend more time in Chapters 11 and 13 exploring how quantitative data can be collected and analysed.

Qualitative research strategies

There is an implicit tendency to define qualitative research strategies by the absence of quantification. This is probably due to the rather large and nuanced methods of data collection that can be used in qualitative research. What can be used as qualitative data is really quite varied.

Traditionally, qualitative research has placed an emphasis on the information produced by 'open' interviews with people and participant observation 'in the field'. The data associated with these methods of collection tend toward being 'textual' in nature. This involves putting the things that people experience, and how they understand those experiences, into words. The resulting interview transcripts or field notes then form the basis for analysis.

Qualitative research is often guided by the broad aims of interpretivism. This involves the interpretation and understanding of actors in particular places at particular times. In turn, qualitative research adopts an ontology that approaches the human world from the contingent and often dynamic perspective of those individuals and groups who experience it. As a result, qualitative research is often associated with induction. Data are collected and then interpreted using methods of analysis that allow researchers to assess the social and cultural conditions that have helped to shape those understandings. Some of these methods of analysis are quite systematic and rule-bound, whereas others can be much more creative in nature. The focus of qualitative research can also vary from being very small in nature (micro), to something very large (macro), as well as something in between (meso). In some

I WISH I'D KNOWN . . . THE RANGE OF MATERIAL THAT CAN BE USED FOR QUALITATIVE RESEARCH 7.1

To emphasize interviews, focus groups, and ethnography would be to underestimate the often surprising range of things, objects, and material that can be used for qualitative inquiry. Digital methods are increasingly exploring sentient analysis; sensory methodologies emphasize sight, sound, and even touch. Objects of material culture can also be used to examine social life. Songs, photographs, websites, and even things like rubbish have all been used for qualitative research.

cases, those who initially provide data actually become the researchers themselves. 'Action research', for example, both involves people as co-researchers and is designed specifically with the aim of changing policy, practice, or experience.

Again, this short overview cannot do justice to the different types and varieties of research that exist in this particular research strategy. From ethnomethodology to participant action research, and then to appreciative inquiry, qualitative research is a very broad church. We will explore some of these ideas in more detail in Chapters 12 and 14.

Mixed methods

There are some instances, however, where you might want to collect different types of data in the same project. Mixed methods research refers to the ways in which data, and methods of data collection and analysis, can be combined. There are some very good reasons to do this. Standard research strategies involve the researcher interacting with a single form of data. The researcher generates an idea, plans their study, collects and analyses one form of data, and writes up their findings. This is a perfectly acceptable way of doing research. However, in relying on a single source of data, there is no way to assess the legitimacy of any results or where there might be divergence from those initial findings. After all, the human world is a complex place where there are often many different perspectives. Mixed methods research gives us the opportunity to find out more about the topic we are interested in.

One way to enhance our findings is to simply introduce a second source of data to the research. This alternative can then be compared and contrasted with our first form of data to examine whether, where, and how there might be agreement. This method of cross-referencing is typically called triangulation. The term is actually taken from geometry and broadly involves the researcher observing two points of interconnected data. If you were to plot this relationship on a piece of paper, imagine a circle with you at the edge. Now pick any two other points on the circumference. You should now be able to draw a triangle between you and those two points, with the final line between the points themselves (see Figure 7.1). You can easily imagine how your field of vision has expanded by triangulating your viewpoint.

The 'mixing' of research can be achieved in two ways: **within** paradigm and **across** paradigm. Mixing data within paradigm basically means using two or more types of data that are either qualitative **or** quantitative in nature. Across paradigm refers to the process of using both qualitative **and** quantitative data.

Mixing within paradigm is generally considered to be less challenging than working across paradigm. This is mainly because the underlying assumptions made about the nature of the data tend to be relatively consistent in terms of ontology and epistemology. These assumptions can become incongruent when working across paradigm. This is not to suggest that it cannot be done. However, it should be highlighted that there might be some issues in doing so.

Figure 7.1 **Triangulation**

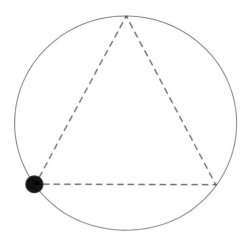

☾ WORKING WITH YOUR SUPERVISOR 7.1

In a review of the literature, Denzin (2012) found that triangulation is actually used in four different ways in the research process:

- Data triangulation—comparison of the different forms of information and material that can be constituted as data
- Researcher triangulation—comparisons are made between the findings of researchers, sometimes working with the same data, and sometimes working with different data
- Theory triangulation—combining aspects drawn from two different theories to illuminate data
- Methodological triangulation—the use of two or more different methods of data collection

If you are unsure about what type of triangulation you might use to build your project, ask your supervisor.

It would also be easy to think that mixed methods provide a fairly straightforward resolution to the disadvantages of doing quantitative or qualitative research. Unfortunately, it is not as simple as this, either in theory or practice. Firstly, when using different sources of data, the advantages of one do not necessarily provide a counterweight to the disadvantages of the other. Secondly, you will also be importing the challenges and issues associated with both strategies, and actually adding another. Mixing methods involves at least three processes: collecting and analysing one data source; collecting and analysing another data source; and being able to combine the results in a meaningful way. In the context of a dissertation, this means that you will need to develop expertise in **three** areas, rather than just one.

FINDING YOUR WAY 7.2

Like all methodological decision-making, the choices associated with using a mixed methods research strategy should be based on the needs of study and the associated research questions. Mixed methods should not be employed just to try and gain extra marks!

Introducing another point of data in a research strategy also raises the question of both the sequence and the interaction of your 'mix'. Conceptually, there are four different ways of ordering mixed methods research. Let us suppose there are two forms of data that you are going to use in your research strategy. We'll call these aspect one and aspect two.

In the first instance, it is possible to conduct one **then** two. That is, data collection and analysis of aspect one is completed and then used to inform the data collection and analysis of aspect two. You could also reverse the order and complete aspect two, and then one. However, aspect one could also be conducted **with** aspect two. Here, both parts of the project would be fully intertwined. Data collection and analysis inform each other in the process of doing the research. Finally, one **and** two could be completed at the same time, but remain relatively independent of each other. They would only be brought together when writing up.

These questions of sequence and integration are important for two reasons. First, you will need to have a clear rationale for organizing the different aspects of the project in the way that you propose. You will need to ask yourself what are the benefits of organizing your methods in that way, **and** what might be potentially problematic. Second, you will need to consider some very practical concerns about the time-limited nature of your dissertation and its relation to other aspects of the course you are studying. If you are planning to conduct aspect one **then** aspect two (or vice versa), you will need to make sure that you have enough space in your diary to complete all the component parts of the project. On the other hand, if you are doing aspect one at the same time as aspect two, you will also need to leave enough room in your schedule so you can complete other demands of your course or programme, and have enough scope to take some time off. Mixed methods research can be very demanding in terms of both intellectual energy and time.

These issues of sequencing and interaction become especially important when working across paradigms. This is because different arrangements can be used to achieve specific goals. Creswell (2018) has developed some useful terms to describe the different strategies that can be employed when mixing quantitative and qualitative strategies. We'll take each in turn.

Sequential explanatory strategies place the quantitative element first, followed by the qualitative component. The quantitative part of the research seeks to

FINDING YOUR WAY 7.3

While doing mixed methods research can be challenging, it also offers many different ways of doing research. For argument's sake, let's suggest there are five key data-collection techniques associated within qualitative research:

- semi-structured interviews
- participant observation
- **visual methods**
- focus groups
- **documentary methods**

Remember that there are four ways of sequencing and combining methods in mixed research? This means that there are at least 40 different ways of combining these five forms of data!

establish and articulate the field, often by describing patterns in the data. Once those trends have been discovered, the qualitative element then elaborates by providing a more in-depth explanation of how, and perhaps why, they take the form that they do. So, for example, you might want to use census data to establish how social housing is distributed within a particular region of a city. Once you have established what this looks like, and which areas are marked by diversity or similarity, you could then conduct some ethnographic work or in-depth interviews to explore the experiences of people in those areas.

Sequential exploratory strategies begin with qualitative work, followed by quantitative. The aim is to first qualitatively explore the field to find out what is, and what is not, relevant or particularly interesting. Any emerging trends or patterns can then be mapped more fully by quantitative techniques of research. This type of approach is often used to develop surveys in areas where not much is known about a particular topic. It is also used a lot in the field of audience studies. This is a field of research in media and communication studies that seeks to examine how audiences react to the representation of particular issues. Typically, these studies begin with focus groups, partly because the nature of a group simulates how people watch television programmes or talk about the news. This establishes the type and range of responses. This information is then transformed into survey questions to examine the size and scope of opinion.

Concurrent designs are those that have qualitative and quantitative elements running side by side. In some cases, these elements remain relatively independent of each other during data collection and analysis, with the findings brought together at the point of writing up. This is referred to as a parallel design. In other cases, the elements are more interactive in nature. These are known as convergent designs. Similarly, there can also be a question of weighting, with one aspect being emphasized over another. These are called nested designs.

◯WORKING WITH YOUR SUPERVISOR 7.2

Due to the challenges associated with undertaking mixed methods research, it is important to ask your supervisor whether it is better to focus on one type of data in more detail or use a mixed strategy. There is a fine balance between doing 'less, more thoroughly' and 'more, less thoroughly'.

A good example of a concurrent design is Bader et al's (2010) study of paranormal beliefs. They used the Baylor Religion Survey, a multi-year national random survey of American religious values, to assess national patterns of belief in the paranormal. At the same time as this quantitative data was being collected, they visited several haunted houses, UFO contactee conferences, and Bigfoot groups to examine the very particular practices of those who held what might otherwise be seen as unconventional ideas. They wrote up their findings in the book 'Paranormal America'. Each part of the study was invaluable, and when the quantitative and qualitative elements were put together, it made for a very robust research strategy. The patterns in paranormal belief that they were able to identify in the quantitative element of the study complemented the insight they were able to draw from the qualitative dimension.

WHAT IS A RESEARCH DESIGN?

While research strategies are variously directed toward a general orientation to data, research design is concerned with the manner in which data collection can be focused and arranged. Dissertation-style research can be put together in different ways and for different purposes. The research design you employ will depend on what you are trying to achieve. You will need to think about which of the following five key types of research design your research aims are directed toward:

- Experimental: establishing causal connections
- Cross-sectional: sampling across a population
- Longitudinal: understanding change over time
- Case studies: examining the experiences of people in specific situations and/or institutions
- Comparative designs: making comparisons between different contexts

Experimental design

The principle of an experiment is relatively straightforward. Measure something twice, but make one change between those two measurements. Any difference can then be attributed to that change because it is the only thing that differed between those two conditions. Cause can be confidently associated with effect.

In principle, this can be done on an individual basis or between groups. You might, for instance, take a baseline measure of individual performance, alter some aspect of a participant's experience, and then take another measure. This is what is known as a repeated measures design. On the other hand, you might take a measure from a control group and compare that against an experimental group who have received some sort of treatment. The control provides the yardstick through which change can be assessed. This is called an independent measures design.

Common to the language of experiments are both the IV and the DV, and the null and alternative hypotheses. These terms sound fairly technical but, again, the basic principles are relatively straightforward. The DV—or dependent variable—is essentially the measurement you are interested in taking. The IV—or independent variable—is the thing you change between conditions. A good way to remember this is to simply look at what the terms are describing. The purpose of an experiment is to find out whether a particular measurement is dependent on a variable that is independent in nature.

Given the design of an experiment, it is possible to predict two things from the outset of the study. On one hand, you might predict that the IV will have a demonstrable effect on the DV. On the other, you might surmise that it will have no impact on the DV whatsoever. These predictions are called the alternative and null hypotheses. The alternative hypothesis states that there will be a difference; the null hypothesis predicts that there will be none. The hypothesis that you choose to accept will be dictated by the results of the experiment.

This experimental procedure works incredibly well where you can remove all prior difference between conditions so you are left with a 'pure' relationship between IV and DV. As you might imagine, this is actually quite difficult to achieve in social research. All too often it is not possible to create two conditions where all of the extraneous influences are removed. There are also ethical issues associated with arranging people into one group or another and then testing certain changes on them. This is particularly the case if there is some service provision in terms of education, welfare, or rehabilitation. However, naturally forming experiments and so-called comparator groups are sometimes possible. For instance, it is possible to measure the effect of poverty on education by using eligibility for 'free school meals' as a proxy measure of poverty, with children who are eligible tending to do worse in terms of educational outcomes than those who are not. But the difficulty of maintaining internal validity—that is, ascribing changes in the DV directly to the IV—often remains. In this particular instance, the length of time a child is eligible for free meals has also been shown to moderate the relationship. The longer someone is eligible, the lower their likely outcomes.

FINDING YOUR WAY 7.4

The **'placebo effect'** is the name given to changes in the DV that can occur simply by the participant knowing that they are in a treatment group. This effect can even extend to the researchers in the form of experimenter bias, which is important to be aware of in your research. This is the reason why many scientific experiments will employ a 'double-blind' design whereby neither participants nor researchers know who is in the treatment group. Unfortunately, this is very difficult to achieve in the social sciences, but if you are in the process of designing an experiment it is worth thinking critically about 'demand characteristics'. These are the expectations and interpretations participants make about the experiment's purpose, who then change their behaviour to fit that interpretation.

Cross-sectional design

Cross-sectional designs are those that collect data from a sample of cases at a specific point in time. These designs are prevalent in survey research, but are also commonly used with a variety of techniques that include: structured observation, diaries/blogs, administrative data, and official statistics. The potentially wide-ranging nature of the samples associated with cross-sectional designs make them particularly useful for quantitative research, especially where statistical generalization is a key concern. However, with some careful attention to issues associated with sampling (see Chapter 10), cross-sectional designs can also be used with qualitative strategies.

There are three key points of issue in cross-sectional designs. The first is a concern with comparison across a sample of participants. Typically, a relatively large sample of participants is selected in order to examine the full range of variation that exists within a population. In quantitative contexts, random samples are generally preferred because they are more likely to capture the full range of this variation. The second point is the requirement that data collection occurs at a specific point in time. This is, in effect, an attempt to provide a stable context in which meaningful comparisons between people can be made. However, in working across a specific point in time, the chronological ordering of variables is not possible. This final point of issue means it is not possible to manipulate variables in order to examine the effect of one variable on another. In fact, making causal inferences from cross-sectional designs is difficult because of problems associated with internal validity. Instead, researchers tend to concentrate on the relationships that might exist between variables and cases.

FINDING YOUR WAY 7.5

Internal validity concerns the extent to which it is possible to attribute change in the dependent variable to the independent variable. Variables that might otherwise interfere or obscure this connection are known as confounding variables. Internal validity is of particular concern where causation is a point of issue. You will need to consider issues associated with internal validity if you are planning to conduct an experiment in your dissertation.

On the other hand, external validity refers to the extent to which the results of the study can be meaningfully transferred from sample to population. It is typically strong in research designs that incorporate random sampling. This is likely to be a point of concern if you are planning to use a cross-sectional design.

Longitudinal design

The main goal of longitudinal research is to examine change over time. Longitudinal designs involve collecting data from a sample, and then repeating the process on at least one further occasion. Often these points of data collection will be a year apart, and sometimes more. Obviously, it isn't possible to collect your own data like this in a time-limited dissertation, but it would be possible to achieve with secondary data (which has already been collected). Both qualitative and quantitative research strategies can be used in conjunction with longitudinal designs.

Broadly speaking, there are two types of longitudinal design: the panel study, and the cohort study. Panel studies involve collecting data from the **same** sample at different points in time. Cohort studies, on the other hand, collect data over time from samples that share similar characteristics. These commonalities may be a shared experience, event, or demographic indicator—the point being that in a cohort study the people in the sample change with each iteration of data collection. Although some attrition is to be expected in longitudinal research, panel studies tend to be much more stable in terms of composition.

Longitudinal designs that are employed in conjunction with a quantitative research strategy have a distinct advantage over their cross-sectional counterparts because they can be time ordered. This means that independent variables can be identified in an early wave of data collection, with its effects measured in a later one. To be clear, this doesn't necessarily solve the problem of confounding variables, but it does mean that it is possible to identify an order in which variables might occur.

However, longitudinal research is not limited to quantitative strategies. The Mass Observation project, for example, is a panel study that regularly collects qualitative data in the form of diary-style entries on a range of issues. It originally ran from the mid-1930s to the mid-1950s, but was revived in 1981 and continues to ask panel members to write about their experience of contemporary issues.

Evidently, there are substantial costs associated with longitudinal research and, given the time and expense, they are relatively uncommon for dissertation purposes. This is especially the case for longitudinal studies that are qualitative in nature. However, it is worth highlighting that many surveys that are delivered

I WISH I'D KNOWN . . . HOW TO IDENTIFY AND ANALYSE DATA TRENDS 7.2

Time series analysis is a particular form of longitudinal research that aims to identify patterns in a sequence of observations. These patterns are then used to forecast future values. Typically, these patterns take the form of trends and seasonality. Trends are general rises or falls in data, whereas seasonality concerns the identification of systematic intervals over time. Employment figures are commonly associated with time series analysis, as are things like gross domestic product, inflation, and crime rates.

annually can, when combined, constitute longitudinal research. For example, much of the data contained in 'Eurostat', the statistical office of the European Union, can be used longitudinally. A dissertation that incorporated this material could prove to be very interesting given the quality and range of their data, all of which is free to download from their website (see Chapter 11).

Case studies

Case studies involve the intensive study of particular locations, communities, or organizations. While case studies are particularly associated with qualitative strategies of research, and ethnography in particular, they can be successfully integrated with quantitative and mixed strategies. What distinguishes case studies from their cross-sectional counterparts is that **the case** is a key focus of interest and the researcher has a direct interest in examining the features of that case that make it unique. Foote Whyte (1943) was interested in the 'corner boys' of Boston's north-end; Armstrong (1998) directed his attention to the activities of Sheffield United's 'Blades Business Crew' (a football hooligan group); and Becker (1963) famously examined how people learn to smoke, and enjoy, marijuana.

What constitutes a 'case' can be quite varied. It can involve a single community or organization; a particular family or school; or a specific individual or event. It might involve a particular meeting of people, a particular town or village (which is often the case in anthropological studies), or a particular community-based initiative such as a local food bank or charity event. The crucial point is that the particular case is a point of interest and an in-depth examination of it is the aim of the research.

Cases may come in a wide variety of shapes and sizes, but some researchers have attempted to classify the different sorts of case studies that are possible. Yin (2014), for example, has distinguished between five different types of case:

- **Critical case studies** involve the researcher developing a theory, and then choosing a particular case that enables them to 'test' that idea. A property associated with that case is deemed to be critical in demonstrating the verisimilitude of the original theory.

- **Unique cases** occur where researchers select the case based on some outstanding feature that is not usually found elsewhere. This uniqueness can then be used as a basis to better understand situations where these properties are absent.
- **Typical cases** are those that best exemplify a broader category of cases. Findings can then be instructive, if not exhaustive, of that broader category.
- **Revelatory cases** are those cases that are original in some aspect, either because a researcher has not had access to it before, or because it has simply not happened before.
- **Longitudinal cases** are those that are investigated at two or more distinct points in time. Many case studies will be longitudinal in nature by virtue of the length of the research, but longitudinal case studies specifically have two or more definite repetitions of data collection that are built into the design.

It should also be noted that two or more of these types of design may be present in a single case.

A generic criticism of case studies is the claim that findings cannot be used for statistical generalization. However, this is not the purpose of a case study. Instead, intensive study of the case is made and then directed toward theoretical development and analysis. The resulting theory can then be applied to other cases beyond the original to see where to further augment the analysis. This process is often referred to as 'analytic generalization' or 'theoretical generalization'.

FINDING YOUR WAY 7.6

'Ecological validity' is the term given to the extent to which conclusions are meaningful beyond the confines of the original research. It is often considered to be high in research that involves observing and interacting with participants in naturalistic settings, as would be typical in case study research. Ecological validity is particularly likely to be worth considering if you are developing a case study.

Comparative design

The final type of research design uses identical methods to compare and contrast two or more cases. In this respect they can be thought of as a multiple case study. The logic that underpins comparative designs is that we are able to better understand particular cases by examining them in relation to similar social phenomena. This approach enables similarities **and** differences between cases to be articulated more fully. Comparative work allows unusual features and properties of an individual case to be identified, while also highlighting patterns that are common across contrasting situations.

This type of design can be used in conjunction with quantitative and qualitative strategies, although mixed methods strategies are also common. Like their case study counterparts, comparative designs can be used to examine particular communities or organizations, but they can also be employed at regional or national levels. There are many examples in the social science literature that have successfully incorporated comparative designs to conduct cross-cultural research. Antonucci (2016), for example, used a comparative design to explore student experiences of higher education and social mobility in the contrasting welfare regimes of England, Sweden, and Italy. Using questionnaires and interviews, she travelled across six cities in these countries and found evidence to suggest that, rather than helping to relieve social inequality, higher education may actually reinforce it.

Obviously, sustained cross-cultural research that incorporates qualitative fieldwork is unlikely to be an option for dissertation research. The costs associated with travel, not to mention the time spent away from university, are likely to be insurmountable. However, quantitative comparisons using the data sets provided by Eurostat, the 'International Social Survey Programme' and the 'World Values Survey', make comparative designs more accessible than they ever have been before. It would also be possible to draw comparative data from a number of different national surveys to achieve the same effect.

Comparative designs are not limited to regional, national, or international comparisons. It is important to remember that they can be directed at much more local levels too. This makes them more achievable in a dissertation project. For instance, it would be possible to attempt something of a replication of Antonucci's study, albeit on a much smaller scale. It would be perfectly feasible to collect questionnaire and interview data and compare student experiences of different universities within a city or a region. Many national data sets also include place-related variables that could enable regional variations to be explored. Of course, you would require a strong rationale to do this, but it would be more than achievable.

CONCLUSION

Choosing an appropriate research strategy and design will shape the nature of your project. It will help you provide a response to the aims and objectives of your research and provide the structure through which you will collect data. However, there are many choices you can make in terms of strategy and design. What you need to make sure of is that your choices resonate with your research aims and objectives. Using the wrong strategy or design is likely to vitally undermine your findings, and your project more generally. So taking the time to make sure that your strategy and design correspond with one another is a crucial point of development. If you have any questions about this, then speak with your supervisor to make sure you get going in the right direction.

WHAT DO I NEED TO THINK ABOUT?

- Do you understand what the terms research strategy, research design, and research method refer to, and why they are important in your dissertation?
- Do you understand how these areas might fit with your research project?
- Are you aware of the limitations of different research designs, strategies, and methods, in addition to the positive aspects?
- Are you clear about how different strategies, designs, and methods may fit with your research aim(s) and objectives?

WHAT DO I NEED TO DO?

- Make sure you understand the difference between a research strategy, a research design, and a research method.
- Examine your research aims and decide what sort of strategies and designs might be suitable for your research. Think about the research methods that might follow on from those decisions.
- Consider any methodological or practical issues associated with those strategies and designs that might limit your capacity to deliver the project on time. Factor this into your planned schedule.
- Revisit your rationale for research and plan a research strategy and associated research design.

Access the online resources **www.oup.com/uk/brymansrple** to help you to successfully complete your social research project or dissertation.

DELVE DEEPER

The Centre for Innovation in Research and Teaching has produced some very accessible material on mixed methods specifically. This includes 'when to use mixed methods', 'choosing a mixed methods design', and 'mixed method data collection'. There are a number of slides and videos to accompany the text, including an interview with 'mixed methods expert', Professor John Creswell. There are also suggested readings that detail issues associated with doing mixed methods research in more detail. https://cirt.gcu.edu/research/developmentresources/research_ready/mixed_methods/overview (Accessed 12 December 2018)

The Centre for Research Quality, based at Walden University, has produced a variety of multimedia material associated with research design and other aspects of the research process. Much of this supports their own programmes of learning, but it will be of use to students from elsewhere. The material is well produced and contains information relating to 'general research design', 'qualitative design and analysis', 'quantitative design and analysis', and 'mixed methods'. Their YouTube pages also feature short videos on research design and mixed methods, as well as overviews of quantitative and qualitative research.

https://academicguides.waldenu.edu/researchcenter/resources/Design
https://www.youtube.com/channel/UCExoTv-rLUa13TxyZwV8flQ/feed
(Accessed 10 December 2018)

Creswell, J. (2018). *Research Design: Qualitative, Quantitative and Mixed Methods Approaches* (5th edition). London: Sage. Now in its fifth edition, this has been the 'go to' text on research design for social science since it was first written in 1994. It has sections on 'selection', 'the use of theory', as well as 'mixed methods procedures'. Authoritative and readable, it includes empirical examples drawn from the literature to demonstrate how ideas can be put into practice.

Eurostat (European Statistical Office) provides statistical information to the institutions of the European Union (EU). This includes general and regional statistics, economy and finance, population and social conditions, industry, trade, and services, as well as a plethora of other material. The list is so long that it is difficult to summarize concisely! You can browse statistics by theme, or explore the database using their 'data explorer'. Much of the material is longitudinal in nature.

https://ec.europa.eu/eurostat/web/main/home (Accessed 1 October 2017).

Gibbs, G. (2013). *Research Design: Youtube playlist.* Graham R. Gibbs has some excellent videos on his YouTube pages that concern research design. They are taken from a series of lectures given to graduate students at the University of Huddersfield about social research methods and research design. There are 29 videos in the playlist on social research methods and design, many of which elaborate on the issues in this chapter. This includes material on case studies, experiments and surveys, as well as quasi-experiments and the nature of social research.

https://www.youtube.com/playlist?list=PLirEzjzoHKvxaX8zZuFUSAi4jdukeexwx
(Accessed 5 December 2018).

Gorard, S. (2016). *Research Design: Creating Robust Approaches for the Social Sciences.* London: Sage. This is a no-nonsense textbook that explores the importance of research design in making convincing research-based claims. With very useful sections on 'identifying researchable questions', 'identifying the sample or cases', 'preparing for comparative claims', and 'how big is a difference?', it offers a thoroughgoing guide to designing social research. Illustrated with case studies of real-life examples as well as craft tips, this is particularly suitable for those using more robust designs that provide concrete answers to research questions.

CHAPTER 8

ETHICS

WHAT DO I NEED TO KNOW?

- What are ethics?
  - The moral and legal rationale for ethical practice in social research
- The key principles of ethical practice
  - Informed consent
    - Internet research and the use of social media
    - Working with vulnerable groups
  - Harm
  - Deception
  - Privacy
  - Anonymity
  - Confidentiality
- Ethical review boards and committees
  - Plagiarism and academic malpractice

INTRODUCTION

You will not be able to start collecting data without gaining ethical approval to undertake empirical research—and, even when this is granted, there are any number of things in the field that you will need to negotiate with professional responsibility. This means that ethics are a vital part of the research process. They provide a set of value-based principles that enable us to conduct research in an appropriate manner. This chapter will introduce you to the practice of ethics in social research. It will provide an outline of basic ethical practice, before introducing the nature and purpose of ethical review boards. It will demonstrate how ethical rules of thumb are often more complicated when encountering them 'in the field', before finally exploring how ethics also informs the process of writing up research.

WHAT ARE ETHICS?

In many undergraduate textbooks, ethics are dealt with by listing the key concerns of:

- informed consent
- confidentiality
- anonymity
- avoidance of harm
- privacy

These principles are usually illustrated with some accompanying examples of severe ethical transgressions, such as Milgram's (1963) 'shocking experiments' which involved participants being encouraged to administer 'fake' electric shocks. However, the process of undertaking an ethical research project involves much more than avoiding such extreme outcomes. The reality is that all empirical projects have to address and negotiate issues of ethics—and this process cannot be taken for granted. Ethical practice involves gaining approval from ethical review boards, accessing participants and interacting with people as living, breathing individuals. You then have to write the whole thing up in a manner that accurately represents your data **and** in accordance with the agreements you have made with your participants. This means you need to be sensitive to potential ethical issues at all stages of the research process, and make sure that you operate within the ethical guidelines set out by your institution.

I WISH I'D KNOWN . . . ABOUT ETHICAL RESPONSIBILITIES 8.1

"*On the one hand dissertation ethics entails a rigorous set of guidelines with which primary research must comply. But all researchers, including those doing 'desk-based' work, should consider their responsibility to the communities they are writing about before, during and after the research journey. Is it possible to 'give something back'?*"
— Dr Michael Pugh, Lecturer in Politics, University of the West of Scotland

Ethics are often thought of as a set of rules by which individuals and societies maintain standards. This idea of ensuring integrity is also central to ethical practice in social research. Research ethics help to make sure that the relationships you build during the process of doing social research are respectful and constructive, and that your project does not endanger either yourself or those who you come into contact with.

However, social researchers can have different opinions about ethical issues and questions. While the key principles of ethics often appear straightforward, there is some uncertainty about what constitutes ethical research and what does not. So, although ethics **are** based on principles of what is right and wrong, they also involve challenges and dilemmas that do not necessarily fit neatly into either camp. This means that ethical research often has to take account of conflicting interests of those involved in the research process. What is 'right' for one participant or group might be 'wrong' for another.

There have also been many times in social research when, in the attempt to do 'right', researchers have done something that can be considered highly questionable. For instance, Humphreys's (1970) infamous 'Tearoom Trade' study might have been orientated toward raising awareness of inequalities in society, but the way he conducted the study was problematic, and the ends may not have justified the means. He conducted a covert ethnographic study of casual homosexual encounters whereby he acted as lookout for his 'participants'. During the

FINDING YOUR WAY 8.1

While you can prepare for some potential ethical challenges, you may not be able to predict others. So, you need to think about potential challenges in advance wherever possible, but also be prepared to consult with your supervisor regarding any unexpected ethical challenges that arise, and how they can be addressed. Failure to plan is likely to lead to challenges in the long run.

process of conducting the research, he also recorded car registration numbers and then used his contacts in the police to obtain the names and home addresses of 134 men. About a year later he contacted these individuals to interview them about their socio-economic position. In doing so he did challenge stereotypes of gay men, which often portrayed homosexual men as 'perverts' who were 'down and outs'. However, his research also violated the core ethical issues of informed consent and deception. This led to a public outcry when the study was published.

This is why ethics are one of the earliest things you will think about when you first meet your dissertation supervisor. Your supervisor will be able to play an important role in helping you think about ethical issues, as those initial discussions will not only focus on research topics and potential research questions, but also identify the ethical issues you may face in meeting those aims. Without an awareness of these issues you are unlikely to be able to undertake your research project successfully. In the first instance, you will need to meet institutional requirements and fulfil the needs of 'ethical approval'. Then you will need to make sure that you operate ethically 'in the field', not to mention when you come to write up your project. 'Ethics' also forms an important section of your final dissertation, usually in your methodology section. Here, you discuss ethics at the same time as your deliberations about design and explanations about the research process.

The moral and legal rationale for ethical practice in social research

Contemporary approaches to ethics in research can be dated back to the Second World War and the appalling abuse perpetrated on Jews by the Nazi doctors. These atrocities, many of which were committed in the name of 'scientific progress', led to the Nuremberg Code (1949). This set out what were to become the basic principles for research on human beings. This code was then superseded by the Declaration of Helsinki (1964)—which also sought to balance the interests of research subjects with scientific research—and the spirit of both documents continues to be present in the various ethical guidelines that can be found today.

I WISH I'D KNOWN . . . ABOUT ETHICAL CODES
OF CONDUCT 8.2

It is common for academic disciplines to have specific ethical codes or guidelines. These are really useful in helping you think about ethical research practice. When developing your research proposals, and when writing up your research, you should try to make reference to them. For instance, if you are doing a research project or dissertation in sociology, then look at the British Sociological Association's code of ethics. If you can't find a disciplinary code, use the Social Research Association's ethical guidelines. You can freely access both online.

https://www.britsoc.co.uk/media/24310/bsa_statement_of_ethical_practice.pdf (Accessed 12 December 2018)

http://the-sra.org.uk/wp-content/uploads/ethics03.pdf (Accessed 2 December 2018)

Ethical guidelines tend to have two overarching purposes. The first is a concern with the values of research; and the second with the more instrumental protection of the researcher, the participants, and the institutions that the research operates within. We will deal with each in turn.

When thinking about the values of social research, we are thinking about the ideas and actions that inform social research practice, and the consequences that might flow from it. In these terms, ethics is often about ensuring that the research process is conducted in a way which ensures the dignity and welfare of all parties involved in the research. Researchers not only have obligations to participants, but also to universities, funding bodies, and research organizations, not to mention the broader community of academia. So, as a researcher, the purpose of **doing** ethics is to make sure that you have an awareness of your own actions and that you act in a way which avoids:

- **misrepresentation**—any statement or action that amounts to an assertion that is false or erroneous and not in accordance with the facts
- **harm**—physical and emotional distress associated with participating in the research
- **discomfort**—making someone feel unduly anxious or embarrassed as a result of the research process
- **bias**—prioritizing one person or group's responses over another
- **misplaced loyalty**—showing loyalty in a situation that you shouldn't; also it can make you biased towards a person or institution, so that you defend the person or institution for wrong reasons

You will need to be honest with yourself, and the people you come into contact with, regarding their involvement and how the information will be used.

In the second instance, there are formal, and often more instrumental, reasons why you need to consider ethics when undertaking your research project. These not only refer to the need to 'pass' the ethical review process, but also the legal requirements that can impact on research practice. If something is illegal for the general public, then it is also illegal for social researchers. This is not a problem for most research, but can create dilemmas for researchers who wish to study illegal activities or who uncover illegal activities in the process of their research. For instance, if you were undertaking a project on the distribution of resources in households and a participant disclosed that they were encountering financial and domestic abuse, what should you do? Do you maintain a confidential approach, which is common practice in research, or do you report it to the relevant authorities? While legislation is always country-specific, in many cases your data are likely to be subpoenable, whereby a writ could be issued by a government agency to compel you to give testimony or order you to produce your evidence. Assurances you might make regarding confidentiality are also unlikely to hold up in court. In the case of the UK, for example, the Children Act 1989 requires you to waive anonymity if a minor is considered to be in danger, and you would be legally obliged to report this to the relevant authority.

You may also have certain legal obligations under legislation on data protection. The UK's General Data Protection Regulation (2018), for example, requires that all personal information should be obtained fairly and lawfully and should not be processed unless certain conditions are met. This includes keeping material safe from unauthorized access, accidental loss or destruction, and not keeping it for longer than is necessary. This legislation is designed to make sure data is handled properly and securely. So, the use of password-protected computers and keeping any paper-based research in a locked drawer are almost inevitably required. When the data has been analysed and is no longer required, a suitable time period (and method) for disposal of the data should also be decided. It is common practice to agree this at the point of informed consent, a principle we will discuss shortly. In some cases, where you plan to undertake further work with the data, you may want to keep the data for a longer period of time. If you plan to use the data for other purposes than your dissertation, such as an article for a student journal, this should be agreed with the participants. You may wish, for example, to specify that 'data collected from participants can be used in future research or publications once it has been made anonymous' in the agreement you make with the participant prior to starting the research.

It is important to remember that research ethics is also concerned with thinking about unintended events. For instance, if you have collected sensitive data and this is stored in the Cloud, or maybe on a USB stick which is left on public transport, you need to know that the data is secure. You need to think about what you can put in place to protect participants, yourself, and your university.

THE KEY PRINCIPLES OF ETHICAL PRACTICE

There are five key areas of ethical practice that will help you to begin to negotiate this complex mix of institutional administration, law, morality, and history. These are:

1. informed consent
2. harm
3. deception
4. privacy
5. anonymity and confidentiality

Informed consent

According to the Social Research Association (SRA), informed consent is 'a procedure for ensuring that research participants understand what is being done to them, the limits to their participation and awareness of any potential risks they incur' (SRA, 2003: 28). This involves making sure that participants are provided with all the information they need to decide whether or not to take part in the research. This consists of information about the study, including its methods, expected benefits of the study, and any risks involved in taking part in the research. It also includes information about data storage, information about confidentiality and anonymity, and what to do if ethics procedures are not followed.

To make sure that the process of informed consent is documented, it is common practice to use an informed consent form (see Appendix 8.1). It is preferable to do this in a written format, including the participant's signature, as it can act as a contract between you and them. This will be a standard requirement in many universities. In fact, some universities will provide templates of these forms that you can use. In addition to creating a clear record of agreement, the consent form can also help to build trust between the researcher and participant because both parties know where they stand and what is required of them. Oral consent can be considered to be acceptable in some circumstances, but this is likely to need clear justification. It is also worth highlighting that in some circumstances, such as ethnographic

I WISH I'D KNOWN . . . ABOUT HOW INFORMATION GAINED FROM PARTICIPANTS CAN BE USED 8.3

Information gained from participants should only be used for the specific purposes associated with your project and as outlined in the participant information sheet. This applies even if the circumstances are similar to the purpose specified in the research or you are pretty sure that a participant wouldn't mind. If you have said you will give the participants an opportunity to see what they have said and verify the content, then you must offer them the opportunity to do so.

research, it is not always practical to gain informed consent from everyone who is present. This is not necessarily a problem, but should not be done without reflecting on other ethical concerns around likelihood of harm and privacy.

In addition to a consent form, an information sheet is often provided to the participant. This might actually be your first point of contact, so the tone of this document should be friendly and clear. There's an example of an information sheet in Appendix 8.2. You will see that it reflects the key areas of agreement detailed in the consent form. It introduces the research, presents participants with the opportunity to be involved in the research, but is also explicit that people don't have to take part if they don't want to. It explains what involvement means, what will happen to the data, as well as the fact that the project has been ethically reviewed and approved. There's also contact information should the person want to discuss their involvement further. This particular example also states the potential benefits of being involved. For this project, you can see that an incentive was offered to participate, but this is less common in undergraduate research projects (see Chapter 10).

Developing appropriate informed consent forms and information sheets can often be a time-consuming process, and they will sometimes need trying out with friends to make sure they are easy to understand.

FINDING YOUR WAY 8.2

Find out whether your department or university has any examples of information sheets or informed consent forms that you could adapt for use in your dissertation. This can help save time and enable you to negotiate the ethics review process more efficiently.

Internet research and the use of social media

The use of social media is becoming more common in research, and this raises some particular issues in relation to informed consent. While 'internet research' in the form of questionnaires or email interviews can generally follow the same guidance as 'face-to-face' delivery, some researchers argue that conventional ethical practices cannot easily be applied to Facebook, LinkedIn, Twitter and other social media sites. Unfortunately, material discovered in forums or chatrooms also might not be 'free to use' for the purposes of social research.

Denscombe (2017) argues that the decision about whether or not to seek consent to use information needs to be made on whether it is intended for public or private consumption. So, if the material is in the public domain and intended to reach a wide audience there would not normally be a requirement to gain consent. Using a popular website for the purposes of analysis, for example, wouldn't ordinarily pose too many risks. However, while some information is clearly in the public domain, there may also be information that people are keeping, or trying

WORKING WITH YOUR SUPERVISOR 8.1

If you are thinking of using social media as a source of data, we suggest you discuss the issue carefully with your supervisor before submitting your proposal to the research ethics committee.

to keep, private—if it is behind a 'login' page, for example. The fact that you may be able to access this information doesn't necessarily mean you should use it for your own purposes if that wasn't the original intention of the author. Violating someone's online privacy is ethically as problematic as violating their privacy in person.

The problem is that there is no consensus among social scientists as to what is private and what is public in such instances. Some researchers **do** use material they find online for the purposes of social research without asking permission, and don't believe that it is necessary, or practical, to always ask for specific consent.

To this end, if you plan to conduct internet research, it is worth considering expert opinion on the issue. The Association of Internet Researchers (AoIR), for example, offers insights and guidance into this relatively new form of research. The AoIR is a group of international academics located in a range of disciplines that focus on internet studies. They have produced ethical guidelines (rather than rules) for ethical internet-based forms of research.

Working with vulnerable groups

Further consideration of informed consent is also required when working with 'vulnerable groups'. It is generally held that 'vulnerable' tends to refer to those individuals or groups who might not be able to fully consent to participation. That is to say that if you suspect their judgement may be compromised in some aspect—whether they are too young or lack the cognitive capacity to understand the consequences of involvement—then you need to tread very carefully. If you suspect that your research might involve a 'question mark' in this area, careful thought should be given to why and how 'vulnerable' groups are being involved, and how you can protect your participants. To this end, Lewis and Porter (2004) have developed a series of questions that need to be asked when planning to conduct research with any group who might be considered to be vulnerable:

- Has the participant's ability to give fully informed consent been assessed and discussed with other appropriate people such as parents, caregivers, or teachers?
- Have ways of checking for understanding of confidentiality/research purposes been explored?
- Have all possible steps been taken to ensure anonymity, given that this may be particularly difficult to achieve with minority populations?

- Will participants, at appropriate intervals, be reminded of their right to withdraw?
- When providing feedback, have steps been taken to ensure the information has been understood? This can be done through, for example, asking a familiar person to talk with the individual, or offering pictures with simplified text or case study material.

This doesn't necessarily mean that research with such groups is impossible. For instance, if you wanted to conduct research with children you could gain written consent from their parent, guardian, or school. In fact, many projects will need the consent of both school and the parent/guardian. You might also produce a special participant consent form and information sheet that is designed for children. If you were conducting research in school, it is also likely that you would need a Disclosure and Barring Service (DBS) check in the UK. Similarly, if you were researching a particular aspect of dementia and you wanted to access participants through a hospital, you would be likely to have to adhere to some specialist regulation that governs research in healthcare settings. Research in the UK's National Health Service, for instance, needs to abide by the Department of Health's Research Governance Framework for Health and Social Care. This provides key principles and responsibilities in relation to parties involved in health and social care research. Gaining this sort of approval can be time-consuming, and universities may advise against research which requires additional ethics approval.

FINDING YOUR WAY 8.3

If you do not build in the necessary time for ethical approval, you could be delayed in starting your research. Therefore, it is also worth thinking about research alternatives in case you do not receive ethical approval.

Harm

It is important to ensure that participants are safe from harm, and you should make every effort to identify basic risks involved in carrying out your project. Researchers need to try and anticipate whether their research may cause harm, be perceived as intrusive, cover sensitive or upsetting issues, or threaten beliefs in a way that could have negative psychological impacts. You will also need to take careful consideration of the physical safety of your participants, anticipating any threats associated with the location of the meeting, travel to the location, or the possibility of retribution towards participants. For instance, if your research is about street gangs and confidentiality is not ensured then this may create a physical risk if negative comments about other gang members can be attributed to a particular individual.

Having said that, assessing psychological harm can be difficult, especially when researching sensitive topics. Most of us are not trained counsellors and lack the training needed to deal with certain situations. Therefore, it is often difficult to determine what 'harm' might mean in the context of social research, and whether it is occurring at all. Murphy and Dingwall (2007), for example, have argued that the 'harm' that can result from participating in social research is qualitatively different from the harm that can be caused in more scientific research. The risks associated with participating in a clinical trial are substantively different from the harm that can occur when, say, interviewing someone about how they coped after the death of a sibling or the closure of their business. In some situations, an interviewee getting upset might actually be viewed positively. Harm is often a subjective experience in social research.

One way of guarding against such difficulties is to provide participants with contact details of people or organizations who could support them, making sure they know they can withdraw at any time and that they have the right to refuse to answer any of the questions without issue. Even then, you might need to be able to show empathy and consider terminating interviews if the content is causing distress to participants.

However, it is not just the risks of harm to your participants that you will need to consider. Ensuring your own personal safety is just as important as ensuring that your participants do not come to any harm. So you also need to have strategies in place to ensure that you are safe 'in the field'. This might include: making sure someone knows where you are and when the research engagement

I WISH I'D KNOWN . . . MORE ABOUT WHAT MIGHT BE HARMFUL PRACTICE 8.4

If you ask questions that the participant considers to be 'out of bounds', or fail to understand the significance of their answers, this can lead to problems in the research process. Hunt's experience of being a participant in the study *A Life Apart* by Miller and Gwynne (1972) provides a nuanced example of a research project where those on the receiving end of the research thought it was 'harmful'. After originally agreeing to be part of a project that Hunt believed would explore the 'social death sentence' of patients in a care home, he was shocked to read how the resulting publication focused on researcher and care worker viewpoints. He was so unhappy, he actually produced a questionnaire for those 'researched' to help them decide whether researchers would be on their side, and whether they want to participate. Hunt's paper, 'Settling Accounts with the Parasite People: A Critique of "A Life Apart" by E. J. Miller and G. V. Gwynne' (Hunt, 1981), has acted as a cornerstone for those researchers that have gone on to develop the social model of disability.

should be finished; being contactable in an emergency; and having established procedures in place if there are any problems. While there may be reasons why research has to be conducted in someone's own home, such as mobility or care commitments, using a public space such as a café is a much safer option. It might also be worth teaming up with one of your peers if you are concerned about issues of safety. You might, for instance, get a friend to accompany you at the research site and wait for you outside the location of the interview. We know of one situation where a student was doing some empirical research in an area considered undesirable and was not contactable for some time after this (several days). Eventually this led to some concerned relatives notifying the police. In the end, it turned out the student had gone away for a couple of nights with their partner straight after the interview and not told anyone of their plans or taken a phone charger!

Deception

It is generally considered that you should not deliberately mislead your participants in the name of social research. This is largely because it violates the principle of informed consent and/or could cause harm. How can someone meaningfully agree to participate in research if they do not really know what the research is about, or what it is trying to achieve? Not only is such practice likely to harm the reputation of your department, institution, and discipline, such an invasion of privacy could also lead to anxiety in the mind of your participants.

An example of research where the researcher deliberately misled his participants was the work of the German researcher-journalist, Wallraff (1985). He pretended to be a Turkish migrant. He worked with his research participants, ate with them, and participated fully in daily activities, but did not disclose that he was undertaking research on them with the intention of writing a book. When the findings emerged, German society was surprised at the working conditions of migrant workers that he revealed in his work. However, he was also criticized for concealing his identity and intentions in order to benefit his research process.

Wallraff's research presented a number of ethical dilemmas. If Wallraff had been open and honest with his participants, it may have affected the reaction of participants, and even the validity of his findings. These 'demand characteristics' often need reflecting on when carrying out particular types of fieldwork, not least because people will often change their behaviour when they know they are being observed. But if Wallraff hadn't carried out his research in the way that he did, German society may not have had crucial information of the lived experiences of migrant workers.

There may also be occasions when it is simply not feasible or desirable to be completely open and honest with participants. If you are conducting an

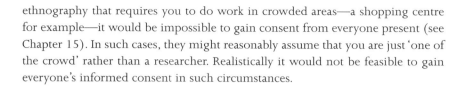

ethnography that requires you to do work in crowded areas—a shopping centre for example—it would be impossible to gain consent from everyone present (see Chapter 15). In such cases, they might reasonably assume that you are just 'one of the crowd' rather than a researcher. Realistically it would not be feasible to gain everyone's informed consent in such circumstances.

Privacy

Privacy is often considered to be one of the basic rights of living in a democratic society. It refers to an individual's right to control the disclosure of what they deem personal or non-public information about themselves. In a 'research' sense, privacy is taken to be a person's right to be free to withhold information that they may deem personal. For instance, in an interview or questionnaire, participants have the right to choose what they reveal and how. There should be no coercion on behalf of the researcher. Similarly, anything they do choose to reveal should remain private and not be routinely released to people who exist outside of the research relationship.

Inevitably, the boundaries around privacy are not always as clear-cut as we might want them to be. For instance, when researching football chants (Clark, 2006), Tom did not routinely attempt to gain informed consent from the crowd he was a part of, as it was neither feasible nor practical. However, in not revealing his identity, he regularly witnessed acts that could have seen people banned or imprisoned if he had been required to report it. Would those people have allowed him to be witness to these events if they knew what he was really doing? Would the football club itself have allowed him into the ground? To what extent was the setting public or private? These are all difficult ethical challenges around the issue of privacy.

Tom navigated this ethical dilemma by, on one hand, being judicious in the field notes he chose to write up. On the other, he also made sure that he completely anonymized events and people, if not the football club. His research was also relatively benign in focus, and always occurred in settings that did not need proprietary access. But you cannot assume that all information collected in public is not subject to issues of privacy. What if you overhear something in a field setting? What if someone says something to you before or after an interview? Can you use this data? There might also be other instances where the people who enabled your access to the research setting don't actually provide the data for your project. These 'gatekeepers' might be fully informed about the research, but not the other participants who come and go within that research setting. Situations where the research setting is both public and private are likely to lead to some difficult decisions for an ethics committee, and may result in you not being able to undertake this kind of research project if risks to privacy are too high.

WORKING WITH YOUR SUPERVISOR 8.2

It might be worth talking with your supervisor about how to approach the issue of your identity. This might include what you are willing to disclose about yourself and your experiences. For instance, if you were conducting research on 'coming out', you would want to think carefully about which aspects of your own sexuality you are willing to disclose before carrying out the research.

Anonymity

Anonymity refers to the process by which participants are protected from identification. Social research does not routinely 'name' the people who cooperated with the research. Any information related to an individual, organization, or place should not be directly traceable to the source of origin.

The most effective way of making sure this is the case is by not collecting identifying data in the first place. Unfortunately, this isn't always possible. For instance, when a researcher needs access to an individual's details to make contact with them, they will necessarily collect material that can identify the participant. To negotiate the problem of anonymity, a pseudonym is often used. This can take the form of a number or a replacement name. It may also be necessary to change other things like titles, events, or places. Qualitative research can be particularly tricky in these respects because you will often find yourself collecting material that is of a very individual nature.

However, there are times when participants may wish to be identified. This is often the case in research where participants wish to have a voice. Some of the participants in Booth and Booth's (2004) study of parents with learning difficulties, for example, were very keen to be identified with the book and were very proud of their involvement in the research. It provided them with a public voice otherwise denied to them. Real names are often also used with elite interviews, such as when interviewing politicians. This is because the process of anonymity would make the content trite or meaningless.

FINDING YOUR WAY 8.4

Cavendish (1982) provides a model example of a researcher taking suitable precautions to ensure that the research participants could not be identified. In her study of working women in a factory, she changed the names of all the individuals involved. She also used a pseudonym to ensure the company wasn't identifiable and invented a name for the workers' trade union. She even changed the location of the factory and made up a product which was different from the one the company actually made.

It is important to identify and recognize where and how issues of anonymity might arise during the course of your research, particularly during the writing up stages. You will normally explain the steps taken to ensure the level of anonymity you are aiming at in the information sheet and informed consent form. Where names or pseudonyms are used it is important to ensure participants are fully aware of the possible consequences of this.

FINDING YOUR WAY 8.5

When using pseudonyms it is useful to store a document with the real names and pseudonyms in a password-protected computer for your own records. This will help you make sure you are attributing the correct quotes to the correct participants.

It may also be the case that your university or organization has rules regarding anonymization and that this is a requirement for ethical approval. You should check your departmental ethics procedure and dissertation handbook if you are unsure.

Confidentiality

Whereas anonymity is concerned with the identification of individual participants, confidentiality is concerned with making sure that the information they provide is not shared with third parties. This is why any data you collect should be kept 'under lock and key', or behind a securely encrypted password.

Of course, there is a central difficulty here. When writing up your project, and providing evidence, you will routinely reveal parts of the data. To guard against inadvertently revealing who your participants are, however, the principle of confidentiality means any specific contribution that does appear 'in print' should not contain information that would enable them to be directly identified. Therefore, anonymity does not just apply to names, but information as well. This is why anonymity and confidentiality are closely intertwined. Making sure that data remains confidential often means changing dates, places, and even some details, just as much as it does changing names. In Armstrong's (1998) study of a community of football hooligans in Sheffield, he not only changed the names of the individuals involved, but also the locations and the names of pubs where the hooligans would often congregate.

Even then, maintaining confidentiality is not always as straightforward as it may first appear, particularly in qualitative contexts, where material is often of an individual nature. It may also be that gatekeepers or other members of the community may be able to use what they know about an individual's identity to work out who the participant is. For instance, an employer may recognize the responses of a particular employee when reading the final report of your study. On one hand, this means you need to be careful regarding definitive claims around ensuring confidentiality; on the other, you will need to think carefully about the presentation of the evidence in your research project, and what it may inadvertently reveal about the participants.

ETHICAL REVIEW BOARDS AND COMMITTEES

It was once possible to undertake small pieces of empirical social research without receiving formal permission to do so from your university. However, undertaking any form of research that brings you into contact with other people is now virtually impossible without receiving some sort of 'stamp of approval' before you step into the field. It should be expected that you will not be allowed to undertake your research project without ethical approval.

The process usually involves submitting a research proposal, and accompanying ethics form, to an ethics review committee or board. In some cases, a risk assessment form may even be required. This ethical review process may be in written form or online. It may also include the submission of information and informed consent forms. They will consider the potential risks entailed in carrying out the proposed research and arrive at a decision regarding whether the well-being of interested parties would be endangered by the research process. If you are required to do an empirically based dissertation as a part of your programme, you can be fairly certain that there will be a set of protocols that you need to follow. So, we suggest that you familiarize yourself with the procedures required by your department, school, or faculty when formulating your dissertation proposal. These guidelines can often be found on your university web pages.

FINDING YOUR WAY 8.6

If you engage with ethics frameworks and guidelines during the process of planning your project, you are more likely to receive ethical approval at the first attempt without the need for changes.

Submissions to ethics committees will be judged according to the broad principles outlined in this chapter, but may also include further specific stipulations depending on the exact context of the study. There are normally three possible outcomes of the ethics review process. Firstly, the proposal is accepted and the research can go ahead without further amendment. Secondly, problems are identified and the project proposal will require some amendment in accordance with the panel's recommendations. In some instances, the board will simply recommend that you think further about the issues, or in others they will require evidence that you have amended your plans accordingly. This usually means that you will have to resubmit the proposal with the changes. Thirdly, the proposal is rejected without the possibility of resubmission. This third outcome is uncommon, and if you have previously met with a supervisor about your research you are likely to be aware if it is potentially problematic and may raise issues.

WORKING WITH YOUR SUPERVISOR 8.3

It is important not to be too intimidated by the ethics form or the procedure of ethical review. It can be really useful in helping you think about your research, especially in terms of access and sample, as well as how you are approaching your research relationships. Fortunately, your supervisor or another designated member of staff should be able to help you with this process by offering you advice about the ethical considerations required for the documentation. This will make the process less daunting.

"*Supervisors are available to help you with ethics. Very often ethics forms are intimidating and undergraduate students have never done one before.*"

— Dr Ruth Penfold-Mounce, Senior Lecturer in Criminology, University of York

I WISH I'D KNOWN . . . THE LENGTH OF TIME AN ETHICAL REVIEW CAN TAKE 8.5

The ethics review process can take some time. Furthermore, if you are doing certain kinds of research where additional ethical approval is required (such as with children in schools) it is likely to take considerably longer. Therefore, it is important to decide on your topic in sufficient time and check how long the ethics review process is likely to take. You need to factor this into your research plan!

Plagiarism and academic malpractice

Ethics is not confined to the field. The process of writing up your dissertation is also informed by ethics, and your research needs to be written in a manner which avoids plagiarism. This means that your final output(s) should be your own work and not written in a way which is biased or discriminatory in tone or expression. If you behave in an unethical manner at this stage of the research process you risk having your research stopped, and you may 'contaminate the field' to such an extent that it prevents other researchers from entering.

Using the ideas of others without acknowledging them appropriately is what is known as plagiarism, and it also constitutes unethical practice. While plagiarism does differ in extent and seriousness, it can include: not using quotation marks where a quote is used; providing incorrect information regarding its source; copying the sentence structure of a source and only changing a few words, without giving credit to the original source; getting someone else to do the 'write-up'; copying or using another student's work; and even resubmitting work taken from another one of your own essays. These are all considered to be serious breaches of integrity.

It is also not worth the risk. Universities and organizations are becoming more sophisticated in spotting plagiarism and often use very sensitive computer software to detect it. The penalties for plagiarism are often severe, and in extreme cases have led to the expulsion of students from universities. We know of one student who sneaked into a number of his housemates' rooms and copied material from their computers. He thought that if he then put the material 'into his own words' he would be able to get away with it. He didn't, and was subsequently removed from his course shortly thereafter.

Unfortunately, students don't always understand what constitutes plagiarism. Perhaps the most common form of plagiarism we see is material that is cut and pasted from internet sources. We have all sat on 'academic malpractice' panels where the student is genuinely surprised to be confronted with evidence of plagiarism. Such formal sanctions could easily have been avoided by citing sources appropriately. While plagiarism may be a deliberate act, it can also be the result of poor note-taking. Make sure that you properly reference your notes and be clear about when you have and haven't changed them from the original source, in order to ensure that you do this in your dissertation and thus appropriately reference text.

In addition to copying and pasting work from elsewhere, purchasing dissertations from the internet is becoming increasingly popular. Evidently, buying work is dishonest. But what is interesting is that they often aren't very good! They are also often easy to spot. Stylistically speaking, it is very hard for a professional writer to actually mimic the writing competencies of a student, and it is easy for tutors to compare and contrast writing styles between past and present submissions.

More generally, it is unclear how much social research is affected by deliberate fraud or misconduct, but there have certainly been fewer high-profile cases than in medicine and science. One infamous example, however, is that of Sir Cyril Burt, a very well-respected British educational psychologist. Much of his life's work was devoted toward research, using 'twin studies', that showed there was a genetic basis for intelligence. A short time after his death, however, it was discovered that he probably falsified his data, and the names of his co-authors. For almost 30 years the research community had been misled.

I WISH I'D KNOWN . . . ABOUT THE DANGERS OF PLAGIARISM 8.6

If you haven't already familiarized yourself with your university's ethics procedures, it really is the time to do so. This should be available in a university handbook or on university web pages. Plagiarism is considered a serious ethical violation, and can lead to significant penalties.

CONCLUSION

Ethical practices are fundamental to social research. This can take many different forms, but developing ethical awareness is vital in enabling you to appropriately complete the ethics review process and carry out the data collection, analysis, and dissemination phases of your research. As such, taking on board the content of this chapter and thinking about ethics during the whole process of research will be a key part of successfully completing your dissertation.

WHAT DO I NEED TO THINK ABOUT?

- ☑ Are you clear about the ethics requirements in your department?
- ☑ Do you understand the key features of ethical practice including: informed consent; harm; deception; privacy; anonymity; and confidentiality; and how you might negotiate them in your dissertation?
- ☑ If you plan to do internet research, such as using social media, do you know how issues of privacy and consent might apply to your project?
- ☑ Are there any ethics requirements or guidance that are specific to your discipline?
- ☑ Are you clear what constitutes plagiarism and academic malpractice, and how to avoid them?

WHAT DO I NEED TO DO?

- ☑ Familiarize yourself with your departmental ethics procedures.
- ☑ Decide what ethical issues are relevant for your project.
- ☑ Develop your informed consent form and information sheet.
- ☑ Complete your ethics application and submit it to the ethical review committee.
- ☑ Ensure that you make any changes resulting from the ethics review and adhere to the specifications of the approved ethics proposal.
- ☑ Avoid any plagiarism and academic malpractice when writing your dissertation.

Access the online resources **www.oup.com/uk/brymansrple** to help you to successfully complete your social research project or dissertation.

DELVE DEEPER

Association of Internet Researchers (AoIR). This is a great place for you to keep up to date with developments and issues in relation to internet research. It provides guidance on how to conduct ethical research. *https://aoir.org/* (Accessed 1 August 2018)

British Sociological Association (BSA). Academic disciplines often have ethical codes or guidelines which are really useful in helping you think about ethical research practice. For instance, the BSA provides guidelines which have some really useful ethical insights, including information about equality and diversity and avoiding sexist, racist, and disablist language. *https://www.britsoc.co.uk/media/24310/bsa_statement_of_ethical_practice.pdf*

https://www.britsoc.co.uk/Equality-Diversity/ (Accessed 7 May 2019)

Dingwall, R., Iphofen, R., Lewis, J., and Oates, J., with Emmerich, N. (2014). 'Towards Common Principles for Social Science Research Ethics' (conference paper). This paper discusses what it calls the fragmented and confused ethics picture in the UK. If you are interested in knowing a bit more about these philosophical and theoretical debates, then you are likely to be interested in the content of this article. *https://www.acss.org.uk/wp-content/uploads/2014/06/Ethics-Final-Principles_16_06_2014.pdf* (Accessed 16 December 2018)

Ransome, P. (2013). *Ethics and Values in Social Research.* **Basingstoke: Palgrave.** This book does a good job of identifying the links between ethics, ontology, and epistemology, and how these affect moral issues. It uses examples and exercises to get you to think about becoming an ethical researcher.

The Research Ethics Guidebook: A Guide for Social Scientists **(online).** This website is designed as a resource for social science researchers. One of its strengths is that it encourages reflection and questioning at all stages of the research process. It provides practical advice on going through the ethics process and how to gather information specific to your project. *http://www.ethicsguidebook.ac.uk/* (Accessed 16 November 2018)

The Social Research Association. This provides a set of guidelines that should be appropriate for all social science projects. The SRA website also provides information about good ethical practice in social research. *http://the-sra.org.uk/* (Accessed 1 June 2017)

Spicker, P. (2007). 'Research Without Consent', *Social Research Update,* **51: 1–4.** This interesting article examines whether consent should always be required when conducting social research. *sru.soc.surrey.ac.uk/SRU51.pdf* (Accessed 10 December 2018)

UK General Data Protection Regulation (2018). This replaced the Data Protection Act (1988). It requires that all personal information should be obtained fairly and lawfully and must not be processed unless certain conditions are met. You need to ensure that your research conforms to this regulation.
https://ico.org.uk/for-organisations/guide-to-the-general-data-protection-regulation-gdpr/ (Accessed 17 October 2018)

Wiles, R. (2013). *What are Qualitative Research Ethics?* **London: Bloomsbury.** This book encourages what it refers to as 'ethical literacy' by showing you how to engage with the ethical issues that emerge during the research process. It explores ethical issues relating to emerging methods such as digital and visual methods as well as more traditional approaches.

APPENDIX 8.1
An informed consent form

'I MIGHT NOT LIVE THAT LONG!' A STUDY OF YOUNG PEOPLE'S PENSION PLANNING IN THE UK

Name of researcher:

Participant Identification Number for this project: Please initial box

1. I confirm that I have read, and understand, the information sheet explaining the above research project and I have had the opportunity to ask questions about the project.

2. I understand that my participation is voluntary and that I am free to withdraw at any time without giving any reason and without there being any negative consequences. In addition, should I not wish to answer any particular question or questions, I am free to decline.

3. I understand that my responses will be kept strictly confidential. I give permission for members of the research team to have access to my anonymized responses. I understand that my name will not be linked with the research materials, and I will not be identified or identifiable in the report or reports that result from the research.

4. I agree for the data collected from me to be used in future research once it has been made anonymous.

5. I agree to take part in the above research project.

6. I agree to assign the copyright I hold in any materials generated as part of this project to the University of Sheffield.

_____	_____	_____
NAME OF PARTICIPANT	DATE	SIGNATURE
_____	_____	_____
RESEARCHER	DATE	SIGNATURE

To be signed and dated in the presence of the participant.

Once this has been signed by all parties, the participant should receive a copy of the signed and dated participant consent form, the letter/pre-written script/information sheet, and any other written information provided to the participants. A copy of the signed and dated consent form should be placed in the project's main record (eg a site file), which must be kept in a secure location.

APPENDIX 8.2
An information sheet

Research project title:
'I MIGHT NOT LIVE THAT LONG!' A STUDY OF YOUNG PEOPLE'S PENSION PLANNING IN THE UK

Invitation paragraph
You are being invited to take part in a research project. Before you decide whether to participate, it is important for you to understand why the research is being done and what it will involve. Please take time to read the following information carefully and discuss it with others if you wish. Ask if there is anything that is not clear or if you would like more information. Take time to decide whether or not you wish to take part.

What is the project's purpose?
There has been much concern about increasing longevity and the implications for future pension costs. In particular, there has been considerable debate about whether people are saving enough for retirement from a young age and whether different types of employment offer sufficient opportunities to contribute to a pension. This project will use interviews with 15 men, aged between 20 and 35 (5 in routine and manual occupations, 5 intermediate and 5 professional and managerial), about their pension contributions, and their attitudes towards retirement and future quality of life, to analyse the implications of employment type on pensions and future quality of life. The findings will then be compared with those from interviews previously conducted with 15 women aged between 20 and 35 to see if there are any differences between men's and women's experiences.

Why have I been chosen?
You have been chosen because you fit the participant criteria.

Do I have to take part?
It is up to you to decide whether or not to take part. If you do decide to take part you will be given this information sheet to keep (and be asked to sign a consent form) and you can still withdraw at any time. You do not have to give a reason.

What will happen to me if I take part?
You will only be interviewed once and this will take between 30 minutes and an hour and a half. The interview will be recorded.

A series of questions will be asked relating to your attitude to saving and retirement. You do not have to answer any questions that you do not wish to.

What are the possible benefits of taking part?
You will receive a £15 voucher for your participation. In addition, it is hoped that this work will contribute to academic and policy debates about pensions and saving.

Will my taking part in this project be kept confidential?
All the information that we collect about you during the course of the research will be kept strictly confidential. You will not be able to be identified in any reports or publications that arise from the research.

What is the legal basis for processing my personal data?
According to data protection legislation, we are required to inform you that the legal basis we are applying in order to process your personal data is that 'processing is necessary for the performance of a task carried out in the public interest' (Article 6(1)(e)). Further information can be found in the University's Privacy Notice: https://www.sheffield.ac.uk/govern/data-protection/privacy/general.

Who is organizing and funding the research?
The research is funded by the University of Sheffield.

Who is the Data Controller?
The University of Sheffield will act as the Data Controller for this study. This means that the University is responsible for looking after your information and using it properly.

Who has ethically reviewed the project?
This research project has been ethically reviewed by the University of Sheffield.

Contact for further information
Please contact [insert your name] at: [insert email address] if you have any further questions.

   [Insert supervisor name and University] at: [insert supervisor's email address] is supervising the project.

CHAPTER 9

WRITING
A RESEARCH
PROPOSAL

WHAT DO I NEED TO KNOW?

- Why do you need a research proposal?
- Key characteristics of a proposal
- Key components of a proposal
  - Title
  - Introduction
  - Literature review
  - Aims and objectives
  - Method and methodology
  - Ethical issues
  - Timetable
  - References

INTRODUCTION

Before you start your dissertation, it is common practice to have to write a research proposal. Not only does a research proposal help you make sense of your own project and what it will look like, it also allows you to connect your research idea to a wider audience so that other people can give you advice about whether, and how, it makes 'research sense'. Often submitted alongside an ethics application, the research proposal is sometimes a requirement of the dissertation process, needing 'approval' before you can undertake your research. This chapter will detail what research proposals look like and why they are important, before outlining the requirements of a typical research proposal.

WHY DO YOU NEED A RESEARCH PROPOSAL?

Developing a research proposal provides an ideal opportunity to make sure you are clear about the direction of your research. Writing a proposal enables you to design a project that interests you, and gives you an opportunity to receive feedback about whether the project is feasible. It will get you thinking about many of the issues you will have to negotiate to deliver the final dissertation, taking into consideration:

- the resources you might need
- the necessary ethical clearance required

- the accessibility of the required sample
- the level of your research skills, and whether they are sufficient to undertake the kinds of analysis that might be required

A good proposal will act as a guide through the research process. That said, research proposals are always tailored to particular audiences. In the context of a dissertation this is likely to be the module leader, personal tutor, or ethics coordinator. They are often responsible for deciding whether or not a project is likely to be successful. The proposal allows a tutor to assess any potential difficulties with the research, and after reading it they might suggest some revisions to strengthen the research. In some institutions, the proposal may even form part of the overall assessment of the dissertation, or be assessed for an associated research methods module.

The formal requirements for a research proposal vary enormously between different institutions, and you must always ensure that you follow the appropriate guidelines. For some courses, a brief outline and a title are all that is required, while others will ask for a full and detailed summary of the proposed project. In some cases, this may actually involve a literature review and an overview of the proposed chapters. It is also not uncommon for a proposal to be accompanied by an ethics application.

FINDING YOUR WAY 9.1

In order to complete your dissertation proposal, it is important to not only understand the requirements for the proposal, but also the final dissertation. This will include information about the word count, and what you need to submit and when. Having an understanding of these factors will help you to plan your project and its scope. Failure to consider these factors could lead to your proposal being too ambitious or too limited.

You may find that you have access to classes about formulating a research proposal, or have to talk through your project with a dedicated member of staff. Some departments will allocate a particular member of staff, such as your personal tutor, to help you with your proposal. If this is the case, then use their expertise to help you think through your ideas for the project, including the potential methods that you might use. If you have to attend taught sessions about proposal writing, make sure you attend and make use of these too.

A full research proposal should ultimately contain sufficient information to persuade members of a review committee that the research is worthwhile, and that it is appropriate in terms of method and ethics. It also provides an opportunity for them to make suggestions on how the study can be improved. As a result,

WORKING WITH YOUR SUPERVISOR 9.1

It is worth asking your supervisor if you can see any examples of previous dissertation proposals. This can be useful to get a sense of style, format, and the level of detail required. At the same time, be careful to pay attention to their format over and above the content—you don't want your proposal to be influenced by their particular subject or problem. It can also be useful to look at peer-reviewed empirical journal articles, and in particular their methods, to get an idea of how projects have been conducted.

proposals need to explain the nature of the research and why it is needed. The proposal should clearly detail what you intend to do, including:

- the scope of the study
- the aims and objectives of the research
- a step-by-step outline of the research methods

It needs to present a convincing case as to why the research should be carried out and that it will be undertaken appropriately. Where possible, you should ground it in the literature by drawing on previous studies and methodological discussion. A well-written proposal will indicate that you have the necessary methodological understanding and sensitivity to successfully undertake the research.

The proposal also acts as a form of contract that will be the basis of the agreement between all parties involved. In most cases this will be you as the researcher and your institution. This means that if you change the nature of the proposal in terms of its topic, methods, or analysis, you may also be required to revise your plan and undertake an additional ethics review if the changes are deemed sufficiently extensive.

FINDING YOUR WAY 9.2

Shortcomings of proposals include:

- Insufficient justification
- It is unlikely to produce useful findings
- Methods that are unsuitable in addressing the aims and objectives
- A lack of coherence between the different components of the project
- The project is too ambitious in scope
- The project involves a vulnerable group

If you are not given permission to undertake your planned research, sometimes it is possible to adapt your proposal to make it more manageable. For instance, you would be unlikely to receive approval to do research with children who have been physically abused, but you may be able to interview members of a voluntary sector organization that provides support for victims of physical abuse. Alternatively, you may wish to consider a totally different dissertation topic. You should discuss these plans with your supervisor or the dissertation tutor.

A well-thought-out and written proposal lays a solid foundation for a successful research project. It is common for an excellent proposal to lead to an excellent dissertation. This is because it helps you to think about the key components of your dissertation and provides a valuable source to refer back to during the research process. It also provides a starting point in terms of identifying and engaging with appropriate literature, and specifically asks you to reflect on methodological issues. In practice, it can take a lot of time to get your research proposal right, but thinking through necessary issues, and writing and revising the proposal, are key parts of the research process.

KEY CHARACTERISTICS OF A PROPOSAL

Perhaps the most important decision you will make when planning your proposal is whether you are going to carry out a project that is qualitative, quantitative, or mixed in terms of its research strategy (see Chapter 7). While qualitative, quantitative, and mixed methods research proposals are similar in scope, there are some differences in emphasis. In some respects, qualitative proposals are harder to develop because they tend to be more inductive in nature. This means that they have more emergent dimensions that are unstructured or unfolding, with the aims and objectives of the research being more exploratory in nature. As a result, specifying 'research questions' isn't always easy. If your university guidelines suggest research questions are required, it might be worth providing them with a caveat that they are likely to change throughout the research process. If a tightly structured qualitative study is planned, the development of the proposal is likely to proceed along similar lines to quantitative ones.

There are a number of key characteristics to bear in mind when writing a research proposal. It needs to be well organized and structured, well articulated, coherent, doable, realistic, ethical, and original. You can tick these off when developing your own proposal:

- ✓ **Well organized** and **structured**—Make sure to take into account any institutional guidance.
- ✓ **Well articulated**—It needs to be pitched at the appropriate level, clearly written and formal in nature. Avoid the use of jargon and also presumptions about what the readership should know. Use clear language that describes your proposed research in a manner which non-specialists can understand.

✓ **Coherent**—Outline clearly what the research will aim to do and how it will be conducted, writing in such a manner that it provides a sense of logic and argument.

✓ **Doable**—There is no point setting yourself up for the impossible. For instance, if you are doing a year-long undergraduate dissertation and state you will interview 100 people, this will obviously raise doubts about whether this can be completed within the time constraints. Alternatively, if you state that you will use multi-level modelling techniques to analyse secondary data, but you have never had any training beyond basic descriptive statistics, you are likely to have to make some revisions.

✓ **Realistic**—While you should 'sell' your project in terms of why it is needed and its value, you also need to be realistic about the scope of the research. In reality, your research is likely to be small-scale and have a limited impact. Being realistic also includes taking into account the designated time frame.

✓ **Ethical**—Make sure to show what ethical questions the research needs to address and how you plan to do this (see Chapter 8).

✓ **Original**—Some dissertation guidance emphasizes the need for research to be original. The notion of undertaking an original research project often fills students with dread. While the potential to generate new knowledge is important in a student project, originality can take many forms (see Chapter 16). For instance, research may be original in terms of the topic, such as a recent political development, the method, or the sample. Remember that 'replication studies' are original in that they explore knowledge in a different time and/or place.

KEY COMPONENTS OF A PROPOSAL

As previously stated, your institution may have particular requirements for what is included in your research proposal, and the order of these components, which should always be followed. For instance, while the aims and objectives are often found following the literature review, they may also be positioned in, or following, the introduction. However, it is common for proposals to make use of particular headings. These will form the basis of the content.

Title

The title is important because your proposal will ultimately be judged with reference to it. Those reviewing your proposal will consider whether the content addresses the title, in a similar way to how they examine whether the research aims and objectives are likely to be addressed by the methods proposed. Remember that the title is the first thing someone looking at your proposal will see and—like other things in life—first impressions count! It should be descriptive and concise, clearly conveying the topic of your research and the key elements in it. For instance, if your research includes exploring the perceptions of older people about crime statistics in a particular place, then you should include the fact that it is about the 'perceptions of older people in a particular place' and 'crime statistics' in the title. If you plan to use a type of method rarely employed, it is often worth specifying this.

FINDING YOUR WAY 9.3

If the title is too long and complex, then you will lose clarity. At the same time, if it is too short it risks not conveying enough about the topic under investigation. You could ask a friend to look at your title and see what it is they think you are going to explore. If they are unclear, you may want to revise the title accordingly.

It is not uncommon for dissertation titles to consist of a statement which may be eye-catching or controversial in some way, with a subtitle that focuses on the specifics of the research. Here are some examples adapted from student dissertation proposals we have seen. These have been carefully crafted to outline the topic and those involved in the research:

- Tequila, takeaways and traffic cones: An investigation of the drinking behaviours of undergraduates at a redbrick university
- A new breed of gamblers? Undergraduate experiences of online betting
- 'Phat' black women: Examining the body image of young British black women
- Unaccompanied asylum-seeking children: What can social workers do to ensure their voices are heard?
- Nursing in crisis? The implications of Brexit on nursing applications from EU nationals
- 'When I'm 65': Older workers' views of the relationship between the Equality Act and age discrimination in employment

It is important to recognize that you are likely to return to your title as you undertake your dissertation project. It is not uncommon for the title to be changed between the research proposal and the final write-up. This is not likely to be a problem. If you stick rigidly to your title you may end up missing many opportunities to make your project more doable or more interesting.

Introduction

In many ways the introduction to a research proposal is similar to those you have already produced for essays. Its purpose is to set the scene for what follows, describing what you plan to investigate, how, and why. It should outline the key problem that leads to the study and establish the reader's interest in the topic. In doing so, it will emphasize key research in the field, and indicate what is original or topical about the project. The introduction will also very briefly outline the methods employed and the sample that you plan to use in the research.

Generally, if the word limit for the proposal is on the shorter side—say 1,000 words or so—the introduction is very concise. However, where the word count is greater, introductions may also provide a brief history of how the issue has developed and the extent of the particular issue. If you are planning to conduct research on the challenges of funding social care for older adults, for instance, then it could be useful to provide information surrounding the nature of the ageing population, the shortage of good-quality social care, the associated costs of provision, and how these issues have emerged.

Regardless of length, the key point of the introduction is to 'set the scene' of the proposal, underlining the reasons for the research while providing an overview of it. As a rule of thumb, the introduction to a research proposal can be framed as a very brief response to the following questions:

- Why is this interesting?
- What is the knowledge gap?
- What are your aims and objectives?
- What will you do to address these?

As surprising as it seems, it is sometimes useful to write the introduction last because, having written the rest of the proposal, you will have a clear idea of what it is you are actually planning to do and what you need to introduce.

Literature review

The literature review should demonstrate that you are familiar with an appropriate range of literature linked to your project (see Chapter 5). It positions the research in terms of what has previously been done in the area, and is basically concerned with articulating what other researchers have said about the topic under investigation. In turn, this provides you with a platform to identify a gap in the literature and introduce the aims and objectives of your project. The literature review is important, as the reader will want a sense of how your project will 'fit' into the body of knowledge that already exists, and what your project may add to this.

The size of the literature review will largely depend on the requirements of the word count. These can vary considerably depending on the discipline and topic. It is usually the largest component of a research proposal, but you will still need to be concise and succinct in your review, referencing work of direct relevance to your study. However, this is not the place for a fully comprehensive review of literature on your topic. It represents a preliminary survey of key literature. There is an expectation that further work will be done on the review when you write your dissertation (see Chapter 6). For the proposal you only need to include enough literature to enable you to situate and justify your project in terms of both theory and substance, linking key existing findings and debates in the area of study.

The literature review should also try and reflect the suitability of your proposed research project in terms of its methods. This can be achieved by referencing comparable studies that have used similar techniques. Let's suggest that you want to explore how attitudes to homosexuality have changed among different age groups over the past ten years, using secondary data from a large data set. In your literature review, you should place an emphasis on drawing on existing studies that have used similar data sets to successfully consider related issues. This will help to give the reader confidence that this type of research can be successfully completed.

Once you have established the key themes in the field, the literature review should then identify and discuss any gaps in relation to the knowledge base. In some cases, these gaps will be substantive in nature; in others they may be more methodological in scope. For instance, if no one has done any research on a particular topic before, or there is a need to see if findings generated elsewhere apply in a new context, then your justification will be more substantive in scope. However, if most of the work conducted on your topic has been done using small-scale unstructured interviews, this may help to justify the need for a more structured quantitative approach to the study that you plan to undertake.

A good literature review is more than a summary of relevant literature in two key respects, as it requires a **synthesis** of the literature that is **critical** in nature. Your review should not simply be a description of what has been published, in the form of a list of research summaries. Instead, it should take the form of a considered argument. There needs to be a distinct progression from identifying and articulating the key themes in the literature, to a critical discussion of the limitations of that body of work. This will enable you to build a gap in the knowledge base, which will provide a clear platform to articulate the aims and objectives of your study.

FINDING YOUR WAY 9.4

Carrying out a well-planned search of the literature will help you to discover whether, and how, the topic has already been studied before. It will assist you in deciding which techniques are likely to be effective for your own study. Ultimately, it will help you to justify why your project needs doing.

Aims and objectives

The aims and objectives often act as a bridge between the literature review and the methods section. Essentially, they provide a clear statement about the intentions of your research. For this reason, they are sometimes included at the end of the literature review or at the beginning of the methods section, or they may be placed under a dedicated heading. For the sake of clarity, we've chosen to discuss them under a single heading, but it's worth checking your guidelines. It's also worth pointing out that in some cases the term 'aims and objectives' is replaced with 'research questions'. It is also possible for both to be included. Research questions are the very specific problems that your project will address, and they are particularly important in quantitative research. However, in many cases, the term 'question' will not apply—particularly if you are working in the more exploratory modes of research—so we prefer to make the distinction between aims and objectives.

Collectively, the aims and objectives represent a statement of intent for your research project. Together they provide a framework for the research and broadly specify what the research is trying to achieve. There are subtle differences between the aim(s) and objectives. Your overarching aims specify the overall focus of the dissertation—and they should be limited in number. In many cases there will be just one overall aim. If you are trying to address several aims you are probably not being focused enough in terms of the purpose of your project. The objectives specifically define the parameters of your aim. They tend to be more detailed than the aim, breaking the aim down into more specific components. They are typically summarized in three or more separate but related points.

Developing your aims and objectives is one of the most challenging aspects of developing a research proposal. They play a role in shaping the literature you use and the methods employed. But the success of your dissertation will be based on how well you manage to address them. This means that the objectives need to clearly indicate the outcomes that should be met if the aims of the project are to be achieved. Generally speaking, objectives should be:

- clear and concise
- answerable
- relevant to the literature
- interconnected

It is often worth presenting the aims and objectives as a series of bullet points, to direct the reader's attention towards them. This example, taken from a project that Liam conducted, shows the link between the aim and objectives.

Aim:

- *To understand women's attitudes and expectations in relation to pensions and planning for retirement in the UK*

Objectives:

- To explore whether women prioritize pensions in their decisions about savings
- To consider how women's knowledge of pension products impact upon those decisions
- To examine whether women's expectations concerning their retirement impact on saving behaviour
- To consider how responsible women feel about their own financial well-being in later life

I WISH I'D KNOWN . . . THE IMPORTANCE OF CLEAR RESEARCH QUESTIONS 9.1

Clarifying your research aims and objectives at the proposal stage is important and will assist you going forward.

"*Students often lack the necessary clarity about what exactly it is they want to find out. If they ensure their research question is clear and well expressed, other important aspects of the research process, for instance what to include in the literature review and methodology choice will become much clearer.*"

— Dr Jacqueline Dynes, Senior Teaching Fellow in Education Policy, University of Warwick

Method and methodology

We tend to think about methods as the techniques and strategies used in order to conduct social science research. Questionnaires and focus groups, for example, are commonly referred to as research methods. However, we can also engage in discussion about those methods. This is essentially the meaning of the term 'methodology'. This section of the proposal is concerned with both of these things. By briefly outlining your methods **and** justifying them, you can be clear about how you will address your aims and objectives. This may include indicating how you intend to approach the study. If you state that you are adopting a feminist methodology, for example, this provides the reader with some idea of the sets of values you are likely to bring to the project. We have also previously noted that positivistic approaches are more frequently linked with quantitative research, and interpretivist research is commonly linked with qualitative research (see Chapter 2). These are not the only theories of knowledge or epistemological positions, but they are the kind of thing you may briefly outline in this section. It is, however, also worth noting that many proposals have very little methodological discussion (if any), and you should find out what your institution's expectation is in relation to this. Sometimes you might also see this section with an alternative heading like 'the research study' or 'the research design'. Again, it's worth checking the guidelines to make sure you get the preferred terminology correct.

Beyond ontological and epistemological orientation, the method and methodology section of the proposal should provide a clear overview of your research strategy, together with important aspects of design, including:

- information about the sample and sampling strategy that will be employed
- detail regarding the data collection, including any research instrument you plan to use
- how your data will be analysed

Of course, every proposal will be different, but your decisions need to be clearly articulated, logical, and planned, noting any limitations where appropriate. You will need to set out which methods you will use in your dissertation, and why, referring to the dedicated literature on research methods in relation to both outline and justification. For instance, if you wanted to conduct work on the experiences of care leavers, it is likely that you would choose an approach that would enable you to collect rich and detailed information, such as semi-structured interviewing. You could then draw briefly on methods literature to both outline this approach and discuss why this kind of approach and techniques are particularly appropriate.

'The methods section' should also highlight important issues around sampling and access: why you have selected your sample (see Chapter 10) and how you intend to access them. This can involve making practical decisions based on issues of gaining access, suitability, and ethics. To return to the previous example, you would need to clearly articulate how you would gain access to this potentially vulnerable group, and this wouldn't necessarily be straightforward. You also need to be realistic here, and try not to exaggerate what you can achieve.

At this stage of writing a proposal it is important to identify the strategy for analysis. In part, this is because not all forms of analysis happen after data collection. Some begins almost as soon as you start to collect data. However, it is always a good idea to be clear how you will process your data. If you are planning to undertake a quantitative study, for example, you would need to briefly explain the

I WISH I'D KNOWN . . . THE IMPORTANCE OF MAKING IT DOABLE 9.2

Making something sound impressive is not likely to convince a reviewer that your project is 'doable'. Remember, you have a limited timescale and budget, and they will have a great deal of experience of what kinds of dissertation are achievable.

"Make sure you choose something doable! Meaning that there is enough material for you to base your research on."

— Mariana Matias, Student, Politics and International studies, University of Warwick statistical tests you propose to use and why these are appropriate. On the other hand, if you are going to conduct a qualitative project, you may need to state the type of analysis you intend to conduct, such as thematic analysis or analytic induction. Qualitative research is often emergent or exploratory. This means that themes and issues of interest emerge over time. If this is likely to be the case, it should be stated. This is acceptable when it forms a logical part of the research process (rather than lazy planning). However, it remains important to explain the basis of this flexibility and how the decision-making process will be used as the project evolves.

FINDING YOUR WAY 9.5

Your process of analysis needs to be compatible with the process of data collection. For instance, it would not be appropriate to carry out structured questionnaires and then attempt a narrative or discourse analysis. Your work is likely to be criticized—and ultimately be unsuccessful—if these two aspects of your proposal do not resonate with one another.

Ethical issues

Regardless of whether or not you think your research will be problematic, your proposal will be expected to outline how ethical issues will be addressed. As mentioned in Chapter 8, this means referring to the ethical guidelines that are set out in disciplinary codes of conduct. Key areas that we would routinely expect to see in the ethics section of a research proposal include:

- informed consent
- confidentiality
- anonymity
- avoidance of harm
- privacy

Your research always has potential repercussions for those you are researching, as well as for you as the researcher. If you wanted to conduct a research project exploring workplace harassment, for example, you would need to think about the fact that some participants may find it traumatic, particularly if they have been victims of such bullying. Ethics need to be thought about in advance of undertaking your research, and discussed in your proposal.

By demonstrating that you have considered how ethical issues will be dealt with in your research at the proposal stage, you will reassure those reading it that you have clearly thought about the challenges involved. Outlining the precautions

FINDING YOUR WAY 9.6

Trying to avoid problematic ethical issues by not acknowledging them is likely to be perceived as a lack of understanding. Rather than 'speeding up' the process, it may actually suggest that you lack the necessary knowledge to carry out the research.

you have put in place to respond to any challenges can help to limit some of the stresses which can occur when undertaking research (although you still need to be alert to unexpected developments in the research process). It is this careful planning that will help to convince the reader that you are an appropriate person to undertake the research.

Timetable

Developing a timetable is really important in terms of getting you to think about the different stages of the research and how long they might take. As discussed in Chapter 3, it is important to develop realistic goals when developing a timetable. Your plan has to be achievable within the specified deadlines. As a result, you should think about where difficulties might arise and how you might overcome them.

It is important when designing your timetable to be aware of the key dates with respect to your institution. These include hand-in dates for draft chapters as well as the final deadline. If you have deadlines for other assessments, it is also worth taking these into consideration in your planning.

I WISH I'D KNOWN . . . HOW LONG RECRUITMENT OF PARTICIPANTS CAN TAKE 9.3

It is not uncommon for students to underestimate the time taken to recruit participants, not to mention how long it can take to process qualitative data. It is important to provide sufficient time for these activities in your timetable.

References

Just as in your other assignments, you are expected to provide full acknowledgement of the work you have used in your proposal. Indeed, not only is a list of references helpful in demonstrating your awareness of the latest literature related to your topic, but it also highlights your understanding of the methods you plan to use. All of the references used in the proposal should be included in the references at the end of the proposal. They should also conform to the referencing method advocated by your university guidelines. While this is likely to be a form of the 'Harvard method' (most likely) or 'Chicago style' (less likely), there are variations of both methods and it is worth making sure that you follow appropriate guidelines.

CONCLUSION

Constructing a research proposal is not simply a bureaucratic task. It is invaluable in ensuring that your research is carefully planned. It demonstrates that you have fully thought through the decisions associated with what you are proposing. Clearly engaging with the research proposal will enhance your chances of producing a good-quality dissertation.

WHAT DO I NEED TO THINK ABOUT?

- Are you clear about why you need a research proposal?
- Do you know where to locate the institutional requirements regarding your dissertation proposal?
- Do you understand the key characteristics of a research proposal?
- Are you clear about how important a well-constructed proposal is for helping to structure and guide your dissertation?

WHAT DO I NEED TO DO?

- Make sure you understand your institutional requirements in relation to the proposal.
- Check with your tutor, dissertation supervisor, or dissertation module coordinator (depending on university guidelines) that your dissertation topic appears viable.
- Construct a well-organized and structured, well-articulated, coherent, doable, realistic, ethical, and original research proposal.
- Ensure that you refer to your research proposal and aims and objectives when writing your dissertation.

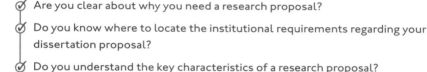
Access the online resources **www.oup.com/uk/brymansrple** to help you to successfully complete your social research project or dissertation.

DELVE DEEPER

The **Center for Innovation in Research and Teaching (CIRT)** provides a short rundown of the key components of developing a research proposal. It also has a linked YouTube video that goes through the process. *https://cirt.gcu.edu/research/developmentresources/tutorials/researchproposal* *(Accessed 5 December 2018)*

Denicolo, P. and Becker, L. (2012). *Developing Research Proposals.* **London: Sage.** This book provides guidance on writing a successful research proposal, addressing all of the key areas you need to consider. It also contains a number of practical activities.

Denscombe, M. (2012). *Research Proposals: A Practical Guide.* **Maidenhead: Open University Press.** This book focuses on the practical development of research proposals. It takes a rather different approach to a number of books by drawing parallels between a research proposal and a sales pitch in terms of being persuasive and selling your idea.

Greener, I. (2011). *Designing Social Research.* **London: Sage.** This covers the practical and theoretical issues in developing a research proposal. It is particularly strong in relation to methodological principles and how they influence your research design. It also examines the use of jargon in social research and the need to write a clear proposal.

Punch, K. (2016). *Developing Effective Research Proposals* **(3rd edition). London: Sage.** This is a really good starting point for you to think about developing your research proposal. It goes through the process slowly, covering all of the sections of the proposal. If you are interested in mixed methods, it is also worth noting that it has a chapter dedicated to developing mixed methods research.

CHAPTER 10
SAMPLING

WHAT DO I NEED TO KNOW?

- Samples, populations, and sampling frames
- Types of sampling: probability vs non-probability
  - Probability samples
    - A simple random sample
    - A systematic sample
    - A stratified sample
    - A cluster sample
  - Non-probability samples
    - A convenience sample
    - A snowball sample
    - A quota sample
    - Theoretical and purposive sampling
- Gaining access
  - Personal contacts/colleagues
  - Gatekeepers
  - Networks
  - Adverts
- How many? When is enough, enough?
  - Cost
  - Population variability
  - Level of precision required
  - Type of method
  - Theoretical (or data) saturation
  - Issues of generalization

INTRODUCTION

Whether your research project adopts a quantitative, qualitative, or mixed strategy, there's little point in asking a few non-random people a few non-random questions as you'll have no idea what those answers might indicate, or whether they might apply in other situations. Therefore, you need to think carefully about your sampling strategy and justify this in your dissertation. This chapter will explain the key principles of probability and non-probability sampling and explore why '**who**' you ask is just as important as '**what**' you ask. We'll take you through the two key stages of sampling: defining the appropriate population for study and developing strategies for recruiting your sample.

SAMPLES, POPULATIONS, AND SAMPLING FRAMES

Dissertation projects will typically involve studying a sample of a population. A sample is simply a smaller part of a bigger whole. Your sample may be made up of certain types of individuals, organizations, or documents that are taken from a larger group. Samples allow you to explore groups of people, organizations, or events that you couldn't explore in their entirety because of size or access issues.

In everyday terms we tend to associate the word population with the whole number of people in a given area, like a city or a country, but in research terms it is used a little more flexibly, even if the general idea is broadly similar. A research population refers to a group of people (or things) that share specific characteristics. This means that we can use the term population on a number of levels. We can, for example, talk about the population of students; the population of undergraduate students; the population of anthropology students; and the population of anthropology students at Yale University.

The process of identifying the population you wish to study requires considerable thought as it shapes the scope of your project. So, before you begin to think about sampling, you need an awareness of who or what the population looks like, and need to ensure that it is defined appropriately with respect to your research aims and objectives. As a general rule of thumb, your sample should reflect your population, and your population should reflect the scope of your study.

In some circumstances, when the population size is small it may be feasible to involve them all in your research. This might be the case if you are doing research in a particular organization that only has ten people in it. Some secondary data sets are also so comprehensive in their coverage that they can be considered to provide population data on a national scale. However, it is usually the case that a dissertation project does not have access to the whole population, regardless of

FINDING YOUR WAY 10.1

Thinking about the representativeness of your sample is important for the success of your project. Representativeness is basically a way of saying that the sample reflects the population. However, making sure your sample represents the population is a difficult task. If you were researching when people could afford to retire and your sample was based purely on professionals and managers, their perceptions are likely to be different from those in routine and manual occupations—who are likely to earn less and find it harder to afford to retire early. So, you need to think carefully about what factors might affect the types of responses you get to make sure your research is as representative of a population as possible.

how specifically it is defined. Dissertation projects typically explore populations that can't be reached in their entirety, either because they are too large or there are not the resources or time to include everyone in the study. This is why some form of selection is required—and if you get this process right and your sample reflects the population, you can say that your study is representative.

Unfortunately, achieving a representative sample isn't always as straightforward as you might wish. Let's say you were interested in studying how full-time workers view unemployment benefits. In the first instance you would need to use your research aims and objectives to identify the population, and then decide on an appropriate way of sampling it. In doing so you would need to identify any possible problems in the relationship between sample and population. This might include the following:

- How 'full-time' workers are defined. This would include things like: how many hours constitute full-time work, and is overtime included in this assessment?
- Are you interested in all full-time workers in the whole country, or those in particular parts of it?
- Whether certain groups of people are likely to be over- or under-represented in full-time work? Does your sample reflect these characteristics, or is the sample linked to a specific place or time? If you decided, for example, to use a sample of full-time workers from a supermarket that you were working at, certain types of people are likely to be over-represented (ie those in low-paid positions).

The choices that you make with respect to sampling are commonly known as a sampling strategy. This is a key part of your research project and it has considerable implications for your results. One tool that can help you to think about the relationship between your sample and the population is what is known as a sampling frame. Denscombe (2017) suggests that a sampling frame needs to be:

- relevant—it should contain things directly linked to the research topic
- complete—it should cover all items
- precise—exclude any items that are not relevant
- up to date—incorporate recent additions and changes and remove redundant items

Sampling frames are commonly associated with quantitative approaches to research, but the logic behind them is very similar to purposive sampling strategies used by qualitative researchers. As we shall see, purposive sampling involves selecting people who 'best fit' the requirements of the study, according to predefined characteristics. Indeed, a sampling frame defines eligibility for inclusion in the study and identifies those features from which you can select particular people. The sampling frame should, as closely as possible, reflect the target population.

WORKING WITH YOUR SUPERVISOR 10.1

When thinking about your sample in the context of your dissertation it is important to be realistic. Your sample size, as we will discuss later in the chapter, should reflect the scope of a dissertation project. For instance, identifying a sample of 50 individuals to interview in your dissertation would certainly be too ambitious. Your supervisor can be a useful source of advice regarding the scale of your sample.

In some projects, and especially quantitative studies, it will actually be an exhaustive list of all of those people (or things) that make up the population. In other situations—such as those where the approach to sampling is more purposive in nature—it may be a more general list of features that are required. The sampling frame is usually specified before a project begins, but some of these more purposive strategies do change their requirements during the course of the research, usually in response to emergent findings.

The task of constructing a suitable sampling frame is not always straightforward, and there are many occasions when you won't be able to obtain the full picture. For instance, a list of all the homeless people in Sydney doesn't exist, and even if it did you probably wouldn't be allowed access to it. Similarly, if you were interested in doing research involving trade union members in a particular organization, a list of members is likely to be available to the union representative but not to you as a researcher. As a consequence, you may need to readjust the scope of your study and be aware of some of the difficulties in extrapolating from your results to that of the wider population. In other cases, especially where the parameters of your population are very specific, it may actually be possible to obtain a suitable sampling frame more easily. If you were only interested in students taking anthropology at a specific university you could potentially access a list of names— you then have a sampling frame!

TYPES OF SAMPLING: PROBABILITY VS NON-PROBABILITY

Perhaps the biggest decision you need to make with respect to your sampling strategy is the type of approach you employ to construct your sample. There are two main types of sampling: probability and non-probability:

- Probability sampling—a sampling strategy which incorporates some form of random selection, meaning that everyone in the population has an equal chance of being included in the study

- Non-probability sampling—strategies that are not random in nature and are commonly associated with qualitative research (but also often feature in quantitative research)

Beyond these broad categories, there are a number of specific sampling strategies that you can use to better meet the aims and objectives of your research. We'll start by describing the most common strategies associated with probability sampling, before moving on to those non-probability techniques.

I WISH I'D KNOWN . . . TO START THINKING ABOUT SAMPLING EARLY IN THE RESEARCH PROCESS 10.1

When writing your dissertation, you will need to think about and discuss which type of sampling you employed and why. As such, you need to know about the different kinds of sampling and be able to justify your approach. Thinking about this early in the dissertation process will help you to do this.

Probability samples

Probability samples offer the best way of making precise estimations about the population of interest. As suggested earlier, the key point to probability sampling is that you must ensure that every unit in the population is available for selection and also has an equal chance of being selected. This central assumption enables probability samples to provide statistical representativeness. As such, it is more likely to be associated with quantitative forms of analysis. Indeed, probability samples allow you to use more sophisticated forms of statistical analysis, such as inferential statistics. These are powerful forms of analyses that enable you to make generalizations about the population from the analysis of the sample.

There are four main types of probability sampling strategies:

- a simple random sample
- a systematic sample
- a stratified sample
- a cluster sample

A simple random sample

With a simple random sample, the cases are drawn entirely at random from the population. This may take the form of drawing names from a hat or using a computer program to randomize your sample. In this respect, a simple random sample is a bit like a lottery where all the balls have an equal chance of being selected.

So, if your population was all members of academic staff from your university— perhaps you wanted to find out their opinion on student fees—then a simple random sample would involve choosing a random selection of them. Each member of staff would have the same chance of being selected.

Unfortunately, one of the problems with simple **random sampling** is that it requires a suitable sampling frame. While these may be likely to be available for some populations (eg organizations such as unions or universities), adequate lists are not commonly available for larger populations such as a city or country (the **census** is an exception). Perhaps more problematically, it involves you then actually speaking to all of the people drawn at random. This is difficult to achieve—and any non-responders will necessarily violate the random nature of the sample because it becomes 'self-selected'. This can have significant knock-on effects when you come to analyse your data, and some of the assumptions of statistical testing rely on the randomness of the sample.

A systematic sample

There are similarities between systematic sampling and simple random sampling. Basically, systematic sampling is a form of random sampling that uses a system for selection. From the sample a starting point is identified at random, and thereafter units are chosen at predefined regular intervals. So, this may mean systematically choosing the xth individual from the sample and continuing this process until you have your full sample. If you wanted to sample ten people in offices in a street with 150 offices, you could choose every 15th office after a random starting point between 1 and 15.

A problem with both random and systematic samples is that they are also often unrepresentative. This is because 'chance' does not always correspond with expectations. Toss a coin 100 times and you will rarely end up with 50 'tails' and 50 'heads'. This can be a problem if you need to try and make sure your sample is representative of all aspects of a population. As a result, there are a number of techniques associated with probability sampling designed to cope with such outcomes.

I WISH I'D KNOWN . . . HOW TO CONTEND WITH THE CHALLENGES OF A LARGE SAMPLE 10.2

Occasionally we have known students collect too much information for them to deal with. For instance, we know one student who sent out an online survey about men's body image and received over 10,000 responses (including to open-ended questions) in one day! Fortunately, they were able to use systematic sampling in order to randomly select cases for analysis.

A stratified sample

This approach is useful when you know there are specific groups in a population who may be different to each other. For example, if you are interested in attitudes toward climate change, you would want to make sure that you included people

WORKING WITH YOUR SUPERVISOR 10.2

You may want to discuss with your supervisor how to approach the issue of stratifying your sample. While the number is often (but not always) proportionate to the number in the population, it may sometimes differ. For example, if you wanted to look at attitudes towards smoking and you knew there were 200 smokers and 800 non-smokers working in a factory, you would want your sample of 100 to represent these groups fairly and would randomly select 20 smokers and 80 non-smokers.

from the full political spectrum, so would want to make sure that you included them all. You wouldn't, for example, want to just involve members of the Green Party because the sample would need to reflect the various strata in the population. The most commonly used stratification in many samples is sex and age, especially in dissertation projects. Other types of stratification may include ethnicity, class, sexuality, etc depending on the questions you are trying to address. It is important to discuss these issues in your supervision meetings.

A cluster sample

If you need a sample from a population that's distributed across a wide geographic region, such as the whole of the UK, you would have to cover a lot of ground to make sure that you actually sampled the units you needed to. Even then, as suggested earlier, your study is still unlikely to be representative. This has led to the development of 'cluster sampling'. This technique usually involves dividing the population into clusters, and randomly sampling from those clusters. So, if you were conducting research about university tuition fees, you could randomly select a small number of universities from the entire population of universities and then survey a number of randomly selected students at each of those universities. By using this approach, only a number of clusters are sampled, with all the other clusters left unrepresented. This is usually beneficial in terms of cost, but certain subgroups of the population are often excluded. Indeed, cluster sampling can become very complex for large populations.

FINDING YOUR WAY 10.2

Whatever sampling strategy you decide to use, it is important to outline your decisions fully in your dissertation. Make sure you discuss, and justify, your reasoning. Let the examiners know you considered alternatives and, although there are weaknesses, picked the most suitable approach—and be sure to state why.

Non-probability samples

There are a number of situations where a probability sample can't be implemented. This may include instances where there is no sampling frame, or where the costs associated with accessing the sample are prohibitive. In others, it may simply not be deemed desirable. In these cases it is likely that non-probability sampling procedures may be useful.

The essence of non-probability sampling is that judgements are made about the specific units or participants included in the sample. These approaches are usually characterized by their purposeful nature, which is why non-probability sampling is sometimes called **purposive sampling**. This means that people are specifically chosen to be part of the study because they correspond with pre-identified features of interest. Non-probability samples cannot be considered to be random, given that all of the units or participants do not have a known chance of inclusion. As a result, they cannot be assumed to produce statistically representative samples, but that is often not what they are designed to do. Patton (2002) argues that the logic of purposive sampling is quite different from that of probability sampling. The goal is to produce information-rich cases that are relevant to the aims and objectives of the project. This is not to say that purposive strategies cannot be instructive beyond the boundaries of a particular project, but it is to highlight that the motivation for using purposive strategies is not statistical generalization.

It is, however, true enough to say that non-probability samples are generally much cheaper and easier to deploy than probabilistic techniques. They can also be much more responsive to emergent data. This makes them particularly useful when taking more inductive approaches to data that are qualitative in nature. However, like all sampling techniques, they need to be used with discretion. We'll introduce you to the four main types of non-probability sampling strategies that are typically used with dissertation projects:

- a convenience sample
- a snowball sample
- a quota sample
- a theoretical sample (also known as a purposive sample)

A convenience sample

Perhaps the most common type of non-probability sampling in dissertation projects is the convenience sample, sometimes called accidental sampling. This is a sort of 'first come, first served' approach to sampling, whereby people that match the target population are asked to participate as and where they are found. It is a form of sampling where participants are 'self-selected' in that they choose whether to respond, but they have to be in the right place at the right time to be asked to participate.

The great thing about convenience samples is that they are readily available to the researcher. For instance, if you wanted to know about attitudes towards the European Union, you could simply ask other students you know, perhaps starting with your flatmates or by putting out a request for volunteers on a student website. Alternatively, you might interview the first 200 people coming into the student union or knock on houses nearby that are known to be 'student flats'.

Obviously, when using such approaches, there is no way to assess the representativeness of your results. As a consequence, there are likely to be significant difficulties in making a statistical estimation of how your results generalize to the population. However, a student project isn't always about doing 'perfect' research. Instead, the process is designed to provide an opportunity to demonstrate critical ability at all stages of the research process. In such cases, a convenience sample is often perfectly acceptable, as long as you explicitly explain why it was used, along with its limitations. Of course, leaving too little time to find a more suitable sample would not be considered a reasonable justification for this. If you are happy to limit your conclusion to something like the students in your particular tutor group, then convenience sampling will be fine. However, if you want to increase the representativeness of your findings, then other forms of sampling may be more appropriate.

FINDING YOUR WAY | 0.3

When using convenience sampling it is important to justify your approach and provide reasons for making that decision. You also need to be careful not to make statistical generalizations about your findings. This is not possible to do with convenience sampling, as your sample is likely to contain biases. While this is less problematic if you are using particular forms of qualitative research where generalization is often not the purpose of the study, it is always important to be very cautious with any claims made, regardless of approach.

A snowball sample

A snowball sample is a form of convenience sample that is often used in projects with people who are difficult to find. Basically, you begin by locating someone who meets the criteria to be included in your study. You then ask them to recommend others they know who also meet the criteria. While this is very unlikely to lead to a representative sample, it is a really useful method when you have limited access to the people who meet your criteria. Snowball sampling is particularly useful when trying to access populations that are hard to find, such as animal rights activists, football hooligans, prostitutes, drug dealers, burglars, or even a population not residing in their country of origin. Liam, for instance, once had a student who was conducting research on the experiences of immigration on deaf asylum seekers. Obviously, this is likely to be both a small population and one that is difficult to find. However, through the use of snowball sampling, the student correctly surmised that some deaf asylum seekers would know other people who met her criteria and she was able to access a sample of her target population.

A quota sample

Quota sampling is similar to stratified sampling in that the sample is balanced in relation to key characteristics. Quota samples aim to reflect a population by using relative proportions of people in relevant categories, such as gender, age, or ethnicity. However, in quota sampling this sample is selected non-randomly. So, if you know the population has 40 per cent women and 60 per cent men, and that you want a total sample size of 100, you will sample according to those percentages.

FINDING YOUR WAY 10.4

Deciding on the quota can be difficult and may require you to be quite creative in your decision-making. For instance, why not use sources of official data like the census in order to 'match' national characteristics? These could include things like the percentages of different ethnic minorities or men and women. Showing you have thought about this when carefully planning your research is likely to be well received by a marker.

Theoretical and purposive sampling

Purposive sampling refers to a range of techniques that involve selecting people according to predefined characteristics. Broadly speaking, samples are chosen based on some aspect of your knowledge of a population, its subgroups, the purpose of the study, and/or your emergent findings. Essentially, you are picking those participants or cases who 'best fit' the (well-thought-out) requirements of the study.

Let's suggest that you are studying experiences of learning and teaching in higher education, and in particular some of the difficulties in making the transition between post-compulsory education and university. You want to conduct qualitative interviews across the student population. Evidently, you can't talk to everyone, so you need to make some choices about which interviews you should prioritize to get the most out of the process. It seems reasonable to assume that these experiences might vary by discipline, but also by type of degree. That is, whether it is a traditional subject, a professional qualification, or somewhere in between. You also want to make sure that your study broadly reflects the demographic make-up of the university in terms of gender and ethnicity. This could be achieved by making sure that across your total sample there is a 50-50 split

☲FINDING YOUR WAY 10.5

There are many different approaches to purposive sampling techniques, and many are particularly suitable for designing more systematic qualitative projects. These include:

- deviant case sampling
- typical case sampling
- critical case sampling
- maximum variation sampling
- criterion sampling

These techniques often allow you to align your sample with your population, as well as the scope of the project, with greater specificity. If you are interested in learning more about these then the 'Delve deeper' section at the end of the chapter is a useful place to start.

in terms of gender, and an 80-20 split in terms of students who self-identify as white or black/ethnic minority. You might also decide to sample three departments—one of each subject type—from each of the four faculties of your university and interview a total of three people from each department. While you might need to do a little bit of further work in planning the exact make-up of your sample, this is an example of a purposive sampling strategy. You have defined a set of characteristics that you think could help 'shape' experiences of the transition into university and have purposefully selected people according to those criteria.

Theoretical sampling operates in a similar manner. However, in the case of theoretical sampling, your choices are driven by theoretical need and emergent data. Indeed, theoretical sampling generally involves making decisions in order to extend or broaden the scope of an existing or emerging theory. It involves jointly collecting, coding, and analysing some of the data before deciding what data to collect next. In this respect, the sampling frame is dynamic, rather than being fixed.

TASK 10.1

Now you have learned about the different forms of sampling, try to see if you can accurately identify the type of sample used by doing the sampling activity in each case (answers can be found at the end of the chapter).

1. If your population was all students and your sample was a selection of students in a lecture you had just attended.

2. If your population was all Police and Crime Commissioners in England and Wales and you selected ten at random to participate in your research.

3. If your population was people of different ages who attend concerts and you interviewed ten people in each of five different age categories—14–18, 19–30, 31–45, 46–59, and 60+ outside an Arcade Fire concert. You continued to conduct interviews until each group was filled up.

4. If your population was all Heads of Children's Services in England and Wales and you wanted to interview 20 of them, you could identify a starting point at random, and then chose the xth individual from the sample, continuing this process until you had 20 participants.

5. If your population was all people entitled to vote on Brexit and you selected a random sample of voters from a list of all voters from the electoral register, ensuring there was an equal number of men and women.

6. If your population was all adults who had been fostered as children in the UK and you accessed someone you knew had been fostered and asked them to identify other adults who had been fostered, who in turn identified other potential participants and so on.

7. If your population was all secondary schoolchildren and the sampling process involved randomly selecting a number of schools (12) from around the country from a list of all secondary schools. You then sent out questionnaires to 50 randomly selected children in each of the 12 schools.

8. If your population was female managers and you selected ten female managers who you thought would have a privileged knowledge on the topic and/or the theory being investigated.

GAINING ACCESS

Having discussed the different forms of sampling, it's now time to think a bit more about the practical aspects of actually accessing your sample. This process is usually referred to as 'gaining access'. It is the term used to describe the process of getting hold of the data that you want to collect (your sample). However, given that this often involves obtaining information from people, there can be real challenges in negotiating access to the material you want.

Fortunately, there are a number of techniques that can be utilized to access your sample. We are going to outline some of these here, and they are particularly appropriate for non-probability sampling. It is worth noting that no method of recruitment is perfect and it is possible to use more than one form of recruitment strategy to access your sample. There are also areas of overlap between the sample strategy used and the method of access. That said, the common strategies you may wish to employ to gain access to your sample include: personal contacts, gatekeepers, networks, and adverts.

WORKING WITH YOUR SUPERVISOR 10.3

You should discuss your ideas for gaining access to your sample at an early stage. Your supervisor may know of a suitable organization or group to be involved in your research. In some cases, your supervisor may even be in the best position to make initial access for you. However, you will then have to take responsibility for making the most of that contact.

Personal contacts/colleagues

You may be able to gain access to your sample through personal contacts that you already have. Indeed, contacts can be made through a current or former workplace, a group or organization you have been involved in, or even your supervisor. In some undergraduate dissertation projects, samples may even be selected through friends or relatives. Using personal contacts in this way can make the process of gaining access much less challenging and can save you much time and effort. However, it is also important to recognize that prior relationships can influence the nature of the data collected. The types of responses may vary as a result of existing relationships. Potentially, the research could even impact on those relationships. Carrying out your project ethically is a must in these situations.

Gatekeepers

From a practical perspective, researchers accessing hard-to-reach populations often do so through what are usually termed 'gatekeepers'. Rather than providing 'data' directly, these are the individuals, groups, and organizations that act as intermediaries between researchers and participants or other forms of data. They are often the people in formal and informal positions of influence in particular groups and communities. They might be a head teacher, community leader, social worker, or the manager of an organization. In some settings, it would not be appropriate to access the particular community in question without first seeking permission from a gatekeeper. This may apply to a school setting, for instance. Some gatekeepers will simply grant you permission, whereas others may assist you with the recruitment process. They are often influential and in a position to encourage people to participate. However, be aware that this may sometimes result in gatekeepers choosing who they would like to be involved in the research. In some cases, they may also ask for something in return, like a copy of the dissertation. Make sure you discuss any such requests with your supervisor.

Networks

You should consider whether your study population is part of a formal network or whether they might use particular services. Think about the types of places your population may gather together, and how you might access such networks for recruitment purposes. It may be that you can send a recruitment letter to a members' list or advertise there, or even use the time prior to or following a meeting to access participants. These networks could include making use of social media platforms like LinkedIn, Twitter, and Facebook. However, you need to be aware of the potential limitations of this too, and be aware that not all of your population might engage with such networks. Make sure you think critically about who you may be inadvertently excluding by using such networks.

Adverts

Adverts can be placed in local papers, internet newsletters, or at organizations. These can catch the attention of your potential sample (Figure 10.1). Sometimes

Figure 10.1 **An example advert**

RESEARCH PARTICIPANTS WANTED!

DO YOU WANT TO EARN A £25 AMAZON VOUCHER FOR
GIVING UP A SHORT AMOUNT OF TIME?

ARE YOU FEMALE AND AGED 24–39 AND EARNING
BETWEEN £24,000 AND £40,000?

WOULD YOU BE INTERESTED IN ATTENDING A FOCUS
GROUP ON PENSIONS TAKING PLACE ON

**WEDNESDAY 24TH FEBRUARY, AT 19.00
AT THE UNIVERSITY OF SHEFFIELD?**

(NO PRIOR KNOWLEDGE REQUIRED)

The Fawcett Society in conjunction with Dr Liam Foster at the
University of Sheffield, kindly supported by Scottish Widows, are
conducting research on women's decision-making in relation to
pensions. Participating would entail attending a focus group discussion on
pensions that will last between one hour and one and a half hours.

*Participants in the focus group will also be entitled to a £20 contribution to
their travel costs.*

**Please email Liam Foster [insert details] to indicate your interest.
Please note this research has ethical approval from the
University of Sheffield.**

FINDING YOUR WAY 10.6

Different types of incentives you might consider using to increase your sample size include:
- access to your findings
- food with the research
- vouchers
- a prize draw
- charitable donations
- reimbursing travel costs

It is also worth noting that the wrong incentive can bias your research and the types of participants you sample. Ethically, there is an issue as to whether incentives make people feel obliged to participate, and in a particular way. This is especially the case with monetary incentives. It is not uncommon for student projects to include no monetary incentives, so don't feel that you must offer one. In fact, some universities will actively discourage their use.

an incentive is used to attract participants to take part (see Finding your way 10.6). Obviously, if you use this method you need to think carefully about what you include in the advert, including the details, purpose, incentive, and timing of the research, emphasizing that it has been ethically approved. Adverts can take the form of posters, flyers, and social media posts. There are even examples in the literature of people using megaphones to attract interest in their research.

HOW MANY? WHEN IS ENOUGH, ENOUGH?

This is a difficult question! The answer depends on a number of considerations. These include: time and money, the population, theoretical (or data) saturation, the methods employed, and the type of analysis you plan to undertake. There may

FINDING YOUR WAY 10.7

It is important to recognize that there is an important difference between sample size in terms of the number of people initially contacted and sample size in terms of the number who respond. It is the eventual sample size that is important. You will need to try and predict the response rate you are likely to achieve and think of ways of encouraging a larger sample if necessary (for example, trying new people or a reminder email). So if you want to have a sample of 200 people in a questionnaire, and you expect the response rate to be about 25 per cent, then you would need to contact 800 people. The number of non-responders—'the non-response rate'—is also worth reporting in your final report.

also be expectations from your department or your supervisor regarding the size of the sample. In some cases you might need to change your plans regarding the size of your sample during the course of the project, particularly if you have access issues. While this can impact on the nature of your sampling strategy, it is not uncommon and doesn't have to be a problem for a dissertation project. However, you do need to be realistic from the outset about the level of responses you are likely to get from potential participants.

Although it happens less frequently, you may even find that you have more time than expected and are able to undertake research with a larger sample than initially expected. If your sample grows unexpectedly, which can sometimes happen when using internet platforms for research, you might have to close access to the research instrument. This is especially the case with qualitative material, so remember to leave enough time to analyse the data.

WORKING WITH YOUR SUPERVISOR 10.4

If you are unable to access as large a sample as you anticipated, speak to your supervisor about the level they think will be appropriate. Discuss your ideas for expanding the sample size and think about how this can be done within the time constraints of the dissertation.

FINDING YOUR WAY 10.8

If you are concerned about the size of your sample, you could:
- explore additional personal contacts
- identify other potentially relevant networks
- advertise your project more widely
- use different approaches to advertising your research (such as social media or posters)
- provide incentives for participation
- broaden your research focus to increase the sample

Alternatively, you may want to consider the use of additional methods. For instance, if you were interested in trade relations between China and the USA and you had been unable to identify and access sufficient elite individuals to interview, you may also decide to undertake document analysis of key trade documents. Potential changes such as this should be discussed with your supervisor.

Your sample size, and when to finish data collection, will depend on several factors which you need to be aware of when planning your research.

Cost

Data can sometimes be very time-consuming and expensive to collect—particularly in qualitative projects. You only want to collect the data that you really require, so your sample size should not be unnecessarily large. Projects have deadlines and you will need to stop collecting data at some point—and it is important to leave enough time to process your data. There may also be direct financial costs that are incurred as part of the research process—travel expenses or postage, for example, so you will need to factor in these things when planning your sample.

Population variability

Where there is greater variability in the population, a larger sample size is usually required. On the other hand, if the population is very uniform, smaller samples are more likely to be acceptable. Doing some initial research about your population, and its relationship to your sample, will help you to think about these issues.

Level of precision required

The greater the level of precision required, the larger the sample that should be used. This is especially the case with probability sampling because a larger sample is likely to provide a more precise estimate. For some statistical tests, a sufficiently large sample size is a necessity. However, it is worth pointing out that as a population gets larger, the sample size needed for an accurate estimate will not get proportionately bigger after a certain point. Of course, statistical representativeness is not always the goal, especially with qualitative forms of research. In such cases, the level of precision may be directed toward quality, rather than quantity. So, the size of a sample that is able to support convincing conclusions is likely to vary according to the purpose of the project.

Type of method

The sample size will also depend on the type of method you are employing. In his comprehensive discussion of 'doing interviews', Kvale (1996: 101) simply states that when interviewing you should include 'as many subjects as necessary to find out what you need to know'. This is probably a good rule of thumb for all research. An undergraduate student undertaking a qualitative project might be expected to interview around 15 well-chosen respondents to make some sustainable conclusions, depending on how 'in-depth' the interviews are, of course. Conclusions drawn from the results of a survey, on the other hand, would usually need to be taken from a much larger sample, with the number largely dependent on the types of analysis you intend to do.

Theoretical (or data) saturation

There may come a time in the data-collection process where you are simply receiving the same types of responses and this may be of limited use to your research. As such, you may feel that the sample is sufficiently large based on your findings. Indeed, 'saturation' implies that no additional data are being found, enabling the researcher to develop properties of the category. This is particularly applicable to qualitative projects. However, you need to be careful using the term, as saturation is often claimed but not justified. To complicate things further, you may also want to allow for some emergence—this involves following (potentially) interesting unanticipated lines of inquiry which arise during the research process.

Issues of generalization

When thinking about the size of your sample it is important to consider the extent to which the findings from your study can be generalized to a wider population—at which point it is worth making the distinction between different types of generalization. Statistical generalization refers to the mathematical process of making inferences about a population from the sample. This is associated with the notion of external validity (see Chapter 4), and there are complex rules that govern whether it is possible to do this. Evidently, this type of generalizing tends to be associated with quantitative research.

On the other hand, there are looser generalizations that can be applied in qualitative contexts. Payne and Williams (2005) term these 'moderatum generalizations' (see Chapter 4). Basically, these are subjective judgements concerning those situations and settings that your conclusions might be instructive in, and those where they are unlikely to apply. It is, however, worth highlighting that the issue of generalization in more interpretivist paradigms is a hot topic of debate.

WORKING WITH YOUR SUPERVISOR 10.5

"*Don't cheat or make massive over claims from your data, which amounts to the same thing and is academically unethical.*"

— Dr Siobhan McAndrew, Lecturer in Sociology with Quantitative Methods,
University of Bristol

Try not to make claims that go beyond the limits of your data. This is particularly the case in qualitative studies, where generalizability may be misrepresented. For instance, if you explored six people's experiences of group drug and alcohol treatment interventions in a particular treatment centre and found that your six participants had all found the experience helpful, it would be problematic to state that because they were effective in this case they should be implemented across the country. It would be better to state that these findings may have implications for other services and warrant further research.

It is also important to recognize that in many instances generalization might not be possible, or indeed desirable, but any conclusions you make need to be supported by reliable evidence. A really good dissertation can be spoiled by exaggerated claims regarding the generalizability of the findings. So be really careful with the claims you make about your research—and always err on the side of caution.

CONCLUSION

The relationship between sample and population is a crucial consideration for social research, and can have considerable implications for your dissertation. The approach you take to identifying and accessing your sample needs to be carefully planned and executed in relation to the aims and objectives of your research. These issues take much thought and need to be planned early in the research process. You also need to be 'prepared for the unexpected' and ready to develop contingency plans if your access to a sample or sample size is problematic.

WHAT DO I NEED TO THINK ABOUT?

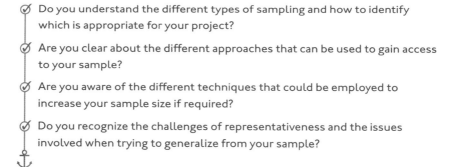

- Do you understand the different types of sampling and how to identify which is appropriate for your project?
- Are you clear about the different approaches that can be used to gain access to your sample?
- Are you aware of the different techniques that could be employed to increase your sample size if required?
- Do you recognize the challenges of representativeness and the issues involved when trying to generalize from your sample?

WHAT DO I NEED TO DO?

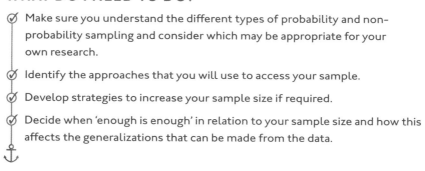

- Make sure you understand the different types of probability and non-probability sampling and consider which may be appropriate for your own research.
- Identify the approaches that you will use to access your sample.
- Develop strategies to increase your sample size if required.
- Decide when 'enough is enough' in relation to your sample size and how this affects the generalizations that can be made from the data.

Access the online resources **www.oup.com/uk/brymansrple** to help you to successfully complete your social research project or dissertation.

DELVE DEEPER

Blair, E. and Blair, J. (2014). *Applied Survey Sampling.* **London: Sage.** This is an excellent book if you want to know more about the different types of sampling you could use in your dissertation. It also covers sampling approaches highlighted but not covered in this chapter. It provides a history of sampling if you want to know more about the emergence of different forms of sampling.

Daniel, J. (2012). *Sampling Essentials: Practical Guidelines for Making Sampling Choices.* **Thousand Oaks: Sage.** This book is helpful in providing a thorough overview of sampling principles and covers, in detail, the requirements for choosing your sampling strategy. It also discusses how to choose the sample size.

Emmel, N. (2013). *Sampling and Choosing Cases in Qualitative Research.* **London: Sage.** This book is particularly useful if you are undertaking qualitative research in your dissertation and need to reflect on your choice of sample. It critically evaluates common sampling strategies, using international case studies from a range of social sciences. It is useful in showing the importance of how cases are used to interpret and explain findings, not just the sample size.

Henry, G. (1990). *Practical Sampling.* **Newbury Park: Sage.** This is a classic text in terms of advancing knowledge in relation to sampling strategies. It engages with the everyday challenges of sampling that you may come across in your dissertation. Its main strength is its ability to show the inter-relationships between research design and sampling choices.

Swisher, M. (2017). *Basics of sampling.* This short online document, aimed at university students, is a useful resource in relation to sampling, explaining the different types of sampling and their limitations in a succinct manner. *https://fycs.ifas.ufl.edu/swisher/6800_18_ELRN/05_06Basics%20of%20 Sampling.pdf* (Accessed 6 November 2018)

Thompson, S. (2012). *Sampling.* **Hoboken: John Wiley and Sons.** This book is useful for those of you who want to know more about the more complex techniques involved in sampling. It is also useful in covering numerous sampling techniques including those associated with clustered, and hard-to-find populations.

The **Web Center for Social Research Methods** has some excellent resources that cover numerous areas associated with social research. It systematically goes through different approaches to sampling. Its strength is in its clear and straightforward descriptions. *https://www.socialresearchmethods.net/kb/sampling.php* (Accessed 29 November 2018)

TASK 10.1 ANSWERS

1. Convenience
2. Simple random
3. Quota sampling
4. Systematic random sampling
5. Stratified random sample
6. Snowball sampling
7. Cluster sample
8. Purposeful or theoretical sampling

CHAPTER 11

COLLECTING
QUANTITATIVE DATA

WHAT DO I NEED TO KNOW?

- The quantitative research process
  - The case for secondary data
  - Sources of secondary data
- Questions, concepts, variables, and data
  - Types of question
  - Variables and levels of measurement
    - Nominal levels of measurement
    - Ordinal levels of measurement
    - Interval and ratio levels of measurement
- Questionnaire design tips
  - Presenting a questionnaire
  - Piloting a questionnaire
- Administering your questionnaire: platforms for delivery and analysis
  - Email surveys and online surveys
  - Postal surveys
  - Household drop-off surveys
  - Structured interviews
- Preparing for analysis

INTRODUCTION

Quantitative methods of data collection can usually be identified by their reliance on number, and the quantification of information. They can be used in conjunction with different research designs, including experiments, cross-sectional or longitudinal designs, as a case study, or used to undertake comparative research (see Chapter 7). Common instruments associated with quantitative data include questionnaires, attitude scales, and 'counts' of things. This chapter introduces you to the basics of collecting quantitative material. It outlines the nature of quantitative data in the context of the research process, before exploring the differences between primary and secondary data. In doing so, it highlights some of the benefits of using secondary data sets for the purposes of dissertation-based research. The chapter then concentrates on examining the relationship between research questions, concepts, and variables, before exploring how quantitative data can be measured at different levels. Finally, it offers some useful tips and advice concerning one technique that is particularly common in student projects—the questionnaire—and demonstrates the different ways in which questionnaires can be developed and administered. As a whole, the chapter aims to both take you through the processes by which quantitative data are constructed, and to prepare you to begin to analyse the data you collect (see Chapter 13).

THE QUANTITATIVE RESEARCH PROCESS

There are any number of interesting and exciting methods of quantitative data collection that can be used for dissertation projects. Despite this, quantitative research is often underused in student projects, especially in social science subjects such as sociology and anthropology. While some students are daunted by what they see as more 'mathematical' approaches to social research, as you will see in Chapter 13, these processes are often relatively straightforward and computer programs such as IBM SPSS can be used to do a lot of the hard work for you. They offer a really useful way of analysing a larger amount of data than could possibly be attempted by a single student working on a qualitative project.

However, like many other forms of social research, quantitative projects do not begin with data collection or analysis. Instead, quantitative research requires substantial planning and thought before you step into the field. You need to know what you are going to do, what data you will collect, how it will be collected, and how it will be analysed **before** you do anything else. Quantitative projects are 'top-down' in that they **begin** with a well-informed general line of reasoning and plan of investigation. This is then carried out to determine what the answer might be. In this respect they tend toward being deductive in nature. A premise is made, and then tested empirically to investigate its veracity. The quantitative research process involves careful design in order to gather useful data, which can be formally analysed to address your research questions.

The case for secondary data

In your dissertation you may wish to use what is termed primary or secondary data. Primary research is defined as any material or information you have collected yourself. This may be gathered through interviews, focus groups, observations, or questionnaires. Secondary data, on the other hand, is generally taken to mean the use of evidence or data which someone else has collected and compiled. Fortunately, there now exists a wide variety of quantitative secondary data sets that can be used for the purposes of dissertation research. While the terms 'primary' and 'secondary' might imply some sort of hierarchy, this is not the case, and pre-existing surveys have some distinct advantages for dissertation projects.

Making use of secondary data sets is actually very common in quantitative research and there are many national and international surveys that you can access for the purposes of your research. A huge amount of money is put into planning, collecting, testing, and analysing this material, so it's often much more robust in terms of coverage and range than can be achieved by a lone researcher. It is also likely to be less time-consuming for you as the data has already been collected. In many cases, the samples are so big and well developed in terms of coverage, they can be taken to be a representative measure of the population. You certainly wouldn't be able to collect all this material by yourself! You could not, for instance, collect data about which region in the European Union has highest educational attainment. However, this data is available to you through secondary data sets like those compiled at Eurostat (see 'Delve deeper', sources of secondary data, 4).

Another great thing about these data sets is that, with a little bit of technical know-how, it is possible to select specific groups for analysis. Not only can you compare and contrast between particular places, you can also explore the attitudes and behaviours of increasingly select groups of people. Given the large sample sizes involved in many of these surveys, you can, for example, choose to look at just men or women, or particular ethnic groups, or socio-economic groups. You can even combine these selections to focus on, for example, young, working-class, white women. Of course, the types of data you can analyse depend on the questions asked in the survey. This means you need to spend time identifying which survey has collected data on topics that best match your interests. You also need to ensure that you are interpreting the data appropriately. Looking at the accompanying documentation, including the full questionnaire, is always advisable before you begin exploring the data you are interested in.

Sources of secondary data

As we've highlighted, there are a plethora of large-scale national data sets covering a wealth of different areas. This typically includes health, crime, employment, housing, and social attitudes. The increase in the number of data sets available— both national and international, longitudinal and cross-sectional—has also been accompanied by advances in technology and, in particular, the development of computers. This means they are very easy to access and use.

The UK Data Service (UKDS), for instance, is fully searchable online and contains data archives of many national surveys that go back a number of years. These include the General Household Survey, the British Social Attitudes Survey, the British Household Panel Survey, and the Crime Survey of England and Wales (formerly the British Crime Survey), to name but a few. The UKDS Nesstar pages (see 'Delve deeper', sources of secondary data, 7) also enable you to explore some of the data sets without having to download them. The British Social Attitudes Information System also has a dedicated website (see 'Delve deeper', sources of secondary data, 1), which allows you to undertake some online analysis. Other providers have similarly made it easy to obtain data. If you are interested in

WORKING WITH YOUR SUPERVISOR 11.1

As well as exploring what data sets are available through UKDS and other online sources, ask your supervisor if they are aware of any particular data sets which map onto your research questions. They may be able to assist.

education, for example, the Higher Education Statistics Agency (HESA) (see 'Delve deeper', sources of secondary data, 3) provides material relating to a range of issues associated with UK higher education. Eurostat (see 'Delve deeper', sources of secondary data, 4) similarly provides a myriad of data that enable cross-European analysis in a number of key areas, and the OECD (see 'Delve deeper', sources of secondary data, 6) provide similar data at a global level. The International Social Survey Programme is also global in nature, as are the World Values Survey and the Survey of International Social Surveys. Again, these are all easily accessible and freely available on the internet. Many of these sites, such as the UKDS, provide opportunities to search for suitable surveys or specific survey questions by theme or topic. This can be a useful way of identifying which data sets contain the types of data you need to address your research questions. There are a number of sources of economic data that can also be analysed. These are particularly useful if you are an economics, international relations, or social policy student. For instance, the United Nations Statistics Division, World Bank, and International Monetary Fund all provide up-to-date data sets which can be analysed quantitatively.

Secondary data sets help you to circumnavigate parts of the data-collection process by providing you with the means to access high-quality data without actually going to the trouble of collecting it all yourself. They allow you to increase the scope and range of your research because they are not limited to your local connections and networks, where generalizability is often a problem. This is not to say that primary methods of data collection should be avoided. It is, however, to emphasize that technological developments have made secondary data sets more and more accessible, and readily usable for dissertation projects. The advantages of using this material for a time-limited project such as a dissertation are certainly worth considering.

QUESTIONS, CONCEPTS, VARIABLES, AND DATA

Regardless of whether you choose to make use of primary or secondary data, before you collect any material you will need to understand how survey questions or items relate to concepts, how concepts become measurements, and the different types of data that can be created by those measurements. Understanding this process will help make your analysis much easier to carry out.

Types of question

Broadly speaking, the questions that are asked in a survey or questionnaire can take three different forms: open, closed, and contingency questions.

Open-ended questions do not specify a predetermined range of answers. Instead, they encourage a richness of responses. They can be useful when you are unsure about the possible answers you might receive or where those answers are complex. However, when developing questionnaires, open questions should not be used because you think it is easier than trying to think through what the closed-ended options should be. While they can produce more detail, open questions can make the analysis more difficult because you'll have to interpret the answers post hoc and without additional context. Instead, it is often a good idea to try to come up with categories, and code them before you administer the questionnaire (see Chapter 15).

I WISH I'D KNOWN . . . WHEN IT IS APPROPRIATE TO USE OPEN-ENDED QUESTIONS 11.1

A large number of open-ended questions can make questionnaires too burdensome for respondents to complete, so they should be limited in number. As such they can impact negatively on response rates so think carefully about when they should be used.

Closed-ended questions offer a set of pre-designed responses. They may consist of yes/no responses, multiple choice options, or may provide respondents with the opportunity to choose from a selection of categories. Generally speaking, they are easier to process than open questions, but are naturally more restrictive. Closed questions may come in various forms. These include:

- **Lists**—These provide respondents with a list of possible responses (they may have the opportunity to tick several responses that apply).
- **Category questions**—These are designed so that only one response is possible. For instance, it could involve requesting that a respondent pick their favourite choice from a list.
- **Ranking questions**—These require respondents to rank responses in order of preference. For instance, you might ask respondents to rank order their party political preferences. This should, however, be done with caution as the results can be difficult to analyse.
- **Scale questions**—This is where respondents are asked to indicate how strongly they agree or disagree with a particular statement.
- **Quantity**—The response is a number which may be exact or approximate, providing the quantity of a particular characteristic.

Filter questions (or contingency questions) are used when it is necessary to ask a respondent one question in order to determine whether they are qualified or experienced enough to answer a subsequent one. For instance, if you were interested in the extent to which students use overdrafts, you may want to ask a first question about whether a respondent uses an overdraft, with follow-up broadly concerned with how much they are currently overdrawn. Those who answer 'no' to the first question would then be instructed not to answer the second. This can help a questionnaire remain focused on relevant characteristics. However, filter questions can make a survey difficult to follow, particularly where there are multiple filters. If the filters become too confusing for the respondent, they may give up altogether. Fortunately, some web-based questionnaire software will make this process much easier by automatically applying the filter for you.

However, before you start to think about asking specific questions and building a survey using these types of questions, you need to understand the relationship between your aims and objectives and your specific questionnaire items. To do this you need to understand what a variable is and what it can measure.

Variables and levels of measurement

Let's suggest that you have an overarching objective to 'assess how smoking varies by ethnicity'. In the form of a research question, this might be framed more specifically as 'how does smoking vary by ethnicity?' The question asks you to collect data that will allow you to examine patterns of smoking in respect to ethnic group. It is likely that you need to collect the data in the form of closed-ended questions. But to develop the specific survey instrument that will allow you to do this, you first need to understand what concepts you need to measure **and** how you will measure them.

In the first instance, a concept is simply a construct or an idea that helps us to frame our understanding of the human world. Can you see what concepts are present in the research question 'how does smoking vary by ethnicity'?

There are two: smoking and ethnicity. So, in order to conduct the empirical research that will enable you to answer this question, you need to find a way to use numbers to make these things 'visible'. This is essentially what is meant by the term 'variable'. Variables are a type of concept which can be seen to vary in amount or quality, and they are frequently measured by the items in a survey. However, it is worth stating that while variables can be entirely constituted by a single question, not all questions constitute a variable. In some cases, variables will be derived from a combination of questions. Socio-economic status, for example, is often worked out from looking at the data from a range of different questions. Likert scales similarly combine data from a range of items.

FINDING YOUR WAY 11.1

You need to plan and understand your methods of data collection and how you will analyse your variables before you think about actually stepping into the field to deliver your survey or questionnaire.

Different variables also record data in different ways—or what are technically referred to as **levels of measurement**. Understanding these levels is crucial because they have different techniques of analysis associated with them. That is to say that how you summarize and interpret quantitative data is entirely dependent on the level of measurement that you have. This is why quantitative projects tend to be front-loaded in terms of the research process.

With that in mind, look at these examples:

Q1. Do you smoke cigarettes?

Yes   No

Q2. Do you consider yourself to be a:

Non-smoker light smoker medium smoker heavy smoker

Q3. How many cigarettes have you smoked in the last seven days?

_____ _____ (write here)

Each of these questions represents the variable 'smoking behaviour' that we are interested in. However, while these questions are concerned with smoking, they are recording the information in subtly different ways. In fact, each question corresponds to a particular level of measurement. These levels are called **nominal**, **ordinal**, and **interval**. We shall deal with each in turn.

Nominal levels of measurement

Look again at the first question.

Q1. Do you smoke cigarettes?

Yes   No

Here, the question constructs a category between cigarette smokers on one hand, and non-cigarette smokers on the other. It assumes that all people can be divided into two separate groups. In this particular case, you are either a cigarette smoker or you are not. There is no middle ground. When you are dealing with variables that measure categories such as these, you are dealing with variables that are operating at a nominal level of measurement. Nominal simply means 'name'.

It is, however, worth noting that nominal variables are also sometimes called 'categorical' variables because they measure distinct categories. **Dichotomous variables**, on the other hand, are simply nominal variables which have only two categories. Although the smoking variable used in this example is a dichotomous variable—you are either a smoker or you are not—not all nominal variables are binary. Ethnicity, marital status, nationality, geographical location, and occupation are all commonly used forms of nominal data in dissertation projects.

Here is an example of a variable that is measured at the nominal level: ethnicity. It was included in the 2011 census:

Q4. What is your ethnic group?

Choose one section from A to E, then tick one box to best describe your ethnic group or background

A. White

English / Welsh / Scottish / Northern Irish / British

Irish

Gypsy or Irish Traveller

Any other background, write in:

_____

B. Mixed / Multiple ethnic groups

White and Black Caribbean

White and Black African

White and Asian

Any other Mixed / multiple ethnic background, write in:

_____

C. Asian / Asian British

Indian

Pakistani

Bangladeshi

Chinese

Any other background, write in:

_____

D. Black / African / Caribbean / Black British

African

Caribbean

Any other Black / African / Caribbean background, write in:

_____

E. Other ethnic group

Arab

Any other ethnic group, write in:

_____

Notice the instruction at the start: 'Choose **one** section from A to E, then tick **one** box to best describe your ethnic group or background'. You are either in group A, B, C, D, or E; there is no sliding scale between White, Mixed, Asian, Black, or Other. Once you have decided which category you are in, you now have to 'tick' which subset of that category you belong to. The categories are mutually exclusive. There is no intrinsic order or inherent scalable quality. What is also important to recognize here is that all possibilities are covered: everybody who responds to the question will fall into one of these categories.

FINDING YOUR WAY 11.2

If you are developing your own variables it is worth exploring how these have been measured elsewhere. For instance, you may find it useful to replicate the categories used in a national or multinational data set. This can save time and energy.

Ordinal levels of measurement

Ordinal variables have two or more categories like nominal variables, but the categories can also be ordered or ranked, usually moving from greater to smaller values or vice versa. So an opinion poll might ask how likely you are to vote for a particular political party at the next election, with the possible options: 'very likely', 'likely', 'not sure', 'unlikely', or 'very unlikely'. Another example would be if you asked someone to provide an answer to the statement: 'I do a lot of exercise' on a similar scale from 'strongly agree' to 'strongly disagree'.

An integral feature of ordinal measurements is that it is impossible to say whether the distances between the points on the scale are equal as it will depend on individual perception. What is a lot of exercise will vary from person to person. As a result, the scale cannot be considered to be continuous.

Look again at Question 2 from our smoking example:

Q2. Do you consider yourself to be a:

Non-smoker   light smoker   medium smoker   heavy smoker

Like Question 1, this question is still concerned with smoking but it is a little more refined as it suggests there is some sort of order to the answer. It is still possible to divide people into non-smokers and smokers, but the question gets a little more specific about how the respondent perceives what type of smoker (or not) they actually are. Unlike Question 1, there is some room for shading between those categories. However, while there is something of a scale here, it is non-specific and there is a lot of room for interpretation; the categories are not neat and well bounded. What 'heavy smoking' means for one person may be 'light smoking' for another. In this sense, the distances between the points on the scale are not equal or well defined.

Ordinal variables can also be used to group together 'counts' of things. For instance, the following scale, also a smoking variable, is also constructed at the ordinal level:

Q5. How many cigarettes do you smoke a day?

I never smoke   Less than one per day   1–19   20+

Notice how the range between each point is not equal? However, in this example some additional thought has gone into possible ways of categorizing the number of cigarettes smoked because there is an abundance of literature that defines 20 or more cigarettes a day as heavy smoking. This is not to say that ordinal scales have to have some theoretical basis. Some variables that employ an ordinal scale will simply group counts equally as it is an easy way to summarize wide-ranging data. Many variables measuring 'age' will do this.

Ordinal scales are not, however, only suitable for 'perceptions of behaviour', 'aggregated counts', or other forms of ordered data. One of the most popular uses of the ordinal scale is to measure attitudes. A popular version of this is a Likert scale. This is a form of rating scale on which respondents specify their beliefs, attitudes, or feelings about a particular topic or issue. Typically, a Likert scale enables respondents to numerically express the strength of feeling with respect to a specific statement or question topic. Multiple measurements are then made on different items that are constructed around two polar opposites with a number of points in-between. This information is then combined to produce a global measure. The exact number of points on a Likert item can vary, although three-point, five-point, seven-point, and even ten-point scales are popular.

Look at this example of a Likert-like item taken from the last wave of the British Household Panel Survey (see 'Delve deeper', sources of secondary data, 2):

Q6. Please look at the card and tell me how much you agree or disagree with the following statement?

A. **It takes too much time and effort to do things that are environmentally friendly:**

Strongly agree	Agree	Neither agree nor disagree	Disagree	Strongly disagree
1	2	3	4	5

In this example, attitude toward an aspect of environmental friendliness is being measured on a five-point Likert-type scale. By compiling the answers to a set of related questions like this one, Likert scales build a composite picture of a particular attitude, belief, or practice.

Interval and ratio levels of measurement

Interval variables can be measured along a continuum and have a numerical value. The distance between the ranks/attributes is also equal and continuous. However, in the particular case of interval variables there is an arbitrary zero point. A familiar example of an interval scale measurement is temperature, as measured by the Celsius scale. Although the zero point is based on the freezing point of water, it could just as easily be based on the freezing point of alcohol or 'absolute zero'. In any case, interval variables such as temperature are rarely used in social research. Instead, **ratio variables** are much more common. These have all the properties of an interval variable, but also have a clear definition of zero. Age, for instance, has a logical zero point and can be considered to be a ratio variable. Other examples of ratio variables include height, weight, distance, or income. In fact, anything where you are counting something specifically is likely to be a ratio variable.

Let us go back to the third question—it is yet more specific than the first two smoking variables.

Q3. How many cigarettes have you smoked in the last seven days?

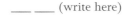 (write here)

This is an example of a ratio variable. It is similar to an ordinal variable in that there is a scale—in this case a count. However, the intervals between the values are equally spaced and the gaps between each point are clear, consistent, and continuous. The difference between one cigarette and two cigarettes is the same as it is between five and six. The gap between each measure is always the same. Where there is no room for individual interpretation between each point on a scale, the distance between points is equal, and there is a non-arbitrary zero point, then it is likely that you are dealing with a ratio measure.

At which point it is possible to return to our original research question: how does smoking vary by ethnicity? Ethnicity is a nominal variable, but smoking is fairly flexible in terms of design. But do bear in mind that if you choose the ratio version of the smoking variable, you could always process down those answers into ordinal and nominal variables at a later date should you wish to.

Now that we've developed measures for our concepts, it would be a relatively straightforward job to process the data into a table for analysis. We'll take you through the process of doing this in Chapter 13.

QUESTIONNAIRE DESIGN TIPS

You should now know how research questions relate to concepts, how concepts can be transformed into variables, and how to identify the levels of measurement of those variables. Assuming that you are not going to make use of a secondary data set, this means we are now in a position to put all of this together and begin to think about how you can develop and administer a questionnaire.

Questionnaires are commonly used in dissertation research because they can provide a relatively quick and inexpensive way of exploring the characteristics, attitudes, and behaviours of a sample. They enable you to collect, describe, and analyse numerical information. So, you might try to discover facts about a group of people such as their age, average income, or gender, or you might look for relationships between variables—how age might relate to internet use or type of newspaper read, for example. Sometimes the term 'questionnaire' is conflated with the term 'survey'. The basic difference between the two is that questionnaire refers to the actual document used to collect data, whereas a survey is the totality of information collected. You use a questionnaire to help you survey a sample of people.

As we've previously highlighted, questionnaires are usually front-loaded in terms of effort and a lot of the hard work comes **before** you actually gather any information. You have to work out what variables you want to measure, how you

I WISH I'D KNOWN . . . HOW TO DESIGN A QUESTIONNAIRE 11.2

There are three interrelated points that you need to consider when designing questionnaire items in order to avoid running into problems:

- Why are you asking the question?
- What are you attempting to measure?
- How you will analyse the information?

will measure them, what you will then go on to do with those measurements, and plan how the resulting analysis will help you to answer your research questions.

With this purpose in mind, we can ask a series of questions that need to be considered when developing a questionnaire.

Why are you asking the question? Perhaps the main reason that people struggle to analyse questionnaire material is because insufficient attention has been paid to the purpose of the questions. All of the questions in a good questionnaire have a specific reason to be there. They should also relate to a clearly identifiable variable that, in turn, will help you to answer pre-specified research questions. In turn, you should also be able to identify what level of measurement your variable will produce **and** what you will do with the subsequent data in terms of analysis. We'll deal with this issue more in Chapter 13, but it is important to consider how you can present the data in graphical or tabular form at this early stage. Poor questionnaire planning will result in problems later in the research process—and mistakes are difficult to rectify. Therefore, it is important to use well-constructed questions and answers. The purpose of each and every question should be well defined and well understood in terms of the data that it will produce and what that data will be made to do—all of which is worked out **before** any data is actually collected. This means that **before** any questions are asked, not only should you have a sound research rationale in place, with supporting research questions, you also need to know exactly what type of data the items in your questionnaire will provide, and what you will do with the resulting data—that is, how you will analyse it. On top of that, you need to know how that analysis will inform your research aim and objectives. As a general rule, if you don't know why you are asking a question or what you will do with the data, don't ask it.

Do you need to ask more than one question? Questions should only deal with a single issue. That is to say that it shouldn't be a double-barrelled question. For instance, look at the following question: '*What are your feelings towards the Green Party and their current policy on recycling?*'

Can you see any problems? It is two questions rolled into one, and in this instance you should think about splitting it into two separate ones as people may feel differently about the two issues mentioned. Alternatively, imagine that you are interested in migrants' experiences of their adopted country and you asked '*How would you rate your experience of the health and education system?*' Again, there are two questions being asked. What if the respondent had different views in relation to health and education, or they had never had any experience of either?! It is sometimes possible to identify double-barrelled questions by the presence of the conjunction 'and'.

Do respondents have the required information? Let's suppose that you are interested in the differences between online and offline experiences of employment support. You compose the following question: '*Do you think that attending the local Jobcentre plus in person is a better source of information than the job centre online?*' Like the previous example, the respondent will be unable to answer this question if they have not used one of the services and so any resulting data will be relatively meaningless. More problematically, it will obscure the responses of people who did actually use the service as there is no way of separating them after the event. Filter questions are often a good way of establishing whether someone can purposefully answer specific questions.

Does your question have the required level of detail? It is possible to be too specific or too general when building survey items. There is a difference, for example, in asking about general fear of crime, and specific forms of crime such as fear of assault more directly. So try to make sure your question is directed toward the concept you are measuring as much as possible. This is often a case of thinking critically about the variables you are seeking to measure and labelling them appropriately.

Are your questions biased or loaded? It is sometimes the case that our own preconceptions and assumptions tacitly influence how we choose to compose questions, and the answers that follow. So, rather than asking '*is city centre parking a problem?*', it would be better to ask '*what is your opinion about city centre parking?*' and then provide an ordinal scale from '*very good*' to '*very bad*'. Another example would be if you were interested in virtual friendships in online gaming and you asked for a response to the following statement: '*Virtual friendships established during online gaming are not as beneficial as face-to-face friendships*'. If you are to ask a loaded question, it is sometimes worth including another item that is loaded in the opposite direction. That way, you can assess the reliability of the answers.

Will respondents answer truthfully? Ask yourself whether the respondent is likely to skew their answer in some form, either on purpose or by accident. If you can think of a reason why this might happen, consider rewording the question. Some people, for example, do not readily like to provide specific details about their income. So it can be better to give them brackets of income because they don't have to specifically state the figure. However, sometimes even this won't be enough and you may need to include '*I'd rather not say*' as one of the options. This gives people an opportunity to skip specific questions, but also makes it clear why they haven't answered it. In other situations, if you think people might be trying to present themselves in a good light, it can be worth repeating items using different formats to see how their answers compare. However, while this does provide a measure of reliability, it can make the questionnaire appear repetitive.

Can your question be misunderstood? Think about whether the question you plan to ask 'makes sense'. Let's suppose you are interested in alcohol consumption and you ask the question '*how much do you drink per week?*' Given your interests, and the fact that other questions are directed toward alcohol, it would still be better to make direct reference to the fact. The question might be better phrased: '*how many units of alcohol do you drink per week?*' Piloting your questions, as we will discuss shortly, can also help iron out any misunderstandings.

Is there a temporal point of reference to your question? If you are using words such as 'will', 'could', 'might', or 'may', your question is likely to include a temporal element. If it does, think about specifying the time frame you are interested in. If you were to ask *'do you think the Bank of England will raise interest rates?'*, for example, you would need to include a time frame in order for it to be meaningful. This is because the government will, necessarily, raise interest rates at some point.

Are negatives used in the questions? Negatives are notoriously difficult to understand clearly, particularly where a sentence incorporates two or more. It is worth avoiding negatives in questions where possible, as they can lead to confusion. For instance, *'would you disagree that older people are not happy today?'* could easily lead to the question being misinterpreted. Again, piloting can help you avoid these mistakes.

Are you using memory questions? People often have problems remembering past events—and the past is always remembered for the purposes of the present. It is common practice not to ask respondents to try to recall anything beyond six months ago.

Is the language used appropriate? It is important that the language in a question is not prejudicial in any way. It should not cause any undue distress, be too informal, or too colloquial. The question should also be clear and easy to comprehend. Just because it is for an academic piece of work does not mean that you should use overly complicated language.

WORKING WITH YOUR SUPERVISOR 11.2

Ask your supervisor to look through your questionnaire before it is sent out to ensure they think it is clearly presented and the questions are appropriate. Remind them of your research questions and the topics you are specifically trying to address so they can get a sense of whether this is likely to be achieved.

Presenting a questionnaire

It is not just the questions themselves that you need to think critically about. The way a questionnaire is designed is also important in terms of response. Questionnaires which appear unprofessional, cramped, or sloppy will inevitably put people off responding. There are three key issues to consider when presenting your questionnaire: length, sequence, and layout. We'll deal with each one in turn.

Everyone has given up on a questionnaire because it was taking too long to fill out. It's logical to assume that there is an inverse relationship between questionnaire length and response rate; as questionnaires get longer, response rates decrease. Unfortunately, there are no set rules about the number of questions that will cause attrition. It will depend on the topic under investigation, how complex the questions are, and the time it takes to think about the answers. These considerations are a matter of judgement—and it is your job to decide how many questions to include and whether your respondents will run out of patience. Indeed, a voluminous questionnaire could cause your respondents to become fatigued and it could put people off people answering it altogether. Just like everyone else, respondents are likely to have a limited amount of time, and a limited attention span, both of which could affect the reliability of any items. It is probably better to guard against this possibility and exclude items that are not clearly related to your research questions.

You need to give careful consideration to the sequence in which questionnaire items are asked. This means thinking about the order of questions. Try to make them flow so they make sense. As a general rule, questionnaire items should not jump around from topic to topic, as you risk confusing the respondent. However, you also need to do this with some balance so that apathy doesn't set in. Therefore, placing similar items into sections can be a useful way of organizing your questionnaire so that it has a logical progression, but don't overdo it. When reflecting on the order of the questions it is important to recognize that the content of earlier questions could have the effect of 'priming' a participant's response to a later question. For instance, an earlier question related to the Fukushima nuclear disaster may impact on subsequent responses to questions about nuclear energy by already creating negative images in the participant's mind.

It's also a good idea to think about making the opening questions easier to answer than what follows. These early questions can set the tone for the survey and help your respondent get into the flow of answering. Starting with some straightforward demographic or descriptive questions will often help the respondent get into the habit of answering.

Additionally, if you need to ask respondents about difficult or uncomfortable topics, it is always worth attempting to develop some trust or rapport with the respondent before you present the questions. If you were interested in the relationship between debt and shame, for example, you might want to use a heading like this:

> In this next section of the survey, you will be asked about some potentially sensitive issues relating to your finances. Please remember that you do not have to answer any questions if you do not wish to do so.

It's also worth thinking about where to place your most important questions. If you leave them until the end, your respondents might be too tired to consider their answers in detail, or they may have already given up on the questionnaire altogether. On the other hand, if you introduce them too early in the questionnaire, the respondent might not yet feel comfortable answering them, especially if they concern a sensitive topic. There aren't always easy solutions to these problems. Piloting can help (as we will discuss shortly), but you will have to use your judgement.

FINDING YOUR WAY 11.3

Remember that ethics, including informed consent and protection of confidentiality, apply to the use of surveys. Respondents also need to be informed about the nature and purposes of the survey, who is sponsoring it, and how much time it will take to complete. Refer to Chapter 8 if you need a reminder.

It is also important to use a clear layout and consistent format in your questionnaire. Make sure you provide plenty of space so that people have room to write their responses and don't miss questions. Give clear instructions about when to tick, when to rank, and when to write or type. This will help when it comes to logging the data and undertaking the analysis.

Also be sure to introduce the questionnaire properly. This may take the form of a verbal introduction, a covering letter, or a preliminary note. You should indicate why they should answer your questionnaire and how the findings will be used. A clear statement about ethics, and ethical approval, should also be made, and don't forget to thank participants for their contribution!

Piloting a questionnaire

No matter how much time and effort you have put into developing your questionnaire, there is no real substitute for trying it out in the field with real participants. In fact, sometimes you can take the content for granted so you stop 'seeing' what is actually there. As a result, piloting is a crucial step in the process of developing a good questionnaire. This essentially means 'testing' your questionnaire out on a few willing volunteers to make sure that both the instructions and the questions 'make sense' to likely people of interest. You will want to pick up spelling and grammatical errors, but also any repetition or lack of clarity, and whether the questions are difficult to understand. Always be prepared to change any element of the questionnaire that is not clear. It is also important to pilot the covering letter you send with the questionnaire. Does this clearly explain the purposes of the survey and spell out the value of the research?

I WISH I'D KNOWN . . . THE BENEFITS OF PILOTING A QUESTIONNAIRE 11.3

"I wish I had known to run a pilot of my survey before deploying it publicly. There are questions I wish I had included and certain questions I wish I had rephrased so that they made more sense to my respondents."

— Jesse Hocking, student, BSc Criminology and Sociology, University of Surrey

As something of a guide, it is worth asking the following sorts of questions when piloting:

- Did you understand the information with the questionnaire and your rights as a participant?
- How long did the questionnaire take to complete?
- Were the instructions provided sufficiently clear?
- Were you in a position (able/willing) to answer all the questions? If you were not, specify which ones and why this was the case.
- Did you find any of the questions problematic to comprehend? If so, which questions and why?
- Do you think that there are any questions which are not currently included in the questionnaire that should be? If so, what might these be?
- Was the layout clear?
- Were the questions in an appropriate order?
- Any other comments?

This information will allow you to adapt the questionnaire if required prior to distributing it more widely.

ADMINISTERING YOUR QUESTIONNAIRE: PLATFORMS FOR DELIVERY AND ANALYSIS

Once you have piloted your questionnaire and made any necessary changes, it is now time to deliver it! Actually, you should have thought about this before designing it, but suffice it to say that there are various ways in which questionnaires can be administered. These include: email surveys or online surveys, postal surveys, household 'drop-off' surveys, and structured interviews. Each has strengths and weaknesses that need to be considered in order to identify the most appropriate method for your needs. We'll take each in turn.

Email surveys and online surveys

These types of surveys are frequently used in dissertations and are now much more common than the other methods of administering a questionnaire outlined here. In fact, I am sure you have all received plenty of emails asking you to complete a student survey of one kind or another! They are very inexpensive and allow for great flexibility in terms of design. Data is also automatically collected without the danger of transcription errors. They can reduce social desirability bias as people feel less compelled to answer questions in a self-enhancing way. However, they are also very easy to delete or ignore. There is also a concern around sampling and unequal access to the internet among certain groups, including older people and those on lower incomes.

There are a range of software programs that can be used to administer your questionnaire. Many enable you to design the survey to skip particular questions and present people with only the questions that are relevant to them. SurveyMonkey is probably the most popular online questionnaire tool, although Google Forms is increasingly used for dissertation research. Both enable users to create their own web-based surveys and can collect responses through web links, email, or social media. They have the added benefit of automatically tracking responses and displaying results.

Postal surveys

Postal surveys are particularly useful if your target sample do not have internet access. There are four main advantages to this type of delivery. In the first instance, postal surveys are relatively inexpensive to deliver. Second, they allow you to send the exact same questionnaire to a wide range of people. Third, the respondent can complete the survey at their own convenience. Fourth, they avoid issues of bias that can result from the interview process. It is also possible to cover a wide geographical base. All of these factors help to reduce the time and financial costs associated with travelling to interview people. Of course, there are also some disadvantages. Response rates from postal surveys are often very low, particularly where literacy may be an issue, and once distributed you have no understanding of the kinds of interpretations people make when answering the questions. Like online surveys, the layout, instructions, and questions must be extremely clear to ensure they are unambiguous and understood in the manner you intend. It is also not possible to observe the respondent's reactions to items of the questionnaire, or provide further clarification where it might be needed.

Household drop-off surveys

Relatively common in dissertation research, the household drop-off survey requires visiting the respondent to physically hand the questionnaire to them. In some cases, the respondent is asked to return the questionnaire by post; in others, the researcher returns to collect it. Like postal surveys, the respondent can answer the questions when it is convenient for them. Generally, this approach is more time-consuming than a postal survey, but you can expect to increase the response rate.

Structured interviews

A structured interview is quantitative in nature and differs from semi-structured and unstructured forms of qualitative interviewing where there is a much greater deal of flexibility in terms of question order and consistency of questions. In a

I WISH I'D KNOWN . . . HOW TO ENCOURAGE ADDITIONAL RESPONSES 11.4

When administering your questionnaire, you need to ensure you get enough responses. If you have not thought about how to recruit additional respondents, you could end up with a poorly constructed sample or insufficient data. This could delay the dissertation process. So developing strategies to encourage responses is a good idea. This might include a strong and persuasive cover letter, with follow-up emails or calls to encourage completion. You might also want to consider the use of a small incentive such as entering them into a prize draw (see Chapter 10).

structured interview, you work directly with the respondent either face-to-face or over the telephone. This personal component has both advantages and disadvantages. You are able to record the context of the interview if required, including any facial expressions, and unlike email and postal surveys, the interviewer has the opportunity to clarify questions. Structured interviews are also used with the longest and most complex questionnaires. However, this type of delivery tends to be very resource-intensive and quite time-consuming. Also be aware that aspects of your identity—such as your appearance, tone of voice, and manner—can affect the respondent's answers. Structured interviews tend to yield a higher response rate than other approaches, but this tends to come at a higher (time) cost depending on how many interviews are conducted. While telephone interviews are less resource-intensive, they can be problematic if you only have access to certain telephone numbers. It can also be a challenge to get people to respond positively and convince them you are not doing market research or selling them something!

PREPARING FOR ANALYSIS

The final consideration when deciding on how to deliver your questionnaire is to begin to make preparations for analysis. You need to plan how your analysis will look to ensure that your questionnaire will provide you with the material you need. This means thinking through how you will process your data. If you are using postal surveys, for example, you will need to think about how you will transcribe or log the data. If you are using email surveys, you will need to think about the forms of data that you can download. All of which requires piloting to make sure you can actually do what you think you can.

To this end, the process of preparing for analysis consists of three key elements: screening the data for accuracy, logging the data, and making data transformations.

When a respondent has completed a questionnaire, you should check that the data contained in it is accurate. This is particularly important when piloting your questionnaire as it allows you to go back to the respondent to clarify any problems or errors. There are several issues that you might want to look out for:

- Can you read all the responses?
- Is there any 'missing data'?
  - Have all the important questions been answered?
  - Are all the responses complete?
- Has all the contextual information you require been recorded?

The quality of your measurements will be crucial to your analysis and your research more generally. So taking the time to check your data to screen out any inaccuracies will help to improve the overall quality of your research.

It is also important to establish procedures for logging your data and keeping track of it until you are ready to carry out the analysis. To do this, you might record the data using a spreadsheet, such as Microsoft Excel or Google Sheets, or use statistical programs such as IBM SPSS. When entering the data, given that it is easier to analyse numeric data than a mixture of characters and letters, it is a good idea to try and code all of your data numerically. You will also have to keep a record of how, exactly, you have coded your data (see Chapter 13).

It is important when assigning codes that:

- there is no overlap—one code must not be used for more than one category
- the categories need to accommodate all possibilities—including missing data
- there are rules about how they have been applied to ensure consistency

It is almost always necessary to transform some of the data into variables that are easier to use in the analysis. This may involve collapsing data into categories. For instance, you may want to transform an income variable into ranges. This process of identifying and implementing appropriate categories will make it easier to analyse the data.

CONCLUSION

This chapter has outlined the process of collecting quantitative data. It has identified the different types of data, including primary and secondary data, and how these are both valuable in quantitative research. You have seen how to identify different levels of measurement and the importance of being able to construct variables at levels appropriate to your research aims. This has implications for the development of different types of questions in questionnaires. These are one of the most common forms of research design in dissertation projects. This chapter has shown how they should be developed or 'built' and the different approaches that can be employed to administer questionnaires. In doing so it has highlighted that careful planning and piloting of the questionnaire are likely to improve the quality of your project and result in the collection of data which can be analysed to address your research questions.

WHAT DO I NEED TO THINK ABOUT?

- Do you understand how the quantitative data collection fits with the rest of your dissertation?
- What are the benefits and limitations of using primary and secondary data collection in a dissertation?
- Are you clear about the difference between questions, concepts, variables, and data and why these are important in the process of collecting data?
- What is the most effective way to administer your questionnaire?
- Do you know how to prepare the data you have collected for analysis?

WHAT DO I NEED TO DO?

- Decide whether you are using primary or secondary data in your dissertation project.
- Ensure your data collection clearly links to the rest of your dissertation.
- Develop a carefully constructed questionnaire bearing in mind how the different levels of measurement affect the analysis.
- Decide on the most appropriate way to administer your questionnaire and collect your data.
- Prepare your data for analysis.

Access the online resources **www.oup.com/uk/brymansrple** to help you to successfully complete your social research project or dissertation.

DELVE DEEPER

> **Blair, J., Czaja, R. and Blair, E. (2014).** *Designing Surveys: A Guide to Decisions and Procedures.* **London: Pine Forge.** If you are looking for a book which covers the whole survey research process, this is one of the most comprehensive available. It is presented in an accessible format using a timeline in relation to survey research. This includes steps involved in preparing for, designing, and implementing survey research. It will not only help you to conduct your own survey in your dissertation but also to assess surveys done by others.
>
> **De Vaus, D. (2013).** *Surveys in Social Research* **(6th edition). London: Routledge.** This long-established classic text does a useful job of demystifying the survey research process by breaking it down into manageable components. It emphasizes the links between theory and research, the

logic and interpretation of statistics, and the practices of social research. It provides an excellent comprehensive account for those wanting to know more about the use of surveys in social research.

Olsen, W. (2012). *Data Collection: Key Debates and Methods in Social Research.* **London: Sage.** This book provides an introduction to key practical methods needed for data collection through the use of interdisciplinary examples from around the world. While it focuses on all forms of data collection, it has specific chapters on experimental and systematic data collection and survey methods.

Oppenheim, A. (2000). *Questionnaire Design, Interviewing and Attitude Measurement.* **London: Continuum.** This classic text provides considerable guidance about survey design, including extensive details about how to develop questionnaire wording and plan to carry surveys out. It is an excellent source of information if you want to develop a questionnaire in your dissertation or know more about measuring attitudes.

Sapsford, R. (2007). *Survey Research.* **London: Sage.** The central message of this book is that theory, technique, and practical application are not separable when it comes to doing or thinking about research. Echoing key principles of this chapter, it takes you through the research process when using surveys. It carefully covers the process of collecting data. It is useful and informative if you want to develop a survey.

Smith, E. (2008). *Using Secondary Data in Educational and Social Research.* **Maidenhead: Open University Press.** This book focuses on collecting and using secondary data in social and educational research. It is excellent for those of you who are new to the field of secondary data analysis. It includes practical strategies for locating and assessing potential data sets. Another of its strengths is in providing guidance on accessing, managing, and preparing large data sets for analysis.

SurveyMonkey is probably the most popular online questionnaire tool, although Google Forms and Survey Gizmo are also worth considering if you are developing a survey in your dissertation. SurveyMonkey provides free, customizable surveys and data representation tools. It includes more extensive paid options too, that some students may consider.
https://www.surveymonkey.com/ (Accessed 5 May 2013)

Vartanian, T. (2010). *Secondary Data Analysis.* **Oxford: Oxford University Press.** For those who want to know more about secondary data and its application this pocket guide is really useful. It provides information about a variety of secondary data sets in the social sciences. It offers an insight into understanding data sets and how they can be used in research on clinical and policy research.

SOURCES OF SECONDARY DATA

1. The **British Social Attitudes Information System** offers data from the annual British Social Attitudes survey, which tracks the social, political, and moral attitudes of people living in Britain.
http://www.britsocat.com (Accessed 12 November 2018)

2. The **British Household Panel Survey** contains data from a representative sample of individuals over a number of years.
https://www.iser.essex.ac.uk/bhps/ (Accessed 7 May 2019)

3. The **Higher Education Statistics Agency** (HESA) publishes data on all aspects of the UK higher education sector.
https://www.hesa.ac.uk/data-and-analysis (Accessed 12 November 2018)

4. **Eurostat** is the statistical office of the European Union, which provides high-quality statistics for Europe. Eurostat provides a myriad of data that allow cross-European analysis in a number of key areas, enabling comparisons between countries and regions.
https://ec.europa.eu/eurostat/web/main/home/ (Accessed 7 May 2019)

5. The **International Monetary Fund (IMF)** offers a range of time series data on topics such as IMF lending, exchange rates, and other economic and financial indicators for analysis through the IMF.
https://www.imf.org/en/Data (Accessed 5 October 2018)

6. **The Organisation for Economic Co-operation and Development (OECD)** provides statistical information about its 36 members on a variety of topics.
http://www.oecd.org/statistics/ (Accessed 5 October 2018)

7. **United Kingdom Data Service Nesstar pages** provide a useful starting point for those of you who want to undertake secondary data analysis using a UK data set. It provides valuable information about a number of surveys, the sample size, and the questions asked. There is also the possibility of exploring some of the data sets without having to download them.
https://www.ukdataservice.ac.uk/get-data/explore-online/nesstar/nesstar (Accessed 12 November 2018)

8. **The United Nations Statistics Division** compiles global statistical information which can be used to explore comparative statistical analysis.
https://unstats.un.org/home/ (Accessed 5 October 2018)

9. **The World Bank** hosts numerous data sets and other resources. It also contains collections of time series data on a variety of topics that could be used in your dissertation.
https://data.worldbank.org/ (Accessed 5 August 2016)

10. The **Yale University Library** curates a list of databases that can be used for the purposes of dissertation-style research. Providing links to statistical and data resources, some are country- or region-specific, whereas others are international resources. This is a useful place to access data sets. *https://guides.library.yale.edu/data-statistics/general-data-resources (Accessed 5 October 2018)*

CHAPTER 12

COLLECTING
QUALITATIVE DATA

WHAT DO I NEED TO KNOW?

- Qualitative interviews
  - Types of qualitative interview
  - Planning a qualitative interview
  - Conducting a qualitative interview
- Participant observation
  - Situating participant observation
    - Gaining access
    - Insider or outsider?
    - Research roles
  - Doing participant observation
  - Writing field notes

INTRODUCTION

While we are all familiar with the idea of interviewing and observing, actually collecting qualitative data is not as easy as it might first appear to be. In fact, when doing qualitative work, it is easy to become overwhelmed by the amount of information you collect, and your research can quickly grind to an uncomfortable halt. But with some purposeful planning, piloting, and practice, you can avoid some of the pitfalls associated with qualitative data collection. Focusing on qualitative interviewing and participant observation, this chapter will introduce you to some of the common issues that arise when gathering qualitative data and offer useful advice concerning the planning and practice of collecting data 'in the field'.

QUALITATIVE INTERVIEWS

Qualitative interviews attempt to generate data about how people understand and experience particular aspects of the human world. They are usually directed toward topics that are not easy to measure or observe directly, and are often used to respond to research aims and objectives that begin with 'how' and 'why'. It is, perhaps, the most popular method of data collection for the purposes of dissertation research because interviews can be directed toward almost every aspect of the human world. This makes them useful across the breadth of the social sciences.

Rather than being a fixed question/response exchange, qualitative interviews can be thought of as a guided conversation that is participant-led. The interpersonal nature of the engagement also means that rapport is an important dynamic in the relationship between interviewer and interviewee. The information-rich data that interviews can produce—usually in the form of a written interview transcript—are particularly suited to generating theory. Interviews also tend to be very good for projects where the people of interest are not usually heard from or where not much is known about the topic.

Types of qualitative interview

Generally speaking, there are four overarching types of qualitative interview: the structured interview; the semi-structured interview; the unstructured interview; and the focus group.

The emphasis for 'structure' in the structured interview is usually on the question rather than the answer (see Chapter 11). Questions are usually fixed in that all respondents work through them in exactly the same way, but the answers to those question are left 'open'. This type of approach is typically seen in online surveys that include open boxes in which participants type their answers. However, the technique can be used in interpersonal contexts too. Structured interviews tend to aid reliability and can be used to tightly define the content of the interview. This can aid comparability across data too. However, this can come at the cost of flexibility, and a structured approach can place constraints on the capacity of the interviewer to change course according to the needs of the interview.

In comparison, semi-structured interviews are more open with respect to the flow of questions, and the conversation is much more dynamic. A series of potential topics are identified and explored in a manner that is responsive to the purpose of the interview **and** the needs of the interviewee. Using this format can be quite challenging because it requires planning, listening, and adapting on behalf of the interviewer—and often all at once. They need to manage the interview based on the demands of the interview schedule **and** the emergent detail of the conversation. This requires them to be well informed but not 'leading', and flexible without straying too far from purpose. This takes a reasonable level of social and technical skill, and often requires some practice.

I WISH I'D KNOWN . . . ABOUT PHOTO ELICITATION 12.1

Photo elicitation is the practice of using photos as a prompt in the context of an interview. Participants are often given a camera beforehand and asked to take pictures of what they consider significant in relation to the aims of the research. This material is then produced in the context of the interview, with participants invited to talk about the significance of the pictures they have taken. The process can easily be adapted for use with other objects of interest.

Unstructured interviews are typically used in conjunction with oral life history, and narrative and biographical research. They are very open in respect to theme, question, and response. Often only the briefest of direction is offered to the participant, who then responds on almost entirely their own terms. This makes unstructured interviews very flexible in terms of content, but this responsiveness comes at the cost of reliability. Data can be wide-ranging and difficult to compare across the sample, with the interviewee also needing to have the confidence to shape the interview space.

Historically, focus groups have been associated with market research and they were first introduced into the social sciences by Paul Lazarsfeld and Robert Merton to help contextualize survey data. They are popular in media studies—audience studies particularly—but are also common in political studies, evaluation research, and organizational research. This is largely because the focus of a focus group is the group, not the individuals themselves. Focus groups offer a distinct method of generating data on the basis of group interaction and discussion. There is a subtle, but strong, assumption that opinions and attitudes are shaped within and through interaction with others. This means that focus groups are particularly appropriate where social process and group context is important in the formulation of a research rationale. Focus groups should not typically be used as group interviews designed to efficiently increase sample size.

Like the vast majority of qualitative research, potential members of focus groups should be purposively selected according to the needs of the research aims and objectives. That said, focus groups tend to be marked by either heterogeneity of homogeneity. That is, broad characteristics are used to select people who are unfamiliar with the topic and/or each other, or people are chosen because they are similar in some way. Focus groups can also be structured or semi-structured. However, they can also be task-based, or involve some sort of sensory stimuli, where photos, video clips, adverts, or vignettes are used to elicit discussion.

FINDING YOUR WAY 12.1

Running a focus group can be difficult; it is definitely not an easy way out! The role of the interviewer includes:

- facilitating interaction and discussion
- enabling contribution
- focusing discussion
- controlling dominant discussants
- controlling flow of discussion

It can be particularly difficult to manage 'polyphonic conversations', particularly where there are dominant actors in the group. If you are using this method, be prepared to manage the conversation and, where necessary, direct it toward other voices. This will help the balance of your data.

Planning a qualitative interview

Regardless of type, there are a number of steps involved in planning an interview. The first thing to do is to ask yourself what it is, exactly, that is puzzling you about your topic of research. This will help you to frame your planning because it creates a clear goal for the interview process. Once you've done this, you will need to use your research aims and objectives and generate some broad topics of interest. Think about what you need to know in order to respond to these objectives. Write your answers down in a list and you will have the beginnings of an interview schedule.

An interview schedule is simply a guide to the interview. It provides a framework that will inform the content and direction of the interview. Although it appears relatively 'fixed' on paper, it can actually be a dynamic tool that can vary both within and between interviews. So, if you are working in a semi-structured or an unstructured format, you do not need to follow it exactly, in the interview or in the future. Interview schedules often change over time as you refine your research focus.

Interview schedules are typically made up of themes, questions, and probes. You should already have a broad outline of your themes: now you need to formulate questions associated with those themes. But before doing that, it is worth highlighting that there are different ways to ask a question—and different types of question produce different types of information. The types of question generally associated with qualitative interview schedules are listed in Table 12.1. This is why it is important to think carefully about what you want to find out. It will enable you to see the type of information you want with more clarity, and allow you to choose the type of question that will best allow you to generate that data.

Interview questions are typically accompanied by probes. These act as planned prompts that are designed to elicit further material. They might take the form of a question, but probes can also be pre-identified areas of interest that help to direct participants towards particular issues or ideas. They are especially useful in

Table 12.1 **Types of interview question**

Types of interview question	Example . . .
Detail-oriented	'What happened . . . ?'
Invitation-oriented	'How do you think . . . ?'
Challenge	'But earlier you said . . . ?'
Amplification	'Can you tell me more about . . . ?'
Explanatory	'How does that work . . . ?'
Category	'How is that different to . . . ?'
Significance	'Why is that important . . . ?'

preventing the interviewee from getting 'stuck'. They can also be used to try and get an interviewee to talk about something in more detail.

When designing probes, it is often a good idea to ask yourself the question you have designed and imagine how you might answer it. As a general rule of thumb, if a question can be answered with a 'yes' or a 'no', it will be. For example, there is a very subtle, but crucial, difference in the questions 'what do you think?' and 'do you think?' The first requires elaboration, the second only agreement or disagreement. If you are in danger of asking a question that has a binary answer, be sure to design some probes that will help you to generate further material. Generally speaking, the more your interviewee talks, the better the interview.

Once you have developed your interview schedule, the time has come to try and pilot it. This is a crucial stage in the process as it will demonstrate the sort of data that your schedule will produce, but also where there might be problems with how participants interpret the questions. Where possible, it is often a very good idea to pilot the interview schedule with two or three people as it will help you to spot patterns in their responses and where further development of the schedule is necessary. If you do not have ready access to your sample, or do not want to 'waste' an interviewee on the pilot, it is worth trying the schedule with a friend. They will at least be able to offer some feedback on whether the questions/probes make sense or not.

FINDING YOUR WAY 12.2

Figure 12.1 is an example of an interview schedule that was designed to explore the learning experiences of higher education students at the end of their first year at university. We've added an accompanying commentary to explain the purposes of the questions.

Conducting a qualitative interview

When you have completed your pilot, the time has nearly come to actually conduct the interview! But don't go rushing into things—there are still a few important things you need to do before the actual interview takes place. Firstly, you need to consider where the interview takes place, and context does really matter. In some cases, you might actually be led by the needs and requirements of the interviewee, but try to think about how power relations, formality, noise, and interruptions might help to shape the nature of the interview. Secondly, you will need to check your equipment works, and that you are comfortable using it so that it does not intrude on the interview. If you are using an audio recording device, it is worth experimenting with the placement of the microphone and learning about

Figure 12.1 An example interview schedule

Interview schedule	Commentary
Remember to make sure the respondent understands the purpose of the study, what will happen to their data, and confirm that they are happy to participate by asking them to sign the consent form	
[demographic detail] Age Gender Subject studied Date	This is general demographic detail to help contextualize the data. It is also material that may help reveal patterns in the data.
[university life] So, how are you finding life at university?	This is an introductory question that is invitation/detail-oriented. It is designed to make the interviewee comfortable. These sorts of questions should be relatively easy to answer in some detail as they are deliberately directed toward personal experience.
[decision-making process] Can you describe the process by which you came to be here? • Background: family, school, friends • When did you decide to come? • Why did you decide to come? • What sorts of things influenced your decision to come to this university in particular? • What do you hope to achieve while here?	This is another invitation/detail-oriented question. It is accompanied by a series of probes that are designed to explore specific areas of interest. They allow the interviewer to pursue material that might be missed by the interviewee if they are not specifically highlighted.
[expectations vs reality] So, is it different from what you expected?	This is a category question that is largely designed to get the interviewee 'in the mood' for talking. While it might provide some useful avenues for further investigation, it also helps to introduce the topics that follow.
[first impressions] Looking back, what were your first impressions of the university?	Another invitation/detail-oriented question. This one is designed to elicit general material with more specific topics of interest to follow.
[early learning experiences] What were your first lectures/seminars like? • How did they compare with what you were used to?	The first question here is an invitation/detail-oriented question, with the follow-up designed as an explanatory category question. In combination they are designed to 'tease out' similarities and differences in styles of teaching and learning between further education and higher education.

(Continued)

Figure 12.1 (*Continued*)

Interview schedule	Commentary
[early assessment experiences] How did you find your first assessments? • What sort of help did you get? • How would you do things differently if you were us?	An explanatory question first, followed by a detail-oriented and another explanatory one. Like the previous question they are designed to tease out differences between further and higher education, but are worded in a way that helps to prevent repetition.
[academic workload] How are you finding the workload? • How does it compare to what you expected?	Explanatory question, followed by an explanatory/category question. Category questions are useful in providing contrast. That is, they allow the interviewee to articulate something with more clarity by stating, in part, what it is not like. Also, notice how this is not phrased as 'is it more or less than you expected?' as this would invite a short answer. Instead, this question allows the interviewee the space to fill as they see fit.
[time management] What techniques do you use to help you manage your time? • Diary/Google Calendar • Routine Why do you find these techniques useful?	Detail-oriented, with some additional probes/areas of interest, followed by a significance prompt. It's also worth noting that the focus is still on the interviewee: the questions are directed toward how they think and feel.
[facilities] What do you think of the facilities at the University of Sheffield? • Union • Entertainment • Sport • Societies • Shops • Department • Teaching spaces • Library • Sports facilities	Invitation/detail-oriented question followed by a list of probes that are essentially areas of interest. It should be noted that these could take some time to get through and flexibility to develop the interview as appropriate would be essential here.

Remember to thank them for their time, remind them what will happen to the data, and confirm whether they are happy to be contacted about the project in the future.

the limits of the technology that you are using. You need to ensure it is fully charged and has sufficient battery life. This is particularly important with focus groups or if you are planning to conduct the interview where background noise might be intrusive.

FINDING YOUR WAY 12.3

There are different ways to record the data associated with qualitative interviews. In some cases, how you choose to record the data might actually depend on the participant or the research topic/questions. Recording options include:

- video recording
- audio recording
- 'shorthand' notes during the interview
- notes immediately after the interview

You should try to think about the impact that your chosen method has on the interview situation and how surroundings may impact on recordings (light, sound intrusion, interruption etc). But also consider the quality of the data. Audio recording is preferable as it provides a concrete record of what actually occurred—and many smartphones are now equipped with very usable recording technology. If you are conducting your interview over the telephone, it is possible to buy relatively inexpensive adapters that can be fitted to the handset connection to facilitate recording. It is also worth highlighting that you should confirm that the interviewee is happy to be recorded. This cannot always be taken for granted.

There are also some specific issues that you might want to consider during the interview:

- Sort out issues of ethics at the start of the interview (see Chapter 8).
- Check how much time the interviewee has available, and try to give them an indication of how long the interview will take.
- Begin with unthreatening questions. Basic, factual questions that the participant will find easier to answer will get the interview flowing in the right direction.
- Don't disagree with your interviewee, unless you have good reason. If you are going to ask questions that you suspect will be more challenging, it is often better to place them toward the end of the interview.
- Be patient with your questioning—try not to be too pushy.
- Try to build rapport by adopting a reassuring, supportive and interested tone.
- Depending on the type of interview you are conducting, you might not ask all the questions on your interview schedule.

- Be prepared to return to a theme if you want to explore it further.
- Try not to participate in the exchange too much. Only do so carefully and reflectively, and remember that the emphasis is on them not you.

I WISH I'D KNOWN . . . HOW TO DEAL WITH SILENCE 12.2

How you deal with silence in the context of an interview will largely dictate how your interviewee will deal with it. People often need time to think when they have been asked a question, so be prepared to let your interviewee collect their thoughts where necessary. However, you do need to be able to tell the difference between someone who is struggling with the question, and someone who is thinking about their answer. Only interrupt the silence if you think they are having difficulty understanding the question. Their body language can be a key indicator that the question needs rephrasing or clarifying.

Once you have finished the interview, thanked the interviewee for their time, and reminded them about what will happen to their data, there are still some things to do immediately after you've said goodbye.

Firstly, check the recording has worked. If it has not—and don't worry, this happens to everyone at some point—try to quickly write down any important issues that emerged. This will, at least, preserve something from the interview. Secondly, make notes on anything that you were unable to record, or any immediate ideas or thoughts that might be worth developing further. Third, try to transcribe the interview fully while it is still fresh in your mind. This will help you to make sure you interpret the conversation appropriately and aid the quality of the transcription.

FINDING YOUR WAY 12.4

Take the time to reflect on how your interview went. Think about the sorts of information that your questions produced, and how your phrasing of particular questions either facilitated or constrained the exchange. Remember that the interview schedule can be a dynamic tool, so be prepared to change it where necessary.

Transcribing the interview is very important as this is what functions as data for analysis. Unfortunately, there is no uniform manner in which to transcribe a qualitative interview—and you will need to make decisions on how you transform the recording into a transcription. The spoken word does not always lend itself to the written word. That is to say, how we actually talk is not exactly the

I WISH I'D KNOWN . . . HOW TO TRANSCRIBE A FOCUS GROUP | 2.3

Transcribing focus group data can be particularly tricky because you need to retain a sense of who is speaking. It is often a good idea to get each person to introduce themselves at the beginning as it will help you to clearly identify each voice. Given the nature of the focus group, you are also likely to have to pay more attention in recording the dynamics of group interaction. Taking notes during the focus group is one way of doing this—particularly if you make a note of the time. Also be prepared to 'step outside' of the transcription and insert descriptive points of interest about those dynamics where necessary.

same as how we might write, so you will have to choose how to best represent the essence of **what** was said and **how** it was said.

The process of transcription does take a lot of time, and hearing the sound of your own voice can sometimes feel awkward. However, it does help you to develop a familiarity with data. Not only will it consolidate your knowledge of what your interviewees said, and how they said it, but transcribing offers you the opportunity to reflect on the nature of the interview and helps you generate avenues for further investigation. You may also find that working with textual data can help generate ideas for analysis.

PARTICIPANT OBSERVATION

Participant observation is directed toward capturing the rich detail and diversity of experience that occurs 'out there' in the human world. As the name might imply, it involves both participating in, and observing, everyday and/or professional life **as it happens**. Although the terms are often used interchangeably, participant observation tends to refer to the practice of actually collecting data while ethnography is the written product that emerges from that process.

The practice of participant observation was first used by anthropologists who were studying 'exotic' cultures. However, it was adapted by sociologists who began to use the method to study their own environments and it is now widely used across the social sciences. 'Fieldwork' tends to take place over a considerable length of time, with the focus for investigation being a particular place, a particular group of people, a particular organization, or even a particular event. Data collection usually takes the form of the researcher writing field notes, which are then used as a focus for analysis—and when you actually do participant observation for the first time you quickly become aware of the complexity that happens around you all the time.

FINDING YOUR WAY 12.5

The requirements of both access and time spent in the field mean that a full-scale ethnography is often difficult to achieve in the context of a dissertation project. However, micro-ethnographies are possible. Typically, this involves working in the field over a much shorter period of time on a much more specific topic. This might involve working in an organization regularly on a particular afternoon over a few months, or spending a more concentrated burst of time at a particular venue or event.

The inherent richness of participant observation can be demonstrated through a simple thought experiment. Sit quietly in your current location and simply try to focus on all the things that you are sensing. Consider all the visual information that you're picking up as you just sit in a room, all the different arrays of colour and the dynamics of depth that you can perceive. Then think about all the sensations of heat that envelop you; think about the sensations of smell; think about your sensations of movement; and, of course, all the things that you can hear.

Now try to think about how you might describe some of that detail by attempting to put it into words. For example, try to describe the smell of the room you are sitting in—what does it smell like? What does it feel like?

The point of this thought experiment is to demonstrate that the world is full of sensory information—we just choose to ignore it most of the time. We attune to bits of it at certain points, but we screen out most of it. Participant observation is the attempt to re-attune ourselves to that material and use it to explore everyday and/or professional lives.

This is what you are attempting to do when writing field notes, and it actually isn't a very easy thing to do, for two reasons. Firstly, sometimes the words in a particular language do not actually describe some things very well, and secondly, there is simply so much going on! Writing down 'what is happening' is actually quite a skilled task, and when conducting work in the field you can't just say 'hold on a minute, can everyone just stop doing things because I need to write these notes down!' Life will carry on regardless, and you've got to try and think about strategies to capture what is happening around you.

I WISH I'D KNOWN . . . ABOUT "NETNOGRAPHY" 12.4

Netnography is a form of participant observation that is conducted online. It is an ethnographic approach to virtual phenomena that heavily relies on observation, but it can also be supported by online interviews and other forms of data collection. It is particularly useful for the investigation of communities that exist exclusively on the web, but it also recognizes the interaction between online and offline worlds. It is sometimes referred to as 'virtual ethnography', 'webnography', or 'online ethnography'.

Situating participant observation

There are any number of sites where you can actually carry out participant observation—all you need is people. Typically, it will involve visiting that field site and observing what is happening and perhaps participating to some degree. It can also involve talking with the people you meet there, whether formally in an interview format, or informally as a conversation. You can even draw on documents produced by different groups or different organizations for the purposes of ethnographic work.

The idea of both place and people is actually a little more flexible than you might first imagine too. Networks of individuals that exist online can be the focus for an ethnography, as can large-scale multiplayer online role-playing games.

I WISH I'D KNOWN . . . ABOUT VISUAL ETHNOGRAPHY 12.5

Visual ethnography uses photographs, films, and associated digital material to capture the rich experience of social life. It is almost always supported by other techniques of data collection such as observation and interviewing, but visual ethnography emphasizes the role of visual culture in everyday and professional life. It can be particularly useful to employ in dissertations.

However, there are particular features of the field that can help to shape the nature of your engagement with it. Issues of gaining access are concerned with whether the site is open or closed, and the extent to which you are afforded physical or social access. There is also the issue of how you act in the field, including whether you are an insider or an outsider, whether you operate in an overt or covert manner, and your associated research role. We'll examine each in turn.

Gaining access

We've already covered the issue of gatekeepers in Chapter 10, but there are specific issues of access in participant observation that are worth exploring in some detail. Firstly, there is a key distinction to make between an open space and a closed one—and, in practice, this places large constraints on what sorts of participant observation might be possible for dissertation-style research. Closed settings are those that require proprietary access and have substantial barriers to prevent outsiders from entering. These barriers can be physical, bureaucratic, or social. As a result, these settings are private rather than public. Examples of closed settings include social service departments, educational institutions, and private organizations. Open settings, on the other hand, have few barriers and are relatively open to access for outsiders. Public places such as parks or sports arenas can be considered open settings as there are few restrictions on those who wish to participate. For instance, a shopping precinct is a space that is open to the public. People can, by and large, come and go freely as they please. You don't need permission to go shopping and permission to enter is not required.

While the distinction between open and closed settings is analytically useful, this is also somewhat context-dependent. To return to the example of a shopping centre, whilst it may be relatively open, access to a particular shop and the staff cultures that may exist there may be much more closed.

In practice, differences in the nature of the setting constrain what you might be able to observe and participate in. Therefore, you need to consider how likely you are to receive permission to enter the field site, who you need to ask, and what you might need to do to access it. This includes thinking about the ethical requirements that might be associated with doing fieldwork. In some cases, these requirements will be very well drawn by the research host; in other cases, you will need to make decisions about how to act in an ethical manner, particularly where informed consent is concerned. Where these demands are high, you will need to factor this into your wider research plan (see Chapter 8 for further discussion).

There are, however, further considerations when you do actually access your fieldwork site. In the first instance, you need to be aware of the difference between physical access and social access. Physical access refers to the ability to make contact with the field; social access is concerned with gaining acceptance within the research group itself. Unfortunately, physical access does not ensure social access, and having material contact with a group is not the same as being accepted by it. Trust, rapport, and credibility are all frequently highlighted as being important in facilitating social access. In part, this is exactly why ethnographies take such a long time. Relationships in the field need cultivating and developing.

Insider or outsider?

This issue of your social status in relation to the field is frequently described as being an insider or outsider. This consideration leads to the related epistemological problem of 'other minds'. The first concern is directed toward your conceptual affinity to the field in terms of your understanding and values. This might involve closeness or distance—and both have opportunities and challenges. You might, for example, think that 'being one' is neither necessary nor sufficient to understand others and distance can better facilitate the knowing of others. Your outsider status will enable you to see things that are taken for granted within your field site, and you might be able to find different explanations to commonly held assumptions. Fieldwork is not necessarily about reproducing accepted understandings.

But, although distance can be a useful thing, so can closeness, particularly if you are working **with** a particular group. Supportive research outcomes are difficult to achieve by maintaining 'objective distance'. Ethnographic work also often involves moving from the 'front stage' of a field and into its 'backstage'. What is staged in the 'shop front', for example, is often quite different from what happens in the stock room. Developing some insider knowledge is crucial to getting past the surface veneer of the field, and penetrating the backstage can help to reveal some of the discrepancies between official representations and unofficial ones. Some insider status can, therefore, uncover the gaps between external claims and internal realities, public rhetoric and private thought, and differences between ideology and practice. Gaining some closeness, some 'insider' knowledge, is likely to be crucial to this process.

These concerns are closely related to what is often termed 'the problem of other minds'. This is a weighty epistemological issue that is concerned with the question 'can we ever "know" someone else?' The philosopher Thomas Nagel (1974) used an interesting thought experiment to illustrate the point—he asks us to simply 'imagine what it's like to be bat'. The answer, at least for Nagel, is that you can never imagine what it is like to be a bat, because it will always be you imagining what it is like to be a bat—this is necessarily not what it is like to be a bat because you are not one. Besides, even in the unlikely event that you did manage to imagine what it was like, there would be no way we could ever confirm that your experience matched that of a bat. Not everyone agrees with Nagel's conclusion, but the experiment does demonstrate some of the difficulty associated with trying to overcome your subjective position to see the world from a view that is not your own. To some extent, research will always be your stories of other people's stories.

For some social scientists, particularly in the fields of gender, ethnicity, and disability, the answer to the question 'do you have to be one to know one' is an unequivocal 'yes'. These 'standpoint theorists' argue that as females, non-white (or non-western), or disabled people they are necessarily different from wider society. Their experiences of society and their resulting knowledge of it are fundamentally and essentially not the same as those in other areas of society (namely male, white, non-disabled). Therefore, the knowledge that these groups have is not only different from wider society, but at the most radical position, essentially unknowable to those outside.

Research roles

The success of your fieldwork is almost entirely dependent on you and your relationship with the field. However, there are many different roles that you can undertake during your time in the field that will ultimately shape the data that you collect. These range from just observing to fully participating, and everything in-between.

At the most basic level, you will need to choose whether you will take an overt or covert role. Overt methods are those in which the researcher makes themselves known as a researcher to those engaged in the research process. Covert methods, on the other hand, are those in which the researcher identity is not revealed to those the researcher is investigating.

WORKING WITH YOUR SUPERVISOR | 2.1

In practice, the ethical requirement for informed consent means that the vast majority of dissertation research that makes use of participant observation is overt in nature (see Chapter 8). However, there are instances where a more covert role is permissible. Sometimes gaining consent from everyone in a field site is simply not practical. There are also some instances where acting overtly would invalidate the research. It is always best to consult with your supervisor about the relationship between ethics and the role you want to take in the field.

In a classic paper entitled 'roles in sociological field observations', Gold (1954) introduced a basic typology of fieldwork roles. These include: the complete observer; the observer as participant; the participant as observer; and the complete participant.

The complete observer is sometimes referred to as a 'veranda-style' approach to participant observation. This is a term that is derived from the anthropological practice of observing exotic cultures solely from the position of the veranda! It involves very little interaction with the people at the field site. Typically, the observer remains unknown to those that they are observing and instead operates by 'systematically eavesdropping'. This includes both listening to and observing people as they go about their daily lives. This type of role often occurs when working in open, public settings where it would impractical to gain informed consent. It is also common in the earlier parts of participant observation where familiarization with the field is the main goal. The distance between observer and observed also means that the chances of 'going native' are small. 'Going native' is said to occur where the researcher uncritically accepts the position of people in the field. However, while the complete observer is unlikely to 'go native', they are also in danger of misunderstanding the field because they, by and large, remain completely outside of it.

The 'observer as participant' can be thought of as an 'on-the-spot' reporter. The research is usually conducted overtly and requires some observation, with points of formal clarification coming in the form of interviews. Contact with informants tends to be both brief and relatively impersonal. This serves to keep some distance between the observer and the field, with engagement coming only where necessary. Again, there is little danger of the fieldworker 'going native' in such a role, but this comes at the cost of understanding. Indeed, Gold (1954) argues that misunderstandings are most likely when operating in this way. This is because the observer comes into contact with more varieties of people, but with insufficient time to fully appreciate their perspective.

The 'participant as observer' operates in an overt, but personal manner. They develop relationships with informants over time and are likely to do more participating than observing. More formal interactions tend to take place toward the start

FINDING YOUR WAY 12.6

When working in an overt role, there are also a number of approaches that you can adopt with respect to the research relationships you develop in the field. The naive student, the advocate or sympathizer, the underdog researcher, the professional, or even the mascot are all commonly cited in the literature.

of fieldwork, with social access being achieved as the people in the field begin to trust the researcher. Gold argues that over-identification with informants is a danger when operating in this role because the lines between stranger and friend become blurred. Therefore, some effort needs to be directed toward reflecting on the nature of relationships as and when they develop.

The final role is that of 'complete participant'. This occurs when the researcher is operating covertly in a setting, but is fully immersed in it. Typically, this approach requires 'role pretence' as there is usually a requirement for the researcher to have some apparent purpose for the people in the field. They might, for example, be working in the setting, or engaging with it in some other capacity, perhaps as a member of a particular fandom culture or as a volunteer. This type of role is often difficult to achieve in the context of dissertation research because of issues around ethics, and deception specifically, but also because of the time needed to fully access such sites. That is not to say this approach is impossible, but it is relatively infrequent (see Chapter 8 for further discussion).

I WISH I'D KNOWN . . . WHAT A 'BREACHING EXPERIMENT' IS 12.6

A breaching experiment is a form of ethnographic encounter that is directed toward understanding the social norms that shape everyday life. Originally conceived by Harold Garfinkel, they are specifically designed to breach social convention (Garfinkel, 1984). This involved asking his students to do various breaching tasks and observe the consequences. This included: treating their home as a hotel; deliberately not trusting the 'other' in a particular conversation; haggling; rubbing out a competitor's move in a game of noughts and crosses; and, invading 'personal space' during a random conversation. Breaching experiments often reveal how social forces help to shape the nature of interactions.

Doing participant observation

Generally speaking, fieldwork is an inductive process. Theory is generated from data and ethnographers typically try to avoid making too many presumptions about what they expect to find before they enter the field. This means that ethnographic work is an iterative process of development that requires fieldworkers to refine observations, ideas, and analyses with time and experience.

However, while fieldwork is inductive, it isn't blind, and before entering the field some effort needs to be made to become sensitive to issues of potential interest. Of course, you cannot know beforehand what you will encounter, but if you attempt to conduct fieldwork without having thought carefully about what you will be exploring in more detail, you will not be seeing much or will quickly become overwhelmed by the data. All of which is to say that you need to identify your frames of interest.

Frames of interest are basically a schedule of things that you might look for in the field—and although people often forget this principle, you do actually have to design observation. These designs are quite loose, and very flexible, but you do plan fieldwork, and this is exactly what identifying your frames of interest will help you to do.

Spradley (1980) offers a useful account of the things that can be used to help frame your fieldwork. These include:

- Space: the physical place
- Actors: the people
- Acts: single actions that people do
- Activities: the things they do
- Events: a set of related activities that people carry out
- Goals: the things that people are trying to accomplish
- Objects: things that are present
- Time: the sequencing of events
- Feelings: the emotions that are expressed

In the first instance, you might want to examine the environment you are working in. That is, how spaces are transformed into places by people. This might include asking questions about how the physical space is arranged and how those arrangements shape interactions. Then there are the actors who actually move about within those places. These are the people that constitute the field: who they are, what they look like, what kind of demographic characteristics they possess, and, of course, how they interact.

An act is a single unit of action undertaken by an actor. It might involve someone talking with someone else, or doing a very particular thing. However, acts are often used in conjunction with one another to produce activities. These are the more complex things that actors do both as individuals and groups, with attention being paid to the detail of action and behaviours in a setting. Although we often take it for granted, people usually do very specific things in particular ways. By deliberately focusing our attention on what people do in a general series of actions, we can begin to understand what ethnographer Richard Jenkins (2014) has termed 'who's who and what's what'.

Events are even larger sequences of related activities that people carry out, often involving different actors who are connected and working together. They are often considerable in terms of their planning and execution because they rely on an inter-dependent series of acts and activities by actors working in coordination with one another. Events are often designed, either formally or informally, to achieve specific ends. Therefore, examining the goals and motivations that exist in the field is often important in understanding what is going on and why. These are the things that people are trying to accomplish in the setting: what acts, activities, and events **do**. Objects can also be important in accomplishing such goals. These are the material things that are used by actors in support of those acts, activities, and events: what objects exist in the setting, how are they used (or not), and by whom? Similarly, time can also often be an important component in terms of the sequencing of acts, actions, and events: how do things begin, what do they begin with, how do they continue, and how are they finished? Last but not least is the issue of emotion. This is a concern with the affective experiences of actors in specific contexts: how do they feel about the things they do, and how do they experience one another?

Some frames of interest will follow very easily from your proposed rationale; some will take more work. One way of beginning to develop your frames of inter-est is to do one or two preliminary visits to your research site. The other is to use the literature to help develop theoretical sensitivity to the types of things that might be relevant to your research. Once you have identified some frames of ref-erence, you can then dedicate specific visits to examining those particular aspects of the field. In turn, this will produce new insights and questions for develop-ment, which will require further fieldwork. Indeed, frames of reference should be thought of as dynamic in that they are refined over time.

Writing field notes

Once you have sensitized yourself to the field, and perhaps even paid a visit to it, you can then think about actually producing data. Unfortunately, while there is often much discussion of field notes in research methods textbooks, they very rarely show you what they look like. There are some reasons for this, confidenti-ality and space being two, but this absence can make it difficult to know what you should be recording and how.

The first thing to recognize is that field notes tend to be written. This is mainly because written material better supports the analytical process. That is not to say that other material is unimportant to participant observation. Researchers will often draw on photographs, sound recordings, and documentary material associ-ated with the research site in the process of data collection. However, written field notes are the primary form of data used in ethnographic work.

Second, it is worth highlighting that field notes are highly personal in nature, and there are not really any hard-and-fast rules about how they should be written.

As a general rule of thumb, what they are actually about in terms of content should be guided by the frames of interest you have identified.

That said, it is possible to identify three types of field notes: mental notes, scratch notes, and full notes. In most cases, the formation of one supports the construction of the other—and the process of writing field notes usually involves at least two stages of writing and sometimes more. Mental notes are used to build scratch notes, which are themselves written up as full notes as soon as possible after fieldwork.

Mental notes are simply a promise to yourself to remember something of significance. They are particularly useful when it is not possible to actually take notes. Of course, the problem with mental notes is that they are reliant on memory, and in the 'cut and thrust' of fieldwork it can be easy to forget things. This is even more likely to be the case as the distance between event and making a record of it increase. In some cases, it may be possible to take a photograph as a reminder of significance.

What is much more common, however, is to take the first opportunity to turn a mental note into a scratch note. There are many 'tales from the field' that recount stories of ethnographers writing scratch notes in all sorts of unusual places! A scratch note is a short written reminder of something significant. They are often just a few words or lines in length, and they are typically a prompt for further development. Often written very quickly, scratch notes need to detail enough of what is important so that you can then 'write up' those notes in full at a later date. Small notepads are often useful to write scratch notes because they are very portable and self-contained, but you could also make notes on your smartphone.

Scratch notes usually form the blueprint for 'full notes'. These are the attempt to write an account of the fieldwork session in as much detail as possible. They are

FINDING YOUR WAY 12.7

For many researchers, the goal of fieldwork is '**thick description**'. This is a term introduced by Geertz (1973: 16), who described it in the following manner: 'Ethnography is thick description. What the ethnographer is in fact faced with [...] is a multiplicity of complex conceptual structures, many of them superimposed upon or knotted into one another, which are at once strange, irregular, and inexplicit, and which he must contrive somehow first to grasp and then to render.' Put another way, thick description involves 'defamiliarizing the familiar'—that is, looking again at all the things that you may once have taken for granted. It also means recording as much contextual information as you can, plus any immediate analytical thoughts. This may include how you feel, as well as what you see.

usually quite long 'warts and all' records of the ethnographic encounter. In some respects, when they are placed side by side, they act like a personal diary of data collection.

When writing full notes, the subjective nature of fieldwork quickly becomes apparent. It is not possible to write up everything, so you will need to make choices about what to focus on and how. This is why it is important to keep your frames of interest close at hand when writing up your notes, because it will help guide some of those decisions. In some cases, your notes might be quite realist in the sense that they attempt to accurately record 'what happened'. In other cases they might be more interpretivist in scope. Although they don't have to be, field notes are also often written up as something of a narrative, and they can be descriptive, exploratory, or reflective in nature. They might also be very experimental with respect to style and form, and they can often include ideas for further avenues of examination or analysis. They will vary in length, but they do tend to be quite detailed, so they are often fairly substantial.

It is a very good idea to write up your field notes as soon as possible. This enables you to better capture the essence of what you remember to be important about the encounter. It will also allow you to reflect on the process of data collection and the ongoing focus of your attention. This will, in turn, help you to attune to those areas of interest in future fieldwork sessions.

CONCLUSION

Collecting qualitative data can be hugely rewarding for dissertation research. However, the detailed nature of both qualitative interviewing and participant observation is relatively hard work and time-intensive. Given the necessary involvement of other people, it can also mean that qualitative research projects can often be subjected to unexpected delays. Careful planning and organization are necessary to ensure that you can make the most of the advantages associated with these techniques. Both methods of data collection that we have introduced here produce rich data that are grounded in the understanding and experiences of people as they go about their personal and professional lives. This data can then be used to generate theory that closely reflects and represents those realities.

WHAT DO I NEED TO THINK ABOUT?

- What sorts of research aims and objectives are particularly suitable for qualitative data collection?
- What are the benefits of using interviews for dissertation research?
- What are the key steps in building an interview schedule?
- What sorts of challenges might you encounter when conducting a qualitative interview?

- Where can participant observation be conducted?
- Why are issues of access important in participant observation?
- What roles can you take 'in the field'?
- What are you trying to capture when writing field notes?

WHAT DO I NEED TO DO?

- Select the most appropriate method of qualitative data collection that will allow you to answer your research aims and objectives.
- Use your research aims and objectives to develop your interview schedule or frames of interest.
- Plan the process of your fieldwork, making sure you have given sufficient time to issues associated with accessing your field and actually collecting data.
- Go out and collect the data, making sure a record is kept of the data collected.

Access the online resources **www.oup.com/uk/brymansrple** to help you to successfully complete your social research project or dissertation.

DELVE DEEPER

Brinkmann, S. and Kvale, S. (2018). *Doing Interviews.* **London: Sage.** Very readable and packed full of 'hands on' advice, this book is likely to be an invaluable guide for the would-be interviewer. Drawing on a wide range of research examples, it covers all types of interview and very clearly examines the nuts and bolts of an interview. Highly recommended.

Gibbs, G. (2013). *The Research Interview.* **YouTube playlist.** The ever reliable Graham Gibbs has a playlist dedicated to the practice of interviewing. He methodically works through the interview process, detailing the pros and cons of interviewing, the types of interview, the interview schedule, types of question, and good practice. There are also examples of both good and bad interviews, and a video about transcription, available elsewhere on his YouTube pages.
https://www.youtube.com/playlist?list=PL0C3243FC24FC639C (Accessed 5 December 2018)

Edwards, R. and Holland, J. (2013). *What is Qualitative Interviewing?* **London: Bloomsbury.** As part of the National Centre for Research Methods' 'What is?' series, this freely available resource was written as an authoritative introduction to interviewing. Beginning with a short history of interviewing, it goes on to describe key aspects in the process of interviewing. This includes the various forms of interviewing, how interviews can be situated, as well as the mechanics of actually carrying them out. It is an excellent overview, and the fact it is freely available makes it all the more attractive.

http://eprints.ncrm.ac.uk/3276/1/complete_proofs.pdf (Accessed 1 October 2017)

Based at the University of Manchester, the Morgan Centre for Research into Everyday Lives has a number of freely available toolkits that are designed to introduce researchers to innovative methodologies. This includes: using self-interviews; using telephone interviews; using walking interviews; and using email interviews.

https://www.socialsciences.manchester.ac.uk/morgan-centre/ (Accessed 27 October 2018)

QualPage is a collection of resources that are dedicated to examining the world through qualitative inquiry. They have blog posts, papers, and podcasts on a range of issues associated with qualitative inquiry. This page is one such example—it provides a quick guide to taking field notes.

https://qualpage.com/2017/04/07/tips-for-observing-and-taking-field-notes-in-qualitative-studies/ (Accessed 1 November 2018)

Social Research Update is published quarterly by the Department of Sociology at the University of Surrey. It is designed to introduce researchers to emerging methods and techniques associated with social research. It has a number of entries that are related to interviewing and participant observation. These include: computer-assisted personal interviewing; walking interviews; writing ethnography; telephone interviewing; focus groups; the use of vignettes in qualitative research; the importance of pilot studies; telephone focus groups; tools for audio recording; in-depth interviewing through instant messaging. There are almost too many to list!

http://sru.soc.surrey.ac.uk/ (Accessed 1 February 2016)

CHAPTER 13

ANALYSING
QUANTITATIVE DATA

WHAT DO I NEED TO KNOW?

- Working with your data
- Descriptive statistics
  - Nominal and ordinal data: frequencies, bar charts, proportions, and pie charts
  - Exploring associations in categorical data
    - Working with larger tables
  - Interval variables: histograms, line graphs, and scatterplots
  - Presenting graphs and tables
  - Measures of central tendency
  - Measures of dispersion
- Inferential statistics
  - Univariate, bivariate, or multivariate analysis
  - Statistical significance
  - Which statistical test should I use?
- Discussing your data

INTRODUCTION

Once you have planned your research project, worked out the research aims, and designed and collected your data, you can move on to the analysis. This chapter introduces you to the two approaches you can use to analyse your quantitative data: descriptive statistics and inferential statistics. Descriptive statistics allow you to summarize and describe data, whereas inferential statistics enable you to infer answers from your data using hypotheses. Both approaches can be extremely useful. The chapter will detail some of the techniques associated with these approaches, and help you to choose which techniques are appropriate for the data you have collected. Showing you how to present your data appropriately, we'll also explore how to discuss your findings in an evidence-informed manner. By introducing you to some of the basic ideas involved in quantitative analysis, the chapter will provide you with skills that can be employed in a quantitative dissertation. Quantitative data analysis might not be as hard as you think!

WORKING WITH YOUR DATA

There are now an increasing number of powerful and (relatively) user-friendly statistics programs that can be used to assist you in organizing and managing the data you have collected. Perhaps the most widely used computer package in social

FINDING YOUR WAY 13.1

Clearly organizing your data will make the job of analysis much easier. Table 13.1 is an example of how data could be coded for a project that looked at self-reported levels of depression and demographic characteristics (obviously you would need a much larger number of respondents). It would be relatively easy to do this on software like IBM SPSS. Presenting the data in this way would allow you to look at the relationships between variables. You could, for example, see whether there were any differences in gender and level of self-reported depression.

Table 13.1 **An example of how data could be coded**

		Variable			
		Age category	Ethnicity	Gender	Self-reported level of depression (1–5) 1 = very high levels, 5 = very low levels
Respondent number	1	18–24	White British	Male	3
	2	55–64	Indian	Female	4
	3	35–44	White British	Female	2

science dissertations is IBM SPSS. It is a comprehensive package that can perform complex data manipulation and analysis. You can enter primary data that you have collected, such as questionnaire data, or import data from the secondary data sets that we discussed in Chapter 11.

There are also a number of other popular programs—such as R, SAS, and STATA—that will all do something similar to IBM SPSS. You can even make use of Microsoft Excel or Google Sheets. In some cases, students will collect responses in the form of tally charts. However, it is important to recognize that collecting data in this way can be problematic, especially where you are working with a large number of responses. It is very easy to make a mistake in your calculations without realizing it.

While computer-assisted analysis can be a very efficient means of processing your data, particularly as it avoids the need to work things out by hand, you will still need to understand the underlying analytical techniques that are available to you and when it is appropriate to use them. If you employ the wrong type of analysis for the type of data, your results will be meaningless regardless of whether you have used a computer or not.

Similarly, it is important not to lose sight of what you are trying to accomplish and the research aims and objectives you are attempting to address. Using

FINDING YOUR WAY 13.2

It is important to remain focused on your research questions and how the analysis you conduct relates to them when undertaking your analysis. This will help you achieve good marks.

computer programs for the purposes of data dredging—analysing data without stating what point you're trying to prove—is generally considered to be very bad practice! Analysis is actually part of a process, which starts with the research design. As we highlighted in Chapter 11, you need to understand what you will do with your data before you collect it. These types of software can help you organize and process data, but they will not plan the analysis for you. Instead, you will have to select which variables to use and which statistical techniques are most appropriate. You will then need to carry out the analysis, interpret any results appropriately, and understand how that information will enable you to answer your research aims.

It is for these reasons that we are not going to go into much detail about how to input and analyse data using IBM SPSS or other platforms. If you are using quantitative data in your dissertation and want to know more about how to do this then there are lots of useful books that will help you get to grips with these programs. We've detailed some of these in the 'Delve deeper' section at the end of the chapter.

But now you know enough about what this software can and can't do, we'll begin with a key distinction you need to be able to make when you are trying to understand your data. As we said in the introduction to this chapter, broadly speaking, there are two ways of analysing quantitative data: descriptive statistics and inferential statistics. Descriptive techniques allow you to summarize and describe data. They enable you to answer questions like 'how many' or 'how often' something takes place. This may involve calculating proportions or averages to describe patterns in your data, or showing the distribution of a variable in visual form. Descriptive techniques reveal overarching trends in data and provide an important way of summarizing complex information. Inferential statistics, on the other hand, enable you to infer whether you have enough evidence of something in your data to answer a specific question. They are a powerful means through which you can move beyond a random sample to suggest something greater about a population. They allow you to say something about 'the bigger picture'. It's also worth pointing out that even if you do not plan to use a quantitative research strategy, having an understanding of the process of analysis is useful when reading articles that make use of statistics that you might encounter while doing your literature review.

WORKING WITH YOUR SUPERVISOR 13.1

Different disciplines, departments, and supervisors may have different expect-ations regarding whether you should use descriptive or inferential statistics. Some supervisors may insist that you move beyond descriptive techniques and use inferential techniques. Others will be less demanding. It is certainly worth clarifying these expectations with your supervisor.

DESCRIPTIVE STATISTICS

In Chapter 11 we discussed different types of variable. Understanding these dis-tinctions is really important because the type of descriptive techniques that you can implement depend on the type of data collected. Categorical data that you might collect from nominal and ordinal levels of measurement need to be pre-sented differently from the continuous data you get from interval and ratio variables.

Use Table 13.2 to guide your decisions about what summary statistics, graphs, and figures are associated with each level of measurement.

Table 13.2 **Guide to which summary statistics, graphs, and figures are associated with each level of measurement**

Levels of measurement	Descriptive statistics	
	Summary statistics	Figures and graphs
Nominal	Frequencies, proportions, crosstabulations (bivariate), mode	Bar charts, pie charts
Ordinal	Frequencies, proportions, crosstabulations (bivariate), mode, median, range, interquartile range	Bar charts, pie charts
Interval/ratio	Mean, mode, median, range, interquartile range, standard deviation	Histograms (univariate), line graphs (bivariate), scatterplots (bivariate)

Nominal and ordinal data: frequencies, bar charts, proportions, and pie charts

When working with nominal or ordinal data you are dealing with categorical data. As a general rule of thumb, frequencies, bar charts, proportions, and pie charts are particularly useful when working with categorical data. We will deal with each in turn.

Frequency tables allow you to identify the amount, or counts, associated with the different categories of a variable. They enable you to summarize the different responses clearly so you can answer questions such as:

- How many divorced people are there in our sample?
- How many people agree with capital punishment?
- How many people prefer living in a rural environment?
- What are the most common qualifications that workers have in a particular factory?

A frequency distribution is calculated by identifying the categories within a variable and counting the number of appearances they make across your sample. This allows you to see how your data is distributed. For example, if you were interested in socio-economic status and you collected data from 178 individuals you could create a frequency chart like that in Table 13.3. From this table you can see that from the 178 people surveyed, the professional or managerial class is the least common value with 14 of the total respondents. Routine or manual workers are most common with a total of 135.

Table 13.3 **Frequency table of socio-economic class**

Occupation	Frequency
Professional or managerial	14
Intermediate	29
Routine or manual	135
Total	**178**

If you also surveyed the 178 people about their highest educational attainment level you could produce another frequency table (Table 13.4). Here you can see that the most common highest educational achievement in our sample is 'A levels', while 'no educational achievement' ('none') is the least common. It is easy to see that frequency tables are useful for presenting the values associated with our variable simply and clearly.

Table 13.4 **Frequency table showing the highest educational attainment**

Educational level	Frequency
Degree+	35
Intermediate	23
A levels	45
GCSEs	30
Other	30
None	15
Total	**178**

Given that both of these tables focus on one variable, they are examples of univariate analysis. This type of analysis is often the cornerstone of descriptive statistics.

Bar charts are also commonly used with categorical data contained in frequency tables. While the exact frequencies are difficult to determine from bar charts, they can be usefully employed to visually summarize the distribution of categorical data. Look at Figure 13.1. This shows the frequency of current marital status of respondents. It is possible to see how the relative height of the bars helps us to see how the counts compare with one another. 'Married' is the most frequent group, followed by 'living with a partner'. The least frequent group is 'in a civil partnership'.

Do you remember that nominal data has no mid-points between the categories? Answers are either in one or the other, never in-between. So the categories are mutually exclusive and non-continuous. Similarly, remember how we highlighted that the scaling of ordinal data is often difficult to determine and as a result ordinal data should not be treated as continuous? Look again at Figure 13.1. The gaps between the bars indicate that the data you are working with is not continuous. This is why you use bar charts, not histograms, to describe nominal and ordinal data.

Figure 13.1 **Bar chart showing the frequency of current marital status**

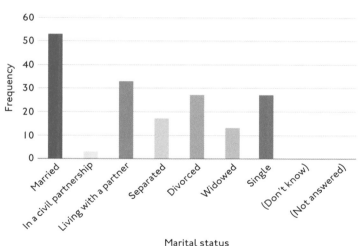

It's also worth noting that too many categories make a bar chart very difficult to read—you wouldn't want many more categories than the ones in Figure 13.1.

Proportions, like frequencies, are another method of summarizing nominal and ordinal data numerically. While there are (generally) no hard-and-fast rules on when to use proportions and when to use frequencies, proportions are really useful if you want to compare two categories that have markedly different sample sizes, as they summarize all data on a scale of 0–100. Where possible, it is common to use proportions as well as frequencies in tables.

Table 13.5 **Frequency and proportion showing the socio-economic class**

Occupation	Frequency	Proportion
Professional or managerial	14	7.9%
Intermediate	29	16.3%
Routine or manual	135	75.8%
Total	**178**	**100.0%**

Fortunately, proportions are relatively easy to work out. It is the same as a percentage. All you have to do is divide each particular value by the total number in the sample and multiply by 100. In Table 13.5, for example, 14 divided by 178 is 0.0787. Multiply this answer by 100 and you have 7.87. Therefore, 14 is 7.87 per cent of 178. If you decide to work to one decimal place, this means that the professional or managerial class make up 7.9 per cent of the sample total. You can see that routine and manual employees are most common. If you collected this data in your dissertation, you might want to reflect on how these figures compared with the national average and why the proportion of routine and manual workers was so high. It might, for instance, be due to particular characteristics of the place where the information was collected.

FINDING YOUR WAY 13.3

While proportions can be a useful way of summarizing data numerically, they also need to be used with caution. For instance, if you had a small sample—let's say 50 or fewer—and presented the information as a proportion without presenting the frequency this would be potentially misleading. This is because a relatively small change in frequency can result in a relatively large change in proportion. This is a common problem when a small sample has been used in a dissertation.

Pie charts are a good way of visually representing proportions. They help you to see all the categories that make up a 'whole' variable, giving you an immediate sense of which attribute contains more counts. A pie chart presents the categories of data as parts of a circle or 'slices of a pie'. A circle contains 360 degrees (360°), so to convert a proportion to degrees, first divide the particular value by the total in the sample, and then multiply the result by 360. You could then plot this using a protractor, but drawing pie charts by hand can be quite labour-intensive so using some computer-assisted analysis software can save you a lot of time.

Pie charts should either clearly label each 'slice' of the pie or have a separate key to show what the different colours/shadings in each 'slice' represent. The latter is particularly likely if you are dealing with lots of slices, or have some relatively small frequencies. If you are drawing several pie charts on the same subject (such

Figure 13.2 **Pie chart showing the socio-economic class in percentages**

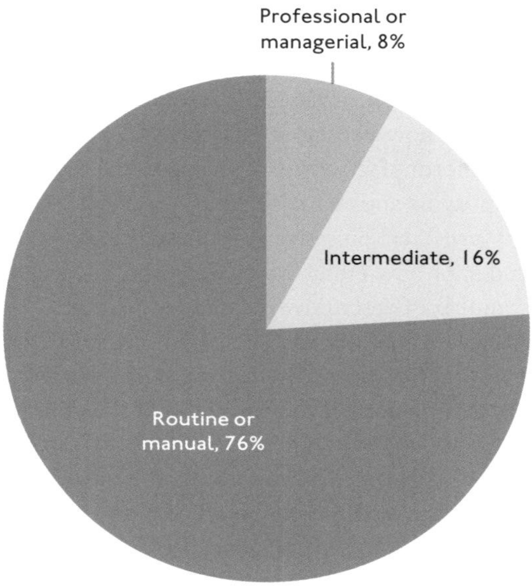

as expenditure in several different countries), always put the categories in the same order on each pie chart as this helps to avoid confusion.

Look at Figure 13.2, drawn from the data in Table 13.3 on socio-economic class. In this example, only the percentages are shown, but some disciplines may require you to show counts and percentages. Pie charts can be useful when you want the reader to notice that there are more people in one group than the others. It is easy to see how routine or manual workers are by far the largest group in your sample, followed by the intermediate group and then the professional or managerial group. Pie charts help an audience gain a sense of the distribution quickly. But in conveying these relative differences efficiently, they do have some limitations. Deciphering the size of wedges in a pie chart is more difficult than comparing the heights of bars, largely because angles are typically harder to compare than lengths. This is why it is always good to provide the numbers too. Pie charts also tend to be used where the number of categories is relatively few, as too many slices can make the chart difficult to read.

WORKING WITH YOUR SUPERVISOR 13.2

If you are in doubt about how to present the data you have collected in your dissertation, and whether certain forms of presentation are not as well received in a particular discipline, it is worth liaising with your supervisor. They should be able to advise you.

Exploring associations in categorical data

Understanding when and how to implement frequencies and proportions is also important for another reason. They form the foundations that help you to begin to explore associations between variables. Indeed, descriptive techniques can be implemented to analyse how particular variables vary in relation to each other. Bivariate analysis is a form of analysis that examines the conjunction of two variables. This can help us to answer those more specific research questions that emerge from your aims and objectives—for instance, how gym membership might vary by gender, or how ethnic status might be associated with fear of racism. There are a number of descriptive techniques that can help us to do this.

Crosstabulations (often abbreviated as crosstabs) are a way to present the joint distribution of two or more variables. In their most simple format, crosstabs are a form of bivariate analysis because they typically show how one variable is contingent to another. This is why they are also referred to as contingency tables. Whereas a frequency distribution provides the distribution of one variable, a contingency table describes the distribution of two or more variables simultaneously.

The most basic format is a 2x2 contingency table. The '2' simply refers to the number of answers that relate to the variable. For instance, if you had collected information about the gender of gym membership, your findings may look something like Table 13.6. Let's imagine that you also collected information about the motivations of people who attend the gym and arranged these into two categories: social (seeing friends, for example) and physical (getting fit) (see Table 13.7). While these tables may be interesting in themselves, they do not tell you anything about how the variables might be related. For instance, were men more or less likely to visit the gym for social or physical reasons? How does this compare with the reasons women go to the gym?

Table 13.6 **Frequency of membership by gender**

Gender of gym member	Frequency
Male	69
Female	124
Total	**193**

Table 13.7 **Frequency of reasons for attending the gym**

Reason for going to the gym	Frequency
Social	98
Physical	95
Total	**193**

In order to find out the answers to these more specific questions, you need to crosstabulate the data in the form of a contingency table. To do this, all you need to do is count how many women also ticked the 'social' box, and how many ticked the 'physical' box. If you do the same for men, you have a table with two categories on the horizontal axis, and two categories on the vertical axis. This is what we mean by a 2x2 table. Table 13.8 shows how this would look. You can now see that the reasons for visiting the gym tended to differ according to the gender of the visitor. It was not possible to see this from the frequency tables alone. In this respect, crosstabs allow you to go deeper into the data and compare and contrast different groups and answers.

Table 13.8 **Reason for visiting the gym by gender**

| | | Reasons for going to the gym | | Total |
		Social	Physical	Total
Gender	Male	25	44	69
	Female	73	51	124
Total		98	95	193

Clustered bar charts can help you to present these types of results visually. You have seen how bar charts can be used to present information about one variable. Clustered bar charts allow you to represent data from more than one variable. Table 13.8, for example, could be presented as a clustered bar chart.

To do this, you first need to convert the frequencies into proportions. This will enable you to present the data more evenly. In Table 13.8, there are more responses from females. If you were to present this data in its raw form, this higher amount would visually distort our results. So, as we are interested in the influence of gender on motivation, we use the row totals for gender to calculate the proportions. It is often considered to be good practice to present the counts (i.e. in brackets) as well as proportions or vice versa. This gives us Table 13.9.

To produce a clustered bar chart, all we need to do now is 'cluster' bars together based on the categories of our variables—with each cluster representing each individual gender with respect to motivation (see Figure 13.3). Presented appropriately, clustered bar charts can help us to interpret complex information visually. They can be a really useful way of presenting information in your dissertation.

Table 13.9 **Reason for visiting the gym by gender (%)**

| | | Reasons for going to the gym | | | | Total (%) | |
| | | Social | | Physical | | Total (%) | |
		Count	%	Count	%	Count	%
Gender	Male	25	36	44	64	69	100
	Female	73	59	51	41	124	100

Figure 13.3 **Clustered bar chart showing reasons for visiting the gym by gender (proportions)**

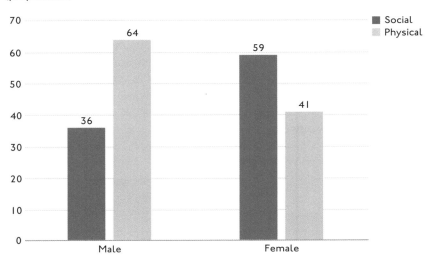

Working with larger tables

Crosstabs can be larger than 2x2 tables. Let's look at an example of data from the British Crime Survey. Table 13.10—a 5x4 crosstab—explores the relationship between ethnicity and fear of racist abuse by examining the responses to the question 'how worried are you about being physically attacked because of skin colour, ethnic origin, or religion?' with reference to the ethnicity of the respondents. This sort of research

Table 13.10 **Worried about being physically attacked because of skin colour, ethnic origin, or religion, by ethnicity**

		Whether a participant is worried about being physically attacked because of skin colour, ethnic origin, or religion				
		Very worried	Fairly worried	Not very worried	Not at all worried	**Total**
Ethnicity	White	877	1170	4889	9482	**16418**
	All black groups	68	61	88	45	**262**
	Indian	89	61	64	29	**243**
	Pakistani/ Bangladeshi	58	44	33	25	**160**
	Other groups	73	65	122	87	**347**
	Total	**1165**	**1401**	**5196**	**9668**	**17430**

Source: British Crime Survey, 2007–2008

question could easily be addressed in the context of a dissertation. As you can see, there is a lot of information contained in this table and making sense of it all might appear to be difficult. However, an effective use of descriptive statistics can help us to identify patterns in the data.

At first glance, it appears to show that the vast majority of people are 'not very worried' or 'not at all worried' about being attacked because of their skin colour, ethnic origin, or religion. Unfortunately, this would not be a robust conclusion to make. This is because although the sample is large (n=17,430), there are a lot more people in the 'white' category than all of the others put together. This has a great deal of influence on the column totals. Looking at the data, it is possible to see that fear of a racially motivated attack might actually vary by ethnicity.

To investigate further, you need to make the values easier to compare. Again, this involves converting the frequencies to within-row proportions. That is, you need to work out the proportions of each cell within a particular category of ethnicity. As you are broadly interested in the impact of ethnicity on fear of racist attack, you need to look at the different proportions associated with each row. This will help you to see the differences in the distribution of the answers between categories more easily.

To do this, you need to divide each cell in your row by the total number of respondents in that row and multiply by 100. For example, the frequency of the 'white' 'very worried' cell is 877. If you divide this by the total number of white respondents—16,418—and then multiply by 100, you get an answer of 5.3 per cent.

Doing this for each cell in your table makes the categories easier to compare. Table 13.11 shows the findings. It is worth emphasizing that you can calculate the percentages of a table in different ways. In Table 13.11, the percentages are calculated as within-row percentages, with the proportion calculated against the row total. However, you could calculate the percentages by the column totals too. The general rule of thumb is to calculate percentages in the direction of the variable that you think is having an impact on a particular measure. As we are interested in the influence of ethnicity on 'fear of racist attack', we calculated the within-row proportions.

A key way to differentiate variables is through cause and effect. This involves being able to clearly identify and distinguish your dependent (DV) and independent variables (IV). As we saw in Chapter 7, a dependent variable is the measurement of the effect, whereas the independent variable is the reason that you are attributing that effect to. When working out the proportions of values in a contingency table, use the

WORKING WITH YOUR SUPERVISOR 13.3

It is worth noting that there are differences between disciplines in terms of how findings are reported. For instance, some disciplines, departments, or supervisors may prefer percentages provided as whole numbers in your dissertation. Again, it is worth consulting with your supervisor (or any additional dissertation guidance) to ensure you are conforming to the requirements.

Table 13.11 Worried about being physically attacked because of skin colour, ethnic origin, or religion, by ethnicity (with proportions)

| | | Whether a participant is worried about being physically attacked because of skin colour, ethnic origin, or religion | | | | | | | | | |
| | | Very worried | | Fairly Worried | | Not very worried | | Not at all worried | | Total | |
		Count	%	Count	%	Count	%	Count	%	Count	%
Ethnicity	White	877	5.3	1170	7.1	4889	29.8	9482	57.8	16418	100
	All black groups	68	26.0	61	23.3	88	33.6	45	17.2	262	100
	Indian	89	36.6	61	25.1	64	26.3	29	11.9	243	100
	Pakistani/ Bangladeshi	58	36.3	44	27.5	33	20.6	25	15.6	160	100
	Other groups	73	21.0	65	18.7	122	35.1	87	25.1	347	100
	Total	1165	6.7	1401	8.0	5196	29.8	9668	55.5	17430	100

Source: British Crime Survey, 2007–2008

totals associated with what you think is acting as the independent variable. In this case, we think ethnicity (the IV) is having an effect on fear of racist attack (the DV).

Let's suggest that you are interested in knowing what factors influence quality of life, level of income, or political affiliation (dependent variables). This could include gender, age, or ethnicity (independent variables). This is to say that quality of life, level of income, or political affiliation are dependent on gender, age, and ethnicity. Often it doesn't make much sense to think about it the other way around: someone's gender isn't dependent on political affiliation.

Although your independent variable might be able to explain the differences between people's responses to your dependent variable, you also need to be a little cautious in your claims. For instance, sometimes there may be another variable you haven't looked at (perhaps it is not available in your data set) that actually causes the dependent variable to change in this way.

FINDING YOUR WAY 13.4

When designing tables, it is common practice to use rows for the independent variable and columns for the dependent variable. You can then use row percentages to compare the characteristics of the variable in the manner outlined in Table 13.10.

So, to return to Table 13.11, you can now go through each 'within-row' category to identify patterns in the data. In this example, it's easy to see that the proportions associated with the 'very worried' and 'fairly worried' categories are much bigger in the non-white ethnic groups.

Once you have analysed the key patterns in a table, your work still isn't over. In a dissertation you need to be able to think and write critically. You need to think about why the results are distributed in this manner **and** account for those findings. Therefore, you have to try to explain the patterns in your data and not just describe them. Data does not just speak for itself.

In this respect, you might ask: why are the Indian group least likely to be 'not at all worried'? Why are the Pakistani/Bangladeshi group most likely to be 'very worried' or 'fairly worried'? The answers to these questions could lie in the way the groups have been measured, the particular histories of the ethnic groups, and the identities, communities, and cultures of those groups. All of which would have to be accounted for in the final analysis. In this particular instance you could probably learn much from both the methodological literature on the British Crime Survey and the more specific literature on ethnicity, racism, and the 'fear of crime'. In fact, you would be expected to be able to draw on some of the information you have already presented in the literature review section of your dissertation. This is why undertaking a thorough literature review will enhance your project.

Interval variables: histograms, line graphs, and scatterplots

As is the case for categorical data, there are different ways of presenting and summarizing interval or ratio variables. In terms of presentation, you can use histograms, line graphs, or scatterplots. Which you choose will largely depend on the demands of your research question. In terms of summary statistics there are particular measures of central tendency and measures of dispersion. We'll introduce you to each in turn.

You should now be aware that if you are working with nominal or ordinal data, then frequencies, proportions, bar charts, and pie charts are particularly useful. There are other techniques of presentation that you might want to implement, but these tend to be key. For instance, it is possible to represent data in the form of maps and other geographic information systems (GIS). These can be a great way of showing levels of poverty in particular regions of cities.

If you are working with interval and ratio data, then the conventions are a little different from their categorical counterparts. This is because the nature of continuous data is different. As a result, there are different ways to present interval data. This might be in the form of a histogram, scatterplot, or line graph.

Histograms provide a visual representation of how often different values occur, how much spread or variability there is among the values, and which values are most typical for the data. They look similar to bar charts, but are different in some key respects. In a histogram, the width of the bar is important. This is because the width can vary with respect to the category it represents. The height of the bar still represents the count or proportion, but the width functions as a summary of the

Figure 13.4 **Histogram showing literacy rate among males aged over 15 years in 44 African countries for which figures are available, 2005–10**
Source: UNESCO Institute for Statistics 2013

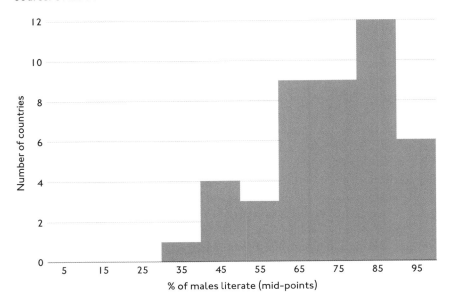

category of the measure. The intervals chosen for the widths are sometimes called 'bins'. For example, if you had a lot of data clustered around a centre point, let's say 40–50, and not much elsewhere, you could summarize that by having a relatively wide bar to represent 0–39 and 51–100, and much thinner bars to represent 40, 41, 42, 43 etc. However, it is more common to have bins of equal-sized intervals, for example ten bins of ten on a scale from 1 to 100, as in Figure 13.4. A histogram also does not feature gaps between the bars because the data is continuous. Figure 13.4 provides an example of a histogram for the ratio variable 'the percentage of males literate in 44 African countries'.

As you can see, histograms are a good method of representation if you want to illustrate a set of data in a simple, easy-to-read manner. It is worth noting, however, that histograms display only the number (or percentage) of observations that fall into each interval, not the actual data. As the data are continuous rather than in discrete categories, the bars of a histogram must touch each other (unlike in a bar chart). The height of each bar represents the frequency (number of countries) in that interval, and the width of each bar must be proportional to the width of the interval on the continuous scale. In this case, all the intervals are the same width, so the bars are also the same width.

When you are trying to examine the relationship between two interval variables, it is often useful to draw a scatterplot (also known as a scattergraph or scattergram).

This is a type of graph where the values for each observation's responses to two variables are plotted against one another. They show you visually whether, and how, two variables might be related to each other. Each axis represents the value of an observation, with the point being where those values intersect.

Scatterplots are used for variables measured at the interval or ratio level, rarely for ordinal variables, and never if either variable is nominal. It only makes sense to use them when it is possible to meaningfully order the values for each of the variables. On a scatterplot, the dependent variable should always go on the y axis (the vertical one) and the independent variable is plotted on the x axis (the horizontal one). Many data are not amenable to being displayed in this way, particularly when there are only a few values for one or both of the variables. One of the most frequent uses of scatterplots is in plotting country trends. Using secondary data in the form of the European Social Survey, for example, you could develop a scatterplot looking at differences in social security spending between different countries, or in trust in the government.

Figure 13.5 shows a scatterplot visualizing the relationship between (median) house prices and the (median) cost of private renting in English local authorities.

Figure 13.5 **Scatterplot showing the median monthly private rent and median house price by local authority**
Source: Office for National Statistics and Valuation Office Agency, 2015

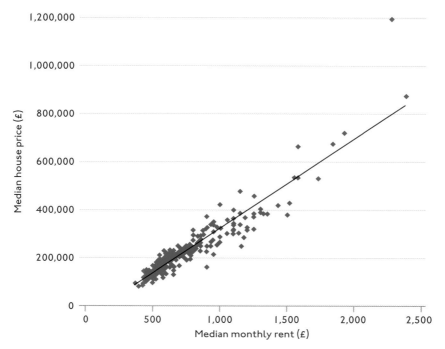

It suggests a fairly linear relationship. Areas that had the highest median house prices also had the highest median monthly rent prices.

Relationships in a scatterplot usually take one of three forms: independence, linear, or nonlinear/curvilinear. Independence is a term used when there is no relationship, essentially because the values are independent of each other. Visually, this looks like a random scatter with no discernible pattern. A linear relationship means that a straight line can be visualized through the middle of the cases from one corner to another. This can be said to have either a positive or negative direction. A positive relationship looks like a diagonal line from the lower left to the upper right, while a negative relationship looks like a line from the upper left to lower right. Nonlinear or curvilinear relationships might mean that the scatter points form a U-curve, right side up or upside down, or an S-curve. They can also start off very 'flat' and then start curving increasingly upwards or downwards, or they can start off going in one direction and then flatten off.

A line graph is similar to a scatterplot but the consecutive points are joined by a line that 'joins the dots'. It is typical for the independent variable to be placed on the horizontal axis and the dependent variable on the vertical axis.

Figure 13.6 is an example of a line graph. It shows the under-18 conception rate for England and Wales between 1969 and 2014, using conceptions per 1,000 women aged 15 to 17 as the measure of interest. The graph enables you to track trends in under-18 conception rates through time and gives you a means through which you can compare how trends have changed. For instance, it shows

Figure 13.6 **Line graph showing under-18 conception rate, 1969 to 2014**
Source: Office for National Statistics, 2016

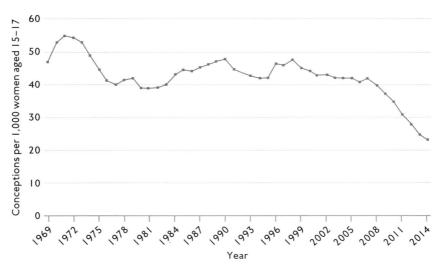

that the conception rate was 22.9 in 2014. This is the lowest since comparable conception statistics were first introduced in 1969 (when the rate was 47.1). You can also see how the 2014 rate continues a steady decline since 1998, when there were 47.1 conceptions per 1,000 women aged 15 to 17, with slight increases found in 2002 and 2007.

When presenting a line graph, be aware that the units of measurement affect the appearance and can make them misleading. Large units can underemphasize change in relative terms because they are not very sensitive, whereas small units can overstate the magnitude of change because they are too sensitive. If you produce a line graph in your dissertation you need to ensure it does not mislead people. Preferably start at zero on the y axis or, if this is not appropriate, at least make it clear to the reader that it does not start at zero by including a break at the bottom of the axis.

Presenting graphs and tables

So far you have seen that there are a number of ways in which you might want to present the data you have collected in your dissertation. While communication is the main purpose of a graph or table, this doesn't detract from the fact that well-designed, aesthetically pleasing presentation can enhance your results. There are a number of conventions which can be used as good 'rules of thumb' to present data meaningfully.

- **Always use the correct type of graph or table for your data.** Ask yourself whether the data are categorical or continuous and then select an appropriate graph or table type according to the needs of your aims and objectives.
- **Label the graph or table clearly.** All graphs and tables should have a clear title explaining what or who the data refer to, and when and where. Both the x (horizontal) and y (vertical) axes of the graph should also have labels and provide the units of measurement.
- **The graph or table should be neat and clear.** Avoid cluttering up a graph with too many bars or lines. Always use the same colours or shadings for the same categories when you have more than one pie chart or bar chart. Also limit the number of different shadings used in a single graphic. If different shadings are used to distinguish bars of a graph, choose shadings that are distinct. Include a key (legend) where appropriate.
- **Include the source.** You will normally know where the data came from (perhaps a secondary data set or your own survey). Put a note below the graph to this effect, for example 'Source: British Social Attitudes Survey, 2019'. Or you can include the source in the title.
- **Be consistent.** For the same type of data, use the same number of decimal places throughout. One or two decimal places should be enough: if you

use more you must have a good reason! Remember some disciplines may prefer no decimal places to be used at all. Check with your supervisor to be clear.

- **Totals and subtotals.** Include relevant totals and subtotals in the table and always check that they add up correctly. In fact, it may also be worth including all of the frequencies in the table. If you have been rounding up to two decimal places, for example, the totals may be slightly out, but do not worry. It may be an idea to indicate in a note below the table that this is the case.

WORKING WITH YOUR SUPERVISOR 13.4

One of the most difficult decisions to make when presenting quantitative data is how many tables and graphs you should include in your dissertation. This is something that is worth getting advice on from your supervisor. It is important to be selective in terms of deciding what to include in your dissertation. There is a temptation to offer graphs and tables for every variable in your study. But it is important to resist this. Instead, try to determine what is important to present in relation to your research questions. A large number of tables or graphs may result in your key findings getting lost in all the detail.

It is important to remember that you choose how to present your data based on what makes things clearer for the reader. They should be both meaningful and relatively easy to decipher. In general, tables must stand alone from the textual explanation. This means that somebody should be able to understand a table without having to read the text before or after it. However, you should always refer to a table in your analysis, picking out the key things to report in order to demonstrate that you understand the material.

Measures of central tendency

Whenever you collect data at the interval level, you are highly unlikely to get the same 'answer' each time you measure the variable. If you wanted to record how many crimes are committed each week in New York City, the answers will vary from week to week. They might be similar, but they will not be exactly the same. There will be some variation and the 'answers' will be distributed across a range of scores. Measures of central tendency attempt to summarize the centre of these distributions of 'answers'. The overall aim is to produce a figure which best represents a mid-point in the data. The mid-point should also be the most common response in the data but, as you will see, this can depend on whether you have chosen the most appropriate measure of central tendency. There are three different ways of doing this: the mean, median, and mode.

The mean is the most familiar of all of the measures of central tendency. It is sometimes referred to as the average. To calculate the mean, it is necessary to add together all of the values and divide the total by the number of values.

So, if you were interested in the age of students taking human geography, you may want to work out the mean for the distribution of age in seminar classes. Although you would want to use a bigger sample, let's show you how to do it with a small class. Let's assume there was a class of seven students of the following ages:

18, 18, 18, 19, 20, 20, 20

The mean would be the total of the ages added together (133) divided by the total number of students (7) giving an answer of 19.

However, there are some weaknesses associated with the use of the mean. It can be disproportionately affected by extreme values in a distribution.

Let us say that one of the 20-year-olds in the seminar group was to change class, and was replaced by a 56-year-old student. The distribution of age now looks like the following:

18, 18, 18, 19, 20, 20, 56

The mean now becomes 24.1 (169 divided by 7). You can see how the introduction of one student considerably older than the rest has dragged the mean up notably, even though the other students are all under 21. This one outlier has skewed the mean and it no longer describes the central tendency of the distribution very well.

Very high or very low values that distort the mean are called outliers. So in this case 56 is an outlier. Outliers can positively or negatively skew the data.

The median is the middle value in a distribution when the scores have been ranked in order of size. Simply line up the scores in ascending order and take the middle value. If you have an even number of scores, take the two numbers either side of the centre, add them and divide by two.

The median age for the original seminar group was 19:

18, 18, 18, 19, 20, 20, 20

This is the value that splits the group in half, with three scores above it and three scores below it.

If an extra student joined the group—aged 21—the median would now be between 19 and 20. So by adding 19 and 20 and dividing by two, we have a median of 19.5.

Unlike the mean, the median is resistant to outliers or extreme values. When the 56-year-old replaced one of the 20-year-olds in the original example, it gave a distribution of: 18, 18, 18, 19, 20, 20, 56. Despite the presence of an outlier, the median would remain at 19 because it doesn't take into account the values of the data. However, while this does make it resistant to outliers, because the median doesn't take into account the actual values in the distribution it lacks the sensitivity of the mean. In other words, it is a less precise measure of central tendency.

The mode is the easiest measure of central tendency to calculate. It is simply the value which occurs most frequently in a distribution. In the example above, when the 56-year-old joined the class, the age distribution was:

$$18, 18, 18, 19, 20, 20, 56$$

The most common age is 18.

Before the 56-year-old joined the group, there was an additional 20-year-old:

$$18, 18, 18, 19, 20, 20, 20$$

In this instance, you can see that there are two modal values—18 and 20—this is an example of a bimodal distribution. More than two modal values would be referred to as a multimodal distribution.

Again, the mode is resistant to outliers, but it does not take into account all the other data—even less so than the median. As a result, it is not a sensitive measure of central tendency.

The mode is the only measure of central tendency that can be used with nominal data, but it can also be used with data at the ordinal level.

Measures of dispersion

In the example provided above, you saw that both the mean and median of the seven students was 19 (18, 18, 18, 19, 20, 20, 20). Let's say you wanted to conduct some further research on the average age of the household that the student lived in before entering university. The first person you chose to ask was one of the 20-year-olds. They had four younger siblings aged 2, 2, 8, and 19 and a mum and dad aged 40 and 42.

So, in order to work out the mean age of the family you would add the seven ages together (2, 2, 8, 19, 20, 40, 42) and divide them by 7. The median is the fourth number in the series—19. Interestingly, the mean and median again turn out to be 19 in spite of there being quite different distributions of age between seminar and family.

Therefore, you need a way to further describe the dimensions of our distributions. In other words, you need to measure the dispersion of the distribution in order to find out the spread of the data.

Fortunately, there are a number of measures which can tell you more about how spread out the values in a distribution are. The measures of dispersion we will discuss are the range, the interquartile range, and standard deviation. However, it should be noted that there are no appropriate measures of dispersion for nominal variables, and when dealing with ordinal data you are restricted to the range and interquartile range. The standard deviation is only calculated for interval/ratio variables. It is also worth recognizing that if you are using a computer program, such as IBM SPSS, these figures can be produced at the click of a button.

The range is calculated by subtracting the smallest value from the largest. It is that simple! If your dissertation was interested in exploring student finances, you may well be interested in the number of hours students work in paid employment while at university. In a situation like this, it would be interesting to look at the range of hours of paid employment.

Let's suppose that you wanted to examine the marks from a Research Methods module in more detail to see if the students had done better from one year to the next.

Consider the two sets of results:

Year one: 85 52 64 51 29 59 47 58 42 37 66 51 (mean 53.4, median 51)

Year two: 62 42 59 45 57 51 46 47 56 55 48 51 (mean 51.6, median 51)

The range in each example is:

Year one: Maximum mark 85, minimum mark 29—the range = 56

Year two: Maximum mark 62, minimum mark 42—the range = 20

Clearly, the similarity of the mean and median for each year hides the fact that the range is very different. It is evident that students who took the module the first time it ran, on average, tended to do a little better and a little worse than those in year two. In fact, one did really well and one did a lot worse than average. When the course ran for the second time, all the marks were much more closely bunched around the mean. So while no one did really well, no one did really badly either.

Although the range can be a useful tool to help us describe our data, it is a rather crude measure of dispersion as it is totally dependent on the two most extreme values—hence it is rather susceptible to outliers. We need to treat the range with caution if these extremes differ substantially from the rest of the distribution.

The interquartile range (IQR) is used to overcome the main flaw of the range by eliminating the most extreme scores in the distribution. The first thing to do is to rank your values in order. Then, the IQR is essentially the range of the middle half of the distribution. Figure 13.7 depicts the idea of the interquartile range. Statistically speaking, the IQR is the difference between the first (Q1) and third (Q3) quartiles. As shown in Figure 13.8, Q1 lies at the mid-point between the first and second quarter of the distribution, and Q3 lies at the mid-point between the third and fourth quarters. Q2 is the median.

Figure 13.7 **Example showing interquartile range**

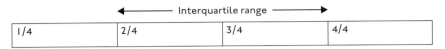

Figure 13.8 **Example highlighting each quartile of the distribution**

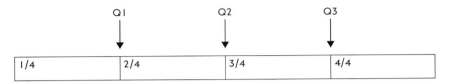

In some cases, Q1 and Q3 will fall quite naturally on the 25 per cent and 75 per cent percentile in your distribution. For instance, if your distribution is 1, 2, 3, 4, 5, 6, 7, 8, 9, 10, 11, then Q1 is 3, Q2 is 6, and Q3 is 9. In other cases, it is a little more complicated—but not much. For instance, in the distribution 1, 2, 3, 4, 5, 6, 7, 8, 9, Q2 is 5 with Q1 being the mid-point between 2 and 3, which is 2.5.

Let us return to the previous example:

Year one: 85 52 64 51 29 59 47 58 42 37 66 51

Year two: 62 42 59 45 57 51 46 47 56 55 48 51

To work out the interquartile range first we need to rank the scores in ascending order.

Year one: 29 37 42 47 51 51 52 58 59 64 66 85

Year two: 42 45 46 47 48 51 51 55 56 57 59 62

Now we need to separate them into four quarters. We have 12 data points so we simply divide 12 by 4. There will be 3 data points in each quarter.

Year one: 29 37 42   47 51 51   52 58 59   64 66 85

Year two: 42 45 46   47 48 51   51 55 56   57 59 62

In year one, it is possible to see that the median, or Q2, is the point between 51 and 52—effectively 51.5. The mid-point between the first and second quarter—Q1—is the average of 42 and 47. So:

$$Q1 = (47 + 42) / 2 = 44.5$$

The mid-point between the third and fourth quarter (Q3) is:

$$Q3 = (64 + 59) / 2 = 61.5.$$

Now all that remains to be done is to subtract Q1 from Q3 (61.5 - 44.5).

The IQR for year one is 17. The IQR for year two is 10 (56.5 - 46.5). Now that the outliers in the distribution have been eradicated, it is possible to see that the distributions for year one and year two are not quite as different as the range might otherwise suggest.

However, the interquartile range doesn't take all the values into account, and it lacks sensitivity as a result. Like the median, the IQR also suffers from the disadvantage that its calculation involves sorting the data. This can be very time-consuming for large samples.

The standard deviation (SD) gives a measure of how widely dispersed the values in a distribution are around the mean. Unlike the range and the IQR, it is sensitive to all of the data in the distribution, not just select parts of it. Of course, this makes it particularly sensitive to outliers, but it does also make it a much more precise measurement of dispersion, as you are no longer ignoring parts of the data.

The standard deviation is relatively easy to work out. You can do it in six simple steps.

1. Work out the mean
2. Calculate how far each individual value is from the mean
3. Square these values (this gets rid of the minus signs, so the negative values don't just cancel out the positive ones)
4. Add up these squared values
5. Divide this by the number of values minus 1
6. Take the square root of this answer

Figure 13.9 **Example of the bell curve**

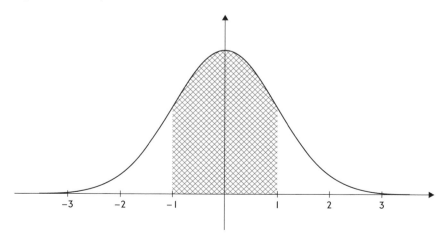

If we do this for year one, we get a standard deviation of 14.68. For year two the SD is 6.21. This gives us a numerical value that suggests that the scores in year one are much more widely dispersed than those in year one. While we would need to seek some further context to make any sort of conclusion as to whether this sort of variation is unusual—possibly in the form of data from further years or across different modules—the SD from one year to the next is effectively twice the size. Because of its sensitivity, the standard deviation should only be used if your data follows a 'normal' distribution, sometimes called a bell curve (see Figure 13.9), where more observations are bunched around the mean and begin to 'thin out' equally at the extremes.

INFERENTIAL STATISTICS

You should now be able to undertake a descriptive analysis of your data in your dissertation. However, what if you want to do something more with your data than describe the properties of your sample? What if you want to infer something about a population based on that sample? This is exactly what inferential statistics are designed to do.

Inferential statistics are employed to make judgements about whether we have enough evidence to suggest that the patterns and relationships we see in our sample are likely to apply to the whole population. In doing so, these statistics allow you to use a sample to make inferences, in the form of estimates or predictions, about the wider population. This makes them really useful for social research. For example, if you asked a random sample of 200 people who they were going to vote for on the day before a local election, you could use inferential techniques to try to predict which party would win the election. While you would never be able to say with certainty who would definitely win the election, inferential statistics do allow us to predict the **likely** outcome or proportion.

There are many different types of inferential techniques, many of which use hypotheses to determine the most likely answers to research questions. Statistical tests such as those associated with differences in scores or measurements between groups

I WISH I'D KNOWN . . . THE IMPACT OF THE TYPE OF SAMPLE ON STATISTICAL TESTS 13.1

Strictly speaking, when working with inferential statistics you should be using data drawn from a random sample of your population. A test carried out on a non-random sample cannot speak with any confidence about the nature of the population. If your sample is not random it may make more sense to spend your time focusing on a thorough descriptive analysis and trying to interpret what is happening in the sample you have collected.

(such as t-tests), associations (such as chi-square), and linear relationships (such as correlations), all allow you to infer an answer from your data using your hypotheses. In each case, the job of the test is to allow you to make an assessment of which hypothesis is more likely to be the 'way things really are' in a population. If you are interested in employing any of these techniques in your dissertation, the 'Delve deeper' section provides details of books which cover these in the detail required.

Univariate, bivariate, or multivariate analysis

Exactly which statistical test you might use will vary depending on the level of measurement, size of the sample, and whether you are testing at a univariate, bivariate, or multivariate level.

You have already seen that univariate analysis is concerned with the analysis of a single variable and is one of the cornerstones of descriptive statistics. However, it is also possible to undertake more sophisticated statistical analysis with this type of data. If you wanted to explore whether the frequency of burglaries was evenly distributed across months of the year, for example, you could undertake univariate analysis in the form of a chi-square 'goodness of fit' test. This would enable you to assess whether the number of burglaries observed was a close fit with what you would expect, or whether those observations deviated significantly from those expectations.

On the other hand, **bivariate** analysis involves the analysis of two variables in conjunction with one another. We have already seen how this may be done descriptively through the use of crosstabs/contingency tables. However, inferential statistics can also be used to examine two variables in conjunction with one another. A chi-square test of association (sometimes called a chi-square test of independence), for instance, can be used to test the association between gender and fear of crime, or age and how people view their local environment. A t-test could be used to assess the differences between exam scores of students in two classes with different teaching styles. A correlation could be used to explore the relationship between age and income.

Multivariate analysis is a form of statistical analysis that explores the relationship between three or more variables. These types of analysis allow researchers to control for lots of confounding factors, search for complex relationships, build multi-level models, and test theories and ideas with more detail. There are three possible contexts where multivariate analysis might be employed for the purposes of an undergraduate dissertation. The first involves so-called spurious relationships. A spurious relationship exists when there appears to be a relationship between two variables, but the relationship is being produced because each variable is itself related to a third variable. Multivariate analysis can be used to isolate the effect of that third variable. Secondly, we might want to ask why there is a relationship between two variables. For instance, let us suggest that you know there is a relationship between people's income and their voting behaviour. One possible reason this may be the case is that people of different incomes vary in their political attitudes, which in turn has implications for their voting behaviour. Political attitudes could, therefore, function as a mediating variable. Finally, multivariate analysis can be used to assess the role of a moderating variable in a relationship. This occurs where a third variable affects the strength or direction of the relation between an independent and dependent variable. For example, the effect of a person's work demands on their job satisfaction might be more negative if they have lower levels of support from their colleagues or the management style of their boss—or both!

While many forms of inferential statistics using univariate and bivariate analysis are relatively straightforward and can be very rewarding, it is worth noting that attempting multivariate analysis often requires significant expertise. If you are thinking about using any of these techniques, we would recommend that you explore some more advanced literature, or fully discuss your plans with your supervisor.

Statistical significance

A key feature of inferential techniques is what is known as 'statistical significance'. But to understand statistical significance, we first need to establish the difference between observed and expected values. When you collect data, the responses you find are known as the 'observed values'. They tell you what you have actually found. But under certain circumstances, it is also possible to calculate expected values too. For example, imagine you and a friend had a pair of six-sided dice and you suspected one of the dice was loaded to land on a specific number more often than the others. If you rolled that die sixty times and every side had an equal chance of coming up you would expect there to be ten rolls of 1, ten rolls of 2, ten rolls of 3, ten rolls of 4, ten of 5, and ten of 6. If after rolling the die sixty times and recording the results you observed that the numbers 1, 2, 3, 4, and 5 came up only five times each, and the number 6 came up thirty-five times, you can clearly conclude that there is a big difference between what we observed and what we would have expected if the die was fair.

This recognition is important because you can use statistical tests to compare the observed and expected values to see whether they are significantly different. Indeed, statistical significance is the threshold level that has been agreed on by statisticians that enables you to make conclusions about the relationship between your sample and the wider population. Specifically, it is the level at which you can say that the difference between what you observed in your sample and what you would have expected if there was no relationship between the variables in the population is so big that we can reject the null hypothesis (ie no relationship). Where the threshold is met, statistical significance enables you to infer that an observed set of values in a sample is likely to be indicative of a wider population.

If it is not met, we cannot be sure if what we observed is really that different from some form of random variation.

Let's take our dice example again. Imagine this time you rolled the die sixty times and the numbers 1, 2, 3, 4, and 5 came up nine times each, and the number 6 came up fifteen times. What we observed still seems quite different from what we might otherwise have expected, but there is still quite a good chance that the die could be fair. We wouldn't want to accuse our friend of cheating without enough evidence! Now, imagine we increased our sample size by rolling the die six hundred times, and this time 1, 2, 3, 4, and 5 came up ninety times each but 6 came up one hundred and fifty times. Even though all of the other die faces are still coming up the same proportion of the time, we can see that the number 6 face is consistently coming up more frequently than any of the other faces. This now makes it very unlikely that the die is fair. So we have enough evidence to reject the idea that all the faces have the same chance of coming up, and can now evidence the fact that our friend is cheating! This example underpins the logic behind most statistics. If there is a big enough difference between what we observed and what we would have expected, or if the difference happens consistently enough in a big sample, we can be more confident that something of significance is happening.

When discussing statistical significance reference is often made to the 'p-value'. This is an assessment of probability concerning the chances of your observed values being meaningful or not. Because p-values can be any number between 0 and 1 (not including zero), the scientific community have chosen significance levels (which are sometimes referred to as critical values) so there is agreement on our conclusions. Conventional significance levels for p-values are $p<0.05$, $p<0.01$, and in some cases $p<0.001$. These are used to show that the probability (p) that we would observe results like this by chance is less than ($<$) 5 in 100, 1 in 100, or 1 in 1,000 respectively. The lower the p-value, the more confident we can be that there is enough evidence to reject the idea of 'no relationship'. Where the p-value exceeds the threshold—that is, it goes above 5 in 100 and the p-value is greater than 0.05—the results are deemed non-significant. This is often denoted by 'n.s.' (not significant).

FINDING YOUR WAY 13.5

You need to be very careful how you interpret your findings in your dissertation. Just because your results are significant at the 0.01 level, this does not mean that your results are any stronger than they were at the 0.05 level. It just means that the chances of your observed values being due to chance are lower. The p-value tells you nothing about how strong the association, effect, or relationship might be; it just gives you an indication as to whether significance can be assumed.

Which statistical test should I use?

There are a large number of statistical tests available which can help you to explore effects, associations, and relationships between variables. While it is important to understand the underlying logic behind the most common statistical techniques, it is also important to recognize that programs such as IBM SPSS are capable of performing such tests without you needing to know the technicalities of their mathematical operations. This can make life a lot easier than working out the test by hand. However, there is still the challenge of identifying the particular statistical test that is required, not to mention the job of interpreting what the findings mean. Remember, if you use the wrong test the findings will be meaningless and you are likely to come to the wrong conclusions.

When choosing which test to use in your dissertation, you will need to know the nature of the variables you are looking at (independent or dependent) as well as their levels of measurement (nominal, ordinal, or interval). You will also need to be aware of the types of question you are attempting to address, and you might be required to use different statistical tests depending on the size of a sample. Assumptions about the distribution of your data (for example, the shape of the histograms of your interval data) will also affect the type of test you use.

WORKING WITH YOUR SUPERVISOR 13.5

If you are thinking about using inferential techniques, you need to make sure you understand the difference between a **parametric test** and a **non-parametric** one. Parametric tests are those that make a series of specific assumptions about the underlying sample data. This often includes assessments about the nature of the distribution, the associated variance, and the scale used to take the measurement. Such parameters can serve to enhance both the accuracy and the precision of the test. As a result, they are generally considered to have more statistical power than their non-parametric counterparts. However, these requirements also mean that they are less flexible in terms of the data that can be used in conjunction with them. The exact requirements vary between tests, so we recommend that you discuss with your supervisor whether parametric or non-parametric tests are appropriate.

The most common kinds of statistical tests that are used for the purposes of a social science dissertation are summarized in Table 13.12. However, there are many different tests that can be used in a variety of contexts, so please do not think that the table is in any way exhaustive. You can find out more about these techniques in statistics texts highlighted in 'Delve deeper'.

Table 13.12 **Common tests used for social science dissertations**

What are you trying to do?	How many variables do you have?	Statistical test	
		Parametric	Non-parametric
Examine frequency counts (in categories)	One	n/a	Chi-square 'Goodness of Fit'
	Two	n/a	Chi-square 'Test of Association'
Look for differences between groups	Two (IV is binary, DV is interval)	Independent samples 't-test'	Mann-Whitney U
	Two (IV is nominal or ordinal **and** non-binary, DV is interval)	ANOVA	Kruskal-Wallis
Look for relationships between variables	Two (IV and DV are interval variables)	Pearson's r	Spearman's Rho (can also be used with two ordinal variables)
	Two (DV is binary, IV is nominal, ordinal, or interval)	Logistic regression	n/a
	One DV, more than one IV (DV is binary, IVs are nominal, ordinal, or interval)	Multiple logistic regression	n/a
	One DV, more than one IV (DV is interval, IVs can be nominal, ordinal, or interval)	Multiple linear regression	n/a
	Multiple DVs, one or more IVs (interval DVs, nominal IVs)	MANOVA	n/a

Source: Author's analysis

WORKING WITH YOUR SUPERVISOR 13.6

Your first decision will be whether you need to use statistical tests. The answer will depend on your discipline and the expectations of your supervisor. Ask your supervisor if these tests are necessary. In many small-scale research projects, simple summary or descriptive statistics convey the information required. When supported by tables and other displays of your data, these techniques can go a long way towards providing what you need to form the basis of your analysis.

DISCUSSING YOUR DATA

Once you have collected your data and analysed it using descriptive and/or inferential statistics, you need to know about how to discuss your findings in your dissertation. The findings and analysis chapter(s) are crucial to your dissertation and provide an opportunity to show what you have identified in the data and how it addresses the research questions, in addition to how it links to existing literature. While there are some structural differences in how the chapters may be presented in terms of how the findings and analysis/discussion chapters are organized in dissertations (this is discussed in more detail in Chapter 17), there are also key considerations that you should make sure you adhere to in these chapters. Remember that the discussion of your data provides a chance to showcase the key points from your data in relation to your aims and objectives. It is not a case of presenting all of the tables and figures you have produced. Instead, you need to decide which ones are most necessary to answer your research questions. You need to tell a narrative using your data. This is also where, in quantitative research, you confirm or disconfirm the initial hypotheses and explain your findings.

A strong and coherent presentation and discussion of your data is crucial to the final mark your dissertation will achieve. It is the place where you link the existing research referred to in the literature review to your individual research. This link to the literature is important in helping you to explain your findings. The process of returning to your initial ideas and reassessing them in the light of your own findings is crucial in presenting a coherent dissertation. If you identified gaps in the literature review you need to demonstrate how your research responds to those gaps. This explanation will help you to demonstrate an original contribution to knowledge (see Chapter 16).

I WISH I'D KNOWN . . . THE NEED TO INCLUDE DATA WHICH REFUTES MY HYPOTHESES 13.2

It may be that your findings do not match with your initial hypotheses and the majority of the literature you have identified. However, if this is clearly related to your research question it should be included. Otherwise it will look like an obvious omission or gap in your analysis. As such, you need to do your best to identify why there may be differences between your findings and the literature. Remember this could be associated with a number of factors which make your data different to previous research in the field. For instance, you are likely to be using a different sample. It may be smaller and it is being collected at a different time period. If these types of factors may play a role in explaining these differences, they should be discussed.

CONCLUSION

This chapter has outlined some of the processes in analysing quantitative data and shown you how these can be used for the purposes of dissertation research. This includes some of the ideas and techniques associated with descriptive and inferential analysis. You will also be aware that, among other things, the types of data you construct have implications for the type of analysis you can conduct. We've also highlighted the importance of presenting data accurately. While quantitative analysis can appear quite daunting at first, taking time to understand some basic forms of quantitative analysis presentation, and how they can be used to describe features of social life, will make exploring more advanced statistical tasks and interpreting their meaning in your dissertation much easier.

WHAT DO I NEED TO THINK ABOUT?

- Do you understand the different levels of measurement and how this affects how you can present your data?
- Are you clear about good practice in relation to presenting data?
- How do you decide which measures of central tendency are useful to use with the data you have collected?
- Do you know the difference between descriptive statistics and inferential statistics and which are most appropriate to use in your dissertation?
- Do you understand what is meant by statistical significance?
- Are you clear about how to describe your data in your discussion section?

WHAT DO I NEED TO DO?

- Decide whether quantitative analysis is appropriate for your project.
- Plan your results in relation to your research aims and questions. This includes being able to:
  - identify when to use frequencies and/or proportions and how you can best present any results
  - understand the different techniques of data visualization, and when and where to use them
  - calculate measures of central tendency and measures of dispersion where necessary
  - understand why you might make use of inferential statistics, including the different types that exist and where they might be appropriate
  - analyse your results, linking your findings to your research questions and literature review.

Access the online resources **www.oup.com/uk/brymansrp1e** to help you to successfully complete your social research project or dissertation.

DELVE DEEPER

Acton, C. and Millar, R. with Fullarton, D. and Maltby, J. (2009). *SPSS for Social Scientists.* **Basingstoke: Palgrave Macmillan.** If you are looking for a very accessible IBM SPSS guide this is one of a number of places you might want to start. It builds on this chapter, providing a detailed guide to producing and interpreting IBM SPSS outputs.

Bryman, A. and Cramer, D. (2011). *Quantitative Data Analysis with IBM SPSS 17, 18 and 19: A Guide for Social Scientists.* **London: Routledge.** This book provides a non-technical approach to quantitative data analysis using IBM SPSS. It is another useful starting place.

Byrne, D. (2002). *Interpreting Quantitative Data.* **London: Sage.** There are very few books focused purely on different types of quantitative data. There are a number of books which cover statistics and IBM SPSS, or general methods texts that touch on various characteristics of quantitative research, but there is a dearth of books covering various quantitative approaches. This book is one of the few that does this.

Field, A. (2017). *Discovering Statistics using IBM SPSS Statistics* **(5th edition). London: Sage.** This book is more advanced (and bigger) than the other 'Delve deeper' recommendations. Written by a psychologist with a love of cats and music (as we are told), it presents statistics in a very didactical and approachable way using a variety of (often quite random but accessible) examples.

Foster, L., Diamond, I., and Jefferies, J. (2014). *Beginning Statistics: An Introduction for Social Scientists* **(2nd edition). London: Sage.** Liam wrote the second edition of this popular book with Ian Diamond and Julie Jefferies. It provides an introduction to working with statistics in the social sciences, clearly explaining how to carry out statistics and present data.

Pallant, J. (2016). *SPSS Survival Manual* **(6th edition). Maidenhead: Open University Press.** This book is an excellent guide to IBM SPSS. It takes you through statistical procedures in some detail using IBM SPSS, but in a step-by-step manner. This makes it extremely accessible and a good starting point for those of you using IBM SPSS for the first time.

The Inter-University Consortium for Political and Social Research at the University of Michigan provides some really useful resources. This includes slides and information about how to interpret frequency distributions, crosstabulations, and many other techniques in IBM SPSS. It builds on many of the concepts learned in this chapter. *https://www.icpsr.umich.edu/icpsrweb/instructors/support/students (Accessed 7 November 2018)*

The Web Center for Social Research is a useful source in relation to many different types of research methods. However, one of its most useful features is the test selector which helps you identify which types of statistical tests are appropriate for your data.
https://socialresearchmethods.net/ (Accessed 7 November 2018)

There are a number of statistical software packages which can be used to analyse numerical data. Some of the most popular include: **IBM SPSS** (https://www.ibm.com/products/spss-statistics), **STATA** (https://www.stata.com), and **R** (https://www.r-project.org/) (Accessed 3 December 2018). If you are interested in using one of these packages you should discuss this with your supervisor.

CHAPTER 14

ANALYSING
QUALITATIVE DATA

WHAT DO I NEED TO KNOW?

- The process of qualitative analysis
  - When to stop?
- Standard features of qualitative analysis
  - Coding
  - Memo writing
- Types of qualitative analysis
  - Analytic induction
  - Thematic analysis
  - Grounded theory
  - Narrative analysis
  - Discourse analysis
- Computer-assisted qualitative data analysis software (CAQDAS)

INTRODUCTION

There are many varieties of qualitative analysis. Some of these approaches are related to specific forms of data, whereas others are more generic in nature. There can also be considerable differences between some forms of qualitative analysis to the extent that they have very little in common with one another. For instance, there are at least four books that detail quite different approaches to grounded theory, none of which really corresponds with the principles that underpin 'performative inquiry'. Given all this diversity, it is not possible for us to adequately address every type of analysis, or provide highly detailed instructions for the more common techniques that we do describe. What we will do in this chapter, however, is introduce you to the general process of qualitative data analysis and some of the techniques that are typically associated with dissertation-type projects.

THE PROCESS OF QUALITATIVE ANALYSIS

In the first instance, it is worth stating that the process of choosing your analytical approach should not coincide with the start of analysis. Instead, you should have thought about the type of analysis you intend to adopt **before** you step into the field. This is because some forms of analysis actually help to direct your research aims and objectives. Others will also influence how you construct your literature review, and some will dictate how you collect your data. This is, in large part, why we suggested in Chapter 9 that writing a proposal is such a key part of the research process. It enables you to make sense of your research **and** how your approach to analysis will influence other aspects of your project.

When considering the type of analysis you intend to take, it is also worth thinking about your approach to theory. Put simply, theory allows researchers to describe, understand, or explain the social world. This often means developing or using higher-order constructs to explain the detail of the phenomena you are interested in. These constructs might be developed from the 'ground up', or be taken from the literature and applied 'top down' to data. The resulting theory can then be supported and/or developed by further data collection, or even further research.

While not always the case, qualitative analysis is usually inductive in nature (see Chapter 2). This means that qualitative researchers tend to use their analysis to construct theory **from** data. Concepts should reflect the demands of the field— they are not necessarily fixed beforehand. This is why qualitative work requires information-rich data. Analysis is often a process of gradual refinement of detail, with theorization being something of an emergent process. This is in contrast to those approaches that stress the need to begin with a theory, which is then tested against observation.

The great advantage of taking a more inductive approach is that theoretical development is not constrained by prior assumptions or commitments. Being 'welded' to a theory, or a particular style of thinking, can prevent you from following up interesting avenues of data. That being said, some qualitative projects do explicitly outline a theoretical position from the outset. Many sociological research proposals that are qualitative in nature, for example, will outline the theoretical position at the beginning.

There is a delicate balance to be made here, and an inductive approach does not mean you enter the field with a completely 'blank slate'. You still need to make sure that you ask meaningful questions and that your research has some greater purpose in terms of the wider literature. Again, while there are different emphases with particular types of approach, qualitative data collection and analysis does not exist in a vacuum: it is informed by the things you are sensitive to. These include: previous data; the wider literature; and, your own interests and experiences.

In this respect, the qualitative researcher is an active constituent of the analytical process. You select: what to focus on; what to record and how to record it; the analytical focus; how to understand that analysis in terms of theory; and how to represent that whole process. There are many opportunities at each of these stages, and you are central to the choices that are made. This is not a neutral process, and it is why critical reflection is so important to qualitative analysis. It acts as a mechanism for both informed decision-making and transparency.

It is also worth highlighting that the process of qualitative analysis is not always as linear as might otherwise be assumed when reading about a project. Typically, the writing of qualitative work requires researchers to introduce the topic in terms of the research and theory, outline the methodology, and then present the results and conclusions—and it looks as if this was how things actually happened. However, what makes sense in terms of writing a narrative for research is not necessarily the same as how things took place, and in what order. While the application of a particular theory might always have been the intended outcome, more often than not theory is more an emergent process.

This is why qualitative research is often considered to be iterative. Analysis is a generative cycle of questions and answers that eventually leads to a desired outcome. Data are collected and an initial analysis is performed. This leads to further questions which, in turn, require further data and analysis. Again, this suggests yet further avenues for investigation, and so on. This general process of inductive analysis in qualitative work is summarized in the following stages:

- Research idea
- Project planning (strategy/design/sampling)
- Data collection
- Analysis
- More data collection
- Refine and develop analysis
- More data collection
- Further theoretical articulation
- Writing up

However, while this is the general process of qualitative analysis, there are significant variations on the theme, and some forms of analysis do not follow this voyage of discovery at all. That being said, the more common forms of analysis that we see when supervising and marking dissertations do follow this sort of pattern. Indeed, the different types of analysis that we detail in the final section of this chapter have these sorts of characteristics, which is why we have introduced the general process here.

When to stop?

At which point, some brief consideration of the issue 'when to stop' is worthwhile. Some types of qualitative analysis have very definite end points. The requirement for 'theoretical saturation' in grounded theory, for example, instructs researchers to complete the analysis when data collection no longer allows them to develop the theoretical properties of their categories. Similarly, the principles of analytic induction suggest the process is complete when data collection no longer identifies any deviant cases that might otherwise refute the analysis.

In reality, both theoretical saturation and the absence of deviant cases are difficult to achieve—particularly so given the time-limited nature of dissertation research. The end of qualitative analysis is often dependent on much more prosaic issues associated with time and cost. In many cases, the analysis ceases simply because the researcher has to stop working on it.

However, more often than not it is possible in dissertation research to reach a point where the rewards of further analysis are considerably less than the effort needed to develop them. You will need to exercise considered judgement here, but where data is being collected and analysed without significant addition, it is time to think about consolidating the findings by formally writing them up. This point is often referred to as data saturation.

STANDARD FEATURES OF QUALITATIVE ANALYSIS

The more common forms of qualitative analysis also share more than a general process of iteration. They also tend to correspond to the more standard techniques of indexing and organizing data. Again, while there are variations in terms of terminology **and** emphasis, the interrelated processes of coding and memo writing are common techniques in qualitative analysis. We will deal with each in turn.

Coding

One of the key components of qualitative analysis is the process of coding. This is basically a system of indexing that enables you to sort your data. By organizing qualitative material into discrete units, codes are shorthand devices that label, separate, and compile data. A code is simply a conceptual label that is written alongside sections of data that describes an 'incident'. These incidents are any points of significance within data. There is little limit to what, exactly, incidents may be deemed significant, but more common types of things that might require a label could include: characteristics, events, actions, attitudes, phrases, people, attributions, or explanations.

When working with transcriptions or field notes, these coded incidents will be a few sentences, or perhaps a whole paragraph. If you are working with more visual or physical material, they could also be any aspect of an image or object. However, the incidents that constitute a code can also be very small, or very large, in scope. For example, when researching the terrace chanting that occurs at football matches, Tom had a series of initial codes that referred to whole songs. Alongside these large codes, he also coded much smaller material, such as a line in a song. Given the highly entropic nature of terrace chants, in some cases a single word actually formed the basis for a code. This process can be seen in Figure 14.1.

Figure 14.1 **Example of coding procedure**

ANY OLD IRON
ANY OLD IRON
WE SING UP THE IRON,
YOU LOOK SWEET
WALKING DOWN THE STREET
BOTTLE IN YOUR HAND
AND BOOTS ON YOUR FEET,
DRESSED IN STYLE,
OLD MAN'S STYLE,
WE SING UP THE IRON,
AND WE DON'T GIVE A DAMN
    ABOUT A CITY FAN,
OLD IRON,
OLD IRON

IRON × 6 (EMPHASIS ON START & FINISH)
OLD × 5
WE × 3 & THEM × 1
SING × 2
STYLE × 2
MAN × 1

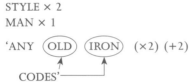

'ANY (OLD) (IRON) (×2) (+2)

    CODES'

OLD:
TRADITION; WELL ESTABLISHED IMPLIED HERITAGE

MEMO
    - IMITATES 'RAG & BONE' MAN
    - BY-GONE DAYS - TRADITION / NOSTALGIA
    - IT'S A UNIQUE SONG
    - IT'S AN OLD SONG
    - REINFORCES NOTIONS OF HISTORY (OLD IRON)
    - IS THERE A CLAIM TO A UNIQUE, 'AUTHENTIC'
TRADITION

IRON:
    - 'THE IRON' IS A NICKNAME
    - SYMBOLIC OF TOWN IDENTITY
    - INDUSTRIAL HERITAGE (STEEL TOWN)

THIS MATTERS TO NAME THE CLUB AFTER ITS INDUSTRY
(ITS PURPOSE) BUT THERE IS ALSO A NEED TO KEEP
REPRODUCING IT AS AN IDENTITY
THIS IS NOT PLURAL. 'THE IRON' IS SINGULAR - EMPHASIS
IS ON THE COLLECTIVE

FINDING YOUR WAY 14.1

Coding has a number of important functions in qualitative analysis:
- It is a system of indexing that allows you to systematically manage your data.
- It requires you to engage in detail with what your participants have told you.
- It enables you to become familiar with, and understand, the content of your data.
- It is the primary means to identify what your findings are.

The process of coding generally tends to take one of two formats: in vivo coding and theoretical coding.

In vivo coding is the term given to the generation of coding labels that are taken directly from the data. The terms and phrases contained in a particular incident are used as a shorthand summation of the code. Data are inspected for incidents, and when something of significance is encountered it is given a label that is taken directly from that incident.

There are some distinct advantages to coding in vivo. By using terms taken directly from the data it is possible to keep as close as possible to the terms and phrases used by the participants. This can be particularly important in the initial stages of analysis where codes, and any associated categories, are being developed. However, some researchers actually warn against the overuse of in vivo coding during the later stages of analysis. This is because it can limit the capacity of the analysis to translate to different contexts within the project itself, and across the wider literature. When using in vivo coding, it can be quite easy to inadvertently amplify particular idiosyncrasies associated with particular people, groups, or locations. These will not necessarily apply elsewhere.

Theoretical coding is the term given to the use of emergent or existing theory to help structure data. This type of coding can be achieved in one of two ways. In the first instance, the coding process will often produce higher-order families that are, in some way, related to one another. These are often referred to as categories. Codes do not usually exist in isolation and will often repeat across data. As you progress through the analysis, for example, you may note that particular incidents in the data are quite similar to codes that have gone before. These incidents can be coded using exactly the in vivo codes that you have already developed.

But some of these codes will become so significant in either quality or quantity that you begin to notice nuances within them. This will often require further articulation to fully appreciate the emerging complexity. This process of 'recoding' incidents within a particular code is a sign that you are now dealing with a more conceptually focused category. Indeed, by comparing and contrasting codes, analysis should be directed toward the similarities and differences in your data and your emerging coding scheme. This helps to develop codes in response to the data.

It is important to keep reviewing the data and the emergent codes and categories so you can expand and modify them where necessary.

In addition to using emergent codes and categories for theoretical coding, you can also use concepts from existing literature as sensitizing constructs to help develop your analysis. This involves using ideas and findings borrowed from elsewhere to help you to illuminate your data and/or orientate the coding process. What, exactly, you choose to borrow will depend entirely on the aims of your project **and** the demands of your data.

The process of theoretical coding also has particular advantages, and some potential drawbacks. To begin with the latter, one danger of utilizing theoretical coding too early in the analytical process is that other, more emergent, aspects of the data can quickly be subsumed by pre-existing theory. Not only does this challenge the inductive properties of analysis, 'forcing' theory can also be inappropriate. While data never speaks for itself, it does need some capacity to be heard! Used judiciously, however, theoretical coding can be used to further articulate categories, and the relationships and interconnections that might exist between them. It can also help the transferability of the analysis to different contexts, both within and beyond your research. This can help your findings to resonate with the wider literature.

In addition to thinking critically about whether you are taking a 'bottom up' or a 'top down' approach to coding, it is also important to recognize that the process of coding is both an ongoing and iterative process. To be clear, this means that it should not be treated as 'a once and for all time' affair, a singular activity that is completed in one go at the end of data collection. Instead, it often accompanies

FINDING YOUR WAY 14.2

Seven tips for coding:
- Familiarize yourself with your data by listening to interviews and/or reading through transcripts, field notes, documents, etc.
- Repeat this process to make sure you 'know' your data!
- Try to begin the coding process as soon as is possible.
- Remember that incidents in the data can be coded in more than one way, or recoded as is necessary.
- Regularly review codes—keeping a code book will help you to do this.
- Be prepared to consider more general theoretical ideas that resonate with the data and the emerging patterns in your coding.
- Remember that coding is only one part of the analytical process—once you have indexed and organized your data, you will still need to examine it further to look for interconnections and relationships between categories. You will also need to interpret your findings in relation to the wider literature.

data collection, and similarly requires revisiting previous data in light of new discoveries. You need to review and evaluate codes on a continuous basis, perhaps even discarding them where necessary. You might also need to relabel codes in the light of later discoveries.

Memo writing

Memo writing is an essential part of the coding process. Memos are simply what is written as an accompaniment to the coding process—and they can vary quite considerably in terms of content, structure, and style. They can be descriptive, explanatory, or summative in purpose, and more or less formal in tone. They do not have to be particularly academic, although they might be. Similarly, they might connect material to the wider research base, or simply refer to the text at hand. In some cases, they might be little more than a couple of words; in others, they are much more substantial.

The key point about memo writing is that it should help you to record your thinking **and** develop your ideas. Memos have two purposes in the process of analysis. They serve as a reminder of your thoughts at the time of coding, and as a way of making sure you do not forget good ideas. Memos also allow you to reflect critically on those initial thoughts. This means you can develop or reject your thinking in the light of new discoveries.

The material contained in memos also provides a way of developing initial thoughts into more concrete theoretical ideas. As codes contain more and more incidents, memos can be used to try and expand codes, and possibly note the nuances that enable them to become more meaningful categories. It is also possible to use memo writing to try and connect the emergent analysis to the wider literature. Memos might highlight a need to discover theoretical constructs that could help account for the data, or act as a sketch pad to explore how an existing theory could be relevant to the material at hand.

It is useful to think of memos as a written record of the process of **your** analysis, and how it is developing. This means that it is not possible to be overly prescriptive about what they should and should not contain, or how they should be written. The style and form that memos take need to be responsive to the requirements of the data, the emerging analysis, **and** how you like to work. Memos might take the form of a research diary, a formal 'code book', a notebook specifically dedicated to jotting down and sketching ideas, or a Word document. You might use this material to draw diagrams on smaller or larger pieces of paper to explore how key categories are emerging, and how they might relate to one another. In other cases, you might want to electronically annotate transcripts or visual material. Some dedicated software programs for qualitative analysis can also be utilized to write memos directly alongside text. These memos can then be searched for key terms at a later date, or reviewed where necessary.

FINDING YOUR WAY 14.3

In your dissertation you can make good use of the 'nuts and bolts' of your analysis to help you structure the findings section.

- Describe categories and their relationships with one another using your memos and codes.
- Use the data incidents contained within codes as evidence for analysis. Select the evidence to include based on clarity, relevance, and eloquence. It should be used to support the point you are making, rather than making the point for you.
- Discuss the significance of your analysis by relating it to relevant research you have used in the literature review **and** in the process of analysis. Again, use any relevant memos you have created to help you to do this.

Perhaps more important than what form they actually take, the key point is that you make some effort to record the process of analysis—particularly as the words you write in your memos can actually become part of the findings sections of your dissertation. As your memos become more and more developed, they often begin to look like key points of discussion—and this discussion can be used directly when writing up your results.

TYPES OF QUALITATIVE ANALYSIS

Beyond the basic operations of coding, categorizing, and memo writing common to qualitative analysis, there are more specific approaches worth outlining in further detail. There are many more opportunities for analysis, but the approaches we detail below tend to be the more common used in dissertations. These are: analytic induction; thematic analysis, grounded theory; narrative analysis; and discourse analysis. We will outline and discuss each in turn.

Analytic induction

Analytic induction is an approach to qualitative analysis that has, perhaps, fallen a little out of favour with researchers. This is, in large part, due to the demands of actually carrying it out. In principle, however, the process of analytical induction is relatively clear. It begins with the following steps:

- Definition of a rough research question
- The development of hypothetical explanation
- Examination of cases/data collection

The logic of analytic induction suggests that any examination of data associated with a case will produce one of two outcomes. Either the case in question will not conform to the hypothetical explanation—in which instance the original explanation will need further reformulation so it can be tested against new cases—or the initial case will confirm the explanation. When no deviant cases appear to contradict the explanation, then data collection ceases.

While this iterative process might sound simple in theory, it is often lengthy in practice. It typically takes much reformulation, and a great many cases, before an explanation is confirmed. Initial hypothetical explanations tend to be somewhat vague, with later iterations becoming more and more complex as the explanation develops. This allows for some theoretical development in the process of analysis. Any deviant case that is encountered necessitates a return to data collection and more and more explanatory reformulation. Unfortunately, there is no explicit number of cases required before the explanation can be confirmed. The decision is largely based on professional intuition, which can be quite challenging for a time-limited student project.

The nature of analytic induction also makes it a somewhat rigid approach to theory construction, and it is not always clear what constitutes a deviant case. Something can look quite different in comparison to something else, but have quite a similar underlying structure. For instance, the notion of the 'ideal type' that was developed by Max Weber (1949) is a way of building theory that attempts to synthesize many diffuse and individual phenomena into a unified theoretical construct. However, in any single case, Weber made the point that any identified properties in such an 'ideal' may be more or less present, or entirely absent, without compromising the integrity of the construct as a whole. This type of theoretical construction highlights a problem in the logic of analytic induction: when, exactly, does something become deviant to the hypothesis? It is not something that is easy to resolve and is likely to depend on professional judgement, rather than explicit instruction.

None of which is to suggest that the process of analytic induction is inappropriate for a qualitatively oriented dissertation research project. However, it is to highlight that there are some difficulties of applying it in practice that need to be considered from the outset.

Thematic analysis

The search for 'themes' is common to much social research. This is exemplified by one increasingly popular approach to the analysis of qualitative material— thematic analysis. While different versions of the general approach do exist, Braun and Clarke (2006) have produced a form of thematic analysis that is particularly noteworthy in terms of its theoretical and methodological transparency. Their approach is also designed to be sympathetic to the emergent themes of interviewees **and** those that are actively chosen by the researcher as being of interest. This makes it particularly useful for dissertation research. Braun and Clarke's method involves a six-stage process:

- *Familiarization:* This may take the form of: transcribing interviews or focus groups; writing and reading field notes; or, inspecting and examining documents and other material.
- *Initial coding:* Thematic analysis follows the basic process of coding described above. Early 'open' coding can be completed using the emergent properties of the data in much the same way as in vivo coding, and then by incorporating theoretical concepts or ideas as they become relevant.
- *Identifying themes:* Again, like the process outlined above, thematic analysis requires the researcher to compare and contrast emergent codes and make interconnections between them. This allows for the elaboration of the properties of a named theme.
- *Reviewing themes:* Emergent analysis is further developed by combining those themes into high-order constructs and by searching for sub-themes or dimensions that help to further articulate the analysis.
- *Defining themes:* A narrative is then developed that describes the theme—and any associated interconnections—in detail.
- *Evidencing themes:* Evidence is then taken from the codes that underpin themes. This supports and substantiates the narrative, and helps to justify the significance of the theme in relation to the wider literature.

Although these stages of analysis are relatively orderly, they do not necessarily have to follow in strict sequence. Braun and Clarke (2006) highlight how the

FINDING YOUR WAY 14.4

A theme can be considered to be (Bryman, 2016: 584):
- a property of the research aims—and perhaps the research questions
- constituted by codes identified in the data
- the platform for theoretical understanding
- a category of interest that occurs across data

When looking for a theme in your data it is worth paying attention to the following, as it might indicate the presence of a theme (adapted from Ryan and Bernard, 2003):
- Repetitions
- Indigenous typologies or categories
- Similarities and differences
- Theory-related material

It is also important to justify why themes are important in your analysis. This can be done by showing how they occur across specific cases, how they relate to the literature, and how they relate to your research focus.

process of coding, identifying, and reviewing themes should be iterative in nature. There is some circular motion between these particular stages, and data collection and analysis more generally. While it is possible to conduct thematic analysis entirely after data collection, it is often helpful to begin analysis while still collecting data. This means your research can be made responsive to the emergent properties of the field, rather than being a more static process of question and response.

Grounded theory

Published in 1967, grounded theory was originally proposed by Glaser and Strauss in their book *The Discovery of Grounded Theory* (Glaser and Strauss, 1967). They sought to provide a series of systematic instructions for qualitative researchers that were designed to 'discover' theory from data in a transparent manner. Grounded theory is an inductive process that emphasizes the need to conduct research based on the demands and requirements of the data, its emergent analysis, and in accordance with the guidelines set by the theory.

While grounded theory has tended to be associated with the analysis of interview transcripts, it is actually compatible with all types of qualitative data. The rich data often associated with interviews, field observations, as well as many types of documentary analysis can all be incorporated into a grounded approach. Similarly, although researchers have tended to use the approach to generate theory at the micro and middle ranges, it does allow for the development of more formal and higher-level theories.

There are seven defining components of grounded theory:

- Data collection occurs in stages and in correspondence to the emergent properties of the analysis
- Codes and categories are generated from the emerging data and not from preconceived ideas and hypotheses
- A method of constant comparison is employed whereby any newly gathered data are continually compared with previous data in order to refine any identified codes and categories
- Theory is advanced at each individual stage of data collection until theoretical saturation is achieved
- Discovered categories are elaborated in order to: specify their properties; define the relationships between categories; identify gaps in the data and analysis
- Sampling is aimed toward theory construction, not statistical representativeness
- The literature review is conducted after the analysis so that the inductive properties of theory generation remain intact

I WISH I'D KNOWN . . . THE DIFFERENCE BETWEEN
OPEN AND AXIAL CODING | 4.|

In the refined version of grounded theory that Strauss and Corbin (1990) went on to articulate, **open coding** refers to the process of breaking down raw qualitative data into more manageable chunks. Through the process of constant comparison, the codes can then be grouped together to construct basic categories. **Axial coding**, on the other hand, is the process of exploring the interconnections and relationships between codes and categories. This involves interrogating the properties of those categories in relation to context, consequence, interaction, and cause. **Selective coding** can then be used to saturate a **core category**, or to discover codes and categories that need further articulation. A core category is simply the main focus of interest around which other categories coalesce.

Unfortunately, while these central components are relatively clear, both Glaser and Strauss each revised the original principles, and subsequent versions of the approach have diverged somewhat. In response to successive critiques that suggested grounded theory was imbued with assumptions of both objectivism and positivism, Charmaz (2000) has also developed a more constructivist account of the approach.

Perhaps more importantly in respect to dissertation research, using grounded theory in accordance with the principles outlined by Glaser and Strauss takes a lot of time and effort. The twin requirements of theoretical sampling and theoretical saturation mean that the demands of data collection and analysis are very large. This point is reached when additional data collection no longer helps to develop the properties of the category. In practice this is very difficult to achieve given the nature of a time-limited dissertation.

There are also other difficulties that can compromise the integrity of achieving the key principles of grounded theory. These include: selective, rather than theoretical sampling; ignoring the emerging properties of the data; using a preconceived theoretical lens; failure to adhere to the constant comparative procedure; and, a reliance on computer programs to identify codes. While many student projects claim to be following a 'grounded' approach, achieving it in practice is actually quite difficult. One way of negotiating this difficulty is to articulate exactly what principles you are attempting to follow with your particular application of the approach **and** those that you cannot, for whatever reason, employ. This will also involve some discussion, perhaps in the methodology or conclusion sections of your dissertation, about the nature of the approach and your claims of implementing grounded theory.

Narrative analysis

Generally speaking, narrative approaches to analysis emphasize the stories people use to understand and represent experience. In some cases, the researcher deliberately uses the phases of data collection to seek out and elicit such stories, and in others, narrative is used as a frame through which to examine pre-existing data. After all, narratives are ubiquitous in everyday life. They are a universal means of ordering understanding, action, and experience.

The narratives researchers utilize for research can be textual, oral, or visual—sometimes in combination. While some narratives may be naturally occurring, they can also be fictional or nonfictional in nature. Narratives may also detail extended periods of time, or be focused toward specific events. Equally, they can be individually driven, or more collectively inspired in terms of both authorship and/or focus. What all of these narratives share is that they detail things over time with some sort of 'plot' to connect them. And, of course, all narratives have some sort of narrator and an audience—whether that audience is real or imagined.

Given the pervasiveness of narrative and its associated purposes, it should be no surprise that there are a number of variations of analysis. These variations have different foci, emphasis, and techniques. Life history research, biographical analysis, and performative inquiry all have narrative components, while the term 'narrative inquiry' is something of an umbrella term for those approaches that seek to examine the nature of narrative in the human world. What all of these approaches share, however, is they tend to be less concerned with the 'truth' of a particular story. Instead, interest is directed toward exploring how narratives are (re)produced, transmitted, **and** received by particular people at particular points in time.

In these terms, much material can be suitable for narrative research in the social sciences. This can include, but is not limited to, the following data: autobiographies, diaries, letters, scrapbooks, conversations, family histories, photographs, films, and even interview material or field notes. Similarly, the range of disciplines associated with narrative research is also quite broad. It is particularly popular in education, sociology, and cultural studies, as well as some areas of human sciences and the humanities.

Narrative approaches also tend to downplay the use of coding in the process of analysis. This is because coding separates data into parts, and disconnects parts of the story from one another. How those parts work in conjunction with each other **as a whole** is a key issue for narrative analysis. The separation of data into discrete units can also serve to divorce the situated meaning of a narrative from its key point of reference—everyday life. In narrative analysis, what is said is just as important as what a narrative is used for, how it is communicated, and the context in which those stories are situated. So, rather than coding, narrative researchers tend to work with narrative frameworks. Broadly speaking, these are the dimensions through which narratives are reproduced, received, and reinterpreted—and rather than being the property of the narrator, they are seen as sets of shared tools that are drawn from wider cultural repertoires.

Riessman (2008) suggests that there are four key arenas of interest for narrative researchers: thematic; structural; performative; and visual. A thematic focus pursues the content of a narrative and/or a set of stories. It seeks to identify key points of issue in those stories and attempts to reveal both their similarities and their differences. Concern is directed toward what, exactly, those narratives are about. Thematic dimensions of any given narrative might include: characters, emotions, settings, events, audience and causality. On the other hand, structural analysis attempts to explore how a story is constructed to achieve particular ends: what does the story do and how are those aims represented in the narrative? To narrate something is to purposefully select, organize, connect, and evaluate events as significant and important to both narrator and audience. Structural analysis of narrative examines what these aims might be, and how they are achieved in practice.

Riessman (2008) suggests that the examination of the thematic and structural properties of a narrative are the building blocks of all narrative analysis. However, beyond these cornerstones, narrative can also be interrogated in terms of their performative and visual aspects. This is particularly the case where the researcher is actively involved in the reproduction of those narratives. Performance refers to the interactive process of delivering and receiving narrative. It concerns both narrator and audience and how the transmission and reception of narratives are interconnected. This is of particular importance to researchers who are interested in the elicitation of narratives from others in the process of research. Data collection is recognized as a means of constructing particular narratives, with the analysis directed toward the context in which those narratives are enacted. Rather than taking those narratives away from people, the focus for such researchers then becomes person-centred, examining how their subjective histories and intentions are embedded in context.

On one hand, visual aspects of narrative can emphasize image, and the relationship between images and words in the production and reception of narratives. However, visual aspects of narrative analysis can also go beyond this to examine how narratives are crafted and curated: that is, how they are positioned among other narratives, and how those narrative ensembles are afforded significance (or not). This involves examining the cultures in which narratives are given visibility. None of which is inevitable.

Regardless of the particular type, narrative analysis is one of those methods that really needs to be integrated from the outset of your project. It is not really an 'off the shelf' method of analysis that exists independently to other aspects of the research process: it shapes the way you approach the investigation of the human

FINDING YOUR WAY 14.5

If you choose to undertake narrative analysis in your dissertation, key questions you should ask include:

- What is the narrative about?
- To what purpose is the narrative being put?
- What does the story accomplish?
- Who is the intended audience?
- What cultural resources does it draw on (or take for granted)?
- Are there preferred, alternate, or counter-narratives?

world, the type of research questions you ask, the format of data collection, **and** the focus for analysis. Again, it is also worth highlighting that there are quite different forms of narrative analysis, so being clear about the particular type of analysis you are thinking of employing is also crucial to its successful utilization.

Discourse analysis

Discourse analysis is broadly concerned with the way in which words and language are used to help to structure particular realities. The term covers a range of approaches, including critical discourse analysis, Foucauldian discourse analysis, and policy discourse analysis. Some forms of conversation analysis have discursive elements, while other approaches are closely related to narrative analysis. What all of these variations share, however, is an emphasis on examining how understanding and action are realized through discourse.

In the context of everyday life, we typically make the sensible assumption that words correspond with **something**. This is essentially what they mean. Language more or less reflects the reality of the social world. Discourse analysts, however, invert that assumption to examine how language structures meaning. That is to ask how knowledge of the social world is reproduced and represented in particular linguistic constructions, **and** what the consequences of those representations might be. In these terms, particular uses of language frame understanding and associated patterns of action, not the other way around. A useful way to think about this is to imagine that discourse is a solution to a problem. The purpose of discourse analysis is to identify what that problem was in the first place, and for whom.

One implication of discourse analysis is to recognize that language is not a neutral instrument. Instead, the knowledge structures that are embedded in particular discourses are thoroughly intertwined with power, with the latter helping to define the former. The capacity for power helps to shape the knowledge that is produced, and language is the key vehicle through which this is achieved and legitimated. This property of discourse analysis has made it very popular with researchers who are interested in the critical investigation of society. Foucault (1967), for example, explored the history of 'madness' to demonstrate how discourse has helped to structure our understanding of, and response to, mental illness. This includes the nature of the illness, what can and should be done about it, and who is entitled to treat it.

While Foucault's focus was at the societal level, discourse analysis can be utilized at micro, meso, and macro levels—and in some cases all three. For example, the linguist Fairclough (1995) developed a three-dimensional model for discourse analysis that broadly correspond to these levels. At the micro level, interest is directed toward the actual textual analysis of discourse; at the meso level the focus is on issues associated with the production and consumption of discourse; and, at the macro level the purpose is to examine the broad sociopolitical context in which discourse exists.

The underlying assumption that language helps to structure reality means that discourse analysis also tends to be anti-realist and distinctly constructionist in nature. They tend to deny that there is 'a world out there' independent to language. Instead, discourse analysts suggest that any representation of reality is always necessarily selective, and it is often imbued with very particular ideologies. To be clear, this means that they are not interested in making comparisons between representation and reality. This is because they question the very nature of reality. Instead, they are concerned with the content and organization of texts, and what sorts of things happen because of those arrangements. In her review of the different approaches to discourse analysis, Gill (1999) suggests five main features of the approach:

- *Discourse is the focus of analysis*: language is not just a means of accessing particular aspects of social reality and is instead the focus of interest
- *Language constructs particular realities*: choices are necessarily made with respect to how reality is being represented in particular discourse
- *Discourse is a means of action*: people use language to do things, and these purposes are contextual in nature
- *Discourse is organized rhetorically*: it is inherently persuasive and cannot be taken for granted
- *Discourse is patterned*: analysis is directed toward identifying those patterns— sometimes referred to as interpretative repertoires—as well as being aware of both silences and absences that exist in a text

The emphasis on language in discourse analysis has meant that it has had considerable application in media and communication studies. However, while its uses for analysing written texts, such as newspapers or articles, is relatively obvious, discourse analysis can also be used with other modes of communication, such as the naturally occurring talk of everyday life, or the material that is constitutive of

FINDING YOUR WAY 14.6

If you are thinking of using discourse analysis, it can often be a good idea to find a paper that does something similar to what you have in mind. This is particularly the case if the paper articulates how they achieved their results because it can serve as a roadmap for your particular process of analysis. Not only does this aid transparency of method, it can also help you to link your research to the wider literature.

an open or semi-structured interview. This means that it has potential uses across the breadth of the disciplines in the social sciences and even the arts and human-ities. It has also had considerable use in the human sciences too.

Unfortunately, due to this diversity it is difficult to provide any sort of 'cookbook' method of discourse analysis. This is further complicated by the fact that many dis-course analysts have actually resisted the idea of explicitly codifying the process. Instead, they often highlight how the analytic mentality required is more like riding a bike, and largely unsuitable to mechanistic description. Many examples that you might find in the literature also have something of a hybrid character that combines a variety of scholarly traditions. Gill's (1999) analysis of sex and relationship advice contained in the pages of *Glamour* magazine, for example, drew on Foucauldian, feminist, and neoliberal critique, as well as more interpretive Weberian influence in the form of Ritzer's (1993) 'McDonaldization' thesis. That said, while lack of trans-parency might be a problem for some, the flexibility it allows can make it an attract-ive means of analysis for dissertation research, particularly where a critical examination of the language is central to the purposes of the project.

COMPUTER-ASSISTED QUALITATIVE DATA ANALYSIS SOFTWARE (CAQDAS)

Before the digital revolution, much of the coding process in qualitative analysis was quite literally achieved by cutting up transcripts and gluing incidents to coded sheets of paper. Obviously, this was a laborious and messy process, particu-larly when dealing with large data sets. Fortunately, there is now a range of com-puter software to help you manage your data. These programs are collectively referred to as Computer-assisted qualitative data analysis software, or CAQDAS for short. While there is no industry leader, NVivo, ATLAS.ti, MAXQDA, Dedoose, and Transana are all popular platforms used for dissertation research.

From the outset, it is important to be clear that the platforms variously associ-ated with CAQDAS will not do the analysis for you. They are not magical 'black boxes' where transcripts are entered into one side with findings coming out the

288 How to do Your Social Research Project or Dissertation

other. Instead, they are tools that allow you to sort, label, and organize your data much more efficiently than you could by hand. The most popular programs tend to operate in the manner of 'code and retrieve'. This is the process of initially coding data, and then collecting it together in a desired sequence so that it can be retrieved in a more meaningful fashion. In doing so, CAQDAS takes over the manual demands associated with physically writing out codes, photocopying transcripts/field notes, cutting out chunks of text, pasting coded text together, and linking codes with associated memos. CAQDAS software also provides space to annotate data and/or codes and categories directly. Many programs will also provide the means for visualizing codes and categories, and any relationships that might exist between them. They can also help you process textual, auditory, and visual material, including, interviews, images, and film.

Unfortunately, when using any software for the first time, there are some start-up costs, and where these costs accumulate, they can become prohibitive. There are two main costs associated with using CAQDAS for dissertation research: finance and time.

CAQDAS platforms can be expensive, particularly so for students. However, you may be fortunate in that your institution has a subscription service to software. In some instances, it might even possible for you to download the software onto your personal devices. In which case, usage becomes much more viable. Some of the major providers also offer free trials of their software, but proceed with caution as it might not be long enough for you to complete your analysis. Some non-commercial software is also available, but functionality can be limited. Given the nature of its independent development, this type of software is also not always updated to be compatible with evolving operating systems.

If access to specific platforms is limited, it is possible to modify word-processing software to function as a means to facilitate your analysis. It would be possible, for instance, to break up large chunks of text by using headings to signify the start and end of a code in a transcript. As the process of analysis progresses and you are able to identify more significant codes, these can then be easily copied and pasted into a new file for further analysis. You can also make use of the search function in these packages to identify keywords. Some also allow for the annotation of text in the form of 'comments boxes'. Again, these should be fully searchable.

The second start-up cost is less easy to assess from the outset. This is because the time necessary to learn how to use the software properly will actually be a product of the particular platform you select, and your own ability to learn and adapt to different software environments. Researching and selecting the platform that you think will best fit your needs only adds to the cost, and evidently, given the nature of a dissertation type project, time is a key concern.

As a very general rule of thumb, if you have less than one hundred thousand words—at around 6,000 words per script this is broadly equivalent to 15 or so semi-structured interviews—the costs are likely to outweigh the rewards for a dissertation-style project. CAQDAS may have its uses beyond that, but it is important to remember that the thoroughness associated with good-quality analysis is a product of the person carrying it out, not the platform it is completed on.

CONCLUSION

Qualitative analysis, regardless of variety, can be a hugely rewarding process. It can also be intellectually stimulating because it involves thinking creatively in interpreting the data. It is, however, also quite labour intensive and requires a certain amount of patience and dedication to keep going over and over documents which, by the end of your analysis, will feel very familiar. Given the time and effort involved, it should not be a surprise to learn that one of the biggest problems we see as supervisors is students who don't sufficiently plan for the amount of time required for analysis in their dissertation. If you are thinking of using one of the approaches outlined above, it is worth starting your data collection and analysis early in the research process as it will stop you trying to do too much, too late.

WHAT DO I NEED TO THINK ABOUT?

- How might your proposed method of analysis impact on your research questions, literature review, and methods of data collection?
- Are there any ontological and epistemological assumptions associated with the type of analysis you might choose?
- Do you understand the key points of technique needed to carry out your analysis, or do you need more specific instructions?
- Can you find any other research papers that follow your proposed method?

WHAT DO I NEED TO DO?

- Make sure you understand the process of qualitative analysis—and where you are currently in your research.
- Choose the most appropriate type of analysis with respect to your focus, your research aims, and your proposed methods of data collection.
- Understand the key techniques needed to carry out your analysis.
- Prepare your data for analysis.
- Conduct your analysis—collecting further data where necessary!

Access the online resources **www.oup.com/uk/brymansrple** to help you to successfully complete your social research project or dissertation.

DELVE DEEPER

Gibbs, G. (2018). *Analyzing Qualitative Data* **(2nd edition). London: Sage.** This is a readable and helpful guide to some of the more common types of analysis that are suitable for qualitative dissertations. It is specifically aimed at undergraduate students, and offers very useful 'how to' guides for all aspects of the analytic process—this includes chapters of preparing data, issues of quality and ethics, and CAQDAS, as well as features of analysis associated with more specific approaches. It is highly recommended for those looking for more practical detail on the aspects of analysis introduced in this chapter.

Bryman, A. (2016). *Social Research Methods* **(5th edition). Oxford: Oxford University Press.** Alan's book has a number of chapters devoted to qualitative analysis. There are extended discussions on grounded theory, analytic induction, narrative analysis, and discourse analysis, as well as a chapter devoted to getting to grips with NVivo, one of the most popular CAQDAS platforms. It will be of particular interest to those who are looking for a more extended discussion of the issues we introduce here.

Braun, V. and Clarke, V. (2013). *Successful Qualitative Research: A Practical Guide for Beginners.* **London: Sage.** This is a comprehensive beginners' guide to qualitative analysis, written by the key proponents of thematic analysis. That expertise is somewhat reflected in terms of content, but the thorough and practical nature of the discussion means that it will be useful across the board. There are particularly useful chapters on preparing data, thinking about analysis, as well as material on quality in qualitative research, and the process of writing up.

Taylor, C. and Gibbs, G. R. (2010). *What is Qualitative Data Analysis (QDA)?* **Online QDA Website.** This website offers a huge amount of resources to help students carrying out qualitative analysis. There is material devoted to specific forms of analysis, as well as tutorials, practical advice, and further reading. Because the site is no longer being updated it does not make use of more recent digital innovations, but CAQDAS aside, much of the content is timeless, and is definitely worth exploring further. http://onlineqda.hud.ac.uk/Intro_QDA/what_is_qda.php (Accessed 11 December 2018)

CHAPTER 15

WORKING
WITH DOCUMENTS

WHAT DO I NEED TO KNOW?

- What are documents?
- The case for using documents
  - Validity
  - Stability
  - Access
  - Cost
- How to appraise documents
- How to work with documents
  - Quantitative content analysis
    - Specifying the research questions
    - Selecting the sample
    - Articulating what is to be counted
    - Coding
  - Qualitative content analysis

INTRODUCTION

While it is not true of all disciplines, much of the data used in social science dissertation projects is produced by interviews, surveys, and participant observation. However, there are other forms of data that can be used for the purposes of social science. This chapter will explore some of this 'documentary' data and how to use it for the purposes of research. Documentary forms of data have some significant advantages that make them particularly useful for student research projects. This does not mean that they are without problems, but this chapter will provide a practical guide for those who are prepared to look beyond familiar horizons. It will make the case for using documents; explore what sorts of things can be included under the broad heading of documents; and introduce both quantitative and qualitative content analysis as a means to analyse documents.

WHAT ARE DOCUMENTS?

Put simply, the primary function of a document is to preserve information across time and place. That act of preservation may take the form of a piece of written text, a sound recording, a picture, or some form of digitized material. Pre-existing

I WISH I'D KNOWN . . . THE WEALTH OF DOCUMENTARY DATA AVAILABLE 15.1

"*Documentary research can be a very fulfilling way of answering research questions, especially regarding non-recent events. Many international archives, such as US presidential libraries, now have a wealth of online resources which could form the basis of dissertation data collection and analysis.*"

— Dr Michael Pugh, Lecturer in Politics, University of the West of Scotland

material used for the purposes of research is also referred to as indirect data; this is the 'stuff' of everyday or professional life that was not produced with research in mind. It might include, but is not limited to: reports in newspapers; Christmas cards; diaries; social media posts; prison records; and governmental legislation. There are even examples of researchers using sightings of the Loch Ness Monster as indirect data! In fact, any discussion of the types of documents that can be used as indirect data is unlikely to be exhaustive—there is simply too much to mention. Given this elasticity, we will interpret the term 'document' quite broadly as any item that preserves information over time and place, but was not produced for the purposes of research. This might be a written document, but could also be a social media message, or a photograph.

Documents can be textual, aural, visual, or digital in nature. They can be written, heard, or seen, and can exist in material or digital formats. Sometimes they might be more than one of these. A film, for instance, can be used as data for the purposes of social science research, and it can exist online or as a physical object. Clearly there are particular challenges associated with working with each of these formats, and further reading is desirable if you are thinking of doing so. The important point to note is that the medium a document takes will help to shape what you can do with it, and how.

Other important dimensions to consider when beginning to think about using documents as a source of data are their authorship and their location. Scott (1990: 14) provides a useful typology to classify the types of document that might be used for research (see Table 15.1).

In the first instance, there is a difference between personal documents and those produced in the routine bureaucracies of contemporary life—the distinction between household and office, so to speak. However, there is also a difference between independent organizations and those of the state. The documents produced in the pursuit of public office are not the same as private business.

In the second instance, there are differences in the availability of documents. Some are 'closed' and only available to insiders who played a part in their production; some are restricted to outsiders only if certain conditions are met; some exist in specific open collections, but require some proprietary access; and, some are routinely published for public viewing.

Table 15.1 **A typology of documents**

		Authorship		
		Personal	Official	
			Private	State
Access	Closed	1	5	9
	Restricted	2	6	10
	Open-archival	3	7	11
	Open-published	4	8	12

Illustrative examples: 1—personal diary; 2—collection of personal papers associated with an individual; 3—collection of personal papers of an important individual lodged in an archive; 4—an autobiography; 5—records of wages or other personal information; 6—organizational records; 7—tax reports; 8—newspaper reports; 9—material protected by the Official Secrets Act; 10—items associated with the 'Black Museum' at Scotland Yard; 11—information held in a national archive; 12—census data.

The important thing to recognize about the typology is that each type has distinct advantages and disadvantages. There is not enough space here to go through each and every one, but generally speaking those sources of documents that are more 'open' in nature are easier to gain access to, and what it is possible to do with the documents associated with the formal administration of state business is different from what can be achieved with private personal documents. For instance, there are numerous research projects that analyse policy documents associated with governance, exploring the language and content of these documents over time. In contrast, there is also much literature that has made use of personal diaries to explore how macro issues are realized and experienced in individual lives.

THE CASE FOR USING DOCUMENTS

There are some straightforward reasons to use the indirect data contained in documents for dissertation research. These include: validity, stability, access, and cost.

Validity

Documentary data can be considered to be what Webb et al (1966) termed an 'unobtrusive measure'. These are measurements that do not intrude on the person or setting that the researcher is investigating. They can be considered to be 'non-reactive'—and it is this lack of researcher interference that heightens validity.

Reactivity refers to the extent to which the researcher interacts with data and how, in one way or another, the researcher might be shaping the information that is collected. A key advantage of using non-reactive data is that it comes from real life as it happened; it is not a reconstruction of it. For example, if participants are aware that what they say and do will be used as data, they may change, nuance, or augment their actions and/or responses. This may particularly be the case if people don't want to feel judged about certain behaviour, such as drug use, drinking, sexual behaviour, or even charitable donations. They may also react differently depending on how particular introductions and questions are phrased, or acquiesce to non-verbal and verbal cues from the researcher.

There is also a long literature that examines how different facets of identity, such as age, gender, and ethnicity, can shape the nature of research engagements. Issues of fatigue, interest, and excitement can also influence how particular research instruments are delivered and received, all of which influences the nature of the data collected. Many direct methods of data collection also occur at a fixed point in time. This means data is often not triangulated across time and place. Webb et al (1966: 1) eloquently summarized the problem of reactivity for social research:

> Interviews and questionnaires intrude as a foreign element into the social setting they would describe, they create as well as measure attitudes, they elicit atypical role and response, they are limited to those who are accessible and who will cooperate, and the responses obtained are produced in part by dimensions of individual differences irrelevant to the topic at hand.

The great advantage of using documents as a form of indirect data is that they are actually records of life, uninterrupted by the researcher and their methods of data collection. They are non-reactive. Documents are often produced from the perspective of the people living those lives, and non-reactive data is high in validity because it allows researchers to access social life **as it happens**, not as a product of a research engagement.

WORKING WITH YOUR SUPERVISOR 15.1

While issues associated with ethics are often lessened when working with indirect data, this is not to say that there are no ethical issues. To take one example, much has been written about the ethics of using social media as data (see Chapter 8). This is largely because informed consent is often not gained at the point of data collated. Some researchers take the opinion that social media is public data and permissible to use providing other ethical requirements are met (confidentiality and anonymity for instance). Others, however, suggest that the practice of 'scraping' data from online spaces and using it for purposes for which it was not originally intended contravenes data protection. The discussion remains unresolved. If you are thinking of using indirect data, it is a good idea to check with your supervisor about the specific issues associated with the type of data you are working with.

Stability

Documents have a tendency to be highly stable: that is, they do not change over time or respond to the demands of the research situation. This stability makes them very reliable. This is not always true of online documents, which can disappear or be amended at the touch of a button, but it does tend to be the case with physical documents.

The great advantage of this stability is that the indirect data associated with documents does not ebb, flow, and change according to circumstances beyond the interest of the research. There are not the problems associated with knowing if you have social access to your field, for example, or whether your interviewee has had a bad morning or not. The data exists in the form that it does regardless of who might be doing the research.

There are, however, some drawbacks to this stability. You cannot interrogate a document or ask questions of it in the same way you can in an interview situation—a document does not talk back! This means your capacity to shape data around your research questions is often constrained. You can only do what the document allows you to do, not necessarily what you want to do: you do have to work **with** documents—hence the title of this chapter. Familiarizing yourself with the documents you want to work with before you formally begin your project is a very good idea. Knowing the limits and potentials of the data at hand will enable you to think more creatively about your project and what you might be able to do with the indirect data you are interested in.

Access

Sometimes it is simply not possible to gain the physical and social access to those arenas of the human world that we are interested in. This may be due to issues of permission, availability, or time. Some groups of people are also simply 'hard to reach'. This can be due to their visibility, geography, or it could be because proprietary access is needed to access the site of interest. Where these permissions are substantial, it can make primary data collection difficult to achieve in the context of a dissertation-style project. For instance, the voluminous requirements of ethics and data protection have made many areas of health-related research difficult to achieve because of the paperwork involved. This can also be true of social work and education research, particularly where the research would involve vulnerable people.

Direct methods of data collection can also be constrained by issues of time and place. This might be because an event has already occurred and the possibilities for data collection have already elapsed, or because physical access is not possible. The people you are interested in might also be dispersed over a wide area, or you might not know where your target sample actually operates. Again, this makes data collection hard to achieve, particularly in resource-limited dissertation research. In other instances, you may have physical access to people, but they might not want to talk to you about what you are interested in. This can severely constrain the validity of the data. There is a difference between having physical access and social access (see Chapter 12).

Used judiciously, the use of documentary data can help circumvent these issues. Tom's research on the prison sentence of British serial killer Myra Hindley, for example, would not have been possible through direct means. In any case, the prison records he examined were so extensive, and written from many different perspectives, that they provided much richer and multilayered data than he could have collected himself. Alan's work on how ethical review boards communicate funding decisions would similarly have been impossible without access to the letters sent by these boards. Elsewhere, discussion boards/online forums, chat rooms, and social media provide the means to access dispersed and otherwise unconnected populations. This is particularly common in areas of fandom, like sport or science fiction.

FINDING YOUR WAY 15.1

Websites, blogs, social media messages, and chat rooms can all be treated as digital documents, and be subject to analysis. However, there are some particular challenges associated with treating the internet as a site of indirect data.

- Search engines only provide selective access to online material, and online searches are only as good as the keywords used to find information. This can serve to obscure the relationship between sample and population.
- Digital material is much more unstable than physical material. Websites and platforms come and go, while others change and evolve. Again, this makes assessments of representativeness and generalization difficult. We recommend downloading and saving the data somewhere safe to avoid this issue.
- Given the rate of technological change, many specific methodologies associated with digital research are somewhat underdeveloped and/or require complex technical understanding.
- It is often difficult to separate meaning from the platform used to create it. This makes the relationship between reality and representation increasingly unclear.

Many of these issues apply equally to many other more conventional sources of data, but they are intensified in digital research.

Cost

Another key advantage of using indirect data is the issue of cost. Collecting good-quality data is difficult. To do it robustly takes time, finance (in some cases), and effort. Evidently, there are constraints on dissertation research in all these respects. Using pre-existing data can help alleviate some of these pressures.

The time saved when utilizing indirect data can also be used elsewhere in the research process. Difficulties associated with primary forms of data collection can often cause slippage in terms of time-management, and many dissertation projects then suffer in terms of depth of analysis and writing quality. Speeding up the process of data collection can allow you to better manage the dissertation process because it can help to remove some of the uncertainties you can encounter when working with people 'in person'. Using indirect data means you can spend more time actually exploring, analyzing, and presenting the data.

None of this is to ignore the problems of using non-reactive data, perhaps the biggest of which is the necessity to shape research aims around the limits of the pre-existing data. Many of these issues reflect the problems associated with secondary quantitative data that we discussed in Chapter 11. Data is always limited, and, as John Scott (1990: 24) highlights in his excellent book *A Matter of Record*, 'even the primary observer may be influenced by illusions, hallucinations, or simple miss-observation ... And both a 'primary' and a 'secondary' observer are liable to negligence and indifference in the reporting of observations and the handling of evidence'. What it is important to note, however, is that there is an interesting and useful array of options beyond having to collect data yourself.

HOW TO APPRAISE DOCUMENTS

In theory, there are two ways to approach documents for the purposes of research. In the first instance, the 'classical' approach to documents is to see them as a particular representation of reality, and when documents are used in conjunction with each other they can be used to reconstruct a narrative that, more or less, represents what actually happened. This sort of approach is common in historical research, for example.

However, a more interpretivist approach to documents is also possible, and perhaps even desirable. Documents do not simply record facts. Instead, they are social and cultural products that are thoroughly embedded in the contexts that gave rise to them. More interpretative approaches to documents focus on the cultural meanings, beliefs, and values that are encoded and transmitted in a document. They make an attempt to place those meanings in relation to the wider context in which they occur. Interpretative approaches to documents include narrative analysis, discourse analysis, auto/biographical analysis, some forms of qualitative content analysis, as well as oral and life history.

FINDING YOUR WAY | 5.2

Biographical analysis is one form of analysis that can be used with those 'documents of life' that are personal in nature (such as diaries). The purpose of biographical analysis is to recognize that the macrostructural is thoroughly intertwined within the micro-social. This means that biographical representations of individual lives can be used to explore the social and cultural concerns of the many. There is a long tradition of biographical research in the field of education, but it is increasingly popular across the breadth of the social sciences.

These broad approaches to documents tend to go hand in hand with one another. On one hand, interpretive work requires some understanding of the actual narrative, and on the other, documents often only 'make sense' when placed in context. This includes other documents, but also the social conditions that create them in the first place.

With this in mind, Scott (1990) has provided four key criteria to assess documents. These criteria are authenticity, credibility, representativeness, and meaning.

Authenticity is simply an assessment of the integrity of the document—is it actually what it purports to be? This criterion is actually a core concern for all research methods. As Scott (1990) highlights, the interviewer needs to be sure that the interviewee is who they say they are, while the ethnographer needs to know they are in the right place to make observations. Knowing the provenance of the document is crucial in knowing whether it can be meaningfully relied on as evidence, and whether it might help you to answer your research aims and objectives. This is actually an increasing problem in research that uses social media messages as indirect data. On top of the general difficulties of reading intent in social media posts and the practice of trolling, the use of bots to artificially inflate public profiles and opinions means that making an assessment of authenticity is difficult. What, exactly, is being measured is often not easy to ascertain.

Credibility is concerned with any distortions that might be present in a document, possibly due to error or evasion. Any single document is unlikely to tell the full story, but credibility draws attention to the sincerity and verisimilitude of the information contained within it. Assessing credibility often involves examining the conditions through which the document was produced: who wrote it, for what purposes, and who for? Asking these questions will enable you to think critically about the information it contains, and allow you to examine it for any implicit biases it might contain.

Representativeness is the extent to which evidence can be judged to be typical or not. This should not be taken to mean that documents should always be typical, but it is to make an assessment of what conclusions might be legitimately drawn from them. Like Scott's other criteria, issues of representativeness are important to all kinds of data collection because it provides a means through which we might move from specific evidence to more general claims of knowledge. To be clear, things that are atypical can be interesting for all sorts of reasons, and the goal of using documents is not to use only those that are typical. Instead, the criterion merely asks us to consider how the item is similar to, and different from, other documents of interest.

Finally, **meaning** relates to whether the evidence contained in a document is clear and/or comprehensible. Again, this is not a call to use only those documents that are simple and straightforward. Instead, it is to consider the messages that are encoded within the document and our understanding of that information. This includes assessment of both the manifest and latent content of the document, but also the contexts in which it was both produced and received. Awareness of this context helps you to interpret the significance of the document in relation to other documents, and also the wider implications of the material.

Collectively, Scott's criteria provide the conceptual guidance necessary to approach and understand documents. The suggestion is not to laboriously go through every document you have collated and formally assess it for each criterion. Instead, they should be used as sensitizing devices that allow you to understand documents and their significance, and as a means for you to think critically about your own process of interpreting them. Indeed, Scott's criteria can actually be used in conjunction with the different forms of analysis that we introduced in Chapter 14. However, there is one further form of analysis that is particularly useful when working with documents, and it has the added bonus of being applicable to both quantitative and qualitative strategies of research. This is content analysis.

HOW TO WORK WITH DOCUMENTS

Content analysis is a form of analysis that aims to classify and categorize the content of communication. Originally associated with the quantitative description of content, there now exist qualitative variants of the technique. This means that it can be applied to a variety of data. This includes words and images, as well as textual and visual material found in both online and offline environments. It is frequently employed in the analysis of newspaper coverage, for example, but it can also be used in conjunction with forms of social media.

The focus of content analysis can also be manifest or latent. This means it can be directed toward asking research questions concerning what documents contain, or the meanings that underlie that surface content. This opens up the possibility for analysis to be directed toward **how** content is represented, as well as **what** is being represented in the first place. Formal descriptions of the approach also tend to emphasize the objective and systematic nature of analysis. In the first instance, objectivity relates to the transparency of the techniques and processes it employs, and in the second, it is systematic because it follows some very specific rules of analysis **in a consistent manner**. Both are designed to reduce any potential biases of the researcher carrying out the analysis. Given the rigour and flexibility associated with it, content analysis has been used across the breadth of the social sciences.

One of the great advantages of content analysis is that it is very flexible and can be applied to a variety of data. It can also be used in conjunction with quantitative and qualitative research strategies. In many instances, content analysis will actually help to facilitate mixed methods research because it can be used to qualify quantity **and** quantify quality. However, in the interests of clarity, we will outline the processes associated with quantitative and qualitative content analysis in turn.

Quantitative content analysis

There are four key processes associated with quantitative content analysis:

- Specifying the research questions
- Selecting the sample
- Articulating what is to be counted
- Coding

Specifying the research questions

Quantitative content analysis requires precise research questions. This is because they guide the selection of the sample, as well as defining what is to be 'counted' and, in the form of a 'code book', how that material will be coded.

Consider, for example, the following aims and objectives:

The research project seeks to analyse how social science research is represented in the mass media, and whether this effects the reputation of social science more generally. It will:

- *analyse newspaper articles that feature social science research*
- *examine the level of social science reporting*
- *explore how this research is represented*

Can you see any potential problems in respect to sample and coding?

In the first instance, there is little clarity about what, exactly, is meant by the term 'mass media'. Second, it is not clear how 'effects' will be measured. Attempts to actually examine the effects of the media are common aims in proposed dissertation research. This is, however, very difficult to achieve in practice and, if proposed, any associated claims to knowledge need to be treated with extreme care. Last, but not least, the research questions themselves are inexact and lack detail. It is not clear what is actually being proposed. This makes it difficult to mobilize the aims and objectives in terms of what to code and count.

It might be better to present the aims and objectives in the following manner.

The research project seeks to use quantitative content analysis to assess the reporting of social science research in the print media over the last five years. It will ask the following research questions:

- *How much social science is reported in the print media?*
- *Are there any differences in the amount of reporting between different national newspapers?*
- *Are there any differences in the locations social science gets reported (news, commentary, special features etc)?*
- *Do some subjects/topics receive greater coverage than others?*
- *How are issues about research quality (ie research methods) communicated?*

Notice how the aims and objectives frame the research questions? In turn, these questions reveal what is to be sampled, and what is to be counted.

I WISH I'D KNOWN . . . ABOUT THE PROBLEMS ASSOCIATED WITH MEASURING MEDIA EFFECTS | 5.2

Trying to assess the impact of the media on the public is difficult to achieve in dissertation research. This is largely due to issues related to research design. For example, many dissertations are nominally directed to the impact of media images of 'size zero' models on body image. Another common example is the effect of violent cartoons on child behaviour. To examine these sorts of issues in terms of cause and effect, you would need to design an experiment that preferably had a pre and post measurement, as well as an intervening condition (ie images of 'size zero models' or 'violent cartoons'). The problem being that society is saturated with such images, so trying to make that intervention meaningful is likely to be difficult to achieve, not to mention the fact that the experimental condition is also likely to underestimate the complexity of the relationship. If you are interested in media effects, it is a good idea to talk with your supervisor early in the research process. Indeed, it might be better to 'do less, more thoroughly' and solely focus on the representation of the issue **or** how people perceive it.

Selecting the sample

When planning to conduct quantitative content analysis, it is important to be clear about what, exactly, will constitute your sample. This includes the following issues: what you will focus on; where, how, and what material you will access; and, over what periods of time. This necessarily entails thinking about how the sample of documents relates to the population. In some cases, you might not be dealing with a sample at all and might actually be able to make much more substantive statements about the whole picture.

Let's return to the example of social science research in the news. The second example had 'the British print media' as the focus for research. If we were to leave it at that, we would need to be careful about how we would build a sample that could, in some way, be said to be representative of that population. One means of doing this would be to first specify the region we are interested in. This might be local or national. Then we would need to decide on a selection of newspapers that would be representative of those regions. We might, for example, decide to focus on a mix of tabloids and broadsheets at the national level, while also selecting across political persuasion. Lastly, we would then need to specify the dates of publication; in this case, a period of five years is suggested. In some cases, the period of time to study is easy to decide—for instance, if you are only interested in the reaction to a certain event. In other cases, more nuanced decisions will have to be made. It is also worth noting that while this purposive approach to sampling is one solution to the problem of sampling, principles of both non-probability and probability sampling can be used in conjunction with content analysis.

However, it might actually be possible to include **all** reports of interest. In which case, you would be working at the population level. This would mean that issues of generalization would be considerably less than you might ordinarily expect in dissertation research. Many databases, for example, now allow you to search all major newspapers within a given time frame. One of Tom's dissertation students, for example, conducted a quantitative content analysis on all national newspaper articles that contained the word 'evil' in the title in the previous five years. This enabled her to map contemporary uses of evil in the print media. Indeed, once you have sketched out an idea, it is often worthwhile trying to get a feel of the volume of data you might generate. This will enable you to refine your idea up or down, depending on circumstances. Again, it is worth highlighting the **process** of research in relation to content analysis. While there is no doubt that the relatively fixed nature of indirect data requires precise planning, this planning is not 'blind'. You actually need to familiarize yourself with your data before you can properly plan the process of analysis. This will enable you to see what is, and what is not, possible, and the kinds of research questions you might be able to ask of your data.

Articulating what is to be counted

What you need to actually 'count' in your research will be heavily influenced by your research questions. However, it is possible to provide a list of the types of things that might be quantified within your data. This includes significant actors; words; subjects/themes; and dispositions.

'Significant actors' refers to the main people involved in the document in terms of authorship, subject, and audience. This might include the person who has produced it; the person that it is about; alternative voices present in the document; and, to whom the document is addressed. While these concerns will not be relevant to every document or research project, the main goal of examining significant actors is to reveal the kinds of mechanisms through which documents come into being, and the interests that are embedded in them.

'Words', on the other hand, refers simply to the process of counting the number of instances particular terms occur. While this process is undoubtedly a laborious one if undertaken manually, many documents are now available in digital formats. This makes them much easier to count. Many computer-assisted qualitative data analysis software (CAQDAS) platforms include features that facilitate basic or more complex keyword analysis. In some cases, optical character recognition (OCR) software can also be used to turn printed material into digital formats, which can then be subject to keyword analysis.

It is, however, worth highlighting that this often means 'weeding out' information that is often redundant in nature. You are unlikely, for instance, to be interested in how many times 'and' or 'the' appear in a document. While some programs will provide the means to do this for you, it is always worth checking what is being included and excluded in any given count.

FINDING YOUR WAY 15.3

Computer-assisted content analysis (CACA) refers to a broad range of software platforms that can help to speed up the process of content analysis. However, these platforms can often do more than simply count particular words. Many have functions that allow particular types of words to be grouped together.

Looking for subjects or themes is also common in content analysis. As you might expect, it involves categorizing material according to the number of times a particular topic occurs. This might be, for instance, the particular type of crime being reported in a newspaper, the gender, age, and occupation of the perpetrator, and the gender, age, and occupation of the victim.

While information relating to subject is often manifest, in some cases the theme of the content might be more latent. In these cases, it will be necessary to ask questions that are deeper in nature, and you will need to infer something from the subjective content of the data. In respect to the previous example, it would be perfectly possible to take a step back from the type of crime being reported in a newspaper article, and instead concentrate on the nature of the offence. This might include whether the crime committed was physical, material, or digital in nature.

Finally, it is also possible to use content analysis to examine disposition—essentially, the temperament, nature, or character of the content. Sentiment analysis, for example, is often used in conjunction with social media and attempts to infer the feelings or judgements that underpin text. This might be whether the message is positive or negative in tone, or whether the message is communicated with certainty or not. It might also include attempting to assess the values or attitudes embedded in a text. Dispositions might also be related to the ideology, beliefs, or principles that are implied in particular representations.

Coding

There are two key elements of coding in quantitative content analysis: the coding schedule and the coding manual.

The coding schedule is simply the form that is used to record the data. It should reflect each dimension of interest that is to be measured. This might take the form of a spreadsheet, a database, or simply a written table. To take a very basic example—if we return to the example of social science research in the media—we might build a table that looks something like the one in Table 15.2.

Table 15.2 **Example of a coding schedule—social science in the media**

Case number	Day	Month	Year	Newspaper	Type of article	Subject	Research quality

Regardless of format, there are a few 'golden rules' of creating a coding schedule. In the first place, the dimensions represented on the schedule should be discrete. That is to say, they should be separate from each other with no overlap between them. This means that categories should be mutually exclusive and that data cannot be coded in two ways. The schedule should also be exhaustive in that all possibilities should be covered. Use categories like 'other' with caution because this can lead to missing important patterns and trends in the data. You need to ensure there is clarity about your units of analysis that will be counted, and how the schedule will serve to record incidents in your data.

The coding manual is what the name suggests: the place where you prescribe the instructions for coding the data. If you imagine that you are not actually doing the analysis yourself, the coding manual should be detailed enough so that another researcher would be able to code the data in exactly the same way as you would. Typically, it will list: all possible categories for each unit of analysis; the codes associated with those categories; and, any associated guidance that will aid the decision-making process. The coding manual explicitly articulates the rules for processing your data.

For example, in Table 15.2 there is a category to record the name of the newspaper the article appeared in. There is also a category for type of article. Table 15.3 shows the codes you could have in your coding manual:

Table 15.3 **Example coding manual for newspaper and type of article**

Newspaper	Type of article
1. The Daily Planet	1. News
2. The Daily Bugle	2. Op-ed (opinion)
3. The Evening Prophet	3. Recurring column
4. Central City News	4. Letter to the editor
5. The Daily Chronicle	5. Special feature
6. The Arkham Gazette	6. Advert
etc	etc

I WISH I'D KNOWN . . . TO THINK ABOUT RATER RELIABILITY | 5.3

You might need to consider the reliability of the coding procedure if you are conducting quantitative content analysis. **Inter-rater reliability** is the term given to consistency of coding between coders. It is particularly important where research teams are collectively coding material. On the other hand, **intra-rater reliability** refers to consistency to which an individual coder records material. This form of reliability is much more likely to be a concern in dissertation research, and a thorough coding manual will help to ensure intra-rater reliability is high. Discussing how you have attempted to ensure reliability, and any limitations, is likely to be well received in your dissertation.

Given the 'golden rules', it is essential that you pilot the coding manual and coding schedule that you have developed. This will help you to identify any potential challenges associated with actually coding the data. Of particular interest are those instances where there are difficulties in applying the codes, or where you find data that does not correspond to the codes you have developed. In either case, you will need to develop and adapt the coding manual to accommodate the data.

Piloting is also useful in identifying units of analysis where a particular category dominates the number of incidents being recorded. If this happens, it is worth examining the data incidents to see whether you can break down the category and produce a more refined analysis.

FINDING YOUR WAY | 5.4

Quantitative content analysis will provide a numeric description of the data you have collected. However, you will still need to interpret that information. One way of doing this is to ask yourself the following questions:

- How do my findings relate to the research questions?
  - What have you found out?
  - What evidence do you have to demonstrate your findings?
- What critiques could be applied to the way I have carried out my research?
  - What might you do differently if you were to do the research again?
- Why do my results remain significant in relation to the wider field of research?
  - Why are your findings important?
- What avenues for further research are suggested by your findings?

Qualitative content analysis

There are a number of different versions of qualitative content analysis, and there is not a definitive guide. Ethnographic content analysis and framework analysis are two popular examples, but even something like interpretative **phenomenological** analysis resonates quite strongly with qualitatively inspired content analysis, particularly where it is applied to interview transcripts. But regardless of the particular format, one of the central questions for those interested in qualitative content analysis is how to preserve the systematic and objective qualities of the approach, while retaining the interpretivist goals of qualitative research.

The solution has been to keep the overarching principles of content analysis, but lessen, and in some cases adapt, the rigidity of the rules that govern the process. It retains the focus on classifying and categorizing the content of communication, but does so without the strict constraints on the quantified coding process. As a result, qualitative content analysis tends to have the following characteristics:

- Involves discovery as well as verification
- Explicitly reflexive in design, and more emergent in nature
- A sampling strategy that can be both purposive and/or theoretical
- Has wider scope in terms of its units of analysis than its quantitative counterpart
- More concerned with validity than reliability

In the first instance, qualitative content analysis tends to pay specific attention to the direction in which codes are generated. Subsequently, it can be used to work in a deductive or inductive manner. Quantitative approaches are, in comparison, theoretically driven, with the coding manual being prescriptively compiled **before** formal analysis. However, the difficulty is that this can shut down emerging points of interest that arise from the data. Qualitative content begins with a coding manual, but is receptive to amending that manual as and where necessary so it more clearly reflects the goals of interpretivism. This also means that data can help elaborate theory, rather than just verifying it.

In part, qualitative content analysis is able to do this because it is reflexive in design and operates in a cyclical, rather than a serial, manner. General codes are created, data is coded, codes can be amended and emergent codes are added to the coding manual, with previous data recoded accordingly. This reflexive approach also means that coding starts **with** data collection, rather than once data collection has been completed.

The sampling strategy used with qualitative content analysis is also more iterative in nature. It is based on the needs of the emerging analysis, rather than the needs of statistical generalization, and theoretical and/purposive sampling strategies are used to develop the coding manual. The selection of cases **is** planned beforehand, but is also informed by the requirements of the emerging analysis.

There is also more focus on units of meaning in qualitative content analysis. While issues of manifest and latent content are still important, the scope of that interest is often less exacting than it is in more quantitative approaches. This tends to result in a larger and more nuanced coding schedule. Rather than producing a spreadsheet of numbers that correspond to categories, it is often the case that the actual data is placed in the coding schedule. In this respect, the 'golden rules' of separation, mutual exclusivity, exhaustiveness, and clarity are made more flexible to accommodate the fuzziness of qualitative data. That is not to say that these rules are irrelevant, but there is more scope for complexity, interpretation, and elaboration.

Finally, while issues of reliability remain important, particularly with respect to the coding manual and schedule, validity is also foregrounded. This is because there is a greater emphasis on the analysis of meaning in qualitative content analysis, and the meaning of text in context more specifically. Instead of making assessments of validity through reliability, and inter- and intra-coder reliability in particular, validity is treated on more ecological terms: that is, whether the interpretations made resonate with the concerns of wider society.

CONCLUSION

Working with documents and other forms of indirect data have a number of advantages for dissertation projects. Given the time constraints that often accompany such work, lessening the burden of primary data collection means that more effort can be directed toward both analysis and writing. Similarly, the non-reactive nature of indirect data can also enhance the validity of a project—indirect data is often a record of life as it happened, rather than a reconstruction of it. Of course, the fact that you cannot interrogate the data beyond what is there means that you might have to think more creatively about what can, and cannot, be achieved with documentary sources. But regardless, working with documents and associated ephemera for the purposes of research can be a rewarding experience.

WHAT DO I NEED TO THINK ABOUT?

- What sorts of indirect data might be associated with your topic of interest?
- How might you make the most of the advantages of indirect data in your research?

What sorts of difficulties do you think you might encounter in the process of your project if you made use of indirect data? Try to identify the gaps in your knowledge.

Do you understand the process of content analysis? Consider whether it is likely to be appropriate for your data.

Do you know of any research in your chosen field that has made use of indirect data? Think about how you could carry out your research in a similar way, and what you can learn from their experiences.

WHAT DO I NEED TO DO?

Make sure you understand what sorts of documents might be suitable for a dissertation project, and how you might access them.

Understand the advantages of using documents, and how and where you might be positioned to make the most of those advantages.

Identify the approaches and methods of analysis associated with working with documents you could employ in your dissertation.

Consider your sample in the context of your research aim(s) and objectives.

Develop a coding schedule and code your data.

Access the online resources **www.oup.com/uk/brymansrp1e** to help you to successfully complete your social research project or dissertation.

DELVE DEEPER

Lee, R. (2000). *Unobtrusive Methods in Social Research*. Buckingham: Open University Press. After Webb et al (1966) introduced the notion of 'unobtrusive measures', any number of researchers have taken inspiration from it to explore what is meant to be used as data, and how. Lee's book is a very readable attempt to try and pull this research together to demonstrate how the idea has developed. It provides a large number of empirical examples that might help you generate interesting and novel approaches to research.

Scott, J. (1990). *A Matter of Record*. Cambridge: Polity. Scott's book is likely to be vital to any student working with written documents. Thoroughgoing, but also very readable, Scott details the different types of documents that can be used for research and, using interesting empirical examples, offers a critical exploration of the issues you might encounter when working with particular documents. He also provides a comprehensive discussion of how to assess documents in terms of authenticity, credibility, representativeness, and meaning.

Webb, E., Campbell, D., Schwartz, R., and Sechrest, L. (1966). *Unobtrusive Measures: Nonreactive Research in the Social Sciences.* **Chicago: Rand McNally and Company.** A classic in the field, this book was the first to really fully explore the idea of non-reactivity, and why 'oddball' methods might be needed. Beginning with a robust discussion of the limitations of obtrusive methods of data collection, the authors then go on to explore a series of creative ways of studying social life in a robust and meaningful manner. Highlighting issues of erosion and accretion, archives, and simple and contrived observation, the intellectual creativity involved in their research really is second to none. This text is actually one of Tom's favourite ever books!

Mass Observation, University of Surrey. Originally designed to record everyday life in Britain between the late 1930s and early 1950s, the Mass Observation Archive draws on around 500 participants to explore all aspects of their day-to-day lives. Asking its writers to submit diary-style responses to subject-specific open-ended questions (known as directives), it contains qualitative material on all sorts of different subjects. This includes, but is by no means limited to: working families; dementia; fraud and scams; the refugee crisis; social mobility; higher education; using animals for research; being 'thrifty'; homelessness; and, the EU referendum. But this is only a small fraction of what they have covered.
http://www.massobs.org.uk/mass-observation-project-directives (Accessed 8 November 2018)

The National Archive. Kew, London. This is one example of an archive: in this case, the official archive of the UK government. It holds a huge array of historical material and public records and, in many respects, functions a bit like a library: you register for a ticket, find documents of interest using their database, and request material, which you can view in their reading room. There are, however, a great many archives, and they all operate differently. Many have a presence on the internet, even if they do not provide the information you are looking for digitally.
http://www.nationalarchives.gov.uk/ (Accessed 7 November 2018)

CHAPTER 16

EVALUATING YOUR PROJECT

WHAT DO I NEED TO KNOW?

- The process of evaluation in social research
- Originality
  - Relevance—how do aspects of your project resonate with the wider body of literature?
  - Timeliness—how do aspects of your project relate to everyday and/or public life?
  - Interest—who might be interested in the different aspects of your project and why?
- Rigour
  - Transparency—have you clearly articulated what you are doing and why?
  - Credibility—is your research based on data that is both reliable and valid?
  - Ethics—how have you conducted your research with key principles of ethics in mind?
- Significance
  - Alignment—are your research aims in alignment with your research methods and your findings?
  - Transferability—have you clearly articulated what you are doing and why?
  - Contribution—how does your project inform current thinking, policy, or practice?

INTRODUCTION

Critical reflection is a key part of evaluating your research project, and a dissertation that demonstrates this is likely to achieve higher marks. Not only does it help to ensure that you do not make claims about your research that go beyond the limits of the evidence, critical reflection also means that you can be more confident in terms of what your research is telling you. However, one of the first things to recognize is that the process of evaluation does not necessarily begin at the end of your project. Instead, issues of research quality are implicitly embedded in all parts of the research process **and** all sections of your dissertation. This is, in part, why we introduced you to the notion of reflexivity in Chapter 4. It is a crucial part of a researcher's toolkit. It prompts you to think about the decisions you make in relation to research, why you have made those decisions, and how they impact on your project. These considerations are threaded through all aspects of doing research **and** writing about it.

However, there does come a point where you will have to begin to think about summarizing key points of issue in your research project or dissertation. This chapter will introduce some key criteria that will help you to evaluate your project and think critically about the research process. It will discuss the importance of originality, rigour, and significance in research, and provide you with key questions to ask yourself about your project. Collectively, these questions will help you to assess and evaluate your research.

THE PROCESS OF EVALUATION IN SOCIAL RESEARCH

There are three overarching principles that are involved in thinking about research quality. These are originality, rigour, and significance. Broadly speaking, the first relates to the purpose of your research, the second relates to the methods you employ to 'find out', and the final principle is concerned with what your research is telling you in relation to the wider body of knowledge.

In practice, these principles can be summarized more concisely by the question 'what am I doing and why?' If you keep asking yourself this question, and answering it, during the process of research you will build the foundations of research quality that are needed to produce an excellent dissertation.

FINDING YOUR WAY 16.1

Keeping a reflexive diary of the process of research can help you to keep a record of any points of significance that might be suitable for future reflection. Entries do not need to be particularly long or written in an academic tone. The point is for you to detail those aspects of **doing** research that you think are interesting or surprising so that you can remember and discuss them in the future, if needed.

It is possible to break down the considerations of originality, rigour, and significance into more specific points of interest that prompt some further questions involved in evaluating your project. These concerns, and the questions that arise from them, are summarized in Table 16.1.

In thinking about these issues you should have a well-developed understanding of your project, and how to think about research quality in relation to it. We'll discuss each of the overarching issues in turn.

Table 16.1 Criteria for evaluating the quality of social research

Criteria	Issues	Ask yourself
Originality	Relevance	How do aspects of your project resonate with the wider body of literature?
	Timeliness	How do aspects of your project relate to everyday and/or public life?
	Interest	Who might be interested in the different aspects of your project and why?
Rigour	Transparency	Have you clearly articulated what you are doing and why?
	Credibility	Is your research based on data that is both reliable and valid?
	Ethics	How have you conducted your research with key principles of ethics in mind?
Significance	Alignment	Are your research aims in alignment with your research methods and your findings?
	Transferability	To what extent might your results be instructive in contexts beyond your research?
	Contribution	How does your project inform current thinking, policy, or practice?

ORIGINALITY

When completing a dissertation project, it is often easy to be overwhelmed by the idea that the goal of research is to make some sort of big leap in knowledge. Furthermore, different institutions may not emphasize the need for originality, but you should check if you are not clear. Fortunately, the (very long and very wide) history of science demonstrates that truly groundbreaking research is the exception, rather than the rule. The reality of research discoveries is usually much more mundane. This is not to say that 'newness' is not important in research. Innovation is part of what is meant by the term originality in the context of a dissertation. But that is not all it is. Originality also incorporates notions of individuality, uniqueness, and veritability. Somewhat fortunately, the nature of the dissertation process is actually primed for you to meet these requirements. After all, the production of your project is unique to you; in many respects it is a 'one off'; and it is, or should be, an open and genuine attempt to produce real knowledge that other people could have an interest in. All of these things constitute originality.

But in being all of these things, any attempt at originality necessarily needs to acknowledge and understand the wider context in which knowledge is being produced. Originality only makes sense in reference to other points of reference

I WISH I'D KNOWN . . . HOW TO MAKE A CONTRIBU-TION TO THE LITERATURE 16.1

Not every aspect of your research needs to be 'groundbreaking'. It may represent original or 'new' research by virtue of the sample you use, or the type of analysis you conduct. For instance, you may be interested in the use of social media in environmental campaigns and find that discourse analysis has not yet been employed to explore the topic. In exploring a new area or in a slightly different way, you are likely to make a contribution to the field.

"I wish I'd known it is not expected of me to revolutionize the field or to come up with a unique, never researched before idea! It took me a while to understand this."

—Roxana Dumitrescu, Student, International Relations with Applied Quantitative Methods, University of Essex

within a field of knowledge or practice. Think about it: to understand individuality you need some sense of collectivity; uniqueness requires knowledge of how your work is similar to **and** different from other work; and, the idea of something being genuine relies on the tacit recognition of something being verifiable. Understanding how, and where, **your** project corresponds with other research in the field and/or wider public life will go a long way in demonstrating originality.

In large part, if you have developed a strong rationale for research and a well-planned research proposal, it is likely that you will already have a good understanding of the relationship between your project, the wider literature, and the types of people who could be interested in what you are doing. Much of this purpose is also likely to be reflected in both your literature search and, ultimately, in your literature review. However, originality is not limited to these phases of the research process. You will also need to be able to take steps of originality when collecting your data, analysing it, and interpreting your results. You will need to think creatively about what questions to ask, how to ask them, how concepts and theoretical constructs can help inform your results, and how your results relate to the wider world. Originality is writ large across the research process, but it does need to be recognized and, where appropriate, formally drawn out. With this in mind, there are a further three questions to ask yourself. These questions relate to the relevance, timeliness, and interest of your project.

Relevance—how do aspects of your project resonate with the wider body of literature?

This is basically the interrelated issue of what you are doing and how your project relates to the research field. Formally speaking, you are likely to demonstrate the ability to do this when writing up your literature review. However, you also need to reflect critically on your approach, your methods, and your findings. All of these aspects of your project will, in one way or another, be informed by the wider literature. You are not making things up as you go along, so where do the ideas you are using come from?

To make sure that your research has relevance, you will need to try and ensure that your reflection is both prospective and retrospective in nature. That is, you will need to consider the literature before you make decisions **and** after the fact. This will help you to understand the range of opportunities available to you **and** help you to assess the impact your decisions might have had on your research practice, not to mention where you might, on reflection, have done things differently. This is something you are likely to need to cover in the conclusion. If you do this at each stage of the research process, you will ensure your project has relevance.

Timeliness—how do aspects of your project relate to everyday and/or public life?

Timeliness refers more broadly to the capacity of your project to resonate with wider issues of interest. This relates to the question 'why is this thing a good thing to do **now**?' This might be a concern of everyday life, or something with more of a policy or practice focus. Thinking about timeliness involves making connections between what you are doing and the sorts of things that make your project an interesting thing to do, for both yourself and those who might engage with it. In doing so, you will be attempting to develop aspects of your project within those wider aspects of the research and human world that provide the context for research. For instance, your topic may be stimulated by policy discussion or more everyday developments. There may be changes in the taxation on alcohol or fizzy drinks that have provided the impetus for your research. Perhaps a ban on smoking in public areas has come into force that has impacted on the way people consume e-cigarettes.

Again, while these sorts of considerations will tend toward being a formal part of the literature review, they are actually also important when thinking about what to include and/or pursue in your data collection and analysis, not to mention how you might situate those results in your discussion. Social science research is constantly evolving, so making sure that you keep up with contemporary debates in the field is an important part of demonstrating originality.

FINDING YOUR WAY 16.2

Making sure you know how to search for literature can help inform the timeliness of your research. In addition to updating more substantively driven searches about your topic, be prepared to search for methodological literature that relates to your project. It can also be a good idea to search databases that contain grey literature to help provide the wider context for research too. This might be in the form of recent policy or practice changes, or more popular coverage of particular issues. As grey literature does not normally undergo a lengthy review process it is often available sooner than journal articles. Of course, you will need to make sure you critically assess any discovered material for quality, but it can help to contextualize your project and any findings.

Interest—who might be interested in the different aspects of your project and why?

What is the point of doing your project, and who might be interested in what you have to say? To answer these questions, it's often a good idea to sketch out the reasons for your project, and the different stakeholders who might have an interest in aspects of it. Stakeholders are exactly what you might think: anyone who has a 'stake' in the research. They might be the participants themselves, organizations associated with your participants, gatekeepers, public bodies, private companies, charities who work in related areas, pressure groups, the popular media, policymakers, or government departments. Again, it will be possible to identify some of these stakeholders because they are tacitly present in your literature review where you outline the rationale for research. However, this sort of consideration can also be useful when thinking about any recommendations that you might make in your conclusions. These recommendations might concern the direction of future research, changes to current policy, or advice for practice. Again, providing recommendations in this way can help demonstrate originality in your project.

RIGOUR

Rigour is an overarching term that is concerned with the thoroughness of research. Typically, discussions of rigour are directed toward methodological issues, often in the form of debates concerning reliability, validity, and generalization. However, while rigour is very important in producing robust research, you actually need to be thorough in other parts of the research process too. Rigour should be a consideration in your literature search, the theoretical constructs you choose to employ or develop, the process of research ethics, and the techniques of analysis you employ. It can even apply to the stages of writing up. After all, writing is a technical skill that needs to be crafted. For instance, if you interviewed 15 police officers about current gun laws and only one or two thought they were problematic in some way, it would be inappropriate to use such views to recommend that legislation needed altering. We will discuss writing up more specifically in Chapter 17, but it is important to highlight that, at each stage of the research process, you will need to ask yourself to what extent your study utilizes research techniques that are both appropriate and sufficient to substantiate your claims.

Unfortunately, there are no hard-and-fast rules in judging what is appropriate or sufficient. Intuition is often a good guide, but you do need to be honest with yourself, **and** not too harsh. On one hand, if you feel confident that you have made every attempt to engage with each phase of the research process thoroughly, you probably have. On the other, if you think you could do more, you are right—you could always do more! But you need to ask yourself whether the rewards are likely to be in excess of the costs, and whether more effort in a particular direction is going to impede you elsewhere. It's worth bearing in mind that researchers never really saturate all avenues of investigation; they make conscious decisions to stop working when they have the confidence to know that they have been as rigorous as is realistically possible.

WORKING WITH YOUR SUPERVISOR 16.1

It is always worth taking a cue from your supervisor by asking them 'have I done this thoroughly?' They can then offer you advice when, and how, to move on to different aspects of your project.

However, with the idea of rigour in mind, it is possible to explore a further set of issues that will help you make sure your dissertation is thorough. These are transparency, credibility, and ethics.

Transparency—have you clearly articulated what you are doing and why?

Social science is absolutely dependent on the process of critique. It ensures that the quality of research is as high as it can be. Basically, you need to make sure your research is made available to public forums so it can be assessed by peers and assessed for its quality. In the case of a dissertation, this public forum is likely to come in the form of those assessing your project; but there are opportunities to publish dissertation work too. Regardless, the process of critique requires that you are as clear as you can be about what you did in your research and why, so interested others can assess the veracity of your study.

This means that, as a general rule of thumb, it should be broadly possible to replicate any social science research project just from reading the methods section of the report. Typically, this section of a report or paper will include key information about the general approach, the sampling strategy, the methods of data collection and analysis, and the process of ethics (see Chapter 17). However, it might also provide a reflexive account of the research process too. This helps to document

I WISH I'D KNOWN ABOUT . . . UNDERGRADUATE JOURNALS AND CONFERENCES 16.2

There are a number of opportunities to disseminate your findings. The British Conference of Undergraduate Research, for example, is an annual interdisciplinary conference that provides a platform for students to present their work. They also curate a list of undergraduate journals. Some of these are institution specific, but many will accept submissions from any student.

http://www.bcur.org/research/undergraduate-journals/ (Accessed 4 December 2018).

In the USA, the Council on Undergraduate Research offers similar platforms.

https://www.cur.org/ (Accessed 4 December 2018).

the reasons behind particular decisions, and the impact that they might have had on the project. In terms of a dissertation, it also helps to demonstrate that you are aware and responsive to the challenges of research.

But again, transparency is not just limited to issues of method and/or writing up. You will need to provide clear justifications for the choices you make at all stages of your project. This includes your initial focus, your literature search strategy, the reasons for your theoretical orientation, as well as specific directions you have taken in both analysis and interpretation.

Credibility—is your research based on data that is both reliable and valid?

To ask whether your research is credible is to assess the nature of your data **and** the assumptions that then flow from it. In part, this concerns the well-established issues of reliability and validity, essentially, the consistency and meaningfulness of your data. However, it is also to ask to what extent your research is based on good evidence, and whether your interpretation of it is both plausible and defensible?

To demonstrate that your arguments are plausible and defensible, you are likely to need to present the evidence necessary to justify your claims. This is particularly likely to be the case in your results section. Select data that helps you to demonstrate the point you are making. Whether it is a table, a quote, or something drawn from your field notes, evidence should help to underline a point, rather than make the point for you. It should be clearly related to the argument you are making, be relatively self-contained, and legible. You will need to ensure that you have taken the time to thoroughly produce and investigate your data. Whether it is in the form of thick description, concrete detail, or adequate representation of a sample, your data needs to be both strong and deep enough to sustain your analysis as well as the interpretations and conclusions that you draw from it. If you have any doubts about the nature of your data, and whether it can be used to illuminate aspects of social life you are interested in, you need to have the confidence to state the limitations of your results. This is expected in a dissertation and should not be seen as some sort of failure of your research. It is about being realistic about your research and what it shows and does not show.

It is also worth considering whether to make the effort to talk to key informants about your project once you have begun the process of analysis and/or writing up. These people may be either participants or actors 'on the ground' who have experience of the kinds of things you are attempting to investigate. What do they think about your work and what you have discovered? Of course, if you are thinking of doing this, you will need to build this process into your research plan as it can take quite some time to gain feedback, not to mention the changes that might be necessary as a result.

I WISH I'D KNOWN . . . ABOUT RESPONDENT VALIDATION | 6.3

Respondent validation is the term given to the process of consulting with key participants once you have your results. It is a way of assessing whether your conclusions are meaningful to those who provided your data. If you are considering using this approach, it is often a good idea to build it into the process of informed consent, making sure that participants are happy to engage with you after the data-collection phases of research. It is also worth noting that this can take a lot of time, so make sure you build it into your research planning.

Ethics—how have you conducted your research with key principles of ethics in mind?

We've already spent some time discussing the importance of ethics in research in Chapter 8, so there is no need to labour the point here. However, it is worth noting that the idea of research quality is often intertwined within institutional codes of ethics. This usually refers to research practice in the integrity of ethical administration and the specific processes associated with documenting informed consent, anonymity, privacy, harm, and confidentiality. But there is more to ethical practice than this, and it is again worth highlighting that ethics are not limited to satisfying institutional requirements at the start of a project. You will also need to consider those situational and culturally specific aspects of ethics that happen both in the field and after you have left it. Again, consulting the more reflexive literature that details ethics **in practice** will be helpful in making sure you consider the ethics associated with your practice as thoroughly as possible.

SIGNIFICANCE

One of the central overarching goals of the social sciences is to extend our understanding and appreciation of the human world. Therefore, a key criterion in evaluating social research is the extent to which your project extends that knowledge base. These contributions might be conceptual, theoretical, methodological, or practical.

All of this means that you need to be clear about the value of your work in relation to those wider fields of knowledge at all stages of the research process. From the outset, a good rationale for research will help you to initially articulate the purposes of your research **and** what sorts of issues are informing those aims. This then needs to be reflected in the process of data collection, and it may be particularly important in terms of recruitment. After all, you will need to persuade potential participants or organizations that are associated with them, that it is worth their time and effort to help you. During the analysis you will have to recognize what sorts of things are significant in your data. Finally, when you have your results, you will need to articulate how they resonate with current knowledge in the form of wider literature, policy, and/or practice.

Alignment—are your research aims in alignment with your research methods and your findings?

In making any assessment of significance, you must first make sure that your project is aligned in a coherent manner. Alignment refers to the extent to which your study is interconnected, and whether those connections are meaningful. That is to say that you need to make sure that your project makes sense in terms of the narrative of research. Your project needs to meaningfully connect literature, aims and objectives, methods, findings, and interpretations with each other. One should follow from the other. There needs to be a rationale for the research where the purpose of the project is made explicit; the methods utilized should then allow you to respond appropriately to those aims and produce findings that clearly answer them **with evidence**; and, your understanding of the whole process needs to be informed by the wider concerns of the literature. Doing so will help demonstrate that you have been rigorous throughout the research process, and provide a platform for you to identify why all of this is significant.

This might all sound a bit obvious, but it is quite easy to underestimate how things can change during the process of research. This is often most noticeable where students write a literature review, then go out into the field, find something quite different to what they expected, but fail to amend the literature review to reflect this change of direction. As a result, the alignment of the whole project can be compromised because it lacks coherence.

FINDING YOUR WAY 16.3

Reviewing your aims and objectives, and any associated research questions, is an important part of the research process. Research ideas can shift during a project—and good intentions do not always reflect what happens in practice: so try to be clear about your research questions at all stages of the research process. Making sure that the methods and findings reflect the purpose of your study is likely to be a key criterion of assessment.

Transferability—have you clearly articulated what you are doing and why?

Transferability refers to the extent that your results are likely to be instructive in contexts beyond your specific sample. That is, how do your findings transfer from one situation to another? Any assessment of the transferability of your findings is implicitly dependent on the nature of your sample and your sampling strategy. This is closely related to the concerns of what is typically referred to as generalization. Unfortunately, this is a term that is often used rather loosely, and often with little precision. Statistical generalization is actually an assessment of probability that is used to indicate the likelihood that a (more or less random) sample is representative of the wider population. When the sample meets specific criteria, it can be considered representative of the wider population, and generalization from the sample is then possible.

However, the logic of generalization in this type of approach is actually quite different from other types of research that do not use random samples, or those that are more purposeful in terms of sampling strategy. In these cases, there may be some very good reasons not to want to take a statistically representative sample, or to generalize to populations. For instance, if you are interested in why a particular programme of intervention designed to get unemployed people into work has been unsuccessful with particular groups, it makes more sense to intensively sample those groups, rather than the whole cohort. This information-rich approach would allow you to make specific assessments about the programme that would be instructive in similar circumstances, but not exhaustive of all situations. That is to say that your findings would transfer across specific contexts without needing to generalize to every context. This is why we use the idea of transferability: it allows us to be more flexible in the way we think about the value of our findings, and whether and where they might, and might not, apply elsewhere.

The issue of transferability requires you to think critically about the nature of your sample and the wider world. What are the key characteristics of your sample, and are there any reasons that you can think of that would be likely to

FINDING YOUR WAY | 6.4

All studies have limitations that can impact on both credibility and transferability. These include, but are not limited to:

- Sample size
- Missing data
- The veracity of self-reported data
- Time
- Measures used for data collection
- Access
- Subjectivity
- Issues associated with research relationships
- Practical considerations like language, cost, or location

constrain or enhance the applicability of your findings about them **to** specific others? For instance, if you are conducting research on how undergraduates use digital technology to enhance their experience of learning and teaching, is the nature of the discipline likely to impact on your results? You might reasonably imagine that media studies students are, for example, likely to engage with technology differently to those studying French. Similarly, would the type of university where you conduct the research be a factor in how far your results will travel? After all, universities do have different student profiles in terms of socio-economic status, ethnicity, and age, all of which might reasonably constrain the transferability of your results.

FINDING YOUR WAY | 6.5

Identifying groups or situations where the transferability of your findings might be problematic is not a bad thing. Instead, it allows you to clearly identify a context where further research is likely to be necessary. This enables you to underline the originality and significance of your work, while also specifically articulating the limitations of it.

Contribution—how does your project inform current thinking, policy, or practice?

Contribution is, perhaps, the central vehicle through which you can demonstrate the significance of your project. Quite simply, how does your dissertation extend understanding? Such change can be conceptual or theoretical, methodological, or of a more practical nature. Assessing contribution involves a considered and con-fident understanding of what the knowledge-base currently looks like, and how it resonates with your conclusions.

In the first instance, you will need to think about contribution when you begin to articulate the knowledge gap that you first construct in your research rationale, and then go on to describe fully in your literature review. This involves working out where, and how, your research is both similar to and different from what has already been conducted in your field of interest.

In some instances, dissertations can also make a methodological contribution to the literature. This doesn't necessarily mean that the project was, so to speak, formally directed to research methods. It might be the case that you have used techniques of data collection that are relatively novel in a particular field, or have tried to triangulate methods or data in a particularly innovative manner. There are many different ways of mixing methods, and not all of these combinations have particularly well-developed coverage. Perhaps you have used an inventive method of recruitment to access your participants, or simply used a previously untapped source of secondary data. In each of these cases, you need to first understand the methodological context of your arena of interest, and what is conventional in that arena. Then you can use the more methodological literature to explore how you have used or developed those techniques in innovative ways, given your topic of interest.

FINDING YOUR WAY 16.6

In some cases, you might find that your research, and any associated results, do not go entirely to plan. Perhaps you have found nothing of relevance in response to your research questions, you don't know what to do with some data, or you have only realized the significance of something after the event and there are gaps in your data. Negative evidence typically refers the non-occurrence of events, an incident that goes unreported, or something that is withheld from inclusion. However, in terms of your dissertation, negative evidence can be use-ful. Discussing any absences in understanding can help you to identify avenues for further research, allow you to demonstrate critical reflexivity in relation to your project, and prevent you from taking your conclusions for granted.

CONCLUSION

Evaluating your research project can feel like a big task. You need to develop the confi-dence to think critically about your practice, and think about what you might have done differently if you were to carry out the project again. But, in critically identifying points of issue in your research project, you also need to retain a sense of purpose about why your project still has relevance, regardless of the limitations. This involves developing key arguments in relation to your findings and making sure that you can evidence those claims. In turn, this will allow you to connect your project to the wider literature and demonstrate both originality and significance. These considerations should reflect, but not repeat, the concerns of your knowledge gap. You need to ask yourself, how does your study extend the knowledge base, why this is important, and what might further research seek to explore?

WHAT DO I NEED TO THINK ABOUT?

- Why is the process of evaluation important in social research?
- Critically reflect on the principles of originality, rigour, and significance for your research.
- Use the key criteria to ask yourself important questions about the research process.

WHAT DO I NEED TO DO?

- Make sure you understand the role of quality in the research process.
- Answer the following:
  - Why was your project an interesting thing to do?
  - What are the limitations of your methodology?
  - Why are your findings important?
  - What avenues for further research are suggested by your project?
- Evaluate your project!

Access the online resources **www.oup.com/uk/brymansrple** to help you to successfully complete your social research project or dissertation.

DELVE DEEPER

Seale, C. (1999). *The Quality of Qualitative Research*. **London: Sage.** If you are looking to read one book about issues of research quality, it should be this one. Comprehensive, but very readable, Seale provides a thorough-going discussion of key issues in the research process. Grounded in empirical examples, this includes chapters on 'contradictions', 'using numbers', 'generalizing from qualitative research', 'reliability and replicability', and 'reflexivity and writing'.

Shipman, M. (1997). *The Limitations of Social Research* **(4th edition). Essex: Longman.** This is a classic text that has stood the test of time. Built around a series of real empirical controversies, Shipman methodically works his way through key points of issue in the research process. Of course, we'd recommend reading the whole thing, but with chapters devoted to particular research designs, and specific methods of data collection, it is possible to pick out issues relevant to your particular project.

The Royal Literary Fund have some useful web pages about critical thinking generally, and making an argument specifically. Informative and concise, they will help you to begin thinking about how to reflect on your project and construct an argument in relation to the key points of issue you have identified.

https://www.rlf.org.uk/resources/are-you-looking-for-an-argument/ (Accessed 10 November 2018)

Tracy, S. (2010). 'Qualitative Quality: Eight "Big Tent" Criteria for Excellent Research', *Qualitative Inquiry,* **16(10): 837–851.** This is an excellent paper that introduces key criteria for thinking about research quality. Highly readable and informative, it is nominally directed toward qualitative research, but the ideas it introduces will be applicable elsewhere. It will be useful for those students who want to supplement their capacity to critically understand the process of research.

The University of Plymouth's Learning Development Team has produced some handy student guides in relation to critical thinking and writing. Offering a wealth of helpful tips on issues associated with 'building an argument', 'critical thinking', and 'reflective writing', they are concisely written and packed with practical advice that can help prepare you to evaluate your project.

https://www.plymouth.ac.uk/student-life/services/learning-gateway/ learning-development (Accessed 17 November 2018)

Williams, M. (2000). 'Interpretivism and Generalization', *Sociology,* **34(2): 209–224.** This is a sensible paper that outlines how you can think about generalization in relation to your project. Moving away from statistical understandings, it specifically develops a rationale for thinking about how far results might travel regardless of epistemology. Highly recommended for those who are looking for a vehicle to outline where and how their results might be relevant elsewhere.

CHAPTER 17

WRITING UP

WHAT DO I NEED TO KNOW?

- The craft of writing
  - Getting feedback
  - Creating an argument
  - Thinking about the audience
  - Principles of academic writing
  - Word limit
- What will my dissertation look like?
  - Title page
  - Contents page
  - Technical list
  - Abstract
  - Acknowledgements
  - Introduction
  - Literature review
  - Method and methodology
  - Findings
  - Analysis/discussion
  - Conclusion
  - Appendices
  - References
- Submitting your dissertation
- What next?

INTRODUCTION

Once you have gone through the process of planning, designing, and carrying out your research, you need to write up your project. Writing is an extremely important part of the research process as a poorly written dissertation will constrain your ability to communicate your findings and limit the final mark you achieve. This chapter will take you through the basic elements of writing a dissertation and introduce you to the structures, forms, and styles that are commonly used to create one. Emphasizing the importance of developing an argument to connect the pieces of your dissertation together, it takes each element of the dissertation in turn and demonstrates how it is 'built'.

THE CRAFT OF WRITING

Writing up your research is an integral part of the dissertation process. Its primary purpose is to share your research with others. While this usually means the tutors who will mark the dissertation, it is certainly not unknown for dissertations to be read by other people and, as briefly mentioned in Chapter 16, some are even published.

However, while dissertations are read 'front to back', the process of writing them up is not a simple mechanical process of starting with the beginning and finishing at the end. Much of the work is completed out of sequence. Don't expect to start with page 1 and write each following page in order. Good dissertations are not usually written in this manner. Writing is an iterative process that involves drafting, redrafting, and revising your work as you move through the research process. You will need to craft your dissertation to answer your aims and objectives in a logical and purposeful manner, and take into account the audience that you are writing for.

Sometimes students think that dissertations consist of a two-step model of first doing the research and only after that is completed, writing it up. This is problematic—and poor dissertations are often the result of leaving the writing until the last minute. The task of writing is not something to be left until late in the process, as writing can be time-consuming, and involve redrafting and revising your work in accordance with feedback. Rather it should take place throughout the process of doing your dissertation. It can also be very daunting to open a blank document and begin writing something that might be as much as 15,000 words long. As a general rule of thumb, the more time you can devote to writing during the research the better, so including writing tasks at all stages of the dissertation process is a very good idea. Writing a dissertation is a marathon, not a last-minute sprint!

Writing can also help you to articulate your thoughts and ideas during a project. It can clarify your thinking, and lead to new insights, thoughts, and developments. The process of writing can be a generative process, a tool for discovery that changes the direction and scope of the study. You should also expect to undertake a series of drafts during the process of writing up. The first draft is usually the hardest to write, but as one supervisor who we've worked with used to say, 'the aim here is to get it written, not to get it right'. By the time you reach the first stage of writing you are likely to have accumulated copious notes and ideas about what you want to discuss. You then need to try and organize these into a coherent structure by connecting it all together. Managing, selecting, and editing are all part of the writing process.

While you need to have read something to write a first draft, you also shouldn't keep putting it off because you don't think that you've read enough. Avoid thinking you can postpone the writing until you can construct the definitive version. Produce first drafts when you can, even if there are a number of limitations. You can subsequently edit any work you do produce at this stage, so you don't need to be overly concerned about quality. By their very definition, first drafts will need developing and refining; but you can only develop and refine when you have something to work on.

Decisions about what to include and the level of depth can also change over the course of writing, but this doesn't mean that first drafts are 'wasted' work. You often need to walk down a wrong path or two to find the right one. Exploring a number of opportunities and **selecting** the best suited to your needs is always better than having to make the best of a bad job. So while you will draft sections as you go along, don't worry about fine-tuning the work too early in the process. Having something written down will improve your confidence and make the task more manageable.

I WISH I'D KNOWN . . . HOW TO CUT SUPERFLUOUS WORDS 17.1

"*Work little and often and the word count soon adds up—10,000 words may seem a lot, but you are very likely to need to cut at the end. Think of it in terms of 50 paragraphs. When you need to make cuts, first strip off flab and make sure you aren't rambling. Then look for whole paragraphs which are the least important in your dissertation as a whole—you can very likely take them out without loss of content and meaning.*"

— Dr Siobhan McAndrew, Lecturer in Sociology with Quantitative Methods, University of Bristol

As you develop your drafts, your writing will become more refined as you move through the research process. While we wouldn't want to put a number on it, most well-written dissertations will go through at least three drafts. Typically, the first will involve churning out the words and is less organized. The second draft becomes more shaped toward a specific end as you work out what you are trying to say; and the third is where word choices, grammar, and structure are reviewed. Of course, this may not happen in all cases and is dependent on time, but it is the sort of thing you should be aiming for.

As you redraft your chapters, you need to think about the 'academic style' of your writing, paying increasing attention to the references you are using. Once you have a final draft, go through it and delete superfluous words to enhance its readability. Everything needs a clear purpose: if you are not sure what a word is doing in a sentence, or what a paragraph adds to a subsection, then change it or get rid of it. Make sure your argument is clearly developed between sentences, from paragraph to paragraph, and chapter to chapter. In fact, introductions and conclusions to individual chapters can play an important role in helping to construct a linked and coherent structure.

I WISH I'D KNOWN . . . THE DIFFERENCES AND SIMILARITIES BETWEEN DISSERTATIONS AND OTHER ESSAYS 17.2

Students are often unaware of the similarities between writing a dissertation and other academic work. This recognition can help to make the task more manageable. Writing up your dissertation may seem like a particularly daunting task, but remember you have written university assignments before. While there are differences between your other assignments and the dissertation there are also similarities. For instance, in your assignments you are also expected to write critically and in an evidence-based manner, while conforming to a clear structure. So you already possess many of the writing skills required to write a dissertation. Some students actually approach dissertation chapters as though they are a series of smaller essays, which can be linked together.

Getting feedback

It is important to make sure you get feedback on your writing. Your supervisors are a key point of contact in this respect. As we pointed out in Chapter 3, given their research experience, and the fact that they are likely to be involved in marking your dissertation, it is important to be guided by their feedback. You need to have a strong rationale if you decide not to adhere to their recommendations—and if you choose not to, you should discuss your decision with them in the first instance. For instance, if the feedback suggests it would benefit from substantial amendments and time is limited, you may need to liaise with your supervisor about which changes to prioritize. Remember, it is normal to have additional work to do on your chapters when you receive feedback from your supervisor, and you should try and factor time for corrections into your timetable for writing. While it can be disheartening to face the prospect of making changes to your work, remember that this is highly likely to result in a stronger dissertation and a better mark.

FINDING YOUR WAY 17.1

When you first receive feedback make sure you understand it and seek clarification from your supervisor if there is anything you are unclear about. Once you are clear about what you need to do, you then need to make a decision about whether to make the changes immediately, or leave them until later. This really is a matter of preference. If you are in the middle of writing a different chapter and you receive feedback, you may prefer to complete the chapter you are concentrating on, before returning to the feedback.

It is also a good idea to get feedback from someone you trust to proofread your work and make sure it is comprehensible. This person could be a friend or family member. You shouldn't see this as a marking exercise: instead, it involves using them—as a lay person—to check your writing and to see whether your arguments 'make sense'. This feedback can help you review and improve your initial drafts. Remember that you need to leave sufficient time for it to be read and to act on any relevant feedback. Build this into your timetable.

(WORKING WITH YOUR SUPERVISOR 17.1

If it is not clear in the dissertation guidance how much work your supervisor can look at, make sure you clarify this at the earliest opportunity. If they are limited in terms of the number of chapters they can read, or the number of times they can look at the same chapter, then seek their advice on which ones you should get feedback on and at what stage. We would advise that you provide your supervisor with drafts of your work to the fullest extent that regulations will allow.

Creating an argument

One of the most common criticisms that tutors make about dissertations is the lack of an argument. An argument is essentially a perspective, a line of reasoning, and the development of an explanation, which has the analysis of your data at its core. It provides a clear purpose for the dissertation. This solid line of thinking takes the reader through the evidence and discussion to show how you came to the conclusions you are making. Your argument should also explore alternative perspectives and explain any issues with these, including why they may not be as applicable.

How you write about your research influences how others will understand it. This is not just about telling a story about what you have found, but also being actively involved in crafting a certain (balanced) view of reality. So, when writing your dissertation, you need to establish a narrative. You need to represent the process of coming to a particular conclusion, providing sufficient contextual information to enable the reader to have a clear understanding of the limitations or constraints on your thinking. Try to write reflexively, as stated in Chapter 16; this means considering the biases you might bring to the research, thinking about how much you can 'speak' on behalf of your participants (especially with qualitative data), and assisting your reader to judge credibility and validity in relation to your interpretations.

I WISH I'D KNOWN . . . THE NEED TO REFERENCE LANDMARK STUDIES 17.3

It is good practice to support your argument by citing landmark studies and grounding your work in the literature. This includes making use of examples and evidence from other researchers. You need to be persuasive in your argument. It is not simply a case of reporting your findings and drawing a few conclusions from these.

Thinking about the audience

In order to write well, it is necessary to keep your reader in mind. Think through what they really need to know in terms of what you did, why you did it, how you did it, and what you found out. You will need to present an intellectual debate which is evidenced-based, informative, and well-reasoned. It needs to be clearly presented and articulate. This will help your reader to understand your argument and evaluate its usefulness. Given that you are writing for an academic audience you should give considerable weight to reviewing academic literature, theories, and methodological accounts. Remember that if the audience, which includes the people marking your work, doesn't understand the messages you are trying to convey then it is going to affect your mark.

Principles of academic writing

There are a number of principles which you should adhere to when writing your dissertation. You may also find it helpful to refer to the hints on getting started with your writing in Chapter 3.

- **Write concisely**—Try to present your work in a precise and articulate manner. There can be a tendency in academic writing to overcomplicate things. This is unnecessary. Go through your work removing words that don't add anything to the meaning. Favour simple sentence structures over complex ones. Make sure your writing can be understood by your audience.
- **Be evidence-based**—Your argument is going to carry more weight and be more transparent if it is clearly evidence-based. Use examples and refer to existing literature to support points that you make.
- **Clearly structure your writing**—Your work needs to be organized so it clearly develops a logical argument. Use headings and subheadings to break up the text and help your audience to navigate your work.
- **Try to avoid sweeping statements**—Make sure your argument has a firm foundation in evidence and is clearly linked to the data or literature. If you do not have sufficient evidence to justify your generalizations, proceed with caution. Do not generalize beyond your data.
- **Define key terms**—Ensure that key ideas are carefully presented and defined. Use the literature to help you outline important features and dimensions of the topic you are interested in.
- **Cut out repetition**—Check your work for words and sentence structures that you use again and again. While some points need to be raised on more than one occasion, continued repetition may both dilute your argument and annoy the reader. Erasing repetition is also a great way of cutting down your word count.

- **Avoid colloquialisms and clichés**—The language that you use in everyday life is not always appropriate for academic work. It is often too informal for a dissertation and can make your work look sloppy or trite.
- **Take care with grammar**—Complex ideas don't need to be communicated through complex sentence structures. There can be a tendency in academic writing to build convoluted sentences. This often obscures the meaning of the message. Try to write in a grammatically appropriate manner, use appropriate punctuation, and if in doubt, keep it simple and clear.
- **Be careful with tenses**—Don't mix past, present, and future in the same sentence or paragraph. This can be challenging in social research given that it normally takes place over a long period of time. Things that were initially written in the future tense in the proposal—ie what was planned—have now taken place and become past tense. If in doubt, keep the focus on the present tense where possible by using phrases such as 'This research examines . . .', or 'This project explores . . .'. In academic writing, many disciplines discourage writing in the first person. However, this is not always the case, and you should check the expectations of your course and your discipline. Regardless of the discipline, there are a number of times when you might find it useful to write in the first person—for instance, if you are reflecting on your role as a researcher. This is something you can discuss with your supervisor as they may have particular preferences.
- **Use appropriate language**—Make sure that the language embraces diversity and is respectful. There are a number of guides provided by professional associations, such as the British Sociological Association, which you might find useful. Remember that language—and what is considered appropriate—changes through time. For instance, the term 'handicap' was used until quite recently (and is still used in some cultures). In fact, up until 1994, the journal *Disability & Society* was called *Disability, Handicap & Society*. Today, it is more appropriate to use terms like 'learning need' or 'mobility requirements'. Your writing should not engender or perpetuate stereotypes.
- **Proofread**—Give yourself time to thoroughly read through your dissertation. Ensure it follows the required style rules and double check your referencing, chapter headings, and numbering. You may also want to proofread your dissertation focusing on grammar and spelling, rather than context.
- **Don't just rely on spellcheckers**—They are useful for spotting spelling mistakes, but they don't tell you if you've used the wrong word when it is spelled correctly.
- **Back up your work**—It would be an awful shame to lose what you have done, especially if you are near the end of your dissertation. Be aware that many universities will not accept computer issues as a reason for late submission. It is important that you save your dissertation as you work on it, and it might be also worth saving the dissertation in more than one place.

Also make sure it is clearly labelled so you know which is the most up-to-date version: this may involve dating copies, or putting the version number—for instance, 'Introduction (Version 3 − 4.5.2020)'.

Word limit

Failure to observe the word limit is likely to lead to some form of sanction being applied to your dissertation. This means that it is useful to consider the number of words when thinking about its structure. Different universities may have different conventions with word count, so check what the expectations are for your course. The length of a section can also vary by strategy, design, and methods of collection and analysis. Another way of assessing 'how many' is to look at past dissertations to get a feel for what is expected.

Don't be concerned if you go slightly over the limit when first writing a chapter. If you find your original word limit was too short, you may need to adjust the words used in another chapter. Remember—you can always cut words later. In fact, this process of refining your work and cutting words usually leads to improved expression. However, this process can also be time-consuming. Being concise is an important skill to learn. Those who are most likely to disregard the word limit have often failed to leave sufficient time to edit and shorten their dissertation.

WORKING WITH YOUR SUPERVISOR 17.2

If you are unsure what 'counts' in the word limit, and this information is not provided in the guidance, speak to your supervisor. For instance, if you are not sure whether references are included in your word count you need to find this out. 'References' tend to be quite a large number of words and can make quite a difference to the length of your writing elsewhere. Also ask your supervisor's advice about the number of words to include in each chapter.

WHAT WILL MY DISSERTATION LOOK LIKE?

There are certain components that make up the typical structure of a dissertation. However, it is important for us to state from the outset that there is often much variation on the theme. For instance, it is common in qualitative research and (to a lesser extent) quantitative research to combine the results with the analysis and discussion chapter. Variations may depend on the type of method utilized (quantitative, qualitative, or mixed methods), the focus of the study, university requirements, and your individual preferences. However, regardless of exact structure, the purpose of a dissertation is the same in that it needs to communicate the research process, the data collected, and what you have found—and it needs to do this in a clear and well-reasoned manner.

I WISH I'D KNOWN . . . TO RETURN TO MY PROPOSAL WHEN WRITING UP | 7.4

When you are writing up it is often useful to return to your proposal. Although the final dissertation includes some different elements to the proposal, it can help you structure and focus your writing.

One common structure for a dissertation is shown here.

Title page

On the title page you are usually required to provide your name and student number, the name of your institution, and the year in which the dissertation is submitted—and the actual title, of course! However, this layout may differ between universities, so you need to follow your institution's guidance.

Contents page

The contents page may simply list the chapter headings or may be more extensive, including details of the headings and subheadings within chapters. The contents page acts as a signpost to allow the reader to find their way easily between different parts of the dissertation. It is useful if they want to refer back to a particular component. If you have figures and tables, these should also be listed on separate pages. The usual convention is for the first table in chapter 1 to be called Table 1.1, the second 1.2 and so on. The first figure in chapter 3 would be figure 3.1 and the second 3.2, etc. Using headers in Word can help to organize this process. Figure 17.1 provides an example of a contents page.

Figure 17.1 **An example contents page**

Table of Contents	
Abstract	iii
Acknowledgements	iv
List of Tables	vii
List of Figures	vii
Chapter One: Introduction	1
Chapter Two: Literature Review	8
Chapter Three: Methods and Methodology	22
Chapter Four: Results	31
Chapter Five: Analysis and Discussion	45
Chapter Six: Conclusion	58
References	63
Appendix	72

Technical list

If your dissertation includes a number of abbreviations, it may be useful to list these in alphabetical order. This is particularly helpful if your dissertation regularly makes use of acronyms. The list acts as a reference point for the reader, alongside a full version of what they stand for.

Abstract

The abstract should briefly summarize your dissertation and is usually between 50 and 250 words. It is often formulaic, concisely identifying the key focus of the dissertation (the topic), stating the methods employed and the nature of the data analysed, before emphasizing the main findings or key argument. This is not the place to include references and figures etc. Try to make your abstract as informative, but lively, as possible. Often, abstracts are written in the form of one or two paragraphs. However, you should check the style guidelines provided by your university. Despite being found at the beginning, its content means it cannot be constructed until you've actually written the rest of the dissertation.

FINDING YOUR WAY |7.2

It is useful to have a look at other examples of abstracts. Journal articles are a particularly useful source of information in respect to style, structure, and content.

Acknowledgements

This is usually optional and represents a personal statement, perhaps thanking those who have helped and supported you through the dissertation process. It should include those who have advised you, provided materials or contacts, or proofread your work. Acknowledgements shouldn't be given at the expense of anonymity as this would compromise ethical practice.

Introduction

The introduction should be immediately engaging to the reader. It needs to get their attention by focusing on an interesting problem, controversy, or opportunity which highlights why the research is required. Identifying 'the research problem', the introduction situates the project in terms of why the research is interesting. Moving beyond this general context, it should also explain the background of your research by briefly outlining what work has been done in this area, where your research 'fits' in relation to this work, and what your project adds to it. It introduces the research aims and objectives, explains your interest in the topic, and methods to be employed. Finally, the introduction provides a brief overview of the organization of the dissertation, often including a very brief description of the main chapters.

In doing these things, the introduction orientates the reader to both the content and structure of the dissertation. It acquaints them with the basic aims of the research, potentially placing it within a historical or theoretical framework. You should write the introduction as though you are setting out the process of investigation, avoiding reference to the discoveries and conclusions you may already have made. Although the introduction is the first chapter, it doesn't have to be the first thing that you write. It can actually be a good idea to leave it until nearer the end of the writing up process, because then you can be sure what it is, exactly, you are trying to introduce.

Literature review

The literature review, discussed in more detail in Chapter 6, surveys previous research on the topic of your dissertation. It shows how your research fits with the field, including the relevant topics, theories, and methods. It is common, but not essential, to write a full draft of the literature review prior to writing the other sections. However, you should expect to have to revise your literature review in the light of your results.

The literature review should provide a comprehensive and critical summary of research associated with your topic. You should report on the state of the literature, including its research directions **and** its current limitations. This will lead to a 'knowledge gap'. Essentially, this is a short statement about what currently remains uncertain in the field of knowledge you are working in. In turn, this gap provides the platform for your research aims, objectives, and questions. It is worth crafting the literature review carefully in accordance with the research aim and objectives you have established.

Remember this section needs to be critical as well as descriptive. Make sure you compare and contrast different interpretations appropriately. It should be clear from a literature review why your study is required, and what it can add to the

I WISH I'D KNOWN . . . TO CRITICALLY ENGAGE WITH THE LITERATURE 17.5

"*Rather than describing what has been said in existing literature, seek to critically engage with it. Consider how one piece of work relates to another—do they agree or disagree? Why is that? Which is the most plausible approach?*"

— Dr Katharine A. M. Wright, Lecturer in International Politics, Newcastle University topic, rather than simply a presentation of everything that has been done in this particular area. It should be written in the form of an argument.

Think carefully about how much space you dedicate to particular authors in the literature review, and consider how important their work is to your study. If something represents a particularly important study that you build on, it will need to be given greater attention than a peripheral study. If you fail to mention a key author in the area, this is likely to be picked up by the marker.

As a rule of thumb, the narrative structure of the literature review considers: what other researchers have said about the topic (research context), what hasn't been said (the 'knowledge gap'), and, therefore, what you will do to address this (aims and objectives). The bulk of the word count will be on the research context, but that discussion needs to specifically lead to a review of 'the gap' in the literature that has emerged in your discussion and, ultimately, a short statement outlining what you intend to do.

FINDING YOUR WAY | 7.3

By using the literature searching skills you developed in Chapter 5, you should be able to survey whether an article is worth focusing on by 'reading' the abstract. This will save you time when completing the literature review. However, don't think you can save time by reading one article and referring to the studies it references without reading them. By doing this there is a real danger you may miss something that is really relevant to your article by not looking at the original source. It is not considered good academic practice, and could lead to criticism by the marker.

Method and methodology

If the purpose of the literature review is to 'ask a question', the purpose of 'the methods' chapter is to detail **how** you will answer that question. This section typically reports what you did during the research. It should state how the data was collected, organized, and analysed in order to address the aims and objectives of the research. At which point it is worth differentiating between method (the techniques associated with what you did) and the methodology (the discussion associated with your method). This distinction is important to note as it gives a clue as to the driving purpose of 'the methods chapter'—and that is to describe what you did, and justify the reasons why you chose to do it in this way.

In the first instance, this chapter should briefly identify the ontological and epistemological basis for your study, and in doing so, demonstrate a good working knowledge of the methods employed. This information doesn't just communicate how the research was conducted, but also allows the reader to evaluate whether your research was carried out in a manner appropriate to the range of assumptions that underpin the study. Whether critiquing or explaining methods, it is important to make reference to methodological literature and debates. This can also give further weight to the choice of a particular method.

In some institutions you may be asked to reflect on how your role as a researcher impacts on the findings. Does your positionality—where you stand in relation to the work—affect the data generated? For instance, if you were a UK national investigating underage marriage in India, you could reflect on how your experience and understanding of UK law and ideologies with respect to childhood influence your approach to the research.

You also need to consider the more technical aspects of your research. This includes explaining the strategy you have adopted and why the design and techniques were used, including the research design, the sampling frame, data-collection techniques, analysis, and ethics. This includes some (brief) discussion concerning why you made these decisions.

Where relevant, describe how your research instrument (such as a questionnaire or interview schedule) was developed and trialled. Provide a narrative of how and when the data was collected—with some justification of why you did it in this way. If the data was recorded and transcribed, state this and explain why you decided to do this. Discuss any significant challenges or problems that led to you deviating from your approach, or affected the data in any way. When outlining the analysis, explain the techniques employed. For instance, if you undertook statistical analysis, you need to indicate the methods of analysis used—such as chi-square, t-tests, or logistic regression—and why.

Finally, the chapter should introduce and address ethical considerations relevant to the study. This includes factors such as informed consent, confidentiality, anonymity, avoidance of harm, and privacy. As previously mentioned in Chapter 8, this also means referring to the ethical guidelines that are set out in codes of conduct for many disciplines.

In some cases, this chapter will also consider the limitations of the methods you have used. However, these can also be given attention in the discussion or conclusion, where you can also use them as a platform to make specific reference to future avenues for research. It will be worth consulting your supervisor to see whether this discussion is best located here or elsewhere.

Findings

Broadly speaking, the findings chapter presents an overview of the important details from your data in relation to the aims and objectives of your research. The results need to be presented in a logical and convincing manner. This means providing a firm description of the data, making sure that your reader can see how your findings fit together.

In your findings, try to present the results of your study; this is why this chapter is sometimes also called 'results'. The discussion section, as we will see shortly, is where you link your data analysis back to the literature you introduced in the literature review. However, it is also worth noting that some people **do** choose to put the findings/results and discussion together in one chapter. Qualitative findings, where the findings and analysis are heavily dependent on a particular theoretical perspective, is one such example. Some dissertations may even include two or three findings chapters in addition to a discussion. This could be the case if a mixed methods approach was taken and you want to keep the findings from the different methods separate. If you are in any doubt, have a discussion with your supervisor about how to structure this part of your dissertation.

Regardless of whether you have taken a quantitative, qualitative, or mixed methods approach to your analysis, you need to be selective in terms of what you include in the findings section. Avoid including anything and everything in the hope that it is relevant. Consider what is necessary to answer your research aims. You should not include every table you have produced as part of your analysis, or every quote or vignette you have transcribed, but you do need to clearly provide evidence of your analysis. Make sure you explain and comment on each piece of data you choose to display, regardless of whether this is qualitative or quantitative—data never speaks for itself.

There are no fixed rules about how to present qualitative data. Quotes and other data should, however, be clearly labelled. This usually involves using a pseudonym and providing a person's age or occupation, depending on the topic of the study. You should (usually) set the quotes apart from the rest of the text by indenting them. Each quotation needs a purpose, and should support the narrative rather than replace it. Quotations should illustrate issues or add context.

When using quantitative data, select the minimum number of tables or figures required to fully evidence your argument. Try not to overwhelm your dissertation with table after table of uninterrupted material. Make sure you choose the most informative statistical analyses and present the data in the clearest way possible. It is also vital that data are supported with associated text. If data may simply be summarized in a couple of sentences, consider whether it is actually necessary to include a table. Is it necessary, for example, to use a table to show the number of women who work on a part-time or full-time basis, or can this information be better presented in written form? More complex data should be presented in figures or tables which are labelled consecutively.

Analysis/discussion

The discussion is the place in which you state how the findings should be interpreted, in relation to both the aims and objectives of your project and the wider literature. The discussion specifically links the key findings from your research to the material you introduced in the literature review, so you will be expected to cite some of it in the analysis. This section is also used to identify the significance of your findings in relation to that literature, and what your project has achieved in relation to the knowledge gap you have identified (see Chapter 16).

It is also important to make sure that in this section you also comment on any results that deviate from expected findings, and try and explain these with reference to the literature. This is, in itself, a research finding. The analysis/discussion chapter provides the reader with a concise and unambiguous explanation of the purpose of your study, its findings, and its significance. It offers you the opportunity to reflexively consider the research study, the results, and the wider literature.

Conclusion

The conclusion provides an opportunity to review the work as a whole. It has three discrete parts. The first is a brief overview of key findings with respect to the research aims and objectives. The second is a short discussion of the limitations of your study. This then provides you with the platform for the third element—future directions of study, given what you have found out.

This is not the place to introduce new materials or new arguments, except for areas for further study. It is not simply a case of reiterating what has been stated in the discussion chapter. Instead, it should identify how the overarching aims of the project have been answered, the constraints on those answers, and their importance going forward. Refer back to the introduction when writing your conclusion and reflect on the project that you set out to explore. If you have not been able to do what you set out, state this and explain why. You should also point out the limitations of your research, but try to provide a convincing rationale as to why your results remain important. So, suggest ways in which limitations could be overcome in the future, and what could have been done differently.

FINDING YOUR WAY 17.4

As it tends to come at the end of the dissertation process, there can be a tendency to not place the required emphasis on the conclusion. This is your last opportunity to create a lasting impression on the marker. It is where you can underline points and demonstrate your ability to think reflexively about the value of your project.

Appendices

Appendices are where you can include material relevant to your dissertation which would interrupt the flow, or take up too much space, in the body of the text. Appendices should not be used as a solution to word count issues, or a place to dump everything there isn't room for in the main body of the text. The kinds of things you might expect to find in an appendix include: sample consent forms and information sheets; questionnaires; detailed tables of data; excerpts from policy documents; an example of coding; a completed transcript. Some students choose to include full transcripts of interviews or field notes; however, this is not usually necessary, and often simply increases your printing costs. Each separate appendix should be labelled Appendix A, Appendix B, etc. It is also worth checking whether the appendix counts towards your word count.

References

This section should include all the sources you have referenced in the main body of the dissertation. This may sometimes be called a bibliography but, in practice, a bibliography differs from a reference list as it also includes sources which informed your thinking in relation to the topic, but are not referenced in the dissertation. It should be presented in the same format you would use for an essay. Make sure you adhere to any guidelines your university has in relation to referencing. For instance, they may specify that a particular form of referencing, such as the Harvard system, is used—and remember that there are different house styles, so make sure you are following the correct one. By the time you come to writing your dissertation there is usually an expectation that you will be familiar with how to accurately reference, and you are likely to be marked down for errors and inconsistencies. The key to referencing is to pay attention to detail.

SUBMITTING YOUR DISSERTATION

It is extremely satisfying to hold that final bound copy of your dissertation in your hand, and it is even more satisfying to submit it. Your department should have provided you with information about how to set out your dissertation, and submission guidelines. It is important that you adhere to these. You don't want to trip up at the final hurdle.

In addition to the written document, it is also increasingly common for students to be required to present dissertations in other formats. You may have to do a short oral presentation of your findings, or develop a poster about your work. The key to such presentations is to ensure you are clear about what is expected of you, and then plan accordingly. Be aware of any time constraints and ensure that you adhere to them. If you are doing a presentation, use visual aids to emphasize key points, including tables or key quotes which you want to share with your audience. Don't just read the slides, but practise using prompts to expand on the information in the slides. As Tom is fond of saying, 'know what you are going to say, not how you are going to say it'. Also, check that you are familiar with the equipment and any technical requirements. While there can always be technical hiccups, familiarity with systems will limit these and reduce anxiety.

Posters, on the other hand, require you to present the key points in as succinct a way as possible, while ensuring you convey the story of the research. You need to carefully consider the key elements to include, and how they are presented. The success of a poster is, in part, based on this presentation. This means paying attention to the use of images, the size of fonts, and the structure. It is not simply a case of filling it with as much information as possible and hoping the viewer can find key information themselves.

I WISH I'D KNOWN . . . HOW MUCH OF A SIGNIFICANT ACHIEVEMENT IT IS | 17.6

"*It has its highs and its lows, but the feeling of handing in your final dissertation is something unparalleled during your degree. It is a significant achievement.*"
— Dr Katharine A. M. Wright, Lecturer in International Politics, Newcastle University

WHAT NEXT?

You may be wondering what next in relation to your dissertation. While submitting your dissertation may represent the last time you look at it (and that is absolutely fine!), there may be ways you can use or develop your research further. For instance, dissertation research may be turned into academic articles, or used to develop newspaper articles, blogs, or reports. And, as we briefly mentioned in Chapter 16, student journals are becoming increasingly common. Your research can make a positive difference on society. In fact, Liam supervised a student who focused on the education of Burmese refugees in the UK. The student was able to develop a report and provide a presentation about educational opportunities in the UK at a centre for Burmese refugees where she had undertaken the research. We have even known a student use their dissertation research to inform evidence submitted to a House of Lords Select Committee on the Olympic and Paralympic legacy. Your dissertation may also act as a foundation for further study. For instance, if you have identified an interesting finding which warrants further attention, this might be something you could explore through further study. As such, doing a dissertation can act as a springboard to exciting and rewarding opportunities.

CONCLUSION

Writing a dissertation is a process. Writing needs to start early and, in itself, can clarify your thinking, lead to new ideas, and give you a sense of progress. By crafting and drafting your dissertation, while remaining focused on your research aims and objectives, you will be able to present an argument that runs through your work. By clearly planning your writing and adopting an appropriate structure it will help you complete your voyage by producing a quality dissertation. Best of luck!

WHAT DO I NEED TO THINK ABOUT?

- ☑ Do you understand the structure of the dissertation?
- ☑ Are you clear about the need to ensure you address your aims and objectives?
- ☑ Are you aware of the key principles of academic writing and the craft of writing?
- ☑ Do you know the amount of work your supervisor can look at, and how often you can see them?
- ☑ Are you clear about the submission process?

WHAT DO I NEED TO DO?

- ☑ (Re)familiarize yourself with the institutional requirements regarding the structure and components of the dissertation.
- ☑ Make sure that in your writing up you are addressing the aims and objectives of your dissertation.
- ☑ Conform to the principles of academic writing.
- ☑ Leave plenty of time to draft and redraft your dissertation, being aware that you are likely to need to cut words.
- ☑ Get feedback on your dissertation from your supervisor, and make any necessary changes.
- ☑ When it is ready, submit your dissertation in accordance with the guidelines.

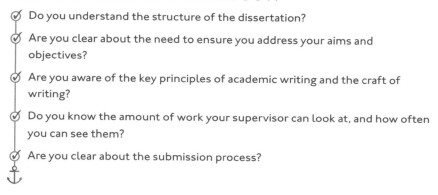

Access the online resources **www.oup.com/uk/brymansrple** to help you to successfully complete your social research project or dissertation.

DELVE DEEPER

Becker, H. (2007). *How to Write for Social Scientists: How to Start and Finish Your Thesis, Book or Article.* **Chicago: University of Chicago Press.** We have previously highlighted this book as excellent in terms of getting you to think about what research means and what it will look like in the context of an independent project. It is also useful in terms of thinking about writing up and what a dissertation looks like.

Gibbs, G. (2015). *Writing up qualitative research.* This YouTube video was a lecture given to students at the University of Huddersfield as part of a

course on qualitative data analysis. It focuses on a range of issues which need to be considered when writing up qualitative research.
https://www.youtube.com/watch?reload=9&v=lFj2ucSP2jc (Accessed 2 November 2018)

Morley, J. *The Academic Phrasebook.* This is a general resource for academic writing, but you may find it particularly useful in terms of your dissertation. It provides examples of the phraseological 'nuts and bolts' of writing, organized around the main sections of the dissertation. It is especially useful for writers who are non-native speakers of English.
http://www.phrasebank.manchester.ac.uk/ (Accessed 2 November 2018)

Murray, N. and Hughes, G. (2008). *Writing Up Your University Assignments and Research Projects: A Practical Handbook.* Maidenhead: Open University Press. This asks and answers key questions such as what is good academic writing and how should I present my written work? Sections of the book address the preparation and writing of dissertations. It is useful in helping you think about your writing style and finding your voice.

The Royal Literary Fund provides support and advice around writing skills for those writing a dissertation. It is not presented as a conventional how-to guide, but rather provides a variety of voices on the process of writing. These are particularly useful in thinking about drafting and rewriting crucial elements of a dissertation.
https://www.rlf.org.uk/resources/introduction-dissertation/ (Accessed 10 November 2018)

Thomson, A. (2008). *Critical Reasoning: A Practical Introduction.* London: Routledge. This book is particularly useful in helping you to improve your skill in analysing arguments. It employs examples to show you how to evaluate the credibility of evidence.

Wolcott, H. (2009). *Writing Up Qualitative Research.* London: Sage. This is especially useful if you have done qualitative research as part of your dissertation. This book focuses on writing up. It is especially useful on how to incorporate theory into this process, something that some students struggle with.

Best of luck with your dissertation or research project!

GLOSSARY

Terms appearing elsewhere in the glossary are in italics.

Action research An approach in which the action researcher and a client collaborate in the diagnosis of a research problem and in the development of a solution based on the diagnosis.

Aim(s) These provide a clear statement about the intentions of the research. The overarching aim(s) specify the overall focus of your project.

Alternative hypothesis In hypothesis-testing, this represents the proposition that there will be a difference between conditions.

Analytic induction An approach to the analysis of *qualitative* data in which the researcher seeks universal explanations of phenomena by pursuing the collection of data until no cases that are inconsistent with a hypothetical explanation (deviant or negative cases) of that phenomenon are found.

Anonymity The process by which participants are protected from identification. Any information related to an individual, organization, or place should not be directly traceable to the source of origin.

Avoidance of harm It is important to ensure that participants are safe from harm, and every effort should be made to identify basic risks involved in carrying out your project.

Axial coding The process of exploring the interconnections and relationships between *codes* and categories. This involves interrogating the properties of those categories in relation to context, consequence, interaction, and cause.

Bar chart Visual representation of data used to describe *nominal* and *ordinal variables*. Bars are used to represent the count, percentage, or *proportion* of each category of the variable.

Biographical analysis A form of qualitative analysis that aims to use biographical representations of single lives to explore and reveal the social and cultural concerns of the many.

Bivariate analysis The examination of the relationship between two *variables*, as in *contingency tables* or *correlation*.

Boolean logic A technique used in literature searching that uses the operators AND, OR, and NOT to connect search terms when using databases.

Case study A *research design* that entails the detailed and intensive analysis of a single case. The term is sometimes extended to include the study of just two or three cases for comparative purposes.

Categorical data *Variables* whose attributes have been categorized. Such *variables* have no numeric value. *Nominal* and *ordinal variables* are categorical.

Causality A concern with establishing causal connections between *variables*, rather than mere *relationships* between them.

Cell The point in a table, such as a *contingency table*, where the rows and columns intersect.

Census The enumeration of an entire *population*. Unlike a *sample*, which comprises a count of some units in a population, a census relates to **all** possible units.

Chi-square test Chi-square (χ^2) is a test of *statistical significance*, which is typically employed to establish how confident we can be that the findings displayed in a *contingency table* can be generalized from a *probability sample* to a *population*.

Closed-ended question A question employed in an *interview schedule* that presents the respondent with a set of possible answers to choose from.

Closed settings Places which require proprietary access and have substantial barriers to prevent outsiders from entering. These barriers can be physical, bureaucratic, or social.

Cluster sample A sampling procedure in which the researcher samples initial areas (ie clusters) and then samples units from these clusters, usually using a *probability sampling* method.

Clustered bar chart Allows you to represent data from more than one *variable*.

Code, coding In *quantitative research*, codes are numbers that are assigned to data about people or other units of analysis when the data are not inherently numerical. In *qualitative research*, coding is the process whereby data are broken down into component parts, which are given labels.

Coding manual In *content analysis*, this is the statement of instructions to coders that outlines all the possible categories for each dimension being analysed.

Coding schedule In *content analysis*, this is the form onto which all the data relating to an item being coded will be entered.

Cohort study A particular form of *longitudinal study* that *samples* a cohort, performing a cross-section at intervals through time. In a cohort study the people in the *sample* change with each iteration of data collection.

Comparative design A *research design* that entails the comparison of two or more cases in order to illuminate existing theory or generate theoretical insights.

Computer-assisted content analysis (CACA) Software platforms that can help to speed up the process of *content analysis*.

Computer-assisted (or aided) qualitative data analysis software (CAQDAS) The use of computer software through which qualitative material can be processed.

Concept/conceptual label A name given to a grouping of phenomena that organizes observations and ideas by virtue of their possessing common features. In *grounded theory*, a concept is a key building block in the construction of a theory.

Confidentiality This is concerned with making sure the information that research participants provide is not shared with third parties.

Constant comparison A central tool of *grounded theory* that entails constantly comparing new data with existing data, *concepts*, and categories.

Construct The same as a *concept* but in much *quantitative research*, construct is the preferred term.

Constructionism, constructionist An *ontological* position (often also referred to as *constructivism*) that asserts that social phenomena and their meanings are continually being accomplished by social actors. It is antithetical to *objectivism*.

Constructivism See *constructionism*.

Content analysis An approach to the analysis of documents and texts that seeks to quantify content in terms of predetermined categories and in a systematic and replicable manner. The term is sometimes used in connection with *qualitative research* as well.

Contingency table A table, comprising rows and columns, that shows the *relationship* between two *variables*. Usually, at least one of the *variables* is a *nominal variable*. Each *cell* in the table shows the frequency of occurrence of the intersection of categories of each of the two *variables* and usually a percentage.

Convenience sample A *sample* that is selected because of its availability to the researcher. It is a form of *non-probability sample*.

Core category In *grounded theory* this is a category that acts as an overarching motif that brings together other categories.

Correlation An approach to the analysis of relationships between *interval/ratio variables* and/or *ordinal variables* that seeks to assess the strength and direction of the *relationship* between the *variables* concerned.

Covert research A term frequently used in connection with *ethnographic* research in which the researcher does not reveal his or her true identity. Such research can violate the ethical principle of *informed consent*.

Criteria-ology A term used to describe the diverse ways of thinking about research quality.

Critical value The point(s) on the scale of a test statistic beyond which to reject the *null hypothesis*.

Cross-sectional design A *research design* that entails the collection of a *sample* of cases at a single point in time. The intention is usually to collect a body of *quantitative* or quantifiable data in connection with two or more *variables* (and often many more than two), which are then examined to detect patterns of association.

Crosstabulation A table of the joint frequency distributions of two *nominal* or *ordinal variables*, sometimes called a *contingency table*.

Data mining This is the automated attempt to extract patterns and trends from huge data sets. It is predominantly used in digital research methods.

Deductive, deduction An approach to social research in which theory drives data collection. Specific research questions are formulated, 'tested' against observation, and an answer is then deduced.

Dependent variable A *variable* that is causally influenced by another variable (ie an *independent variable*).

Descriptive statistics Tools used to describe data and their characteristics.

Dewey Decimal System A numbering system that catalogues and arranges collections of books into themes.

Dichotomous variable A *variable* with just two categories.

Discourse analysis An approach to the analysis of discourse that emphasizes the ways in which versions of reality are accomplished through language.

Documentary methods Techniques used to categorize, investigate, and analyse various forms of text.

Email survey A *survey* in which respondents are sent the survey in an email. This may be embedded in the email or attached to the email.

Empiricism An approach to the study of reality that suggests that only knowledge gained through experience and the senses is acceptable.

Epistemology, epistemological A theory of knowledge. It is particularly employed in this book to refer to a stance on what should pass as acceptable knowledge. See *positivism* and *interpretivism*.

Ethnography, ethnographer Like *participant observation*, a research method in which the researcher immerses him- or herself in a social setting for an extended period of time. It involves observing behaviour, listening to what is said in conversations both between others and with the fieldworker, and asking questions. However, the term has a more inclusive sense than *participant observation*, which seems to emphasize the observational component. Also, the term 'an ethnography' is frequently used to refer to the written output of ethnographic research.

Ethnomethodology A perspective concerned with the way in which social order is accomplished through talk and interaction. It provides the intellectual foundations of conversation analysis.

Evaluation research Research that is concerned with the evaluation of real-life interventions in the social world.

Expected values The values which we would expect to appear if variables are completely independent of each other (ie they happen by chance).

Experiment A *research design* that rules out alternative causal explanations of findings deriving from it by having at least (*a*) an experimental group, which is exposed to a treatment, and a control group, which is not, and (*b*) random assignment to the two groups. Instead of a control group, an experiment may comprise a further group (or groups) that are exposed to other treatments.

Factor analysis A statistical technique used for large numbers of *variables* to establish whether there is a tendency for groups of them to be interrelated. It is often used with multiple-indicator measures to see if they bunch to form one or more groups of indicators. These groups of indicators are called factors and must then be given a name.

Field notes A detailed chronicle by an *ethnographer* of events, conversations, and behaviour, and the researcher's initial reflections on them.

Filter question A type of question that is used in surveys to filter respondents to further questions if specific requirements are met. For example, the filter question might ask respondents whether they have driven while intoxicated. Should the answer be 'yes', respondents would then be asked about the number of times that has happened. If they answer 'no', they will skip to a later question.

Focus group A form of group interview in which: there are several participants (in addition to the moderator/facilitator); there is an emphasis in the questioning on a particular fairly tightly defined topic; and the emphasis is on interaction within the group and the joint construction of meaning.

Frequency table A table that displays the number and/or percentage of units (eg people) in different categories of a *variable*.

Gantt chart A type of chart that illustrates a project schedule.

Gatekeepers These are the individuals, groups, and organizations that act as intermediaries between researchers and participants or other forms of data. They are often the people in formal and informal positions of influence in particular groups and communities.

Generalization, generalizability A concern with the external *validity* of research findings.

Grand theory This attempts to explain and/or understand the whole of society. This type of theorizing is often perceived to be highly abstract.

Grey literature Literature which hasn't been through the process of peer review.

Grounded theory An iterative, and systematic, approach to the analysis of *qualitative* data that aims to generate theory out of research data by achieving a close fit between the two.

Histogram A bar graph used for *interval* and *ratio* (continuous) *variables*.

Household drop-off survey A method of delivering a survey in which the respondent's home or business is visited to hand the respondent the *questionnaire* directly. In some cases, the respondent is asked to mail it back or it is picked up.

Hypothesis An informed speculation, which is set up to be tested, about the possible relationship between two or more *variables*.

Hypothetico-deductive model A form of theorizing that articulates a specific *research question* where two answers are possible.

IBM SPSS Originally short for **S**tatistical **P**ackage for the **S**ocial **S**ciences, IBM SPSS is a widely used computer program that allows quantitative data to be managed and analysed.

Independent variable A *variable* that has a causal impact on another variable (ie a *dependent variable*).

Index See *scale*.

Inductive, induction An approach to the relationship between theory and research in which the former is generated out of the latter.

Inferential statistics Allow inferences to be made about qualities of a *population* from a *sample* drawn randomly from that population. This process is referred to as statistical inference.

Informed consent A key principle in social research ethics. It requires that prospective research participants should be given as much information as might be needed to make an informed decision about whether or not they wish to participate in a study.

Interpretivism An *epistemological* position that requires the social scientist to grasp the subjective meaning of social action.

Interquartile range The difference between highest and lowest values in a distribution of values when the highest and lowest 25 per cent of values have been removed.

Inter-rater reliability The degree to which two or more individuals agree about the *coding* of an item. Inter-rater reliability is likely to be an issue in *content analysis, structured observation,* and when *coding* answers to *open-ended questions* in research based on *questionnaires* or *structured interviews.*

Interval variable A *variable* where the distances between the points of measurement are identical across its range of categories.

Interview schedule A collection of questions designed to be asked by an interviewer. An interview schedule is always used in a *structured interview,* and often employed in a *semi-structured interview.*

Intra-rater reliability The degree to which an individual differs over time in the *coding* of an item. Intra-rater reliability is likely to be an issue in *content analysis, structured observation,* and when *coding* answers to *open-ended questions* in research based on *questionnaires* or *structured interviews.*

Keywords Key *concepts* and terms related to a piece of research. They can be theoretical, methodological, or substantive in focus.

Labelling theory Concerned with how the process of labelling influences the identity and behaviour of individuals.

Levels of measurement The different ways in which variables record numeric data. There are four levels of measurement: *nominal, ordinal, interval,* and *ratio.*

Life history research Emphasizes the inner experience of individuals and its connections with changing events and phases throughout the life course. The method usually entails life history interviews and the use of personal documents as data.

Likert scale A widely used format developed by Rensis Likert for asking attitude questions. Respondents are typically asked their degree of agreement with a series of statements that, when combined, form a multiple-indicator or -item measure. The *scale* is deemed then to measure the intensity with which respondents feel about an issue.

Line graph A diagram in which lines are used to indicate the frequency of a variable.

Literature search The action of conducting a search for literature published on a research topic.

Longitudinal research A *research design* in which data are collected on a *sample* (of people, documents, etc) over time.

Mean This is the everyday 'average'—namely, the total of a distribution of values divided by the number of values.

Measure of central tendency A statistic, like the *mean*, *median*, or *mode*, that summarizes a distribution of values.

Measure of dispersion A statistic, like the *range* or *standard deviation*, that summarizes the amount of variation in a distribution of values.

Median The mid-point in a distribution of values.

Meta-analysis A form of systematic review that involves summarizing the results of a large number of *quantitative* studies and conducting various analytical tests to show whether or not a particular variable has an effect across those studies.

Methodology This is concerned with the discussion of *epistemological* and *ontological* aspects of a *research strategy*.

Micro-level theory A very specific theory that concentrates its attention on everyday human interactions. Small-scale in focus, it largely uses interpretative techniques to examine how interpersonal encounters are achieved 'in practice'.

Middle-range theories These theories seek to understand more particular aspects of social life. Typically, this type of theorizing occurs at a more substantive level.

Missing data Data relating to items or cases that are not available—for example, when a respondent in social *survey* research does not answer a question. These are referred to as 'missing values' in *IBM SPSS*. The term non-response is often used to refer to unanswered questions.

Mixed methods research A term that is increasingly employed to describe research that combines the use of both *quantitative research* and *qualitative research*. The term can be used to describe research that combines just different *quantitative research* methods or that combines just different *qualitative research* methods. However, in recent times, it has taken on this more specific meaning of combining *quantitative* and *qualitative research* methods.

Mode The value that occurs most frequently in a distribution of values.

Multivariate analysis The examination of *relationships* between three or more *variables*.

Narrative analysis An approach to the elicitation and analysis of data that is sensitive to the sense of temporal sequence that people, as tellers of stories about their lives or events around them, detect in their lives and surrounding episodes and inject into their accounts. However, the approach is not exclusive to a focus on life histories and can be used with a wide range of mediums.

Narrative review An approach to reviewing the literature that is often contrasted with a *systematic review*. It tends to be less focused than a *systematic review* and seeks to arrive at a critical interpretation of the literature that it reviews.

Netnography A form of *ethnography* which is applied to online or largely online communities. It has mainly been used in relation to topics in the fields of marketing and retailing.

Nominal variable Also known as a *categorical variable*, this is a *variable* that comprises categories that cannot be rank ordered.

Non-parametric test A statistical test which needs fewer assumptions about the distribution of values in a sample than a *parametric test*.

Non-probability sample A sample that has not been selected using a *random sampling* method. Essentially, this implies that some units in the *population* are more likely to be selected than others. In qualitative research strategies, this is often done purposively.

Null hypothesis A *hypothesis* that suggests there will be no difference in measurement between two conditions.

NVivo A *CAQDAS* package that facilitates the management and analysis of *qualitative* data.

Objectives Specifically define the parameters of your *aim(s)* by breaking them down into more specific components.

Objectivism An *ontological* position that asserts that social phenomena and their meanings have an existence that is independent of social actors.

Observed values The values that are actually obtained when taking measurements.

Online surveys Surveys/questionnaires that are delivered electronically through internet platforms. Respondents are typically contacted by email, with a link provided to the electronic survey. Popular examples include Google Forms and SurveyMonkey.

Ontology, ontological Discussion directed toward the nature of social entities. See *objectivism* and *constructionism*.

Open coding The process of breaking down raw *qualitative* data into more manageable chunks. Through the process of constant comparison, the *codes* can then be grouped together to construct basic categories.

Open settings Ethnographic settings that have few barriers of entry and are relatively open to access for outsiders.

Open-ended question A question employed in an *interview schedule* or self-administered questionnaire that does not present the respondent with a set of possible answers to choose from.

Ordinal variable A *variable* whose categories can be rank ordered (as in the case of *interval* and *ratio variables*), but the distances between the categories are not equal or cannot be interpreted consistently.

Outlier An extreme value in a distribution of values. If a *variable* has an extreme value—either very high or very low—the *mean* or the *range* will be distorted by it.

Overt research Methods in which the researcher makes themselves known as a researcher to those engaged in the research process.

Panel study A particular design of *longitudinal study* in which the same *sample* is followed at specified intervals over a long period, often many years.

Paradigm A term deriving from the history of science, where it was used to describe a cluster of beliefs and dictates that influence what should be studied, how research should be carried out, and how results should be interpreted.

Parametric test A form of inferential statistics where a series of specific assumptions about the underlying *sample* data are made. This often includes assessments about the nature of the distribution, the associated variance, and the *scale* used to take the measurement. It is generally seen to be a stronger form of testing than its non-parametric counterpart.

Participant observation Research in which the researcher immerses him- or herself in a social setting for an extended period of time, observing behaviour, listening to what is said in conversations both between others and with the fieldworker, and asking questions. Participant observation usually includes interviewing key informants and studying documents, and as such is difficult to distinguish from *ethnography*. In this book, participant observation is used to refer to the specifically observational aspect of ethnography.

Peer-reviewed literature Literature which has gone through a peer review process prior to publication.

Performative inquiry This offers practitioners and researchers a way of engaging in research that attends to critical moments that emerge through creative action.

Personal documents Documents such as diaries, letters, and autobiographies that are not written for an official purpose. They provide first-person accounts of the writer's life and events within it.

Phenomenology, phenomenological A philosophy that is concerned with the question of how individuals make sense of the world around them and how the philosopher should 'bracket out' preconceptions concerning his or her grasp of that world.

Photo elicitation A *visual* research method that entails getting interviewees to discuss one or more photographs in the course of an interview. The photograph(s) may be existing images or may have been taken by the interviewee for the purpose of the research.

Pie chart A graph used to describe the distribution of *nominal* or *ordinal* data. A pie chart presents the categories of data as parts of a circle or 'slices of a pie'.

Pilot study A small-scale, preliminary study conducted to test the research instruments prior to undertaking a full-scale research project.

Placebo effect The name given to changes in the research that can occur simply by the participant knowing that they are in a treatment group.

Plagiarism Presenting someone else's work or ideas as your own, with or without their consent, by incorporating it into your work without full acknowledgement.

Population The universe of units from which a *sample* is to be selected.

Positivism An *epistemological* position that advocates the application of the methods of the natural sciences to the study of social reality.

Postal survey A form of self-administered *questionnaire* that is sent to respondents and usually returned by them by mail.

Postmodernism A position that displays a distaste for master-narratives and for a realist orientation. In the context of research *methodology*, postmodernists have a preference for *qualitative* methods and a concern with the modes of representation of research findings.

Post-positivism A reformulation of *positivism* that attempts to recognize the difficulties of remaining 'objective'. Rather than emphasizing the independent relationship between researcher and researched, post-positivism accepts that the researcher's background, values, and theories will influence the research. While research can remain 'value-free', effort needs to be directed toward detecting and eradicating bias.

Primary data Data used in research that is obtained through the direct efforts of the researcher through *surveys*, interviews, and direct observation.

Privacy A person's right to be free to withhold information that they may deem personal.

Probability sampling, sample A *sample* that has been selected using *random sampling* and in which each unit in the population has a known probability of being selected.

Proportion Very similar to a percentage, the main difference being that a proportion can take any value from 0 to 1 inclusive, while a percentage usually takes a value from 0 per cent to 100 per cent (although percentage changes greater than 100 per cent are possible).

Purposive sampling, sample A form of *non-probability sample* in which the researcher aims to sample cases/participants in a strategic way, so that those sampled are relevant to the research questions that are being posed.

'P-value' When discussing *statistical significance*, reference is often made to the 'p-value'. This is an assessment of probability that your results are indicative of the wider *population*.

Qualitative research Qualitative research usually emphasizes meaning rather than quantification in the collection and analysis of data. As a *research strategy* it is *inductivist*, *constructionist*, and *interpretivist*, but qualitative researchers do not always subscribe to all three of these features.

Quantitative research Quantitative research usually emphasizes quantification in the collection and analysis of data. As a *research strategy* it is *deductivist* and *objectivist* and incorporates a natural science model of the research process (in particular, one influenced by *positivism*), but quantitative researchers do not always subscribe to all three of these features. Compare with *qualitative research*.

Questionnaire A research instrument consisting of a series of questions for the purpose of gathering information from respondents.

Quota sample A *sample* in which participants are non-randomly sampled from a *population* in terms of the relative proportions of people in different categories. It is a type of *non-probability sample*.

Random sampling Sampling whereby the inclusion of a unit of a *population* occurs entirely by chance.

Range The difference between the maximum and the minimum value in a distribution of values associated with an *interval* or *ratio variable*.

Ratio variable An *interval variable* with a true zero point.

Rationale This is a brief explanation of why your research topic is worthy of study and how it makes a significant contribution to the body of already existing research.

Reflexivity A term used in research *methodology* to refer to a reflectiveness among social researchers about the implications they generate for the knowledge of the social world. Often directed toward their methods, values, biases, decisions, and mere presence in the very situations they investigate.

Relationship An association between two *variables* whereby the variation in one *variable* coincides with variation in another *variable*.

Reliability The degree to which a measure of a *concept* is stable.

Replication, replicability The degree to which the results of a study can be reproduced.

Representative sample A *sample* that reflects the *population* accurately, so that it is a microcosm of the *population*.

Research design This term is employed in this book to refer to a framework or structure within which the collection and analysis of data takes place. A choice of research design reflects decisions about the priority being given to a range of dimensions of the research process (such as *causality* and *generalization*) and is influenced by the kind of *research question* that is posed.

Research proposal A plan of research that describes the context, the rationale, and the methods for research. The proposal helps you make sense of your project and what it will look like.

Research question An explicit statement in the form of a question of what it is that a researcher intends to find out about. A research question not only influences the scope of an investigation but also how the research will be conducted.

Research strategy A term used in this book to refer to a general orientation to the conduct of social research (see *quantitative research* and *qualitative research*).

Respondent validation Sometimes called member validation, this is a process whereby a researcher provides the people on whom he or she has conducted research with an account of his or her findings and requests feedback on that account.

Restudy The adaptation of an existing study. Also known as a replication study.

Sample The units of the population that are selected for research. Essentially a subset of the *population*. The method of selection may be based on *probability sampling* or *non-probability sampling* principles.

Sampling frame The listing of all units in the *population* from which a *sample* is selected.

Scale A term that is usually used interchangeably with *index* to refer to a multiple-indicator measure in which the score a person gives for each component indicator is used to provide a composite score for that person.

Scatterplot This is a type of graph where one observation is plotted against another. They provide a visual representation of whether, and how, two *variables* might be related to each other. Each axis represents the value of an observation, with the point being where those values intersect.

Scoping studies The rapid gathering of literature in a given area where the aims are to accumulate as much evidence as possible and map the results.

Secondary data Data used by researchers who will probably not have been involved in the collection of those data. Secondary data may be either quantitative data or qualitative data.

Selective coding Used in some forms of *grounded theory* to saturate a *core category*, or to discover *codes* and categories that need further articulation.

Semi-structured interview A term that covers a wide range of types of interview. It typically refers to a context in which the interviewer has a series of questions that are in the general form of an interview guide but is able to vary the sequence of questions. Questioning is somewhat more dynamic than that typically found in a *structured interview schedule*. The interviewer usually has some latitude to ask further questions in response to what are seen as significant replies.

Significance level The point(s) on the scale of a test statistic at which, given the sample size, quantitative findings are deemed to be statistically significant. Significance is usually reported at $p<.05$ and $p<.01$ (ie if we assume that the null hypothesis is correct, the probability of the observed result being due to chance is lower than 5 per cent or 1 per cent).

Simple random sample A *sample* in which each unit has been selected entirely by chance. Each unit of the *population* has a known and equal probability of inclusion in the sample.

Snowball sample A *non-probability sample* in which the researcher makes initial contact with a small group of people who are relevant to the research topic and then uses these to establish contacts with others.

Spurious relationship A *relationship* between two *variables* is said to be spurious if it is being produced by the impact of a third variable (often referred to as a confounding variable). When the third *variable* is controlled, the *relationship* disappears.

Standard deviation A measure of dispersion around the *mean*.

Standpoint theorists People who argue that an individual's experiences of society, and their resulting knowledge of it, is fundamentally and essentially not the same as those in other areas of society. Common in areas of feminism, disability studies, and postcolonialism.

Statistical significance (test of) Allows the analyst to estimate how confident he or she can be that the results deriving from a study based on a randomly selected *sample* are *generalizable* to the *population* from which the sample was drawn. Such a test does not allow the researcher to infer that the findings are of substantive importance. The *chi-square test* is an example of this kind of test. The process of using a test of statistical significance to generalize from a *sample* to a *population* is known as statistical inference.

Stratified sample A *sample* in which units are *randomly sampled* from a *population* that has been divided into categories (strata).

Structured interview A type of interview usually used in the context of *survey* research in which all respondents are asked exactly the same questions in the same order with the aid of a formal *interview schedule*.

Structured observation Often also called systematic observation, this is a technique in which the researcher employs explicitly formulated rules for the observation and recording of behaviour. The rules inform observers about what they should look for and how they should record behaviour.

Subpoenable Capable of being required by a court of law.

Survey A collection of questions aimed at extracting specific data from a particular group of people.

Systematic review A type of literature review that aims to provide a comprehensive account of the field. It should also be capable of *replication*, and transparent in its approach. Systematic reviews pay close attention to assessing the quality of research in deciding whether a study should be included or not. *Meta-analysis* and meta-*ethnography* are both forms of systematic review.

Systematic sample A *probability sampling* method in which units are selected from a *sampling frame* according to fixed intervals, such as every fifth unit.

Thematic analysis A form of qualitative analysis that is directed toward uncovering key themes. Although there are variations in approach, it is increasingly common in qualitative research.

Theoretical coding The term given to the use of emergent or existing theory to help structure data.

Theoretical sampling, sample A term used mainly in relation to *grounded theory* to refer to *purposive sampling* carried out so that emerging theoretical considerations guide the selection of cases and/or research participants. Theoretical sampling is supposed to continue until a point of *theoretical saturation* is reached.

Theoretical saturation The point when emerging *concepts* have been fully explored and no new theoretical insights are being generated. See also *theoretical sampling*.

Thick description A term devised by Clifford Geertz to refer to detailed accounts of a social setting that can form the basis for the creation of general statements about a culture and its significance in people's social lives.

Time series analysis A particular form of *longitudinal* research that aims to identify patterns within a sequence of observations.

Transcription, transcript The written translation of a recorded interview or *focus group* session.

Triangulation The use of more than one method or source of data in the study of a social phenomenon so that findings may be cross-checked.

T-test A significance test which compares the sample mean with the population mean. The t-test can only be used with random samples and when the data are normally distributed.

Univariate analysis The analysis of a single *variable* at a time.

Unobtrusive measures Indirect methods of data collection that focus on naturally occurring data. As data collection does not typically require direct engagement with research participants, these techniques can be considered to be non-reactive in nature.

Unstructured interview A type of interview in which the interviewer typically has only a very general list of topics or issues that will be covered. The style of questioning is usually very informal. The phrasing and sequencing of questions will vary from interview to interview.

Validity A concern with the integrity of the conclusions that are generated from a piece of research.

Variable An attribute in terms of which cases vary. See also *dependent variable* and *independent variable*.

Vignette A hypothetical situation or narrative to which research participants respond thereby revealing their perceptions, values, or impressions of events.

Visual ethnography A form of *ethnography* conducted using photography, video, or film.

Visual methods Methods that incorporate some kind of imagery into the research process. Images can constitute the research data, the tools through which research data is analysed, or how the research results are communicated.

Vulnerable groups This tends to refer to those individuals or groups who might not be able to fully consent to participation.

Writ A formal written command from a court of law.

REFERENCES

CHAPTER 2: THE SOCIAL RESEARCH PROCESS

Becker, H. (1953). 'Becoming a Marijuana User', *American Journal of Sociology*, 59(3): 235–242.

Glaser, B. and Strauss, A. (1967). *The Discovery of Grounded Theory: Strategies for Qualitative Research*. Hawthorne: Aldine de Gruyter.

Tukey, J. W. (1977). *Exploratory Data Analysis*. Reading, MA: Addison-Wesley.

CHAPTER 4: DEVELOPING A RESEARCH IDEA

Bell, C. and Newby, H. (1977). *Doing Sociological Research*. London: Allen and Unwin.

Bryman, A. (2004). *The Disneyization of Society*. London: Sage.

Johnson, J., Rolph, S., and Smith, R. (2010). *Residential Care Transformed: Revisiting 'The Last Refuge'*. Basingstoke: Palgrave.

Law, J. (2000). *After Method: Mess in Social Science Research*. London: Routledge.

Lee, C. and Dorling, D. (2011). 'The Geography of Poverty', *Socialist Review*, October.

Letherby, G., Scott, J., and Williams, M. (2012). *Objectivity and Subjectivity in Social Research*. London: Sage.

Peach, C. (1999). 'London and New York: Contrasts in British and American Models of Segregation', *International Journal of Population Geography*, 5: 319–351.

Seale, C. (2002). 'Quality Issues in Qualitative Inquiry', *Qualitative Social Work*, 1(1): 97–110.

Townsend, P. (1962). *The Last Refuge: A Survey of Residential Institutions and Homes for the Aged in England and Wales*. London: Routledge.

Wacquant, L. (2008). *Urban Outcasts: A Comparative Sociology of Advanced Marginality*. Cambridge: Polity Press.

Williams, M. (2000). 'Interpretivism and Generalisation', *Sociology*, 34(2): 209–224.

CHAPTER 6: REVIEWING THE LITERATURE

Arksey, H. and O'Malley, L. (2005). 'Scoping Studies: Towards a Methodological Framework', *International Journal of Social Research Methodology*, 8(1): 19–32.

British Council (2014). *Massification of Higher Education in Large Academic Systems: Summary Report*. London: British Council.

Bryman, A. (2016). *Social Research Methods* (5th edition). Oxford: Oxford University Press.

CHAPTER 7: BUILDING YOUR PROJECT

Antonucci, L. (2016). *Student Lives in Crisis: Deepening Inequality in Times of Austerity*. Bristol: Policy Press.

Armstrong, G. (1998). *Football Hooligans: Knowing the Score*. Oxford: Berg.

Bader, C., Mencken, C., and Baker, J. (2010). *Paranormal America: Ghost Encounters, UFO Sightings, Bigfoot Hunts and Other Curiosities in Religion and Culture*. New York: New York University Press.

Becker, H. (1963). *Outsiders: Studies in the Sociology of Deviance*. New York: Macmillan.

Creswell, J. (2018). *Research Design: Qualitative, Quantitative and Mixed Methods Approaches* (5th edition). London: Sage.

Denzin, N. (2012). 'Triangulation 2.0', *Journal of Mixed Methods Research*, 6(2): 80–88.

Whyte, W. (1943). *Street Corner Society: Social Structure of an Italian Slum*. Chicago: University of Chicago Press.

Yin, R. (2014). *Case Study Research Design and Methods* (5th edition). Thousand Oaks: Sage.

CHAPTER 8: ETHICS

Armstrong, G. (1998). *Football Hooligans: Knowing the Score*. Oxford: Berg.

Booth, T. and Booth, W. (2004). *Parents with Learning Difficulties, Child Protection and the Courts: A Report to The Nuffield Foundation*. Sheffield: University of Sheffield.

Cavendish, R. (1982). *Women on the Line*. London: Routledge and Kegan Paul.

Clark, T. (2006). '"I'm Scunthorpe 'til I die": Constructing and (Re)negotiating Identity Through the Terrace Chant', *Soccer and Society*, 7(4): 494–507.

Denscombe, M. (2017). *The Good Research Guide: For Small-scale Social Research Projects* (6th edition). London: Open University Press.

Humphreys, L. (1970). *Tearoom Trade: Impersonal Sex in Public Places*. Chicago: Aldine Publishing Company.

Hunt, P. (1981). 'Settling Accounts with the Parasite People: A Critique of *"A Life Apart"* by E. J. Miller and G. V. Gwynne', *Disability Challenge*, 1: 37–50.

Lewis, A. and Porter, J. (2004). 'Interviewing Children and Young People with Learning Disabilities: Guidelines for Researchers and Multi-professional Practice', *British Journal of Learning Disabilities*, 32(4): 191–197.

Milgram, S. (1963). 'Behavioral Study of Obedience', *Journal of Abnormal and Social Psychology*, 67(4): 371–378.

Miller, E. and Gwynne, G. (1972). *A Life Apart*. London: Tavistock Publications and Lippincott.

Murphy, E. and Dingwall, R. (2007). 'Informed Consent, Anticipatory Regulation and Ethnographic Practice', *Social Science and Medicine*, 65(11): 2223–2234.

Social Research Association (2003). *Ethical guidelines*. http://the-sra.org.uk/wp-content/uploads/ethics03.pdf (Accessed 17 October 2012).

Wallraff, G. (1985). *Ganz Unten*. Köln: Kiepenheuer and Witsch.

CHAPTER 10: SAMPLING

Denscombe, M. (2017). *The Good Research Guide: For Small-scale Social Research Projects* (6th edition). London: Open University Press.

Kvale, S. (1996). *InterViews: An Introduction to Qualitative Research Interviewing.* Thousand Oaks: Sage.

Patton, M. (2002). *Qualitative Research and Evaluation Methods* (3rd edition). Thousand Oaks: Sage.

Payne, G. and Williams, M. (2005). 'Generalization in Qualitative Research', *Sociology*, 39(2): 295–314.

CHAPTER 12: COLLECTING QUALITATIVE DATA

Garfinkel, H. (1984). *Studies in Ethnomethodology.* Bristol: Polity Press.

Geertz, C. (1973). 'Thick Description: Toward an Interpretive Theory of Culture', in C. Geertz (ed), *The Interpretation of Cultures: Selected Essays.* New York: Basic Books, 3–30.

Gold, R. (1954). 'Roles in Sociological Field Observations', *Social Forces*, 36(3): 217–223.

Jenkins, R. (2014). *Social Identity* (4th edition). London: Routledge.

Nagel, T. (1974). 'What is it Like to Be a Bat?', *The Philosophical Review*, 83(4): 435–450.

Spradley, J. (1980). *Participant Observation.* New York: Holt, Rinehart and Winston.

CHAPTER 14: ANALYSING QUALITATIVE DATA

Braun, V. and Clarke, V. (2006). 'Using Thematic Analysis in Psychology', *Qualitative Research in Psychology*, 3(2): 77–101.

Bryman, A. (2016). *Social Research Methods* (5th edition). Oxford: Oxford University Press.

Charmaz, K. (2000). 'Grounded Theory: Objectivist and Constructivist Methods', in N. Denzin and Y. Lincoln (eds), *Handbook of Qualitative Research* (2nd edition). Thousand Oaks: Sage, 509–536.

Fairclough, N. (1995). *Critical Discourse Analysis: The Critical Study of Language.* New York: Longman.

Foucault, M. (1967). *Madness and Civilization.* London: Tavistock.

Gill, R. (1999). 'Mediated Intimacy and Post-feminism: A Discourse Analytic Examination of Sex and Relationships Advice in a Women's Magazine', *Discourse and Communication*, 3(4): 345–369.

Glaser, B. and Strauss, A. (1967). *The Discovery of Grounded Theory: Strategies for Qualitative Research.* Chicago: Aldine.

Riessman, C. (2008). *Narrative Methods for the Human Sciences.* Thousand Oaks: Sage.

Ritzer, G. (1993). *The McDonaldization of Society.* Los Angeles: Pine Forge Press.

Ryan, G. and Bernard, H. (2003). 'Techniques to Identify Themes', *Field Method*, 15: 85–109.

Strauss, A. and Corbin, J. (1990). *Basics of Qualitative Research: Grounded Theory Procedures and Techniques.* Thousand Oaks: Sage.

Weber, M. (1949). *The Methodology of the Social Sciences* (trans. E. A. Shils and H. A. Finch). Glencoe, IL: The Free Press.

CHAPTER 15: WORKING WITH DOCUMENTS

Scott, J. (1990). *A Matter of Record*. Cambridge: Polity.

Webb, E., Campbell, D., Schwartz, R., and Sechrest, L. (1966). *Unobtrusive Measures: Nonreactive Research in the Social Sciences*. Chicago: Rand McNally and Company.

INDEX

Tables and figures are indicated by an italic t and f following the page number.